Social Advantage and Disadv

Social Advantage and Disadvantage

Edited by
Hartley Dean and Lucinda Platt

OXFORD
UNIVERSITY PRESS

OXFORD
UNIVERSITY PRESS

Great Clarendon Street, Oxford, OX2 6DP,
United Kingdom

Oxford University Press is a department of the University of Oxford.
It furthers the University's objective of excellence in research, scholarship,
and education by publishing worldwide. Oxford is a registered trade mark of
Oxford University Press in the UK and in certain other countries

First Edition published in 2016
Impression: 1

Published in the United States of America by Oxford University Press
198 Madison Avenue, New York, NY 10016, United States of America

British Library Cataloguing in Publication Data
Data available

Library of Congress Control Number: 2015944721

ISBN 978–0–19–873707–0 (hbk)
      978–0–19–873708–7 (pbk)

Printed in Great Britain by
Clays Ltd, St Ives plc

Preface

This volume represents, in part, a replacement for the highly successful *Understanding Social Exclusion*, edited by John Hills, Julian Le Grand, and David Piachaud, published in 2002 by Oxford University Press. In the decade since the publication of that volume, the concept of social exclusion, though still relevant, has slipped down the social policy agenda and now vies for attention with reinvigorated understandings of well-established conceptions of poverty and inequality, and with newer and emerging understandings of relative advantage and disadvantage, such as the capabilities approach, social capital theory, and revived preoccupations with social mobility. This book seeks therefore to do more than update the earlier book. Instead, rather than justifying a single conceptual approach to social disadvantage, it engages with an array of approaches. Its aim is first to provide a critical discussion of competing conceptual frameworks and then to illustrate a variety of differing dimensions of social (dis)advantage, drawing upon those frameworks and on both classic and recent research, in both the UK and the broader global context.

Social advantage and disadvantage are catch-all terms with no established definition. They are useful, nevertheless—especially when they are considered in relation to one another—because they can embrace a wide variety of more specific concepts that try and address the ways in which human society can cause, exacerbate, or fail to prevent injustices, divisions, or disruptions that are harmful to some of society's members. The title of the book captures the sense in which any conceptualization of *dis*advantage is concerned with the consequences of a process by which some form of *relative* advantage has been *selectively* conferred or attained. It also captures the increased—and much needed—attention to how inequalities and social divisions are created as much by the cumulative concentration of advantage among the best off as by the systematic exclusion of the less well situated. This book aims to elucidate some of the most important concepts invoked or implied in the analysis of different forms of advantage and disadvantage. It will in particular illustrate the contexts and dimensions in which social (dis)advantage occurs.

Conceptual distinctions between social advantage and disadvantage—of privilege and deprivation—come and go. They are often controversial: not least because they engage with moral or ideological considerations about whether the advantages of social existence should necessarily be for the mutual benefit of all or whether and when they may legitimately accrue more to some than to others in society. The conceptual foundations of such distinctions may complement or they can conflict with one another. Perhaps the oldest of all such distinctions is that between affluence and poverty. Poverty has been a central preoccupation for students of social policy. And yet it represents not so much a single concept as a term with many meanings and uses. In an increasingly affluent era, when it appeared that humanity was capable of combating what we might once have agreed to call poverty, other terms have begun to enter the social policy lexicon, albeit that these too can lend themselves to diverse and sometimes problematic interpretations; terms or ideas such as social exclusion, capability deprivation, rights violation, social immobility, and human or social capital deficiency. In Part One we critically discuss this spectrum of conceptual frameworks and ideas.

Part Two addresses advantage and disadvantage from a life course perspective. It addresses issues of child and family poverty and intergenerational transmission, education, work, income dynamics, and wealth across the life course, working lives, and older people, again including issues of intergenerational transmission. The concern here is to illustrate and explore the ways in which advantage and disadvantage occur at different life stages, the processes by which they cumulate, and how they are linked to different policy contexts.

Part Three considers cross-cutting divides that are implicated in the social construction and maintenance of advantage and disadvantage, including divisions premised on gender, 'race', ethnicity, migration and religion, neighbourhood, and the experience of crime and victimization. An important emphasis in some chapters is placed on how, on the one hand, social policies may sometimes have been implicated in shaping or perpetuating some forms of social (dis)advantage, but how on the other, policy can play a vital role in ameliorating or abating it. We are more than mindful that there are other cross-cutting divides—most significantly, that of disability—that ought ideally to have been included in this section. But at the time the volume was planned we were unable to achieve this, though we have attempted throughout the book to mitigate such deficiencies by emphasizing where relevant the intersecting character of social advantages and disadvantages.

Part Four consists of a single concluding chapter which will consider the extent to which social disadvantage may be considered as something more than a convenient portmanteau term, but as a concept which allows us to reflect on the several dimensions in which advantages may accrue to some in society and the processes by which they are denied to others. It will explore the ways findings are shaped by and have implications for different policy regimes and models of social welfare.

The fifteen different authors who have contributed, all of whom have current or past connections with the London School of Economics, have brought to this volume a variety of contrasting writing styles and intellectual approaches. During the preparation of the book, a majority of the contributors met together at a workshop at which early drafts of our chapters were discussed. We are most grateful to David Piachaud for kindly agreeing to chair the workshop and for his valuable contribution to the discussion. We hope this will have brought coherence to the structure and substance of the volume. However, we have made no attempt to establish a single message or agreed orthodoxy. Our hope is that we might open up to others the debate about social advantage and disadvantage that we have begun among ourselves. It has been and it should continue to be a multi- and inter-disciplinary debate, drawing on a diversity of conceptual and methodological approaches; a debate that will stimulate new thinking, research, and action.

Contents

Contents

List of Boxes and Figures

Boxes

Figures

List of Tables

List of Contributors

Tania Burchardt, Associate Professor of Social Policy and Deputy Director of CASE, London School of Economics.

Jack Cunliffe, Lecturer in Quantitative Criminology, University of Kent.

Hartley Dean, Professor of Social Policy, London School of Economics.

Sonia Exley, Assistant Professor of Social Policy, London School of Economics.

Emily Grundy, Professor of Demography, London School of Economics.

Rod Hick, Lecturer in Social Policy, University of Cardiff.

Sir John Hills, Richard Titmuss Professor of Social Policy and Director of CASE and Co-Director of the International Inequalities Institute, London School of Economics.

Stephen P. Jenkins, Professor of Economic and Social Policy, London School of Economics.

Neil Lee, Assistant Professor of Economic Geography, London School of Economics.

Margarita León, Senior Research Fellow at the Institute of Government and Public Policies of the Universitat Autònoma Barcelona.

Tim Newburn, Professor of Criminology and Social Policy, London School of Economics.

Coretta Phillips, Associate Professor/Reader in Criminology, London School of Economics.

Lucinda Platt, Professor of Social Policy and Sociology, London School of Economics.

Isabel Shutes, Assistant Professor of Social Policy, London School of Economics.

Kitty Stewart, Associate Professor of Social Policy, London School of Economics.

Malcolm Torry, Visiting Fellow in the Department of Social Policy and Director of the Citizen's Income Trust.

Polly Vizard, Research Fellow, CASE, London School of Economics

Part I
Concepts and Theory

1

Poverty and Social Exclusion

Hartley Dean

The concept perhaps most commonly associated with 'social disadvantage' is poverty. When poverty is equated with *dis*advantage it is defined not in terms of the inherent characteristics of poverty, but in terms of an absence, lack, or denial of advantage. A physicist will tell you there is no such thing as cold; only heat. To describe something as 'cold' is to regard it in terms of the absence—or relative absence—of heat energy. By the same token, it has been suggested, there is no such thing as poverty; only the absence of wealth (Jacobs, 1969; and see Piachaud, 2002). Just as heat is a form of energy that is implicated in and necessary for life itself, so wealth is—metaphorically speaking—a form of energy that fuels socio-economic development and personal well-being. Though 'wealth' is a term that may be used (as in Chapter 8, this volume) to refer to personal assets as opposed to income, it is also a term that is widely, if 'loosely', used in everyday parlance as a simple antonym for poverty (Rowlingson, 2008: 15). Poverty, by implication, is a consequence of failure: a systemic failure in the distribution of wealth, or a behavioural failure on the part of those who fail to acquire it.

Of course, it might also be argued that there is no such thing as wealth; only power and competitive advantage. The advantage of wealth lies not in the stored value of goods, money, or capital assets, but in the relations of power through which surplus value is created (Marx, 1887). Human fulfilment, as opposed to wealth, is founded not on the pursuit of relative advantage, but in the very substance and realization of our social existence. Poverty is a process of 'immiseration': if it is a consequence of failure, this is not a failure to create or distribute wealth, but a fundamental failure to meet human needs (Dean, 2010: ch. 4).

Poverty is therefore a socially constructed concept that has been perennially discovered and rediscovered as a form of disadvantage concerned not only with material deprivations, but with symbolic meanings and moral implications (Lister, 2004): meanings and implications for society as a whole; for the relatively advantaged members of society as much as for those identified as 'poor'. Because it is a contested concept, there have been many attempts to introduce synonyms or alternatives. The most salient of these in recent times has been 'social exclusion' (Hills et al., 2002). Yet this term too can capture a variety of quite different understandings or concepts. Exclusion might clearly be a form of disadvantage, but *exclusivity* may as easily be associated with relative advantage. The idea of social exclusion focuses attention on the *processes* (Room, 1995) by which poverty or disadvantage occurs. But just as easily as the idea of poverty, it can also divert attention from systemic effects and focus instead on the supposed defects of those who experience disadvantage, by portraying them as an aberrant minority or as an excluded 'underclass' (Levitas, 1998).

This chapter will begin with a discussion of competing definitions of poverty and different ways of measuring it, before moving on to discuss poverty not as an objective phenomenon, but as a social construction; and finally, to introduce debates about social exclusion, ideas of underclass and their relationship with poverty.

1.1 Definitions and Measurement

The relief of poverty, or its prevention, is one of the essential goals of social policy. But to address poverty, it might be supposed, we must first have accepted ways of defining and measuring it.

1.1.1 *Absolute and Relative*

There is an enduring debate as to whether poverty should be defined in terms of absolute or relative disadvantage, though the distinction can be elusive. In one sense, an absolute definition can be any definition that applies a criterion of sufficiency that pays no regard to the existing social distribution of resources. In theory, therefore, one might arbitrarily apply a more or less generous standard by which to declare a person to be poor or not poor. In practice, the earliest attempts to set such a standard did so having regard to *minimalist* criteria. Charles Booth (1902–3) in his studies of poverty in London in the late nineteenth and early twentieth centuries found it necessary to draw distinctions between 'the poor' (who struggled to obtain the necessaries of life), the 'very poor' (whom he described as living 'in chronic want') and a dissolute class of 'loafers, the vicious and the semi-criminal'. Seebohm Rowntree (1901), who attempted a similar study in York, sought to be more precise. He defined the state of 'primary poverty' in terms of the inability of a household to afford the weekly basket of the goods he adjudged necessary for 'bare physical efficiency'. Rowntree further defined a state of 'secondary poverty', which could arise when a household had sufficient income, but was feckless or improvident when spending it. We can see immediately that absolute definitions of poverty, when based on minimalist standards, may invoke judgements about the different ways in which people manage scarce resources (cf. Platt, 2013: 312).

Rowntree repeated his study of poverty in the 1930s (Rowntree, 1941). But whereas in his initial study the basket of goods required for a household to escape primary poverty had not included such things as a daily newspaper, or such wasteful luxuries as a modicum of beer or tobacco, some thirty-five years later these items were counted as reasonable necessities. Expert opinion as to what is an absolute necessity can vary, but more to the point, living standards and social expectations also vary over time. The contemporary UK equivalent of Rowntree's basket of goods, the Minimum Income Standard (Davis et al., 2014), would factor in the possession of a television and some form of internet access as necessities for an acceptable standard of living; things that were undiscovered and undreamt of in Booth and Rowntree's day. Judgements as to what is minimally sufficient may be more or less relative to the social context. In this sense, there can be no such thing as an absolute definition of poverty.

Later theorists of poverty, most notably Peter Townsend (1979, 1993), began to define poverty in relation not to a basket of goods that households could or couldn't afford, but to the extent to which they could *participate* in society; to which they shared in the living standards of their contemporaries and enjoyed comparable access to decent employment and housing, education, healthcare, public amenities and services. Townsend insisted that deprivation is a social phenomenon: for social beings, disadvantage is axiomatically relative and this is how poverty was to be understood. It is now generally accepted that we might have two broad definitions of poverty. The United Nations distinguishes between so-called absolute poverty, as 'a condition characterised by severe deprivation of basic human needs' and *overall* poverty, which the UN says 'has various manifestations, including lack of income and productive resources to ensure sustainable livelihoods', but which may also be 'characterised by lack of participation in decision making and in civil, social and cultural life' (UN, 1995). Another way of thinking about poverty has been proposed by George and Howards (1991), who envision a continuum ranging from the 'deepest' forms of so-called absolute definition—that may be based either on a 'starvation' standard or a less stringent 'subsistence' standard—through to relative definitions that may be based either on a 'coping' standard, or a more encompassing 'participation' standard (see Table 1.1). This allows us

Table 1.1. Depths of poverty

		People are poor if:
Absolute	starvation standard	they have not enough to eat
	subsistence standard	they lack the means materially to sustain themselves
Relative	coping standard	they are not managing acceptably to 'get by' in society
	participation standard	they cannot play a full and active part in society

Source: Based on George and Howards (1991: 3)

to apply the term 'poverty' as legitimately to the disadvantage experienced by victims of famine in the least economically developed countries of the global south as to that experienced, for example, by low income households struggling to survive in poor housing with minimal assistance in the most economically developed countries of the global north.

1.1.2 *Measure for Measure*

Measurement entails judgement as to what to measure and to what end. Practical measurements have long been used in the course of our everyday lives: a hand-full, a cup-full, an arms-length, and so on. But in the everyday world, poverty has been something to be feared or suffered, not measured. Nevertheless, standardized measurements of poverty provide important insights and enable us to draw comparisons: social, spatial, and temporal comparisons relating, for example, to the poverty of particular social groups, neighbourhoods, or countries, and changes in the incidence of poverty over time. Measurement matters in social policy. But standardized measures are imposed by governmental or scientific decree. They impart a particular judgement as to who is poor and, by implication, who or what might be to blame. Measures of absolute poverty focus on material disadvantage and imply judgements about how individuals or households can or should be enabled to survive. Measures of relative poverty focus on social disadvantage and imply judgements about how society is or should be organized.

Absolute measures of poverty can be more or less arbitrary. The most widely known example is the $1 a day international poverty line first adopted by the UN in 1990, which quantified poverty in terms of the numbers or proportions of people in the poorest countries of the world who were forced to live on less than US$1 a day (at purchasing power parity). The $1 a day standard was uprated by the World Bank to $1.25 a day as indicator of 'extreme' poverty, while $2 a day was taken as a broader indicator (World Bank, 2001; Ravallion et al., 2009; and see Gordon, 2002). Less arbitrary measures of poverty use variations upon the budget standards approach first pioneered by Rowntree by determining the level of income necessary for a person, or more usually a household, to avoid poverty. Such approaches may use a variety of methods to decide what to include in a household budget (drawing on expert or public opinion).

Relative measures of poverty may seek to draw not a fixed poverty line, but a poverty *threshold* defined with reference to the distribution of resources in society. This was the approach pioneered by Townsend, whose concern was with substantive living standards, rather than imputed living costs. Townsend's classic UK study drew up a list not only of consumables, but of life style requirements including people's ability to sustain family life and social activities. His survey of poverty established, on the one hand, the extent to which people were deprived in terms of their living standards and, on the other, the level of income at which people's participation in prevailing living standards was compromised and below which they were disproportionately likely to be deprived. Townsend's work on social deprivation fomented two important ideas that would lead the measurement of poverty in new directions:

- First, the idea of a deprivation threshold expressed not as a fixed income level, but in relation to the social average. This became the basis for one of the most widely used forms of poverty indicator: measurements based on the proportion of individuals living in households with incomes beneath a set percentage of average household income. Variations of this *households below average income* (HBAI) measure have been used in several countries (e.g. DWP, 2014; and see Chapter 7, this volume), but also in various contexts by the EU (as a social inclusion indicator—see Marlier et al., 2007) and the OECD (2014).

- Second, the idea of a measure of social deprivation that is conceptually distinct from—albeit statistically related to—any measure of personal or household income. This became, amongst other things, the basis for poverty measures informed by social consensus: measurements based on the proportion of people who are obliged to live without access to some of the goods, services, and activities that a majority of the population at large would agree to be necessities (Gordon and Pantazis, 1997; Mack and Lansley, 1985; Pantazis et al., 2006). It also, perhaps indirectly, opened the way to a variety of other non-income-related poverty measures.

There is a considerable array of non-income-related poverty measures: too many to be usefully addressed in this short chapter. Some are readily observable 'proxy' indicators, such as whether people lack access, for example, to a working toilet, or a mobile phone. On their own, these may be crude, but telling statistics. The fact that fewer of the world's 7 billion people have access to a working toilet (4.5 billion) than a mobile 'phone (6 billion) reveals that in parts of the world infrastructural investment in sanitation remains woefully inadequate (UN News Centre, 2013), but it also says something about the immense importance human beings attach to effective means of interpersonal communication. None the less, in particular societies, whether for example a person lives in a household with access to a motor vehicle may strongly predict whether or not she is likely to be in poverty by other criteria. Increasingly, we are using complex composite or multiple deprivation indices. These may be local measures, such as the Indices of Multiple Deprivation used to evaluate employment, health, education, housing, crime, and environmental conditions in different parts of England (http://data.gov.uk/dataset/english_ indices_of_deprivation), or highly specialized measures, such as the UN's Food Security Index (FAO, 2013).

The United Nations Development Programme recently introduced a sophisticated non-income-related Multidimensional Poverty Index, based on a combination of weighted indicators (Alkire and Santos, 2010), as shown in Box 1.1. It is currently applied in 104 countries around the world (UNDP, 2013).

1.1.3 *Global Context*

However measured, poverty is very much a worldwide phenomenon. Despite this, a great deal of the literature on poverty has been focused on the persistence of poverty as a form of relative disadvantage occurring in the world's richer countries. We have seen that some of the most significant developments in the study of poverty took place in the UK. At the turn of the twentieth century, using different methodologies, Booth had estimated the incidence of poverty in London to be 30 per cent; Rowntree estimated it in York to be 28 per cent. Over a century later and using more advanced methodologies, the UK Government estimates the incidence of poverty across the UK as a whole to be 21 per cent (when measured as the proportion of individuals living in households with incomes less than 60 per cent of the 2012/13 median, after adjustment for housing costs—see DWP, 2014); while a major study in 2012, involving a team of academics funded by the Economic and Social Research Council, estimated that around 22 per cent of the UK population were unable to afford one or more essential household goods and around 19 per cent were too poor to engage in common social activities considered necessary by the majority of the population (PSE UK, 2013).

Though the extent and character of the problem varies, poverty as a form of disadvantage remains a significant issue within rich and poor countries alike, as may be seen from Table 1.2. The table is presented not as an accurate summary of the global situation, but as an illustration of the very different kinds of data available to us and the limitations and potentially questionable value of the picture they can together present. If, nevertheless, one considers

---

Box 1.1 THE UN MULTIDIMENSIONAL POVERTY INDICATOR (MPI)

The MPI is calculated by multiplying the **incidence** of poverty in a country (the proportion of people who are 'MPI poor') by the **intensity** of poverty in that country (the average MPI score), based on the following ten **indicators**:

Health indicators

Child mortality: has any child in her family died? (1/6 weighting)

Nutrition: is any adult or child in her household for whom there is nutritional information malnourished? (1/6 weighting)

Education indicators

Years of schooling: has nobody in her household completed five years of schooling? (1/6 weighting)

School attendance: is any school-aged child in her household not attending school up to class 8? (1/6 weighting)

Standard of living indicators

Electricity: does her household not have an electricity supply? (1/18 weighting)

Sanitation: does her household's sanitation facility not meet the standard set by the Millennium Development Goals and/or is it shared with other households? (1/18 weighting)

Drinking water: does her household not have access to safe drinking water or safe drinking water in more than a 30-minute round-trip walk from home? (1/18 weighting)

Floor: does her household have a dirt, sand, or dung floor? (1/18 weighting)

Cooking fuel: does her household cook with dung, wood, or charcoal? (1/18 weighting)

Asset ownership: does her household not own a motorcar or truck and more than one of the following items: a radio, television, refrigerator, telephone, bicycle, or motorbike? (1/18 weighting)

- The resulting integer—expressed as a decimal fraction between 0 and 1—is the MPI.
- A person is considered MPI poor if she is deprived on at least one third of the indicators.
- Intensity of poverty is denoted by the proportion of indicators on which a person is deprived.

Note. The MPI replaced an earlier Human Poverty Index, HPI-1, which until 2009 had been used to measure poverty in developing countries. A rather different index, HPI-2, which had been used for highly developed countries, was discontinued, but see Table 1.2 below.

---

the economically powerful countries belonging to the G7 group, it may be seen that poverty appears to be notably worse in the major Anglophone countries (the USA and the UK) than in the major continental European countries (Germany and France) but not quite so severe as in Southern

European/Mediterranean countries, such as Italy. If one considers the emerging economies of the so-called 'BRIC' group (O'Neill, 2001) the variation between them is considerable. On the basis of the measures used in Table 1.2, poverty in Russia is lower than in the other BRICs, though some 17 per cent of Russians were living on less than 50 per cent median household income in 2010 (approximately the same as in the USA). Poverty in Brazil, as in other Latin American countries, has been declining (but income inequality remains relatively high). China and India, the two most populous countries on Earth, still experience high levels of poverty, despite recent improvements, especially in rural areas (World Bank, 2013). If one considers the more recently emerging economies of the so-called 'MINT' group (e.g. Fraser, 2011), there is, once again, considerable variation. Countries like Mexico and Turkey, have already become members of the OECD, but—though their poverty levels are low relative to other developing countries—they are high compared to other OECD countries (20.4 per cent and 19.3 per cent respectively in terms of the proportion of their populations living on less than 50 per cent median income). Indonesia, despite economic successes has a higher MPI score than China and half its population is living on less than $2 dollars a day, while

Table 1.2. Poverty in global perspective

		Human Poverty Index-2 (reported 2009)[1]	% population living on less than 50% median equivalized household income (2010)[2]
G7 countries	Germany	0.101	8.8
	France	0.110	7.9
	Canada	0.112	11.9
	Japan	0.116	16.0
	UK	0.146	10.0
	USA	0.152	17.4
	Italy	0.298	13.0
		Multidimensional Poverty Index (reported 2013)[3]	% population living on less than $2 a day (reported 2013)[4]
BRIC countries	Russia	0.005	0.1
	Brazil	0.011	9.9
	China	0.056	36.3
	India	0.283	75.6
MINT countries	Mexico	0.015	8.6
	Turkey	0.028	9.1
	Indonesia	0.095	50.6
	Nigeria	0.310	83.9

Notes:
1. HPI-2 was intended to measure poverty in highly developed countries and was computed on the basis of four indicators: (i) probability at birth of an inhabitant not surviving to age 60; (ii) functional illiteracy levels; (iii) proportion of households with less than 50% median income; and (iv) long-term unemployment rates. It was discontinued after 2009
2. Source: UNDP 2009 (index calculated on the basis of data from several recent years)
3. Source: OECD 2014
4. Source: UNDP 2013 (index calculated on the basis of data from several recent years)

Nigeria has one of the highest MPI scores in the world and over 80 per cent of its population is living on less than $2 dollars a day.

By the UN's criterion, however, the most extreme poverty is that experienced by the 1.2 billion people living on the equivalent of less than $1.25 a day, for whom—within the smaller officially designated 'low-income countries' (most of which are in sub-Saharan Africa)—prospects of improved living standards appear severely constrained. In these countries, contrary to trends elsewhere, the Aggregate Poverty Gap (the aggregate additional income required to lift every individual out of extreme poverty) has over the past two decades been increasing (Olinto et al., 2013).

1.2 Social Construction

'Poverty' is an ancient construct. As Jeremy Seabrook has observed, 'the word itself conceals a multitude of meanings and does not distinguish the diversity of the ways in which it is possible to be poor.... But we can see in the changing vocabulary the journey of humanity from a poverty created by nature, into poverties manipulated by ruling castes and hierarchies, and thence into the managed penury of "advanced" industrial society' (Seabrook, 2013: 1 and 3).

1.2.1 Discovery and Rediscovery

Certainly, the biblical proclamation—attributed to Moses—that 'the poor shall never cease out of the land' (Deuteronomy 15: 11) implied that poverty was an irremediable feature of the human condition. The poor were a legitimate object of compassion. But the significance of poverty has been subject to continual rediscovery and reinvention. In Europe in mediaeval times, poverty was, if not potentially an honourable status, quite simply the normal condition of the masses (Lis and Soly, 1979). However, the advent of industrial capitalism rendered poverty both visible and problematic. The spectre of dispossessed labour, urban slums, and conspicuous exploitation posed threats to the maintenance of social order and the protection of public health; threats demanding new modes of governance and control (H. Dean, 1991; M. Dean, 1991). By the nineteenth century, poverty was something to be managed. It could no longer be an honourable or a normal status. To be classified a pauper, according to Bentham, was to become an object not of compassion, but of 'wholesome horror' (cited in Spicker, 1984).

In the twentieth century, the hesitant development of 'modern' welfare states in the industrial nations of the global north brought change: initially, because of such nations' concerns for the quality and fitness of their 'human stock' (e.g. Williams, 1989: ch. 6); but later, because of the self-evident need to

11

compensate civilian populations for the consequences of two world wars (Titmuss, 1955). The poor were therefore constituted as objects for improvement and/or as victims of remediable circumstance. Such was the confidence in the administrative capacities of post-Second World War welfare states that there followed an era of complacency in which, it seems, poverty again became largely invisible (Glennerster, 2004). Before long, however, it became clear that the problem of poverty had not been solved. Welfare states were failing to maintain the living standards of vulnerable groups in rich societies (Abel-Smith and Townsend, 1965; Harrington, 1962; and see Room, 1982), and the richest cities in the capitalist world still contained chronically impoverished neighbourhoods (e.g. Lewis, 1966). The concept of poverty now began to acquire new associations. Whereas the risk of poverty under capitalism in peace-time might once have been principally associated with labour market issues and class inequalities, the risk was increasingly connected with social change and demographic trends; and with issues of gender, ethnicity, disability, and age (Bonoli, 2005; Roche, 1992: chs. 3, 5, and 8; Taylor-Gooby, 2000).

For inhabitants of the global north, in a post-material/post-emotional era (Inglehart, 1990; Mestrovic, 1997), poverty has become an ambiguous concept. On the one hand it is increasingly a personalized risk to be worried about, guarded against, and individually managed (Beck, 1992). On the other, it is a misfortune that befalls distant others for whom one might experience a kind of hollowed-out compassion expressed through support for anti-poverty causes (Dean, 2003: 696; and see Dogra, 2012).

1.2.2 Symbolic Meanings

It may begin to appear that poverty is more ephemeral than real. A criticism aimed at Townsend for his attempt to locate a definitive poverty threshold is that such a quest fails to allow for diversity of lifestyle and human behaviour: one person might feel deprived if she could not eat meat once a week, while another might prefer never to eat meat at all. However, the point about poverty, as David Piachaud has put it, is that the term 'carries with it an implication and a moral imperative that something should be done about it' (Piachaud, 1981: 119). To speak of poverty is to make value judgements, as much as scientific statements. The moral significance of poverty lies in its symbolic as much as its material dimensions. Ruth Lister draws a distinction between the 'unacceptable hardship' that constitutes poverty's material core and what she refers to as poverty's 'relational-symbolic aspects', which she lists as: disrespect; humiliation; shame and stigma; assault on dignity/self-esteem; othering; denial of human rights; diminished citizenship; lack of voice; powerlessness (2004: 8).

As we have seen, in days gone by, material deprivation might not invariably have been associated with negative emotions, such as shame or humiliation, but most certainly they can be. In eighteenth-century Scotland, for example, Adam Smith (1776: 691) famously observed the culturally constituted sense of shame that could befall a day-labourer were he so poor as to be unable to present himself in public without a pair of leather shoes on his feet, yet in France it appeared that no shame at all attached to appearing in public in wooden shoes or even barefooted. More recently, particular attention has turned to the idea of poverty as a psychosocial effect (Taylor, 2011) or as a form of 'social suffering' (Bourdieu, 1999). Empirical research in seven very diverse countries has suggested that shame is a common denominator in the social framing of poverty (Walker et al., 2013). Shamefulness is a consequence of the social construction of poverty and of 'the poor' as things envisioned through their 'otherness'; as socially, temporally, or spatially distant. There is a parallel to be drawn here with Foucault's claim that changing social constructions of sexuality and criminality created processes by which distinctions between normal and abnormal behaviour are imposed (Foucault, 1977, 1979). The same might be said about social constructions of poverty (H. Dean, 1991). Qualitative research consistently demonstrates that people experiencing material poverty are inclined to deny that they are poor. Poverty is imagined as something that happens to others: to people in different social circumstances, to people who lived in the past or to people in distant countries (Dean with Melrose, 1999).

1.2.3 The Relativity of Disadvantage

To suggest that poverty is socially constructed is not to deny its reality, but to implicate the whole of society in the nature of its meaning. When Townsend sought to define poverty in terms of relative deprivation he was mindful that the problem of poverty might just as well be regarded as a problem of riches (cf. Tawney, 1913), not only in the sense that it is the rich who monopolize society's material wealth, but in the sense that they actively shape society's standards and values: they are responsible for the 'proselytisation of lifestyles' (Townsend, 1979: 367). However, the relationship between rich and poor—the privileged and the deprived—can be understood in another context. Scott has drawn attention to the common etymological origins of 'privilege' and 'deprivation' in the Latin word 'privatus', which refers to a thing or person that is private or withdrawn from public life (Scott, 1994: 150). The terms privilege and deprivation therefore convey the sense that rich and poor respectively are supposedly withdrawn from the realm of ordinary lifestyles. Riches and poverty represent extremes that lie beyond the pale of the 'normal' social continuum. If this is so, the proselytization of lifestyles entails mediated processes of transmission. This was illustrated in Runciman's (1966) classic study of relative deprivation in England, which demonstrated that people tend by and large to compare their material circumstances with social reference groups that lie within the horizons of their daily lives and personal experiences. Any sense of relative privilege or deprivation is limited by those horizons. This finding has been supported in more recent research, which has confirmed that in an unequal society people may have a limited or distorted sense of how relatively rich or poor they themselves are. However, it also suggested that people's fear of poverty and their horror for the imagined lifestyles of the poor are greater than their desire for wealth and their fascination with the imagined lifestyles of the rich (Dean with Melrose, 1999). By and large, people may worry lest they should ever descend into poverty; they think it might be fun to be rich; but their primary aspiration is to be just 'comfortable'—to achieve or maintain a lifestyle within the bounds they perceive to be ordinary or normal.

1.3 Social Exclusion

This leads us to a discussion of a concept that attained particular fashionability in the 1990s and 2000s, namely 'social exclusion'. It has been suggested that the concept may be distinguished from the concept of poverty insofar as it is concerned with *relational* issues and focused on processes of disadvantage, whereas poverty is concerned with *distributive* issues and focuses on states of disadvantage (Room, 1995). This is helpful up to a point, but three things should be borne in mind:

- Social exclusion, like poverty, is a protean concept with competing and contradictory definitions;
- Social exclusion has been widely used as a synonym for poverty, or else has been casually conflated with the concept of poverty;
- Some conceptualizations of poverty—as we have seen—are very much concerned with relational issues and processes of disadvantage and already effectively embrace the idea of social exclusion.

1.3.1 *Paradigms, Discourses, and Clubs*

This section will draw on three overlapping conceptual frameworks relating to social exclusion. The first is that of Hilary Silver (1995) who defines three *paradigms* of social exclusion: the 'solidarity' paradigm, which is concerned with the failure of a society fully to incorporate all its members as social participants; the 'specialization' paradigm, which is concerned with the difficulties an industrialized society can have integrating some of its members into its complex division of labour; and the 'monopoly' paradigm, which is concerned with the way dominant classes in society mobilize so as effectively to exclude subordinate classes. The second framework is that of Bill Jordan (1996), who extrapolates from a version of economic club theory to argue that—from the level of the global clubs established by rich nations (such as the G7 or the European Union) down to the level of local amateur sports and social clubs—the world is divided into competing and mutually exclusive communities or clubs: clubs, which by regulating competition among their own members can mobilize more effective competition against rival clubs. Jordan's approach connects with key elements of Silver's solidarity and monopoly paradigms. The third framework is that of Ruth Levitas (1998), who identifies three political or popular *discourses* of social exclusion, each identified by a three letter acronym: the 'social integration discourse' (SID) resonates with key aspects of Silver's specialization paradigm insofar as it is preoccupied with the social consequences of labour market exclusion; the 'redistributionist discourse' (RED) resonates with some aspects of Silver's monopoly paradigm insofar as it is preoccupied with the exclusionary consequences of unequally distributed resources; the moral underclass discourse (MUD) is preoccupied— as we shall see below—with the dysfunctional consequences of the behaviour of aberrant social minorities.

Focusing for a moment on the *solidarity* paradigm, it may be seen that the concept of social exclusion has certain roots in an older concept of 'marginalization'; with concerns, for example, about the exclusion of minority ethnic immigrants in the 1920s from dominant White Anglo-Saxon Protestant culture in the USA (Park, 1928); or the plight of impoverished rural–urban migrants in the 1980s throughout much of Latin America (Faria, 1995; Germani, 1980). The origin of the term social exclusion is widely attributed to Lenoir (1974), whose concern was with the exclusion of those social groups in France who had slipped through the protective net of the welfare state. The International Labour Organisation has explored the concept of social exclusion (Rodgers et al., 1995) framing it in terms of a process by which groups or even entire populations can be excluded from the benefits of social protection and the right to social development.

The *specialization* paradigm became dominant in Western Europe with the development of the EU's Social Inclusion process and Social Inclusion strategies (Marlier et al., 2007). The seeds of that process had begun with the European Poverty Programmes in the 1970s but, it has been suggested, the subsequent flowering of the EU 'social agenda' had been impeded in the 1980s—at least in part by the opposition of the Conservative government in the UK, which denied the existence of poverty as a significant problem and objected to the use of the term (Bergman, 1995). The impasse was strategically resolved by the adoption of the language of social exclusion. Such language

15

was whole-heartedly embraced across the whole of Europe during the subsequent 'Third Way' reform era (Lewis and Surender, 2004), dominated as it was by a neo-liberal economic consensus that prioritized social inclusion through labour market activation (Levitas, 1998).

The *monopoly* paradigm is portrayed by Silver as an essentially socialist or social democratic approach. More radical examples of the genre may be found, for example, in the work of Byrne (2005). And Jordan's club theory approach captures the sense in which privileged communities by excluding deprived communities, monopolize access to resources: 'communities of choice' have the freedom unfairly to maximize their advantages, while the options open to 'communities of fate' are unjustly constrained (Jordan, 1996: ch. 5).

An influential strand of ideologically moderate scholarship that *combines* the focus on distributive and social justice issues associated with the monopoly paradigm with an emphasis on participation similar to that of the solidarity paradigm is to be found in the work of the Centre for the Analysis of Social Exclusion (CASE) at the LSE. CASE's working definition of social exclusion is essentially consistent, if not coterminous, with Townsend's definition of relative poverty:

> An individual is socially excluded if he or she does not participate in key activities of the society in which he or she lives . . . [including] Consumption (the capacity to purchase goods and services); Production (participation in economically or socially valuable services); Political engagement (involvement in local or national decision making); Social integration (integration with family, friends and community). (Burchardt et al., 2002a: 30–1)

CASE's intention was that the definition should inform an integrated approach, capturing different layers of social exclusion, effected by influences operating at a variety of levels, ranging from the individual to the global (Burchardt et al., 2002b: 7). This they illustrated with the 'onion' diagram reproduced as Figure 1.1.

1.3.2 *A socially Excluded 'Underclass'?*

We turn finally to address the notion of 'underclass'. The MUD discourse identified by Levitas may encompass certain implicit as well as explicit notions of underclass. The 'New' Labour government in the UK in 1997 created a Social Exclusion Unit with a broad cross-departmental remit to tackle complex social problems. Its definition of social exclusion was pragmatic:

> A short hand label for what can happen when individuals or areas suffer from a combination of linked problems such as unemployment, poor skills, low incomes, poor housing, high crime environments, bad health and family breakdown. (SEU, 1997: 1)

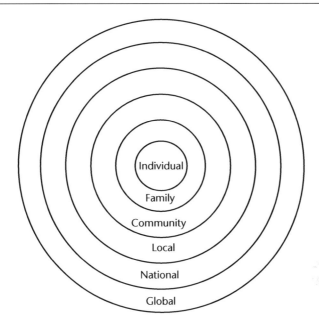

Individual: e.g. age, gender, race, disability, preferences, beliefs, and values

Family: e.g. partnership, children, caring responsibilities

Community: e.g. Social and physical environment, schools, health, and social services

Local: e.g. labour market, transport

National: e.g. cultural influences, social security, legislative framework

Global: e.g. international trade, migration, climate change

Figure 1.1. An integrated approach to social exclusion

Source: Burchardt et al. (2002b: 7), by permission of Oxford University Press

Though this makes no explicit mention of 'underclass', there is nonetheless an implication that social exclusion is associated with undesirable outcomes at the margins of society. Early initiatives undertaken by the SEU were focused on such aberrant behaviours as rough sleeping, teenage pregnancy, school truanting, and young people not in education, employment, or training (SEU, 1998a, 1998b, 1999a, 1999b). This use of the term social exclusion is redolent of past concerns with what the English Victorians had called society's 'residuum' (Stedman-Jones, 1971); with the dysfunctionality of the class Booth had defined as the 'very poor' and the corrosive presence of 'loafers, the vicious and the semi-criminal' (see above); with what policymakers in the inter-war years had alluded to as 'social problem groups' (Macnicol, 1987).

The term, 'underclass', first emerged in the USA in the 1960s where it was associated with a conspicuously racialized conception of poverty (Myrdal, 1963) and in some contexts this has continued to be the case (as may be seen in Chapter 12, this volume). But it was popularized in the 1980s, partly by a journalist, Ken Auletta, who claimed to have observed a social stratum of destitute and/or state welfare-dependent people, including 'the passive poor ... the hostile ... the hustlers ... [and] the traumatised' (Auletta, 1982: xvi); and partly through the arguments of the controversial paleo-conservative political scientist, Charles Murray. Murray's claim was that the USA was beset by a rising tide of 'illegitimacy' (i.e. unmarried motherhood), violent crime, and labour-force drop out. His quest was to reintroduce traditional family values, the work ethic and the idea of moral blameworthiness (Murray, 1984). The rise of this 'underclass' Murray attributed to the perverse incentives created by the welfare state, a trend he later also detected in Britain (1990), so refuelling a debate ignited by interpretations of Oscar Lewis's 'culture of poverty' thesis (see above) and a belief that such a culture was transmitted from generation to generation (e.g. Welshman, 2002).

However, the notion of an 'underclass' has not invariably been associated with moralistic accounts of social exclusion. A number of commentators have sought to define an underclass in structural rather than behavioural terms. Most importantly, William Julius Wilson (1987) used the term 'ghetto under-class' when describing the social ecology of inner-city neighbourhoods rendered dysfunctional by job-losses, out-migration, and the dislocation of communities. There have been other attempts to legitimize the idea that social groups systemically excluded from the benefits of labour market participation in advanced industrial societies constitute a class in itself, rather than a detached portion of the working class (Field, 1989; Runciman, 1990). Critics nevertheless suggest that the concept is too deeply discredited: estimates of the size of the underclass in countries such as the US and the UK vary wildly (from 1 per cent to 12 per cent of the population); the posited membership of the underclass is too diverse and transient for it properly to be accounted for as a class; and there is little satisfactory evidence for the alleged existence of a distinctive underclass culture (Dean and Taylor-Gooby, 1992; Lister, 1990, 1996; Shildrick et al., 2012).

Use of the underclass concept has been largely confined to the Anglophone world, but despite the controversy it has generated it continues to surface in a wide variety of contexts. In the UK, a Conservative think tank with significant influence on the Coalition government that came to power in 2010 used it to identify those whose lives are 'characterised by dependency, addiction, debt and family breakdown' (CSJ, 2007: 5). The UN-HABITAT agency has used it in relation to the condition of the world's 1 billion slum dwellers (UN-HABITAT, 2003). And various terms that are in many respects similar to 'underclass'—such as 'informal proletariat' (Davis, 2006) and 'the detached' (Standing, 2009)—continue regularly to emerge.

1.4 Summary and Conclusion

This chapter provides a foundation for the book by tracing the contours of some of the classic debates relating to social advantage and disadvantage.

The original conceptual framing of social advantage and disadvantage is to be found in ideas and concepts of wealth and poverty. The chapter has briefly visited the well-worn distinction between absolute and relative poverty: concepts that articulate different, but not necessarily incompatible, criteria or standards by which to determine what constitutes advantage and, by implication, disadvantage. Of particular importance is the conceptualization of poverty as relative deprivation: as a form of disadvantage that can only be understood in the context of what is adjudged advantageous to human well-being. The measurement of poverty imposes assumptions about what is meant by advantage and disadvantage. As a result, advantage and disadvantage can be indicated by a variety of means. Contemporary poverty measures allow us insights into the variation and extent of advantage and disadvantage in a global perspective.

Secondly, the chapter has focused on the social dimension and has illustrated how the meaning and significance of poverty has been socially constructed and reconstructed throughout history. Insofar as poverty has been regarded as an inevitable background to the human condition it has not always impinged on general awareness and its visibility may fluctuate according to the social context. Poverty is more than material or economic disadvantage: it has symbolic meaning that is constituted through the processes by which social advantage may be acquired. Poverty is or can be 'otherness'. It can entail social stigma. Advantage and disadvantage are social experiences and relative deprivation results from the awareness of social difference and the moral and emotional significance that attaches to social differences and degrees of social difference.

Finally, the chapter has discussed concepts of social exclusion that, arguably, either subsumed or broadened our thinking about poverty as a form of relative deprivation. Concepts of social exclusion focus on the systemic processes by which advantage may accrue to some and be denied to others. However, that focus may be directed to different kinds of exclusion: to exclusion from social rights, from social belonging, or from the social division of labour. The term social exclusion can also be used to refer to the exclusion of a supposedly morally culpable minority or 'underclass'.

Poverty and social exclusion are, self-evidently, contested or even contro-versial concepts. But they are concepts that provide much of the language, the social science, and the moral grammar through which social advantage and disadvantage may be apprehended.

References

Abel-Smith, B., and Townsend, P. (1965). *The Poor and the Poorest*. London: G. Bell & Sons (Occasional Papers in Social Administration, No. 17).

Alkire, S., and Santos, M. (2010). 'Acute Multidimensional Poverty: A New Index for Developing Countries' Working Paper No. 38. Oxford: OPHI, Oxford Department of International Development.

Auletta, K. (1982). *The Underclass*. New York: Random House.

Beck, U. (1992). *Risk Society: Towards a New Modernity*. London: Sage.

Bergman, J. (1995). 'Social Exclusion in Europe: Policy Context and Analytical Frame-work'. In G. Room (ed.), *Beyond the Threshold: The Measurement and Analysis of Social Exclusion*. Bristol: The Policy Press.

Bonoli, G. (2005). 'The Politics of the New Social Policies: Providing Coverage for New Social Risks in Mature Welfare States'. *Policy and Politics*, 33(3): 431–49.

Booth, C. (1902–3). *The Life and Labour of the People in London*. 17 volumes. 3rd edn. London: Macmillan.

Bordieu, P. (1999). *The Weight of the World: Social Suffering in Contemporary Society*. Cambridge: Polity.

Burchardt, T., Le Grand, J., and Piachaud, D. (2002a). 'Degrees of Exclusion: Developing a Dynamic, Multidimensional Measure'. In J. Hills, J. Le Grand, and D. Piachaud (eds), *Understanding Social Exclusion*, pp. 30–43. Oxford: Oxford University Press.

Burchardt, T., Le Grand, J., and Piachaud, D. (2002b). 'Introduction'. In J. Hills, J. Le Grand, and D. Piachaud (eds), *Understanding Social Exclusion*, pp. 1–12. Oxford: Oxford University Press.

Byrne, D. (2005). *Social Exclusion*. 2nd edn. Maidenhead: Open University Press.

Centre for Social Justice (CSJ). (2007). *Breakthrough Britain: Ending the Costs of Social Breakdown*. London: CSJ.

Davis, A., Hirsch, D., and Padley, M. (2014). *A Minimum Income Standard for the UK in 2014*. York: JRF.

Davis, N. (2006). *Planet of Slums*. London: Verso.

Dean, H. (1991). *Social Security and Social Control*. London: Routledge.

Dean, H. (with M. Melrose) (1999). *Poverty, Riches and Social Citizenship*. Basingstoke: Macmillan.

Dean, H. (2003). 'The Third Way and Social Welfare: The Myth of Post-emotionalism'. *Social Policy and Administration*, 37(7): 695–708.

Dean, H. (2010). *Understanding Human Need*. Bristol: The Policy Press.

Dean, H., and Taylor-Gooby, P. (1992). *Dependency Culture: The Explosion of a Myth*. Hemel Hempstead: Harvester Wheatsheaf.

Dean, M. (1991). *The Constitution of Poverty: Toward a Genealogy of Liberal Governance*. London: Routledge.

Department of Work and Pensions (DWP). (2014). *Households below Average Income: An Analysis of the Income Distribution 1994/95–2012/13*. London: DWP.

Dogra, N. (2012). *Representations of Global Poverty*. London: I.B. Tauris.

Faria, V. (1995). 'Social Exclusion and Latin American Analyses of Poverty and Deprivation'. In G. Rodgers, C. Gore, and J. Figueiredo (eds), *Social Exclusion: Rhetoric, Reality, Responses*. Geneva: ILO.

Field, F. (1989). *Losing Out: The Emergence of Britain's Underclass*. Oxford: Blackwell.

Food and Agriculture Organisation of the United Nations (FAO) (2013). *The State of Food Insecurity in the World 2013*. Rome: FAO/IFAD/WFP.

Foucault, M. (1977). *Discipline and Punish*. Harmondsworth: Penguin.

Foucault, M. (1979). *The History of Sexuality*. London: Allen Lane.

Fraser, I. (2011). 'Fidelity is confident its MINTs won't suck'. *Bloomsbury Information QFINANCE*(10 May). http://www.financepractitioner.com/blogs/ian-fraser/2011/05/10/fidelity-is-confident-its-mints-wont-suck-emerging-economies, accessed 5 August 2015.

George, V., and Howards, I. (1991). *Poverty amidst Affluence*. Aldershot: Edward Elgar.

Germani, G. (1980). *Marginality*. New Brunswick, NJ: Transaction Books.

Glennerster, H. (2004). 'Poverty Policy from 1900 to the 1970s'. In H. Glennerster, J. Hills, D. Piachaud, and A. Webb (eds), *One Hundred Years of Poverty and Policy*. York: Joseph Rowntree Foundation.

Gordon, D. (2002). 'The International Measurement of Poverty and Anti-poverty Policies'. In P. Townsend and D. Gordon (eds), *World Poverty: New Policies to Defeat an Old Enemy*. pp. 53–81. Bristol: The Policy Press.

Gordon, D., and Pantazis, C. (eds) (1997). *Breadline Britain in the 1990s*. Aldershot: Ashgate.

Harrington, M. (1962). *The Other America: Poverty in the United States*. Harmondsworth: Penguin.

Hills, J., Le Grand, J., and Piachaud, D. (eds) (2002). *Understanding Social Exclusion*. Oxford: Oxford University Press.

Inglehart, R. (1990). *Culture Shift in Advanced Industrial Society*. Princeton, NJ: Princeton University Press.

Jacobs, J. (1969). *The Economy of Cities*. New York: Random House.

Jordan, B. (1996). *A Theory of Poverty and Social Exclusion*. Cambridge: Polity.

Lenoir, R. (1974). *Les Exclus*. Paris: Seuil.

Levitas, R. (1998). *The Inclusive Society? Social Exclusion and New Labour*. Basingstoke: Macmillan.

Lewis, J., and Surender, R. (eds) (2004). *Welfare State Change: Towards a Third Way?* Oxford: Oxford University Press.

Lewis, O. (1966). 'The Culture of Poverty'. *Scientific American*, 215(4): 19–25.

Lis, C. and Soly, H. (1979). *Poverty and Capitalism in Pre-Industrial Europe*. Brighton: Harvester.

Lister, R. (1990). *The Exclusive Society: Citizenship and the Poor*. London: Child Poverty Action Group.

Lister, R. (ed.) (1996). *Charles Murray and the Underclass: The Developing Debate.* London: IEA.

Lister, R. (2004). *Poverty.* Cambridge: Policy.

Mack, J., and Lansley, S. (1985). *Poor Britain.* London: Allen and Unwin.

Macnicol, J. (1987). 'In Pursuit of the Underclass'. *Journal of Social Policy*, 16(3): 293–318.

Marlier, E., Atkinson, A., Cantillon, B., and Nolan, B. (eds) (2007). *The EU and Social Inclusion: Facing the Challenges.* Bristol: The Policy Press.

Marx, K. (1887). *Capital*, i, 1970 edn. London: Lawrence & Wishart.

Mestrovic, S. (1997). *Postemotional Society.* London: Sage Publications.

Murray, C. (1984). *Losing Ground: American Social Policy 1950–1980.* New York: Basic Books.

Murray, C. (1990). *The Emerging British Underclass.* London: Institute of Economic Affairs.

Myrdal, G. (1963). *A Challenge to Affluence.* New York: Random House.

O'Neill, J. (2001). 'Building Better Global Economic BRICs'. Goldman Sachs & Co. Global Economic Paper, 66.

Olinto, P., Beegle, K., Sobrado, C., and Uematsu, H. (2013). 'The State of the Poor: Where Are the Poor, Where Is Extreme Poverty Harder to End, and What Is the Current Profile of the World's Poor?'. Economic Premise Series, Poverty Reduction and Economic Management Note # 125, World Bank.

Organisation for Economic Co-operation and Development (OECD). (2014). *Society at a Glance 2014: OECD Social Indicators.* Paris: OECD.

Pantazis, C., Gordon, D., and Levitas, R. (eds) (2006). *Poverty and Social Exclusion in Britain: The Millennium Survey.* Bristol: The Policy Press.

Park, R. (1928). 'Human Migration and the Marginal Man'. *American Journal of Sociology*, 33: 881–93.

Piachaud, D. (1981). 'Peter Townsend and the Holy Grail'. *New Society.* 10 September.

Piachaud, D. (2002). 'Capital and the Determinants of Poverty and Social Exclusion'. CASE paper 60. London: LSE.

Platt, L. (2013). 'Poverty'. In G. Payne (ed.), *Social Divisions* (pp. 305–31). Basingstoke: Palgrave Macmillan.

PSE UK. (2013). *The Impoverishment of the UK—PSE UK First Results: Living Standards.* Bristol: PSE UK.

Ravallion, M., Chen, S., and Sangraula, P. (2009). 'Dollar a Day Revisited'. *World Bank Economic Review*, 23(2): 163–84.

Roche, M. (1992). *Re-thinking Citizenship.* Cambridge: Polity.

Rodgers, G., Gore, C., and Figueiredo, J. (eds) (1995). *Social Exclusion: Rhetoric, Reality, Responses.* Geneva: ILO.

Room, G. (1982). 'Understanding Poverty'. In J. Dennett, S. James, G. Room, and P. Watson (eds), *Europe Against Poverty: The European Poverty Programme 1975–80*, pp.163–84. London: Bedford Square Press.

Room, G. (ed.) (1995). *Beyond the Threshold: The Measurement and Analysis of Social Exclusion.* Bristol: The Policy Press.

Rowlingson, K. (2008). 'Wealth'. In T. Ridge and S. Wright (eds), *Understanding Inequality, Poverty and Wealth*, pp. 15–36. Bristol: The Policy Press.

Rowntree, B. S. (1901). *Poverty: A Study of Town Life*. London: Macmillan.

Rowntree, B. S. (1941). *Poverty and Progress: A Second Social Survey of York*. London: Longman.

Runciman, G. (1966). *Relative Deprivation and Social Justice*. London: Routledge & Kegan Paul.

Runciman, G. (1990). 'How Many Classes Are There in Contemporary British Society? *Sociology*, 24(3): 377–96.

Scott, J. (1994). *Poverty and Wealth: Citizenship, Deprivation and Privilege*. Harlow: Longmans.

Seabrook, J. (2013). *Pauperland: Poverty and the Poor in Britain*. London: Hurst & Co.

Shildrick, T., MacDonald, R., Webster, C., and Garthwaite, K. (2012). *Poverty and Insecurity: Life in Low-pay, No-pay Britain*. Bristol: The Policy Press.

Silver, H. (1995). 'Reconceptualising Social Disadvantage: Three Paradigms of Social Exclusion. In G. Rodgers, C. Gore, and J. Figueiredo (eds), *Social Exclusion: Rhetoric, Reality, Responses*. Geneva: ILO.

Smith, A. (1776). *An Inquiry into the Nature and Causes of the Wealth of Nations*. 1900 edn. London: George Routledge.

Social Exclusion Unit. (1997). 'Social Exclusion Unit: Purpose, Work Priorities and Working Methods'. Briefing document. London: Cabinet Office.

Social Exclusion Unit. (1998a). *Rough Sleeping*. London: The Stationery Office.

Social Exclusion Unit. (1998b). *Truancy and School Exclusion*. London: The Stationery Office.

Social Exclusion Unit. (1999a). *Bridging the Gap: 16–18-year-olds Not in Education, Training or Employment*. (Cm 4405) London: The Stationery Office.

Social Exclusion Unit. (1999b). *Teenage Pregnancy*. (Cm 4342) London: The Stationery Office.

Spicker, P. (1984). *Stigma and Social Welfare*. Beckenham: Croom Helm.

Standing, G. (2009). *Work after Globalization: Building Occupational Citizenship*. Cheltenham: Edward Elgar.

Stedman-Jones, G. (1971). *Outcast London*. Oxford: Clarendon Press.

Tawney, R. (1913). 'Poverty as an Industrial Problem'. In R. Tawney (ed.), *Memoranda on the Problems of Poverty*, ii. London: William Morris Press.

Taylor, D. (2011). 'Wellbeing and Welfare: A Psychosocial Analysis of Being Well and Doing Well'. *Journal of Social Policy*, 40(4): 777–94.

Taylor-Gooby, P. (2000). 'Risk and Welfare'. In P. Taylor-Gooby (ed.), *Risk, Trust and Welfare*. Basingstoke: Macmillan.

Titmuss, R. (1955). 'War and Social Policy (a lecture originally given at King's College London)'. In P. Alcock, H. Glennerster, A. Oakley, and A. Sinfield (eds), *Welfare and Wellbeing: Richard Titmuss' Contribution to Social Policy*. 2001 edn. Bristol: The Policy Press.

Townsend, P. (1979). *Poverty in the UK*. Harmondsworth: Penguin.

Townsend, P. (1993). *The International Analysis of Poverty*. Hemel Hempstead: Harvester Wheatsheaf.

UN News Centre. (2013). 'Deputy UN Chief Calls for Urgent Action to Tackle Global Sanitation Crisis'. 21 March. http://www.un.org/apps/news/story.asp?NewsID=44452#.U8-Sz00g8bI, accessed 23 July 2014.

United Nations. (1995). *The Copenhagen Declaration and Programme of Action: World Summit for Social Development*. New York: UN.

United Nations Development Programme (UNDP).(2009). *Human Development Report 2009—Overcoming Barriers: Human Mobility and Development*. New York: UNDP.

United Nations Development Programme (UNDP). (2013). *Human Development Report 2013—The Rise of the South: Human Progress in a Diverse World*. New York: UNDP.

United Nations Human Settlements Programme (UN-HABITAT). (2003). *The Challenge of Slums—Global Report on Human Settlements 2003*. London: Earthscan.

Walker, R., Kyomuhendo, G., Chase, E., Choudry, S., Gubrium, E., Nicola, J., and Ming, Y. (2013). 'Poverty in Global Perspective: Is Shame a Common Denominator?'. *Journal of Social Policy*, 42(2): 215–33.

Welshman, J. (2002). 'The Cycle of Deprivation and the Concept of Underclass'. *Benefits: The Journal of Poverty and Social Justice*, 10(3): 199–205.

Williams, F. (1989). *Social Policy: A Critical Introduction*. Cambridge: Polity.

Wilson, W. (1987). *The Truly Disadvantaged*. Chicago: Chicago University Press.

World Bank. (2001). *World Development Report 2000/2001*. Oxford: Oxford University Press.

World Bank. (2013). *Global Monitoring Report 2013: Rural-urban Dynamics and the Millennium Development Goals*. New York: IMF/World Bank.

2

The Capability Approach to Advantage and Disadvantage

Tania Burchardt and Rod Hick

How should we evaluate advantage and disadvantage? Amartya Sen, pioneer of what has become known as the capability approach, argues there are three principal alternatives. The first is to focus on people's resources—typically, their income and wealth; the second, on their utility, or happiness; the third, on what people are able to do or be, or what he calls people's capabilities. In this chapter, we present an outline of the capability approach and discuss the contribution it might make to the study of advantage and disadvantage.

Recent years have seen growing attention to inequality in addition to the more traditional concern with poverty (Piketty, 2014; Atkinson and Piketty, 2014; Milanovic, 2011, inter alia)—or, following the theme of this volume, with *advantage* as well as with disadvantage. But while poverty is increasingly conceptualized and measured multi-dimensionally, including using the capability approach, the debate on inequality has focused overwhelmingly on single dimensions—usually income or wealth, and sometimes health or education. In contrast, the capability approach requires us to examine advantage and disadvantage across a range of dimensions.

The capability approach has been influential internationally, most prominently through the concept of human development, which provided the underpinning for the measurement of the United Nations' Human Development Index (HDI) comparing levels of education, health, and standard of living across countries. The capability approach has received much less attention in Social Policy—despite its relevance for understanding poverty and disadvantage. We believe the capability approach can 'add value' to the study of advantage and disadvantage compared with other metrics, though we recognize it raises methodological challenges, especially in a context of focusing on advantage.

The following section outlines three competing ways to understand advantage and disadvantage, discusses the motivation for adopting a capability perspective, presents some issues that arise in applying it, and briefly outlines some key critiques that have been levelled at the approach. The second section assesses the distinctive features of capability analysis for the study of disadvantage, drawing on existing work, and its potential for conceptualizing advantage, where considerably less work has been conducted. The third section reviews some prominent applications of the approach, and the concluding section summarizes the 'value added' of the capability approach, as we see it, for understanding advantage and disadvantage.

2.1 Three Approaches to Understanding Advantage and Disadvantage

There are three alternative ways in which we might evaluate advantage and disadvantage. The first—focusing on people's resources—remains the dominant approach and is more fully explored in Chapters 7 and 8 in this volume. Work of this kind includes studies that examine the proportion of households falling below an income poverty line—understood either in relative terms (e.g. using an income poverty line set at 50 per cent or 60 per cent of national median income; Forster and Mira d'Ercole, 2005), or in absolute terms (e.g. a poverty line set at $1.25 a day; Ravallion et al., 2009). It also includes studies comparing the wealth of nations on the basis of their Gross Domestic Product (GDP) (e.g. World Bank website, n.d.).

The second basis on which we might analyse advantage and disadvantage is subjective well-being, happiness, or utility, and there has been growing interest in this approach in academic circles (e.g. Layard, 2005; Dolan, 2014) and politically, with President Sarkozy in France and Prime Minister David Cameron in the UK both establishing commissions to look into ways of measuring national well-being that include happiness (Stiglitz et al., 2009; BBC, 2010). A key motivation has been evidence which shows that while developed nations have become much more wealthy in the last half century, they have not, in the main, become happier (Layard, 2006). Utilitarianism potentially offers a different goal for societies to that of maximizing GDP.

The third way in which advantage and disadvantage might be understood is in terms of people's functionings and capabilities. A person's functionings are their activities and states of being (Wolff and de Shalit, 2007: 7)—studying, caring for an elderly parent, experiencing poor mental health, living in substandard accommodation, and so forth. It is an inherently multidimensional perspective. A person's capabilities are what they are *able* to do or be. Thus, while a person's functionings represent the outcomes they achieve, their capabilities reflect their real opportunity or freedom to achieve a variety of functionings. Finally, a person's *capability set* is the set of alternative combinations of functionings a person could achieve, from which they select one combination.

2.1.1 *Motivations*

According to Sen, there are two important limitations with the tradition based on resources. Firstly, people have different needs, and thus may require different levels and types of resources to achieve the same outcomes. For example, a person with a disability may need more resources than a person who is not disabled to achieve the same standard of living (understood as a functioning) (Zaidi and Burchardt, 2005). Secondly, a person's resources are just one determinant of what they can do and be; they may also face discrimination or other obstacles. These two arguments suggest that advantage and disadvantage in terms of income and wealth may not coincide with that of other domains. At a national level for example, life expectancy in the USA is lower than in Cuba, despite the GNI per capita of the United States being very considerably higher (UNDP, 2014: 160). A person's income and wealth may not correspond with his or her capabilities, and a country's GDP may not correspond with its level of human development.

On the other hand, the utilitarian perspective is, Sen argues, insufficiently sensitive to objective deprivations. People's expectations and preferences are adaptive—'a person who is ill-fed, under-nourished and under-sheltered and ill can still be high up the scale of happiness or desire-fulfilment if he or she has learned to have "realistic" desires and to take pleasure in small mercies' (Sen, 1987: 14). This relates to Runciman's (1966) study of deprivation referred to in Chapter 1 of this volume, in which he shows that people's sense of privilege or deprivation is relative to those with whom they come regularly into contact. Subjective well-being may be a valuable functioning, but judging advantage and disadvantage solely in terms of happiness, or subjective states more broadly, is inadequate because subjective states are not a good guide to objective deprivations. What matters is not so much whether people feel advantaged or disadvantaged as whether they *are* advantaged or disadvantaged.

2.1.2 *Towards Application*

Moving beyond abstract examples requires us to answer the question of which functionings or capabilities should count towards an assessment of advantage and disadvantage. This question of the 'capability list', which remains one of the most contentious issues within the capability literature (see Hick and

Burchardt, forthcoming, for a discussion). Sen has not identified a fixed list of capabilities, arguing instead that any list must be relevant to the particular circumstances of its application and decided by democratic deliberation and public scrutiny. It may not be helpful to prescribe a list of dimensions in advance when we do not yet know what kind of analysis we are undertaking (an evaluation of a rural development programme in Pakistan; a framework for assessing poverty and wealth in Germany; or a study of elites in the UK).

By contrast, Nussbaum has specified a list of ten central human capabilities that emerge from her Aristotelian analysis of human flourishing and the requirements necessary to secure human dignity. These capabilities are: life; bodily health; bodily integrity; senses, imagination, and thought; emotions; practical reason; affiliation; other species; play; and control over one's environment (2011: 33–4). Nussbaum (2011: 71) argues that it is essential to specify a list of valued capabilities and questions 'whether the idea of promoting freedom is even a coherent political project', since some people's freedoms inevitably limit those of others. Nussbaum discusses the importance of restricting non-consensual sexual intercourse within marriage and suggests that 'any political project that is going to protect the equal worth and certain basic liberties for the poor and to improve their living conditions needs to say forthrightly that some freedoms are central for political purposes and some are distinctly not' (Nussbaum, 2011: 72). As we will argue below, such considerations have a particular resonance in the context of advantage since some forms of advantage may imply highly unequal power relations.

Despite these debates about whether and how a 'list' of capabilities is to be derived, analysis of the dimensions selected by various authors shows that, in practice, 'areas of consensus seem to emerge' (Alkire, 2010: 19, 2002). Similarly, on the question of which dimensions make up quality of life, the Stiglitz–Sen–Fitoussi Commission (2009: 58) notes that 'while the precise list of these features inevitably rests on value judgements, there is a consensus that quality of life depends on people's health and education, their everyday activities (which include the right to a decent job and housing), their participation in the political process, the social and natural environment in which they live, and the factors shaping their personal and economic security'.

An additional challenge emerges when seeking to operationalize the concept of *capability*, namely, considering the alternative functionings a person could have selected but did not, as well as the actual functionings observed. Most empirical analyses rely on information about people's actual achievements (i.e. their functionings) and make inferences about their capability sets. It may be that a particular functioning is sufficiently basic that deprivation can be assumed to have arisen from a lack of real opportunity to achieve a better outcome, so the functioning and the capability are coterminous. For other dimensions, and in particular where preferences may play a role, additional information may be brought to bear in order to draw inferences about whether a particular outcome arose from choice or constraint. Such information may include asking people directly, or looking at their resources, or at their other achieved functionings (Hick, 2014). The more we move away from assessing disadvantage towards assessing advantage, the more significant the distinction between functioning and capability becomes, and the more pressing it becomes to find an appropriate empirical strategy.

2.1.3 *Critiques*

One common misapprehension is to regard the capability approach as a comprehensive theory of justice. It is not. It provides an answer to the question, 'equality of what?' that sets it apart from resource-based or utilitarian perspectives, but is does not address the question of, 'how much inequality is unjust?' In particular, endorsing a particular capability is not to say that advantage on that dimension is just, but simply that the dimension matters and should be included in the metric. A supplementary ethical or political theory is required to judge what degree of inequality, if any, is acceptable.

Even with such an addition, some have questioned whether the approach can be successfully operationalized. Sugden (1993: 1953), for example, notes that 'given the rich array of functionings that Sen takes to be relevant, given the extent of disagreement among reasonable people about the nature of the good life, and given the unresolved problem of how to value sets, it is natural to ask how far Sen's framework is operational'. It is certainly the case that the capability approach is more complex to apply than approaches based on resources or utility. Nonetheless, the period since Sugden expressed this reservation has witnessed a wide range of more or less successful applications of the approach, some of which we discuss in this chapter.

A second criticism levelled at the capability approach is that it is too individualistic and that it neglects the ways in which people's capabilities are interdependent. Dean (2009) argues that human beings are defined through relationships, which both contribute to, and constrain, their autonomy as individuals. One person's capabilities may be exercised in ways which limit those of another, or which enhance them (Dean, 2009: 273). Stewart (2005: 190) argues that groups also need to be given a greater emphasis within the approach, because group membership and group achievements 'affect one's sense of well-being', because groups can have an instrumental impact on individuals' well-being by achieving greater resource shares for their members, and because groups can influence their member's preferences and behaviours.

Dean and Stewart are clearly right that what a person is able to be or do depends crucially on what others have done in the past and are doing in the present. Moreover, people identify with, formulate their goals in relation to, and operate as members of, multiple groupings—families, ethnic groups, political parties, and social classes to name but a few—as Sen has also analysed (2006). But we do not see that acknowledging this interdependency invalidates the assessment of the degree to which an individual has a more or less valuable capability set than another individual. The capability approach, is, in essence, seeking to 'evaluate and interpersonally compare overall individual advantages' (Sen, 2010: 242), whichever collectivities—including families and partnerships—those individuals are also part of, and however their capability sets have been created and influenced.

Robeyns (2005) distinguishes between ethical and ontological individualism. Ontological individualism, 'states that only individuals and their properties exist, and that all social entities and properties can be identified by reducing them to individuals and their properties. Ontological individualism hence makes a claim about the nature of human beings, about the way they live their lives and about their relation to society' (Robeyns, 2005: 108). The capability approach is certainly not individualistic in this sense. By contrast, the capability approach *does* subscribe to ethical individualism, which, 'makes a claim about who or what should count in our evaluative exercises and decisions. It postulates that individuals, and only individuals, are the units of moral concern' (Robeyns, 2005: 107). Ethical individualism is shared by almost all contemporary approaches to evaluating advantage and disadvantage, including theories of human needs, which place normative value on *individuals* rather than collectivities. Communitarianism is the exception (Taylor, 1985), which places value on cultures and identities, over and above the interests of the individuals who make up those groups.

A third line of critique of the capability approach comes from consideration of the needs of future generations. Liberal egalitarian theories developed in an era when the central questions were about fair distributions within nation states, and, sometimes, between them, but with increasing concern about environmental sustainability, analysis of distributional justice must adapt to include future populations as well as those currently living. Gough (2014) argues that the absence of a universal list of central human capabilities (or even an agreed method to derive one) makes the capability approach inadequate to the task, since it is not clear which capabilities we should be interested in preserving for future generations, or, for that matter, protecting for the currently living against the potentially limitless demands of future lives.

In practice, as noted above, there is a reasonable level of agreement between 'lists' about valued dimensions, whether these are derived from a capability approach, a theory of human needs, or an analysis of the human rights that have been claimed. One reason for this overlap could be that there is a degree of universality in basic human requirements and goals. Thus, we do not believe that a capability approach and a human needs approach are contradictory; on the contrary, there is scope for greater engagement between the two.

Finally, the capability approach is criticized for adopting an abstract, naive, or technical approach to the definition of what matters. Whether a capability list is derived in a philosophical way, following Nussbaum, through democratic deliberation, following Sen, or in an ad hoc way based on data availability (as is common in practice), Marxists point to a lack of appreciation that definitions of need are contested and negotiable, and that what is recognized now as a need or entitlement is the product of historical struggles rather than being an abstract or fixed entity (Dean, 2009). This is an important reminder about the contingent status of any capability list.

2.2 Advantage and Disadvantage through the Lens of Capabilities

2.2.1 Distinctive Features of Capability Analysis of Disadvantage

The vast majority of applications of the capability approach have focused on *dis*advantage. Disadvantage is viewed as being a restricted capability set—the inability of people to live a life that they value and have reason to value. This requires a multidimensional assessment of disadvantage, which can be contrasted with the unidimensional approaches based on resources or subjective well-being.

Applications of the approach have assessed disadvantage in a range of dimensions. For example, Brandolini and d'Alessio (1998) employed the approach to support a multidimensional poverty analysis focusing on health, education, employment, housing, social relationships, and economic resources, while Bonvin and Dif-Pradalier (2010) have emphasized the importance of the capability for work and the capability for voice.

Thus, the conception of disadvantage includes, but is not limited to, disadvantages which are imposed by resource constraints. This can point to quite different policy implications, than analysis which focuses on resources alone. For example, one of the most startling outcomes of the recent recession in Europe has been the rise in youth unemployment (i.e. for people under 25 years) which peaked at almost one quarter of all young people across the twenty-eight EU Member States in 2013—and affected more than one-half of all young people in Greece and Spain (rates of 59.5 per cent and 55.5 per cent, respectively) (Eurostat, n.d.). While unemployment in many cases leads to income poverty, the disadvantage associated with unemployment cannot be remedied successfully solely by income transfer nor does it merit concern only when income poverty arises. Subjective well-being, health, relationships, skills, subsequent employment prospects, are also affected (Sen, 1997).

People's capabilities can also be curtailed for reasons other than a lack of resources. One such example is immigration regulations, which can prevent a person from moving from one place to another in search of work or, indeed, restrict the ability of economic migrants to leave one employer to work for another (see also Chapters 9 and 13 in this volume on aspects of the quality of work—security, dignity, and worth—that are not captured by an exclusive focus on the financial rewards of employment). A prominent international example of this is the restrictions on Nepali migrant workers in Qatar, who may not be able to leave one employer to join another, or even to exit the country, without their employer's permission. More generally, immigration regulations form an important non-income impediment to human capabilities, especially, though by no means exclusively, for people from the global south.

2.2.2 *How Advantage Might Be Conceptualized in a Capability Framework*

In contrast to disadvantage, considerably less work has been conducted on the capability approach to conceptualize *advantage*. Here we take some tentative steps towards considering what a multidimensional and freedom-focused assessment might contribute. The approaches we discuss are descriptive and analytical—identifying relative advantage and disadvantage in terms of a given set of functionings or capabilities, and analysing the relationship between the creation of advantage and disadvantage. They do not reflect a comprehensive normative position, because the capability approach is not in itself a theory of justice; it requires a supplementary ethical or political theory to define which distributions or processes are to be considered unjust.

As a starting point, advantage can be conceived of as having a larger capability set: having additional (combinations of) functionings available to you, compared to a more disadvantaged capability set. These functionings could be of at least three types: (i) higher levels of achievement on commonly available functionings that people value and have reason to value (for example, accessing higher education rather than just the statutory minimum); (ii) functionings in *combinations* unavailable to less privileged individuals (e.g. enjoying time off work *and* avoiding material deprivation); and (iii) functionings wholly unavailable to most people (e.g. influencing public opinion, or being insured against the effects of natural disasters).

Which of these types of functionings is relevant to an assessment of advantage will depend on the purpose of the evaluative exercise. If we are interested in advantage as a contrast with disadvantage, in order to see more clearly who is in need and to understand the disparities that exist between people, we may wish to explore the distribution of achievement on commonly available and widely valued functionings—such as nutrition, shelter, education, physical security, and social participation. Advantage and disadvantage are in this case evaluated in the same 'space', and the focus is likely to be on actual achievement (functionings), rather than capabilities. Some indicators permit full distributional analysis (such as life expectancy or educational achievement), while others depend on examining the proportions of different population sub-groups who obtain functioning above or below a given threshold (for example, the proportions of men and women who are victims of violence).

However, one of the interesting ways in which advantage may manifest itself, and which the capability approach is particularly well-suited to explore, is the extent to which people are freed from trading-off between achieving their valuable ends. As discussed in Burchardt (2010), while a well-paid professional may be able to increase her leisure time without incurring material deprivation, a low-income couple with children may face a trade-off between time poverty and material poverty, and a lone parent with few educational qualifications may be able to escape *neither* time poverty *nor* material poverty, however she allocates her time across activities. To examine trade-offs, we can retain the focus on basic and central capabilities commonly used in analysis of disadvantage, but we need to move from consideration of functionings to capabilities. Such an approach is undoubtedly complex, especially if we are to consider trade-offs on more than two dimensions, and capabilities are, notoriously, not susceptible to direct observation or measurement. Nevertheless, examining the *combinations* of functionings (standard of living, health, and leisure) enjoyed by different groups (for example, men and women in higher and lower social classes) provides an indication of the range of possibilities open to people with that set of characteristics, and which combinations are unavailable to the less well-off. This can be supplemented with survey data on respondents' own assessments of the extent to which they have 'autonomy' or choice and control over key aspects of their lives (see Burchardt, Evans, and Holder, 2015).

Finally, we may be interested in evaluating advantage because we think that advantage, and the mechanisms which secure and sustain it, contribute to the creation of disadvantage. Thinking about the causal relationship between advantage and disadvantage pushes us beyond thinking about the usual set of basic and central capabilities or functionings, because it is not only the fact that some people have higher educational achievement, for example, that disadvantages those with lower educational attainment (in relative terms), but also the fact that the privileged exercise their power in all sorts of ways that impede the chances of the less well-off. We thus need to consider functionings wholly unavailable to disadvantaged people, to identify what it is that the privileged can do and be that others cannot, and how this contributes to the creation and maintenance of inequalities.

But which of the infinite set of possible functionings are relevant here? For disadvantage, analysis typically focuses on a group of dimensions which would be valued in any context—goals which are shared by all people, whatever else they value (see Hick, 2014 for a discussion). However, once we turn our attention towards the study of advantage, there is no reason to assume that valued capabilities would coalesce around a common core; instead, people might value and have reason to value very different capabilities. We could call this the *challenge of pluralism*, following Rawls (1988: 255–6).

Moreover, if our motivation is to understand the ways in which advantage and disadvantage are causally connected, we must consider the exercise of power that is harmful to others. Sen emphasizes that capabilities are what people 'value and have reason to value', and this excludes, by definition, the ability to harm others (e.g. murder), on the Kantian grounds that one cannot have reason to value a capability unless one can at the same time wish everyone else to have that capability too. So consideration of the exercise of power that is harmful to others implies going beyond capability space as defined by Sen.

An alternative is offered by what Goerne (2010) calls the *descriptive* as opposed to *normative* aspects of a person's capability set. The former reflects all of the things that a person is able to do and be—their raw freedom—while the latter refers solely to beings and doings which a person has reason to value—true capabilities in Sen's sense. While analysis of disadvantage can concentrate on normative capabilities, specifically basic and central capabilities that people have reason to value, a comprehensive analysis of advantage must extend into descriptive capabilities to make room for examining raw freedoms that are actually or potentially harmful to others. This would include, for example, the ability to perpetrate violence or threaten violence on others; to avoid or subvert legal challenge; to exercise exclusive rights over land, natural resources, and scientific advances; to exploit labour (paid or unpaid); to exert disproportionate political influence; and to define cultural norms and values. This is not an exhaustive list, but provides an indication of the very different types of freedoms that are relevant to the evaluation of advantage than those commonly used to assess disadvantage. The fact that the privileged possess and use some of these freedoms to their advantage is of course part of the mechanism that generates and sustains disadvantage for others, and exploring these connections opens up important areas for further debate and research.

Two features of the capability approach, extended in this way, are relevant. The first is once again its multidimensionality. Whilst individuals who are advantaged in the areas listed above are all likely to be comparatively wealthy, they could have quite different levels of wealth—a warlord, a global entrepreneur, and a TV presenter, for example. If we consider advantage solely in terms of income and wealth, we may miss some of the mechanisms that operate on other dimensions.

The second feature is the inclusion of potential beings and doings as well as realized outcomes. A person in a position of power does not actually have to perpetrate violence or subvert justice or dismiss someone from his employment in order to gain advantage, he just needs other people to know he is in a position to do so if he chooses to.

The discussion in this section indicates that conceptualizing and evaluating advantage using the apparatus provided by the capability approach is not simply the flip-side of thinking about disadvantage. In particular, to understand the connections between the mechanisms of advantage and disadvantage, we may need to add 'raw freedoms', including those that have the potential to harm others, to the more familiar list of central and valuable capabilities. But key features of the capability approach—its multidimensionality, the way it captures trade-offs between valuable ends, and its focus on potentials as well as realized outcomes—suggest that it could offer important insights into the nature of advantage.

2.3 Applications

In this penultimate section we review a number of applications of the capability approach, each of which serves to highlight some of its distinctive features.

2.3.1 *The Human Development Index and the Multidimensional Poverty Index*

Perhaps the most prominent of all applications is that of the UN Human Development Index (HDI), which has formed the basis of the United Nations Development Programme's (UNDP) Human Development Reports since their inception in 1990. The HDI is an aggregated measure of income, life expectancy, and education, and was proposed by the Pakistani economist Mahbub ul Haq to shift attention from *economic* development (as encapsulated by GDP per capita) to *human development* (which would be partially captured in HDI rankings).

In focusing on just three dimensions, the HDI is a highly reductive form of the capability approach, as Sen himself has noted: 'These are useful indicators in rough and ready work, but the real merit of the human development approach lies in the plural attention it brings to bear on development evaluation' (Sen, 2000: 22).

One of the limitations of the HDI, is that its three component measures do not come from the same data source. This means that while it can provide country rankings, it is not possible to explore the coupling of disadvantages *within* households. Partly for this reason, Alkire et al., (2015) have proposed a new Multidimensional Poverty Index (MPI) (see also Chapter 1 in this volume). This index is comprised of ten indicators relating to standard of living, health, and education but, importantly, the data are all collected in the same survey, enabling the examination of simultaneous deprivations within households (Alkire and Santos, 2010: 8). It thus allows combinations of functionings to be explored, and subsequently disaggregated by socio-economic and household characteristics, and so forth.

2.3.2 *The Equality Measurement Framework*

The Equality Measurement Framework (EMF) is a capability-inspired framework for monitoring equality and human rights in England, Scotland, and Wales (Burchardt and Vizard, 2011) (Figure 2.1). The framework assesses inequalities between individuals and groups in the 'substantive freedom' they enjoy. 'Substantive freedom' is unpacked into three aspects: achieved *outcomes* (or functionings), *autonomy* (or choice and control), and *treatment* (including issues of discrimination, or conversely, being treated with dignity and respect). This attempt to capture aspects of capability that go beyond observed functionings is one way in which the EMF is distinctive from other capability applications.

The framework incorporates a capability list derived from international human rights covenants, which was refined through deliberative consultation with the general public and with groups at risk of discrimination and disadvantage (Burchardt and Vizard, 2011). The capability list is grouped into ten domains: life; physical security; legal security; health; education and learning; standard of living; productive and valued activities; participation, influence, and voice; individual, family, and social life; identity, expression, and self-respect (Vizard and Speed, forthcoming 2015). The EMF adopts a 'dashboard' approach—meaning that inequalities in the different domains are examined in their own right and are not aggregated into multidimensional measures of inequality. Arguably, this makes it easier to identify potential targets for policy intervention (EHRC, 2010), and to be sensitive to differences between groups and between dimensions, although it has the disadvantage of generating a mass of data which can be intractable, and which cannot readily be summarized or plugged into evaluations of cost-effectiveness.

The EMF adopts a principle of 'systematic disaggregation' of each indicator by a set of equality characteristics including age, gender, disability, ethnicity, and social class as well as, where possible, sexual identity and religion/belief (Suh et al., 2013). It shows how the capability approach can motivate an analysis which looks at the overall spread of achievement across multiple

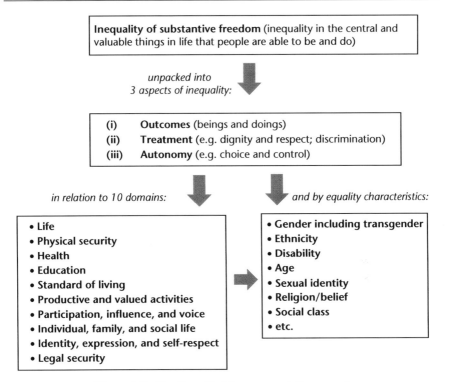

Figure 2.1. The Equality Measurement Framework
Source: Burchardt and Vizard, 2011

dimensions, as well as differences in achievements between sub-groups of the population (Burchardt and Vizard, 2011).

2.3.3 *Hick's Analysis of the Distinctiveness of Multidimensional Assessment*

One response to the greater complexity of multidimensional analysis is to investigate whether the results it produces are distinctive to those produced using a simpler, unidimensional approach, or whether they are effectively equivalent. Hick (2015) has conducted a capability-inspired analysis of the relationship between two measures of material poverty (low income and material deprivation) and seven dimensions of multiple deprivation (health, mental health, housing deprivation, limited autonomy, life satisfaction, financial stress, unemployment) in the United Kingdom, analysing the dimensions individually as well as in aggregate form.

The findings show that the distinctiveness of multidimensional assessment depends significantly on whether one is interested in identifying vulnerable *individuals* or vulnerable *groups* and whether one is analysing aggregate or disaggregated measures. The measures of material poverty and multiple deprivation are found to identify substantially different individuals as being poor and deprived, irrespective of whether disaggregated or aggregate measures of material poverty and multiple deprivation are analysed. Greater consistency is observed in identifying the *groups* at risk of poverty and deprivation, though these remain distinctive when disaggregated measures of material poverty and multiple deprivation measures are employed. When analysing the aggregate experience of material poverty and multiple deprivation for thirty-five population sub-groups, there is a very high degree of consistency (the correlation between groups' aggregate material poverty and multiple deprivation scores was 0.92 in this exercise).

Adopting a more straightforward approach does not, by definition, account for the multidimensional mechanisms of advantage and disadvantage. Nonetheless, Hick's findings suggest that the distinctiveness of multidimensional assessment is not an all-or-nothing affair: it depends on whether one's interest is in identifying disadvantaged individuals or groups, and whether the focus is on disaggregated or aggregated dimensions. If our aim is to identify advantaged or disadvantaged groups (rather than individuals), then a simpler analysis may in fact take us quite far.

2.4 Conclusions

In this chapter, we have provided an outline of the capability approach and a discussion of how it can be employed to conceptualize advantage and disadvantage. We have argued that it offers a distinctive assessment of advantage and disadvantage compared to approaches based on resources or subjective well-being. The distinctiveness derives from two key features: its multidimensionality, and its focus on real freedoms as well as observed outcomes.

Multidimensionality ensures that important dimensions of advantage and disadvantage can be examined in their own right rather than overlooked or misrepresented by focusing on a single dimension like income or happiness, or by using aggregate or proxy measures. We can explore the relative position of individuals, groups, and countries in terms of a core set of central and valuable capabilities such as standard of living, health, education, physical security, political participation, and so on. Low levels of achievement indicate disadvantage while a higher level of achievement on one or more dimensions indicates advantage.

Secondly, multidimensionality combined with attention to what real opportunities are available to people, draws our attention to the different trade-offs that people face. For example, a severely disadvantaged person is likely to be both in poor health and have a low standard of living. Someone with fewer constraints may face a trade-off: they can achieve a higher standard of living but only by taking a job that imperils their health or safety. The truly advantaged are freed of this dilemma: they can obtain a comfortable standard of living from the safety of their armchair! Thus looking at combinations of functionings and the trade-offs between them for different groups is a key and distinctive contribution that the capability approach can make to analysis of advantage and disadvantage.

Finally, both the multidimensionality and the freedom-focus of the capability approach come into sharp focus when considering the causal relationship between advantage and disadvantage—that is, the mechanisms which generate and sustain inequality. Here we have argued there is a need to go beyond central and valued capabilities to a wider field of 'raw freedoms' including the exercise of power that may be harmful to others, such as the ability to subvert the course of justice. This opens up an interesting avenue for further debate and research.

There are however limitations and challenges to the capability approach. Controversy over which capabilities are relevant, how they are to be identified, and whether they can reflect ongoing struggles for recognition of diverse human needs continues (although in practice most capability lists for evaluating disadvantage show considerable overlap). Taking account of interdependency between people is a clear theoretical requirement, but can be difficult to implement empirically. Indeed, the informational and analytical demands of the capability approach are significant and remain an obstacle to reflecting the full conceptual richness of the approach in real-world applications.

Recent years have seen substantial attention devoted to the issue of advantage in addition to the more traditional focus on disadvantage. We would argue that this field has much to gain from a greater focus on the diverse ways in which advantage can manifest itself and, indeed, in the relationship between dimensions of advantage and their role in generating disadvantage for others. This is a newly emerging field, which despite its conceptual and empirical challenges provides the basis for a critical reframing of essential debates regarding our understanding of social advantage and disadvantage.

References

Alkire, S. (2002). *Valuing Freedoms*. Oxford: Oxford University Press.

Alkire, S. (2010). 'Human Development: Definitions, Critiques and Related Concepts'. Background paper for the 2010 *Human Development Report*. Oxford: Oxford Poverty and Human Development Initiative.

Alkire, S. and Santos, M. E. (2010). 'Acute Multidimensional Poverty: A New Index for Developing Countries'. OPHI Working Paper No. 38. Oxford: Oxford Poverty and Human Development Initiative.

Atkinson, A. B. and Piketty, T. (eds) (2014). *Top Incomes: A Global Perspective*. Oxford: Oxford University Press.

BBC. (2010). 'Plan to Measure Happiness "not Woolly"—Cameron', BBC online, 25 November 2010, http://www.bbc.co.uk/news/uk-11833241, last accessed 24 February 2015.

Bonvin, J.-M. and Dif-Pradalier, M. (2010). 'Implementing the Capability Approach in the Field of Education and Welfare: Conceptual Insights and Practical Conse-quences'. Deliverable 2.1. Workshop-related papers on the application of the cap-ability approach to the study of transitions from education to the labour market. Pavia: W.-M. C. Work.

Brandolini, A. and D'Alessio, G. (1998). *Measuring Well-being in the Functioning Space*. Rome: Banco d'Italia Research Department.

Burchardt, T. (2010). 'Time, Income and Substantive Freedom: A Capability Approach'. *Time and Society*, 19(3): 318–44.

Burchardt, T., Evans, M., and Holder, H. (2015). 'Public Policy and Inequalities of Choice and Autonomy'. *Social Policy & Administration*, 49: 44–67. doi: 10.1111/spol.12074.

Burchardt, T. and Vizard, P. (2011). '"Operationalising" the Capability Approach as a Basis for Equality and Human Rights Monitoring in Twenty-first Century Britain'. *Journal of Human Development and Capabilities*, 12(1): 91–119.

Dean, H. (2009). 'Critiquing Capabilities: The Distractions of a Beguiling Concept'. *Critical Social Policy*, 29(2): 261–78.

Dolan, P. (2014). *Happiness by Design*. London: Penguin.

Equality and Human Rights Commission (EHRC) (2010). *How Fair Is Britain? Equality, Human Rights and Good Relations in 2010. The First Triennial Report*. London: EHRC.

Forster, M. and Mira d'Ercole, M. (2005). 'Income Distribution and Poverty in OECD Countries in the Second Half of the 1990s'. OECD Social, Employment and Migration Working Papers. Paris: OECD.

Goerne, A. (2010). 'The Capability Approach in Social Policy Analysis: Yet Another Concept?'. REC-WP Working Papers on the Reconciliation of Work and Welfare in Europe, (03-2010). Edinburgh: RECWOWE Publication, Dissemination and Dialogue Centre.

Gough, I. (2014). 'Climate Change and Sustainable Welfare: An Argument for the Centrality of Human Needs'. CASEpaper 182. London: Centre for Analysis of Social Exclusion, LSE.

Hick, R. (2014). 'Poverty as Capability Deprivation: Conceptualising and Measuring Poverty in Contemporary Europe'. *European Journal of Sociology*, 55(3): 295–323.

Hick, R. (2015). 'Material Poverty and Multiple Deprivation in Britain: The Distinctive-ness of Multidimensional Assessment'. *Journal of Public Policy*, FirstView. doi.org/10.1017/S0143814X14000348.

Hick, R. and Burchardt, T. (forthcoming). 'Capability Deprivation'. In D. Brady and L. M. Burton (eds), *The Oxford Handbook of Poverty and Society*. Oxford, Oxford University Press.

Layard, R. (2005). *Happiness: Lessons from a New Science*. London: Allen Lane.

Layard, R. (2006). 'Happiness and Public Policy: A Challenge to the Profession'. *The Economic Journal*, 116, C24–C33.

Milanovic, B. (2011). *The Haves and the Have-nots*. New York: Basic Books.

Nussbaum, M. (2011). *Creating Capabilities: The Human Development Approach*. Cambridge, MA: Harvard University Press.

Piketty, T. (2014). *Capital in the Twenty-first Century*. Cambridge, MA: Harvard University Press.

Ravallion, M., Chen, S., and Sangraula, P. (2009). 'Dollar a Day Revisited'. *The World Bank Economic Review*, 23(2): 163–84.

Rawls, J. (1988). 'The Priority of Right and Ideas of the Good'. *Philosophy and Public Affairs*, 17(4): 251–76.

Robeyns, I. (2005). 'The Capability Approach: A Theoretical Survey'. *Journal of Human Development*, 6(1): 93–117.

Runciman, W. (1966). *Relative Deprivation and Social Justice: A Study of Attitudes to Social Inequality in Twentieth-century England*. Berkeley: University of California Press.

Sen, A. (1987). *Commodities and Capabilities*. New Delhi: Oxford University Press.

Sen, A. (1997). 'Inequality, Unemployment and Contemporary Europe'. *International Labour Review*, 136(2): 155–71.

Sen, A. (2000). 'A Decade of Human Development'. *Journal of Human Development*, 1(1): 17–23.

Sen, A. (2010). 'The Place of the Capability Approach in a Theory of Justice'. In H. Brighouse and I. Robeyns (eds), *Measuring Justice: Primary Goods and Capabilities*, pp. 239–53. Cambridge: Cambridge University Press.

Stewart, F. (2005). 'Groups and Capabilities'. *Journal of Human Development*, 6(2): 185–204.

Stiglitz, J., Sen, A., and Fitoussi, J-P. (2009). 'Report of the Commission on the Measurement of Economic Performance and Social Progress'. Online. http://ec.europa.eu/eurostat/documents/118025/118123/Fitoussi+Commission+report, accessed 15 August 2015.

Sugden, R. (1993). 'Welfare, Resources and Capabilities: A Review of *Inequality Reexamined* by Amartya Sen'. *Journal of Economic Literature*, 31(4): 1947–62.

Suh, E., Tsang, T., Vizard, P., Zaidi, A., and Burchardt, T. (2013). 'Quality of Life in Europe: Social Inequalities'. *Eurofound Third European Quality of Life Survey*. Luxembourg: Publications Office of the European Union.

Taylor, M. (1985). *Philosophy and the Human Sciences: Philosophical Papers 2*. Cambridge: Cambridge University Press.

United Nations Development Programme (UNDP). (2014). *Human Development Report 2014: Sustaining Human Progress: Reducing Vulnerabilities and Building Resilience*. New York: United Nations Development Programme.

Vizard, P. and Speed, L. (2015). Examining Multidimensional Inequality and Deprivation in Britain Using the Capability Approach. *Forum For Social Economics*, Published Online 03 Feb 2015, doi: 10.1080/07360932.2014.997267

Wolff, J. and de-Shalit, A. (2007). *Disadvantage*. Oxford: Oxford University Press.

World Bank (n.d.). 'GDP per capita, PPP (current international $)'. Online. http://data.worldbank.org/indicator/NY.GDP.PCAP.PP.CD, accessed 15 August 2015.

Zaidi, A. and Burchardt, T. (2005). 'Comparing Incomes When Needs Differ: Equivalization for the Extra Costs of Disability in the UK'. *Review of Income and Wealth*, 51(1): 89–114.

3

The Human Rights and Equalities Agenda

Polly Vizard

The contemporary idea of human rights is embodied in the Universal Declaration of Human Rights (1948). This suggests that all individuals everywhere have basic entitlements to a core set of freedoms—civil, political, economic, social, and cultural—which should be secured on the basis of non-discrimination and equality, regardless of country, nationality, and citizenship, or characteristics such as gender, age, race, and ethnicity, or other characteristics or status. This idea of human rights is widely invoked worldwide in struggles against oppression and campaigns for social justice. Historically speaking, antecedents of the idea of human rights—such as earlier notions of natural rights in the Western tradition—have been axiomatic to challenges against the arbitrary and unjust exercise of power for more than two thousand years.

This chapter considers the role of human rights in addressing social (dis)advantage. It suggests that human rights can play an important role in addressing the social as well as the political dimensions of advantage and disadvantage and in framing the claims of those who are disadvantaged and the corresponding duties of those in a position to help. Poverty and other aspects of socio-economic deprivation such as hunger, starvation, lack of access to healthcare and education, and exploitative working conditions, were downgraded and neglected as human rights concerns for much of the second half of the twentieth century. However, there is now substantially more international recognition and acceptance of a broader characterization of human rights incorporating social, economic, and cultural rights as well as civil and political rights; and positive as well as negative duties. Economic and social rights are being translated into bills of rights and positive law in many different countries and contexts and are increasingly cited as underpinning policies and strategies that aim to address poverty and multidimensional deprivation at the global, regional, and national levels. Campaigns to combat social disadvantage increasingly appeal to notions of human rights both internationally and in the British context.

The chapter examines these developments and explores the potential of a human rights approach to (dis)advantage. The first section discusses the links between human rights and (dis)advantage. The second explores foundational debates in ethics. The third considers issues of legal status and enforcement. The fourth discusses the more general role that human rights can play in influencing social outcomes beyond the Courts—for example, through public policy mechanisms, as instruments of regulation and in broader processes of social change. The concluding section reflects on the possible limitations of a human rights approach.

3.1 Framing the Discussion: Human Rights and (Dis)advantage

For many decades, the international human rights agenda focused almost exclusively on civil and political rights. Poverty and other aspects of multidimensional deprivation such as lack of access to food, water, shelter, housing, education, and/or healthcare were not recognized as 'legitimate' elements of the international human rights agenda. Whilst recognition of economic and social rights dates back to the Universal Declaration of Rights (1948), for much of the second half of the twentieth century, these issues were excluded and downgraded. Underlying factors here included the politics of the Cold War and ideological struggles over the concepts of individual freedom and human rights. In the United States, despite early support for the notions of freedom from want, the liberty-focused view of human rights had the ascendency—with economic rights viewed exclusively as rights of capital rather than as rights of individuals (Alston, 2009; Stiglitz, 2012).

As a result of this downgrading and neglect of poverty and multidimensional deprivation as human rights concerns, the international human rights framework was widely perceived as failing to provide foundations for a broad concept of disadvantage, taking account of the different dimensions (civil, political, economic, social, etc.) that this concept entails. This is not to imply that the non-fulfilment of civil and political rights such as torture, inhuman and degrading treatment or punishment; lack of access to justice (for example, a free and fair trial); and nonparticipation in political and public life (for example, free elections) are not critical elements of the concept social disadvantage. However, as noted in Chapter 1, poverty and deprivation in basic needs such as health and education are central to the concept of disadvantage (see also Dean, 2015). Whilst the international human rights agenda was dominated by civil and political rights concerns, discussions about social disadvantage and advantage on the one hand, and discussions about human rights on the other, were rarely linked.

3.1.1 *International Recognition of Economic and Social Rights*

In contrast, there has been substantial evolution and broadening of the idea of human rights over the past two decades. Economic and social rights are codified in key international human rights treaties such as the International Covenant on Economic, Social and Cultural Rights (ICESCR) which, as an international treaty, is legally binding on state parties under international law. There were 161 such state parties by July 2014. The ICESCR is part of the International Bill of Human Rights, which, with its sister treaty the International Convention on Civil and Political Rights, sets out the core human rights that are recognized internationally. The ICESCR recognizes the right to an adequate living and freedom from hunger (article 11); the right of everyone to the enjoyment of the highest attainable standard of physical and mental health (article 12); the right of everyone to education (article 13) and compulsory primary education, free of charge (article 14); the right to work (article 6); and the right to just and fair conditions of work (article 7) and the right to social security (article 9). By signing up to this treaty, states are obliged 'to take steps, individually and through international assistance and co-operation, to the maximum of its available resources, with a view to achieving progressively the full realisation of these rights' and to guarantee non-discrimination (article 2). Other key international instruments recognizing economic and social rights are highlighted in Figure 3.1.

3.1.2 *International Recognition of 'Positive Obligation'*

The international human rights framework has also undergone a substantial evolution and broadening over the past two decades in the way in which the obligations on states to guarantee human rights are characterized. It has become increasingly accepted that all human rights—civil, political, economic, social, and cultural—give rise to positive duties on states to protect and promote human rights as well as negative duties on states to refrain from undermining human rights. This shift provides an important step in the development of a formal theory of human rights towards a substantive understanding of human rights that takes into account the things that in practice people can *do* and *be* (Vizard, 2006).

Fredman (2008) provides a detailed examination of positive obligation in international human rights law. She notes that human rights were long understood only in terms of negative duties and providing protection for

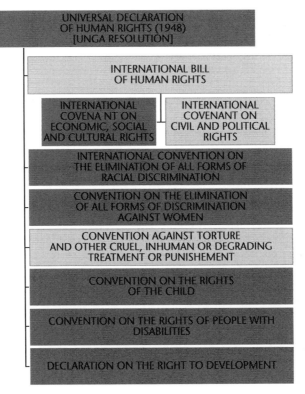

Figure 3.1. The human rights framework in the UK—protection of economic and social rights

individual negative freedom against an intrusive state. However, the emergence of a positive understanding of duties constitutes an effective 'transformation' of the idea of human rights—away from a paradigm which involves being 'left alone' towards a richer view which takes into account of a person's ability to exercise their freedoms in practice (Fredman, 2008).

The evolution and broadening of international standards relating to positive obligation is an ongoing process. The international human rights framework has traditionally put a central emphasis on states as duty holders. However, recent international standards put increasing emphasis on protection from violations by third parties (e.g. private companies) and on collective obligations (e.g. The Maastricht Principles on Extraterritorial Obligations, 2012).

3.1.3 *A Human Rights Approach to (Dis)advantage*

Whilst the idea of human rights remains contested, the international human rights framework can still play an important role as a pragmatic starting point for characterizing disadvantage in terms of the denial of a broad set of critical freedoms (civil, political, economic, social, and cultural), which are basic entitlements of all individuals everywhere, on the basis of non-discrimination and equality. This includes international recognition of the human rights to an adequate standard of living, health, housing, and education, as well as freedom from torture and inhuman or degrading treatment, and the right to a free trial and fair elections (Vizard, 2006; 2007). This approach has been applied in the context of inequality monitoring by the British Equality and Human Rights Commission (on which, see Burchardt and Vizard, 2011, and Chapter 2).

Human rights can also provide an analytical bridge between the idea of (dis) advantage and the concepts of responsibility, obligation, and accountability. Logically speaking, human rights are not simply descriptive characterizations of critical freedoms, but are linked to normative obligations on the part of others to guarantee the freedoms involved. Consider the following questions. Do those who are advantaged and who are in a position to help have obligations to address social disadvantage? Do governments, international organizations, and private companies have duties to address disadvantage within a domestic context and/or globally? The international human rights framework provides a starting point for addressing these questions and for developing an overall framework of accountability and responsibility for addressing poverty and multidimensional deprivation (Vizard, 2006; 2007).

3.1.4 *Challenges for a Human Rights Approach*

Yet whilst the human rights approach has considerable pragmatic appeal, the justification, validity, and effectiveness of a human rights approach to the elimination of poverty and multidimensional deprivation raises far-reaching issues across a number of different disciplinary perspectives.

- Foundational debates continue relating to the underlying question of whether the idea of human rights can be justified. Even if the idea of human rights can indeed be justified, its reach extends beyond civil and political rights to cover poverty and the non-fulfilment of basic needs and capabilities remains controversial.

- Human rights standards are increasingly put forward as a basis for legal challenges to poverty and multidimensional deprivation. However, key questions arise in relation to the legal enforcement and justiciability of economic and social rights. Why are international mechanisms for economic and social rights still weaker than for civil and political rights? Should these standards be codified in positive law? Can the corresponding duties be specified and legally enforced?

- In the social sciences, there is now more recognition of the broader role that human rights can play beyond the courts—in public policy, in overall systems for regulation, in providing 'bottom-up' sources of countervailing power, in shaping attitudes, norms and behaviour, and in broader processes of social change. However, important empirical questions remain regarding whether—and the extent to which—these standards can influence social outcomes and result in greater substantive social equality in practice.

These questions are addressed sequentially in the sections that follow. The discussion is necessarily brief and is intended as an introduction and overview to the key issues involved.

3.2 Foundational Debates in Ethics

In many classic theories, concerns with social disadvantage, poverty, and basic needs are classified as beyond the realm of 'legitimate' human-rights-based claims. This is the case not only in the tradition of libertarian theories of justice (e.g. Nozick and Hayek) which focus on the concept of negative obligation; but also in some liberal theories such as that proposed by O'Neill, who strongly argues *against* the proposition that deprivation in basic needs (including hunger and starvation) give rise to human rights based claims. According to O'Neill, precisely specified 'perfect obligations' (relating to the performance of specific actions) can be adequately reflected in a rights-based ethical framework. However, 'imperfect obligations' (relating to the promotion of general goals rather than the performance of precisely specified actions) will be 'unallocated' and 'neglected' in the absence of institutions and systems of special rights and cannot be effectively 'claimed' or 'enforced'. As a result, general obligations to relieve poverty, hunger, and starvation 'can at best have subordinate status in an ethical system in which the concept of rights is fundamental' (O'Neill, 1986; 1996).

3.2.1 *Poverty as a Violation of Human Rights*

There have been a number of attempts to develop broader theories of human rights that incorporate poverty and related concerns. Pogge attempts to avoid the complexities raised by notions of positive (imperfect) obligation by focusing on the characterization of global poverty as a violation of *negative* duties. In Pogge's ethical framework, the more advantaged (specifically, the global rich) are viewed as having stringent negative duties to refrain from supporting socio-economic arrangements that impede the fulfilment of basic social and

47

economic rights. Socio-economic arrangements such as international trade agreements, property rights, and patent rules relating to essential medicines are characterized as having a *causal* role in generating and perpetuating global poverty (Pogge, 2008).

In the broader literature, Campbell argues in favour of a theory of poverty and human rights based on the universal humanitarian obligation to participate in the relief of extreme suffering (Campbell, 2007). Griffin rejects the formulation of some social and economic rights in international instruments (including article 12 of the ICESCR). Nevertheless, he contends that human personhood and agency require both liberty and autonomy; and that 'there is a human right to the minimum resources needed to live as a normative agent' (Griffin, 2008: 206). Beitz develops a political account of human rights informed by contemporary human rights practice including 'anti-poverty rights' (Beitz, 2011).

3.2.2 The Capability Approach and Human Rights

The links between the capability approach, discussed in Chapter 2, and the development of a broad theory of human rights are examined in Vizard (2006; 2007). In Sen's conceptual framework, basic capabilities such as being free from hunger and malnutrition, and having access to education and healthcare, are characterized as human freedoms. Deprivation in basic capabilities of this type are viewed as sources of 'unfreedom' and as an important element of a theory of justice (Sen, 2009).

Building on these arguments, the capability approach provides a basis for the development of a broad theory of individual rights that covers aspects of socio-economic deprivation as well as deprivation in basic liberties. Sen has argued that the importance of certain critical freedoms constitutes the grounds of basic claims on others to safeguard these freedoms and on social arrangements (such as the nature of institutions, positive law, and public action). In this way, the subset of capability-freedoms links to a derived class of 'capability rights' and associated obligations with 'minimal demands of well-being (in the form of basic functionings, e.g. not to be hungry), and of well-being freedom (in the form of minimal capabilities, e.g. having the means of avoiding hunger)' conceptualized as rights that 'command attention and call for support' (Sen, 1985).

By extension, Sen contends that the idea of capability is an important 'element' of a theory of human rights. Human rights denials can relate to deprivation in basic capabilities (such as poverty, malnutrition, and lack of access to education and healthcare) as well as to deprivation in basic liberties and 'many human rights that can be seen as rights to particular capabilities'. Sen has also argued (against O'Neill) that human-rights-based claims can be valid in the context of imperfect obligation (with broadly specified duties) as well as perfect obligation (with narrowly/precisely specified duties). He concludes that a theory of human rights can legitimately include economic and social rights (Sen, 2004; 2005; 2009).

3.3 Human Rights as a Legal Paradigm

Some legal theorists in the positivist tradition have developed their own version of the sceptical philosophical position on economic and social human rights. It has been argued, for example, that the standards set out in international treaties in the field of economic and social rights are too vague and indeterminate to be regarded as 'real' justiciable rights that can be legally enforced. This position has been developed, for example, in the context of Article 2 of the ICESCR. Sceptics argue that the notions of 'maximum available resources' and 'progressive realization' limit the nature and scope of the obligations of states and that the human rights set out in the ICESCR have an aspirational rather than a legal status (e.g. Vierdag, 1978).

The growing body of authoritative international interpretative standards relating to the implementation of economic and social rights challenges this characterization. These are set out in the General Comments of the UN Committee on Economic, Social and Cultural Rights, which oversees the implementation of the ICESCR, and other authoritative international documents. For example, the 'minimum core' obligations approach suggests that the failure to ensure the satisfaction of, at the very least, minimum essential levels of economic and social rights is taken to provide prima facie evidence of a violation (The Maastricht Guidelines on Violations, 1998).

3.3.1 *The South African Model*

The sceptical position is also challenged by the trend towards the incorporation of economic and social rights into regional and domestic law and national constitutions and bills of rights. Internationally, there is a growing body of case law that supports the characterization of human rights covering poverty and other aspects of multidimensional deprivation as 'real' justiciable individual rights that can be enforced in the courts.

For example, the economic and social rights given effect in the South African Bill of Rights are summarized in Figure 3.2. The justiciability of these standards has been established by the South African Court in a series of landmark cases. In the Grootboom case (2000), the Court established that economic and social rights are rights that the Courts can, and in appropriate circumstances should, enforce. It found that whilst the South African State is

Index of sections
7. Rights
8. Application
9.Equality
10.Human Dignity
11/12. Life, Freedom and Security of the Person
13. Slavery, Servitude and Forced Labour
14. Privacy
15. Freedom of Religion, Belief and Opinion
16. Freedom of Expression
17. Assembly, Demonstration, Picket and Petition
18. Freedom of Association
19. Political Rights
20. Citizenship
21. Freedom of Movement and Residence
22. Freedom of Trade, Occupation and Profession
23. Labour Relations
24. Environment
25. Property
26. Housing
27. Health Care, Food Water and Social Security
28. Children
29. Education
30/31. Language, Culture and Linguistic and other Communities
32. Access to Information
33. Just Administrative Action
34. Access to Courts
35. Arrested, detained and Accused Persons
36/37. Limitation of Rights and States of Emergency
38/39. Enforcement and Interpretation

Figure 3.2. Constitution of South Africa (1996): Chapter 2 (Bill of Rights)

not required to go beyond available resources or to realize economic and social rights immediately, it has nevertheless a positive obligation to take steps to ameliorate deplorable living conditions, including by providing access to housing, health-care, sufficient food and water, and social security to those unable to support themselves and their dependants.

In a second landmark decision (the 'Treatment Action Campaign' case), the Court ruled that the absence of a comprehensive and coordinated plan for the roll-out of anti-retroviral drugs could not be regarded as 'reasonable' and compatible with section 27 of the South African Bill of Rights. This case is widely cited as establishing an international model for the judicial enforcement of the right to health. At the same time, however, the case also highlights the limited function of the Courts in providing judicial review in the field of public and social policy. The South African Constitutional Court considered but did not apply the 'minimum core obligations' approach set out in the Maastricht Principles and the General Comments of the UN Committee on Economic, Social and Cultural Rights. Rather, it emphasized the limited and qualified nature of the obligation on the state to take 'reasonable' measures to progressively eliminate deprivation over time.

3.3.2 *Justiciability and Enforcement in the British Context*

The UK has signed and ratified numerous international human rights instruments including the International Convention on Civil and Political Rights, the International Convention on Economic, Social and Cultural Rights, the Convention on the Rights of the Child, the Convention on the Elimination of Discrimination Against Women, the Convention on Torture and the Convention on Rights of People with Disabilities. Whilst these international treaties impose legally binding obligations on states parties under international treaty law, they are not usually viewed as elements of UK domestic law (or as directly enforceable through the British Courts). In contrast, the Human Rights Act (HRA) (1998) incorporates the rights set out in the European Convention on Human Rights (ECHR) into UK domestic law. Under section 6, public bodies providing services such as education and healthcare—as well as private providers providing public functions, such as private providers of social care—are required to be HRA complaint.

Whilst the focus of the HRA is on civil and political rights, it has also been interpreted as providing an element of protection for economic and social rights. In 2005, it was established that the denial of public assistance to a late asylum seeker could amount to a violation of Article 3 of the ECHR (the prohibition on torture and cruel, unusual treatment or punishment). Whilst the threshold for establishing violations was found to be extremely high, this may be crossed if 'a late applicant with no means and no alternative sources of support, unable to support himself, is, by the deliberate action of the state, denied shelter, food or the most basic necessities of life'. Article 3 of the HRA, together with Article 8 (private and family life), is increasingly invoked to challenge neglect in public services. In the Bernard case, the courts ruled that a local council was not merely under a negative duty to refrain from interference in private and family life but also had a positive duty to take steps to maintain the basic physical and psychological integrity of a disabled woman (including the provision of suitably adapted accommodation). Another recent case concerned an alteration in a social care package by Kensington and Chelsea council. Whilst a legal challenge based on human rights standards ultimately failed, the case helped to establish the role of dignity as a legal principle in public services delivery.

The Equality Act (2010) provides a framework of protection against discrimination and establishes a general public sector equality duty (PSED) which requires public authorities to give 'due regard' to equality. This duty is binding on all public authorities such as local authorities, central government, health commissioners, health providers, schools, and other bodies (for example, private social care providers) when they are carrying out a public function. The PSED has been characterized as an important step in moving beyond an individual, complaints-based model and in providing legislative recognition of the need for pro-active measures to promote or achieve equality by characteristics such as gender, ethnic group, and disability (Fredman, 2011). However, a duty 'to have due regard to inequalities of outcome which result from socio-economic disadvantage' has *not* been put into force.

3.3.3 *Human Rights and Austerity*

Human rights and equality standards have been invoked to challenge public decision-making in the context of austerity and fiscal consolidation. A number of cases point towards the necessity of consultation and equality impact assessment as *procedural* requirements. In 2011, in the Rahman case involving Birmingham City Council, the withdrawal of funding from legal advice centres was found to be in breach of the PSED on the grounds that the impact on disadvantaged service users had not been fully assessed. In another case, the High Court considered a council decision to limit social care eligibility criteria to cover critical needs only. It reasoned that the impact of this change on disabled people with substantial care needs had not been fully assessed and the consultation process had been inadequate.

Recent cases establish that the threshold for establishing human rights violations is extremely high and suggest only a minimal, limited role for judicial intervention in public and social policy. In Britain, widely applied principles of administrative law equate lack of 'reasonableness' with 'irrationality' and result in an extremely stringent test for establishing violations. This test is often justified in terms of the 'separation of powers' and the proposition that the judiciary should only rarely interfere with decision-making by the democratically elected executive and legislative branches of government.

This reasoning was reflected in a recent case where the Court of Appeal upheld an earlier decision of the High Court that the Government's housing benefit regulations (2012) (the so-called benefit cap) did *not* violate human rights. The Court highlighted the primary role of democratically elected institutions in decision-making in public policy; and the limited role of the judiciary in undertaking scrutiny. It reasoned that whilst being potentially harmful, the regulations could not be deemed as 'manifestly without reasonable foundation' since they had been subjected to parliamentary scrutiny and could be revised in the future. The Supreme Court similarly ruled that the regulations were not unlawful (although the cap was found to be incompatible with the Government's obligation to promote the 'best interests of the child' under the UN Convention on the Rights of the Child). In another case, the High Court again ruled that new housing benefit rules are *not* 'manifestly without reasonable foundation'. This case now awaits further adjudication.

3.4 Broader Processes and Mechanisms

Beyond the ethical and legal perspectives, there is now more recognition of the instrumental role of human rights standards beyond the courts. Box 3.1 sets out some of the broad mechanisms and processes—beyond individual justiciability and legal enforcement—whereby human rights and equalities standards can influence social outcomes. These include the role of human rights in public policy and regulation; the role of human rights as sources of 'bottom-up' and countervailing power and as a driver of attitudes, behaviour, and social norms; and the role of human rights in overall processes of social struggle and social change.

Arguably, resource allocations, welfare states, public health systems, and other public and social policy measures—not legal codification and judicial enforcement—are necessary to bring about substantive social change. However, human rights and equalities standards and norms now play an important role in motivating such approaches. They are increasingly cited as a basis for social legislation and broader policy initiatives (e.g. the *Bolsa Familia* programme in Brazil). In India, there has been increasing emphasis on judicial enforcement of economic and social rights. This includes, for example, key legislative decisions enforcing the right to food, based on a broad interpretation of the Right to Life under Article 21 of the Indian Constitution, read in conjunction with Directive Principles. However, judicial enforcement has been combined with broader policies and social legislation such as famine relief measures, a school meals programme, the Right to Education Act, the Right to Information Act, and the Rural Employment Guarantee Scheme (on which see Drèze, 2004 and Drèze and Sen, 2013).

Box 3.1 PROCESSES AND MECHANISMS THROUGH WHICH HUMAN RIGHTS AND EQUALITIES STANDARDS MIGHT INFLUENCE SOCIAL OUTCOMES

- Constitutions/bills of rights/statements of basic societal goals
- Justiciability/legal enforcement
- Broader socio-economic arrangements: for example, social legislation, public policy, institutions (e.g. public health systems, welfare states), regulation
- Political influence (e.g. focusing political/media/public attention on a particular issue; helping to precipitate a public policy response; focusing political attention on minority concerns/needs of subordinate groups)
- Accountability and transparency—human rights as source of 'bottom-up' pressure, democratic control mechanisms, countervailing power
- Influencing social norms, expectations, attitudes, and behaviour (e.g. attitudes of girls to going to school)
- Contribution to civil and political activism in bringing about social change (e.g. social mobilization/agitation)

International economic and social rights also increasingly underpin measures to address poverty and multidimensional deprivation at the global and regional as well as national levels (e.g. OHCHR, 2003). The need for global welfare mechanisms and other global social policy interventions in implementing economic and social rights is highlighted in the literature (e.g. Deacon, 2007; Townsend and Gordon, 2002). Related proposals include a Global Resources Dividend, a tax on multinationals to support human development and a Health Impact Fund to support the development of essential medicines (Pogge, 2013).

Several analyses point towards a political economy understanding of human rights. Sen has famously argued that famines do not arise in democracies, citing wide-ranging empirical examples from the Indian Famine of 1947 to contemporary food shortages in Rajasthan. Sen and Drèze establish that democratic forms of government and individual rights can be instrumentally important in protecting and promoting capabilities via a range of different mechanisms including: by disseminating information, facilitating public scrutiny and debate, by building up political opposition, increasing pressure on governments, proving for the correction of 'errors', and helping to precipitate a more effective public policy response. Human rights campaigns can also impact on broader processes of social change through their effects on expectations, attitudes, and social norms (for example, in the emergence of new social norms on girls' right to education in India) (Sen, 1999; Drèze and Sen, 1989; 2002; 2013; Drèze, 2004).

Stiglitz highlights the role that individual rights can play in checking power and abuses. Individual rights to information (e.g. in the form of Freedom of Information Acts) can strengthen transparency and counter informational asymmetries that result in capture by special interests and corruption by government officials. Individual rights to redress can strengthen accountability and help to ensure that appropriate 'democratic control mechanisms' are in place. In general, an active civil society functions as a check on abuses of power and influence and concentrations of power in one domain are checked and restrained by countervailing sources of power in another domain. Participatory processes (including individual rights) provide one such source of 'countervailing power' (Stiglitz, 1999; 2002).

Stiglitz also highlights the complex interdependences between social outcomes, public policy, and social norms. Consider the lack of normative support for economic and social rights as human rights in the United States on the one hand, and the lack of universal health coverage and health inequalities on the other. As Stiglitz notes, 'more than a half-century ago, America led the way in advocating for the Universal Declaration of Human Rights... Today, access to health care is among the most universally accepted rights... America, despite the implementation of the Affordable Care Act, is the exception...with great divides in access to health care, life expectancy and health status' (Stiglitz, 2014).

Besley and Burgess (2002) examine the role of individual rights in ensuring responsiveness to citizens' needs in electoral democracies. They highlight the function of individual rights in public policy in preventing 'capture' by elites and dominant social groups and strengthening the influence of subordinate groups in collective decision-making. Amid an increasing consensus that inequality—especially extreme inequality—is bad for growth (Stiglitz, 2012; IMF, 2014), the limits imposed by inequality and discrimination on social opportunity, participation, and growth are examined in The World Bank (2005). The World Bank is also putting increased emphasis on the role of social protection and universal health in overall processes of development and growth (e.g. The World Bank, n.d.).

A recent assessment of the role of justiciable socio-economic rights in achieving social transformation in South Africa puts particular emphasis on the links between human rights standards on the other hand, and civil activism and social mobilization on the other. Arguably, the role of legal enforcement of economic and social rights in South Africa in achieving change on the ground has been limited. Nevertheless, human rights have played an important role as part of a broader social movement and a focus of civil society organization and activism (Langford et al., 2014).

Dean emphasizes the broader terrain of social struggle over the interpretation of social needs and human rights. He presents a dynamic view of human rights whereby human needs are socially interpreted and translated into rights-based claims. This dynamic process in turn reflects broader social relations, the balance of power between different social groups, 'bottom-up' processes of social agitation, and ongoing processes of social struggle. Dean further contends that, understood in this way, the idea of human rights can play an important role in the development of a global 'post-Marshallian' concept of social citizenship in an era of globalization (Dean, 2008; 2014; 2015).

3.4.1 *Global Poverty, Human Rights, and Equalities*

The Millennium Development Goals (MDG) provide an international agreement on reducing global poverty by 2015. Official evaluations suggest that international public action has been galvanized through the system of outcome-orientated and time-bound targets and indicators. Consider progress against MDG 1 ('eradicating extreme poverty and hunger'). Substantial progress has been made in relation to the $1.25 a day threshold, with the proportion of those in developing regions living in extreme poverty falling from 47 per cent in 1990 to 14 per cent in 2015. Nevertheless, in 2015 an estimated 863 million people lived in extreme poverty based on this definition (UN, 2015).

The international human rights framework makes provision for the 'progressive realisation' of economic and social rights. Nevertheless, some have argued that the MDGs have been a betrayal of international standards—with only weak links to international law, minimalist targets specified in terms of *halving* rather than *eliminating* extreme poverty and hunger, and weak mechanisms for accountability and enforcement. The absence of adequate mechanisms for implementing collective obligations under MDG 8 ('building a global partnership for development') has been highlighted. Other critiques concern the (mis)identification of the global poor (Reddy and Pogge, 2005) and lack of focus on inequalities (Doyle and Stiglitz, 2014).

3.4.2 *Broader Applications in the British Context*

In the British context, equality and human rights have an increasing role beyond the Courts—as the basis for public action, as elements of an overall regulatory framework, and as minimum standards in public policy. Equalities and human rights standards are referred to in a broad range of contexts from child poverty to medical neglect and poor treatment in public services. National institutions (for example, the Children's Commissioners for England) and NGOs increasingly work within a human rights and equalities framework.

The Child Poverty Act (2010) established a legal duty to eradicate child poverty by 2020 (the so-called 'Child Poverty Duty'). The Act establishes both political and legal accountability mechanisms (with a possibility of judicial review) and specifies four time-bound statistical targets for evaluating progress. The legislation has been characterized by the Joint Committee on Human Rights as a 'human rights enhancing measure' that provides a means of implementing Article 27 of the Convention of the Rights of the Child and Article 11 of the ICESCR (Child Poverty Act 2010; JCHR, 2008; Vizard, 2012).

The PSEDs have resulted in a new form of administrative accountability and the publication of equality impact statements is now widespread amongst public authorities such as local and central government, education services and the police. In health the PSEDs cover both health commissioners and providers (e.g. hospital trusts) and are reinforced by new duties to reduce health inequalities (Health and Social Care Act 2012). The revised NHS Constitution also highlights equality and human rights standards.

The Equality and Human Rights Commission (EHRC) is a strategic equality and human rights regulator and undertakes a number of functions in addition to legal enforcement. A recent inquiry on exploitative working conditions in the meat and poultry processing sectors identified evidence of mistreatment and discrimination against migrant and pregnant workers. A further inquiry into home care identified evidence of failure to guarantee respect for the human rights of older people including instances of inhuman or degrading treatment (EHRC, 2010; 2011).

3.5 Limitations, Critique, and Conclusions

Power-based critiques of human rights have been developed in the literature in relation, for example, to the ideological foundation of human rights; the legal adjudication of human rights; and the functions of human rights within global configurations of power. The social control critique highlights the exercise of bureaucratic power, including in relation to the administration of welfare rights and poverty elimination programmes (Dean, 2015). Further concerns relate to the unequal nature of the legal system and unequal access to justice. Access to legal systems can be highly differentiated by social group. As Stiglitz notes, existing inequalities are reflected in legal as well as political systems, with the 'rules of the game' open to manipulation and rent-seeking behaviour (Stiglitz, 2012).

It has been suggested that judicial enforcement of the right to health in some countries and contexts has itself reinforced and resulted in new forms of inequality. For example, in Brazil there has been a rapid increase in right to health litigation over the past decade. Ferraz (2011) contends that the overall effect of such litigation has been to harm rather than benefit the most disadvantaged. Individualistic legal interpretations focusing on individual access to drugs and treatment has favoured litigants (often a privileged minority) over the rest of the population and reallocated resources away from comprehensive programmes aimed at the general population.

Arguably, conventional human rights law puts too much emphasis on resource-constrained states in the global south as duty holders. Under international human rights law, national authorities have traditionally been viewed as being responsible for the implementation and enforcement of human rights. As Stiglitz notes, globalization requires both a *downscaling* of responsibility (for example, to cover non-state actors such as private companies) and an *up*-scaling of responsibility (to the global arena—for example, with more emphasis on collective responsibilities). Multinational private companies, for example, should be held responsible for misuses of power and market manipulation and for human rights abuses under international law. Recent developments here include the Chevron case (involving allegations of responsibility for environmental pollution impacting on health in Ecuador); and the decision of the Indian Supreme Court to reject the patenting of a cancer drug by a private pharmaceutical company. At the other end of the spectrum, there should be more focus on collective responsibility and

57

the duties of the global north and international organizations in the context of global poverty (2013a; 2013b).

The proposition that the elected legislature, rather than the judiciary, should be responsible for public and social policy decisions that have resource implications has been invoked to challenge the legal enforcement of economic and social rights (Gearty, 2011). Another important critique relates to the distinction between formal rights and substantive rights—and whether the formal recognition of economic and social rights within legal instruments can bring about 'real' change on the ground. International mechanisms for implementation and enforcement of economic and social rights remain weaker than in the context of civil and political rights; whilst the textual formulation of the ICESCR qualifies and limits the obligations of states. Arguably, this formulation reduces the 'substantive rights' in the ICESCR to 'minimum standards'. Even if economic and social rights were to be universally enforced, their implementation can only be achieved over time and is consistent with the perpetuation of widespread inequalities.

In responding to these critiques, it is important to recognize that a human rights approach is not the same as a full theory of substantive equality. Indeed, the idea of a human rights approach has been proposed by some as a minimum conception of justice—that is, as specifying the minimum core entitlements and obligations that should pertain in a minimally just society. Likewise, international human rights standards provide a potential basis for limiting extreme social disadvantage and curtailing extreme advantage. However, even if perfectly implemented, these standards would be unlikely to address the full range of social disadvantages and advantages examined in this volume.

Sen has persuasively argued that the incremental elimination of injustices can and should proceed in advance of the specification of a full theory of perfect substantive equality. Whilst it is often possible to agree that some changes would reduce injustice, even if all such agreed changes were to be successfully implemented, we would not necessarily have anything that we can call 'perfect justice' (Sen, 2009: xii). The examples highlighted here suggest that the human rights approach—whilst imperfectly implemented to date and perhaps falling short of a utopian ideal—has an important role to play in achieving incremental improvements towards greater equality.

References

Alston, P. (2009). 'Putting Economic, Social, and Cultural Rights Back on the Agenda of the United States'. NYU School of Law, Public Law Research Paper No. 09–35. doi.org/10.2139/ssrn.1397703.

Beitz, C. (2011). *The Idea of Human Rights*. Oxford: Oxford University Press.

Besley, T. and Burgess, R. (2002). 'The Political Economy of Government Responsiveness: Theory and Evidence from India'. *Quarterly Journal of Economics*, 117(4): 1415–52.

Burchardt, T. and Vizard, P. (2011). 'Operationalizing the Capability Approach as a Basis for Equality and Human Rights Monitoring in Twenty-first-century Britain'. *Journal of Human Development and Capabilities*, 12(1): 91–119.

Campbell, T. (2007). 'Poverty as a Violation of Human Rights: Inhumanity or Injustice?' In T. Pogge (ed.) *Freedom from Poverty as a Human Right: Who Owes What to the Very Global Poor?* (pp. 55–74). Oxford: Oxford University Press.

Deacon, B. (2007). *Global Social Policy and Governance*. London: Sage.

Dean, H. (2008). 'Social Policy and Human Rights: Re-thinking the Engagement'. *Social Policy and Society*, 7(1): 1–12.

Dean, H. (2014). 'A Post-Marshallian Conception of Global Social Citizenship'. In E. Isin and P. Nyers (eds) *Routledge Handbook of Global Citizenship Studies* (pp. 128–38). Abingdon: Routledge.

Dean, H. (2015). *Social Rights and Human Welfare*. Abingdon: Routledge.

Doyle, M. and Stiglitz, J. (2014). 'Eliminating Extreme Inequality: A Sustainable Development Goal, 2015–2030'. *Ethics and International Affairs*, 28(1): 5–13. Available at http://www.ethicsandinternationalaffairs.org/2014/eliminating-extreme-inequality-a-sustainable-development-goal-2015-2030/, accessed April 2015.

Drèze, J. (2004). 'Democracy and the Right to Food'. *Economic and Political Weekly*, XXXIX: 17. Available at http://www.epw.in/special-articles/democracy-and-right-food.html, accessed 24 August 2015.

Drèze, J. and Sen, A. K. (1989). *Hunger and Public Action*. Oxford: Clarendon Press.

Drèze, J. and Sen, A. K. (2002). *India: Development and Participation*. New Delhi: Oxford University Press.

Drèze, J. and Sen, A. K. (2013). *An Uncertain Glory: India and its Contradictions*. London: Penguin.

Equality and Human Rights Commission (EHRC). (2010). *Inquiry Into Recruitment and Employment in the Meat And Poultry Processing Sector*. Available at http://www.equalityhumanrights.com/sites/default/files/documents/Inquiries/meat_inquiry_report.pdf, accessed 24 August 2015.

Equality and Human Rights Commission (EHRC). (2011). *Close to Home: An Inquiry into older people and care at home*. Available at http://www.equalityhumanrights.com/publication/close-home-inquiry-older-people-and-human-rights-home-care, accessed 1 September 2015.

Ferraz, O. (2011). 'Harming the Poor through Social Rights Litigation: Lessons from Brazil'. *South Texas Law Review*, 89: 1643–68.

Fredman, S. (2008). *Human Rights Transformed: Positive Rights and Positive Duties*. Oxford: Oxford University Press.

Fredman, S. (2011). 'The Public Sector Equality Duty'. *Industrial Law Journal*, 40(4): 405–27.

Gearty, C. (2011). 'Against Judicial Enforcement'. In C. Gearty and V. Mantouvalou (eds) *Debating Social Rights*. Oxford: Hart Publishing.

Griffin, J. (2008). *On Human Rights*. Oxford: Oxford University Press.

International Monetary Fund (IMF). (2014). *Redistribution, Inequality, and Growth*. Staff Discussion Note SDN/14/02 prepared by J. Ostry, A. Berg, and C. Tsangarides, IMF Research Department C. Available at http://www.imf.org/external/pubs/ft/sdn/2014/sdn1402.pdf, accessed 24 August 2015.

Joint Committee on Human Rights. (2008). *Legislative Scrutiny: Child Poverty Bill*. London: The Stationery Office. Available at http://www.publications.parliament.uk/pa/jt200809/jtselect/jtrights/183/18305.htm, accessed 24 August 2015.

Langford, M., Cousins, B., Dugard, J., and Madlingozi, T. (2014). *Socio-Economic Rights in South Africa: Symbols or Substance?* Cambridge: Cambridge University Press.

Office of the High Commissioner for Human Rights (OHCHR). (2003). *Human Rights and Poverty Reduction: A Conceptual Framework*. Geneva: United Nations.

O'Neill, O. (1986). *Faces of Hunger: An Essay on Poverty, Justice and Development*. London: Allen and Unwin.

O'Neill, O. (1996). *Towards Justice and Virtue: A Constructive Account of Practical Reasoning*. Cambridge: Cambridge University Press.

Pogge, T. (2008). *World Poverty and Human Rights*. 2nd edn. Cambridge: Polity.

Pogge, T. (2013). Interview with Thomas Pogge. E-International Relations. Available at http://www.e-ir.info/2013/06/12/interview-thomas-pogge/ accessed 24 August 2015.

Reddy, S. and Pogge, T. (2005). 'How *Not* to Count the Poor'. Version 6.2. New York: Columbia University. Available at http://www.columbia.edu/~sr793/count.pdf., accessed 5 August 2015.

Sen, A. K. (1985). 'Well-being, Agency and Freedom: The Dewey Lectures 1984'. *The Journal of Philosophy*, 82(4): 169–221.

Sen, A. K. (1999). *Development as Freedom*. Oxford: Oxford University Press.

Sen, A. K. (2004). 'Elements of a Theory of Human Rights'. *Philosophy and Public Affairs*, 23(4): 315–56.

Sen, A. K. (2005). 'Human Rights and Capabilities'. *Journal of Human Development*, 6(2): 151–66.

Sen, A. K. (2009). *The Idea of Justice*. Penguin: London.

Stiglitz, J. (1999). 'On Liberty, the Right to Know, and Public Discourse: The Role of Transparency in Public Life'. Oxford Amnesty Lecture, University of Oxford, 27 January.

Stiglitz, J. (2002). 'Participation and Development: Perspectives from the Comprehensive Development Paradigm'. *Review of Development Economics*, 6(2): 163–82.

Stiglitz, J. (2012). *The Price of Inequality*. Penguin: London.

Stiglitz, J. (2013a). 'Human Rights and Globalization: The Responsibility of States and Private Actors'. *Journal of Catholic Social Thought*, 10(1): 85–90.

Stiglitz, J. (2013b). 'India's Patently Wise Decision'. Project Syndicate. Available at http://www.project-syndicate.org/commentary/the-impact-of-the-indian-supreme-court-s-patent-decision-by-joseph-e–stiglitz-and-arjun-jayadev, accessed 24 August 2015.

Stiglitz, J. (2014). 'Inequality Is not Inevitable'. New York: *New York Times*. Available at http://opinionator.blogs.nytimes.com/2014/06/27/inequality-is-not-inevitable/?_r=0, accessed 24 August 2015.

The Maastricht Guidelines on Violations of Economic, Social and Cultural Rights (1998). *Human Rights Quarterly*, 20: 691–705.

The Maastricht Principles on the Extraterritorial Obligations of States in the Area of Economic, Social and Cultural Rights (2012). http://www.maastrichtuniversity.nl/web/Institutes/MaastrichtCentreForHumanRights/MaastrichtETOPrinciples.htm, final version 29 February 2012, accessed April 2015.

The World Bank (2005). *World Development Report 2006: Equity and Development.* Washington, DC: The World Bank.

The World Bank (n.d.). Universal Health Coverage mini-website, http://www.worldbank.org/en/topic/universalhealthcoverage, accessed 5 August 2015.

Townsend, P. and Gordon, D. (eds) (2002). *World Poverty: New Policies to Defeat an Old Enemy.* Bristol: The Policy Press.

United Nations (2015). *The Millennium Development Goals Report 2015.* Available at http://mdgs.un.org/unsd/mdg/Resources/Static/Products/Progress2015/English2015.pdf, accessed 24 August 2015.

Vierdag, E. W. (1978). 'The Legal Nature of the Rights Granted by the International Covenant on Economic, Social and Cultural Rights'. *Netherlands Yearbook of International Law,* 9: 69–105.

Vizard, P. (2006). *Poverty and Human Rights: Sen's 'Capability Perspective' Examined.* Oxford: Oxford University Press.

Vizard, P. (2007). 'Selecting and Justifying a Basic Capability Set: Should the International Human Rights Framework Be Given a More Direct Role?'. *Oxford Development Studies,* 35(3): 225–50.

Vizard, P. (2012). 'Evaluating Compliance Using Quantitative Methods and Indicators: Lessons from the Human Rights Measurement Framework'. *Nordic Journal of Human Rights Special Issue—Quantifying Human Rights,* 30(3): 12.

4

Class, Capitals, and Social Mobility

Lucinda Platt

Class is of enduring significance in describing the distribution of advantage and disadvantage across populations and explaining processes of intergenerational transmission. While not synonymous with income (see Chapter 7) or wealth (see Chapter 8) or the dividing power of poverty and riches discussed in Chapter 1, class represents a profound structuring of life chances of individuals and their offspring. Yet, class remains a highly contested term. This chapter provides an account of the disputed territory. It argues that the wealth of national cross-national and cross-temporal analysis on class stratification reveals its key role in social reproduction, and discusses the link to education (see also Chapter 6). Outlining some of the main ways that class has been conceived, specifically by Marx, Weber, and Bourdieu, it then discusses the contemporary class measures that stem from these different approaches. It follows this with a review of evidence of variations in social mobility, focusing on countries in the global north. While not the main focus of the paper, class analysis as applied to post-industrial and industrial economies is increasingly used to interrogate the openness or rigidity of structures of accumulation and intergenerational transmission in developing economies. Such studies reveal ways in which the analysis of class and social mobility may be taken forward in the future.

4.1 What is Class?

Class is a highly contested term that has a proliferation of meanings and forms of measurement. For Marx (1976) there were fundamentally two classes, the owners of capital (or the bourgeoisie) and those who supplied their labour in the service of capital (or the proletariat). Labourers created surplus value for the owners of capital by both being paid less in wages than they created in value and through, additionally, spending those wages on their own maintenance—reproducing themselves for future work as well as engaging in the reproduction of the next generation of workers (Marx, *Capital*, Vol. 1. Part VII, ch. 23).

For Marx, the distinction between labour and capitalists was fundamental and derived from his perception of the massive changes brought about by industrialization alongside the notable emiseration of workers also noted emotively by his collaborator Engels (1969). Marx observed how the owners of industrial capital (the 'bourgeoisie') were succeeding from land owners or the 'rentier' class, as the dominant and dominating class in society, with the proletariat succeeding own account workers, and feudal labourers. He expected this binary distinction to become more polarized, and solidarity with one class or the other to increase, noting how the bourgeoisie recognized their own common interests and in time the proletariat would do the same.

Development over the course of the nineteenth century of an intermediate (salaried) class with substantial status and income but not economic owner-ship complicated this dualistic picture, as Weber, writing some decades later was very aware. Weber like Marx was also attempting to understand the transformations of industrial society; but rather than the binary distinction between labour and capital, he elaborated different dimensions of social position, namely class, status, and power. While class was intrinsically linked to economic rewards and control of production, he argued that status oper-ated on a different dimension: a social position could be a high position but without the same economic rewards as a lower status position. Classes were linked to life chances, but were not communities, while status groups were typically communities. Status was reflected in patterns of consumption and culture, of 'styles of life'. At the same time, occupational groups were also seen by Weber as status groups. Moreover, status was also embedded in ascribed characteristics such as ethnicity or gender. Finally, power was distinguished as a third dimension. While power might often be economic power, non-capitalists could also find themselves in positions of substantial influence or control over the distribution of resources through their position in a bureau-cracy (Scott, 1996). Moreover, for Weber, power could be sought as an end in itself, as a form of social position or 'honour' rather than simply as the means to control the economy.

Among contemporary class analysts, neo-Weberians therefore emphasize the distinction between status and class, as discussed further in the section on measurement below. It has been argued that the conflation of class with status distinctions, that is common to popular discourse (cf. Cannadine, 1998), undermines recognition of the economic basis of class structures and invites inaccurate claims for 'classless' societies where *status* distinctions of language, style, or consumption are less pronounced (Scott, 1996: 31). Some neo-Weberian class analysts have attempted empirically to demonstrate the ways in which class and status operate distinctively and are associated with different aspects of life (Devine, Savage, Scott, and Crompton, 2005). For example, Chan and Goldthorpe (2007a, 2007b) explored different patterns of cultural consumption and argue that class, but not status, influences life chances, while status, but not class, results in more 'omnivorous' patterns of cultural consumption. That is, those who are higher status, rather than having 'elite' tastes enjoy a wider range of cultural consumption, while 'lower status' individuals have a more restricted range. This contrasts with the argument of Bourdieu, to which we turn next.

4.2 Class and Capitals

Unlike neo-Weberian approaches to social class which conceive of a distinction between class and status with each having potentially independent influences, Bourdieusian approaches conceive of the social advantage represented by class maintenance as being implicated in three complementary and reinforcing 'capitals'. The concept of 'capitals' as developed by the French sociologist, Pierre Bourdieu, extends the economic understanding of 'capital' as income and/or wealth to 'cultural' and 'social' capitals (Bourdieu, 1997). For Bourdieu, the term capital represents the process of accumulation across any given domain.

According to Bourdieu, and by contrast with Weber, these three forms of capital are 'fungible' or subject to 'transubstantiation' in that they are not only equivalent in terms of having specific measures of resources linked to them, but can also be exchanged between each other. They are discussed in terms of the ways in which they mutually reinforce one another to enable privilege to consolidate and maintain itself over time, as those with (more) resources continue to accumulate them and transmit them to subsequent generations.

4.2.1 *Economic Capital*

Economic capital is represented by access to monetary resources and the wealth (such as property rights) within which economic resources are institutionalized. See further the discussion of income and wealth in Chapters 7 and 8. Economic capital can immediately be converted into money, whereas the other capitals require investment of economic capital (directly or as time spent) in order that they can prove profitable. While the capitals are discussed as equivalent and in many ways commensurate, Bourdieu also acknowledges that economic capital underpins the other two forms of capital.

4.2.2 *Cultural Capital*

Bourdieu developed the notion of 'cultural capital' in his *Outline of a Theory of Practice* (Bourdieu, 1977). See also Bourdieu and Passeron (1977) and Bourdieu (1997). The relationship between cultural competence and educational advantage is discussed in more detail in Chapter 6. Education provides the means by which cultural capital can first be accumulated, then translated into qualifications, and, through qualifications, into (restricted) access to certain positions and hence into money. Bourdieu disputes the terminology of education and qualifications as 'human capital' as used in the economics literature as he argues that schooling and the acquisition of qualifications is not a matter merely of economic investment, but rather involves the effective transmission of a cultural 'habitus'.

In *Distinction* (Bourdieu, 1989), Bourdieu elaborated the concept, arguing that those with plenty of cultural capital define 'taste'. They make a distinction (which is naturalized and thus accepted as legitimate) between 'high' and 'low' culture. This then denies those who have other 'tastes' legitimacy, and reinforces the position of those with greater economic (and other) capitals to impose their 'refined' tastes on others who are concerned not to appear 'vulgar'. Such tastes then permeate institutionalized systems such as education and the civil service. Thus, this cultural hegemony serves to ensure the (legitimacy) of social reproduction of the ruling class.

Legitimacy for privilege is also obtained, he argues, through the recognition of learning by means of specific qualifications or credentials (compare the discussion in Collins (1979)). The apparently transparent and meritocratic nature of such qualifications enables their holders to justify their advantage and obtain the sanction of entitlement to their privilege from those less advantaged.

4.2.3 *Social Capital*

The third part of the triad of capitals which makes up and serves to reproduce advantaged class locations is social capital (Bourdieu, 1997). For Bourdieu, social capital comprises connections of social obligations. It consists in networks that give access to the resources (the economic, cultural, and social capital) of network members. Hence, social capital is 'the aggregate of the actual or potential resources which are linked to possession of a durable network of more or less institutionalised relationships' (p. 51). A key feature of these institutionalized relationships is that they imply membership of a group, which maintains social closure. Bourdieu argues that social relationships are not specifically pursued for the profit they provide and the solidarity which reinforces their value, but nevertheless, their continuous symbolic maintenance through the exchange of gifts does consciously or unconsciously create durable mutual obligations and hence provide access to the backing implied by solidarity and the reproduction of the group, and the profit derived from the ability to capitalize on others' resources.

This concept of social capital has a number of features in common with that developed by Coleman (1988). Both stress the importance of social closure for the effective working of the network and emphasize the fact that the maintenance of social networks may not be carried out *in order* to ensure the rewards and reproduction that flow from them. Coleman's conception was embedded in the incidental nature of many social contacts. He also illustrated how, as a result, the social capital of a group, such as a collective of parents who benefited their children through surveillance and mutual reinforcement of norms, could be easily and unintentionally disrupted by an individual action, such as a move to a different area. Coleman's account is particular concerned with the way in which social capital can contribute towards education or the formation of 'human capital'. Thus, like Bourdieu he links together social capital with educational attainment. However, Coleman's conception of social capital indicates that it can provide a resource precisely where other forms of advantage are lacking, rather than, as with Bourdieu, the forms being mutually reinforcing.

The stress on social closure within both Coleman and Bourdieu's account contrasts with Granovetter's (1973) account of the importance of extended networks and 'weak ties', rather than close—and closed—groups for instrumental advantage (see also Lin, 2001). This distinction was subsequently taken up by Putnam's (2000) contrast between 'bridging' and 'bonding' social capital. Coleman, however, shares with Putnam the premise that social capital created within-group trust. And loss of trust at the community level, was an aspect that was central to Putnam's consideration of the impact of the perceived decline of social capital in his influential work on *Bowling Alone* (Putnam, 1995, 2000). Putnam conceived of social capital as primarily a community-level resource, emphasizing 'networks, norms and trust', and, by contrast with Coleman, who stressed the importance of the family in the creation and maintenance of social capital, he focused on the aggregate rather than the individual or micro-level. Putnam is also known for his argument that homogeneous communities are better at creating social capital as a public good (Putnam, 2007).

Despite the influence of the concept of social capital and of the instrumental value of social networks, it has been widely critiqued on a number of grounds. First, it is a somewhat chaotic term with a variety of meanings and uses (Fine, 2001). It has also been argued that the usage of social capital, in particular the way it is employed by Putnam, ignores the way social capital can be used for socially destructive aims (Schuller, Baron, and Field, 2000). The idea of social capital as a community resource stresses its benefits rather than the negative aspects of social capital such as monopoly, exclusivity, and exclusion of non-group members from benefits or jobs, and the destructive as well as beneficial aspects of social control, surveillance, and norms of giving (Portes, 1998). Portes (1998; 2000) stressed the importance of clarity and distinguishing among: '(a) the possessors of social capital (those making claims); (b) the sources of social capital (those agreeing to these demands); (c) the resources themselves' (Portes, 1998: 6), elements which, he argued, were typically confused. He specifically critiqued the extension of the concept from individuals to communities as it involves circularity, in that the cause (social capital) and the positive effect (e.g. lower crime rates, greater trust) were mutually implicated. See also the discussion in Johnston and Percy-Smith (2003).

An over-emphasis on social capital and the need for disadvantaged individuals and communities to participate in social activities in order to ensure the health of those communities also risks treating it as a solution or 'catch-all' for all situations (Aldridge, Halpern, and Fitzpatrick, 2002). And it can risk 'blaming the victim' and idealizing the strength of 'homogeneous' communities, while ignoring more fundamental structural issues (Fine, 2005; Halpern, 2005).

4.2.4 *The Continuing Salience of Class*

While there continue to be debates on the exact definition of class, it is broadly recognized as representing a fundamental (economic) distinction between those with different relations to the means of production and differential command over resources. However, class also retains a concept of differential prestige, of differential patterns of consumption, and of particular social relations on the basis that people associate more with those of the same 'class' as themselves. The implications are that measurement of class is typically based on occupation, but there are debates as to whether class measures should (also) map the prestige of the occupation, its employment relations, or patterns of association between occupations. Furthermore there is also ongoing debate on whether classes need to be 'owned' by their members in order to be meaningful (Crompton, 2008). However, most class measures used in evaluating the openness or otherwise of societies do not involve a subjective element. Before reviewing the evidence on class persistence and mobility, we first look at measurement issues and the implications of different measures.

4.3 Measuring Class

To characterize the structure of societies and demonstrate the extent to which they are open or closed (i.e. enable mobility between classes) requires effective measures. Classifications take occupation as their starting point, but then diverge in the ways in which they translate occupations into class categories or class locations.

The various class schemes and scales that are in common use typically reflect adherence to the various theoretical accounts outlined above, and there is ongoing debate about the most appropriate. Proponents justify their choice of classification by its criterion validity, that is the extent to which position in the scheme or scale is associated with life chances; and by their construct validity, the extent to which the measures reflect the principles of class relations that are intended. Even here, though, there is often disagreement as to how well particular schemes or scales 'perform' in practice. In general, nevertheless, they tend to provide largely consistent accounts of class structures—though there are often differences between the story told in relation to class mobility and that told in relation to income mobility (Björkland and Jäntti, 2000; Jäntti and Jenkins, 2015).

4.3.1 *Registrar General's Social Class Schema (RGC)*

An early construction of class, and one that has endured in the UK for many decades despite its declining applicability, is the registrar general's social class schema. This is a 5-class categorical scheme based on occupation that was based on a manual/non-manual distinction. It was developed for analysing and demonstrating the classed nature of fertility decline; but, as Szreter (1996) has discussed, it was strongly embedded in assumptions about the class structure, which already presupposed the relationships between fertility and 'class'. It was not well validated nor based in clear theoretical constructs of class; and the categories that were relevant at the time of its development no longer prevail in the current occupational structure. Thus, for example, the large manual class at the beginning of the twentieth century has reduced substantially. This further limits the explanatory potential of the scheme. It has nevertheless endured in much British analysis, especially epidemiological analysis; and continues to be used to demonstrate classed health inequalities (see e.g. Acheson, 1998; Marmot, 2010).

4.3.2 *Marxist Class Schemes*

Wright (1997; 2005) operationalized a Marxist classification that retained the fundamental distinction between the proletariat and the bourgeoisie. His scheme is conceptually underpinned by the key features of class relations of exploitation and domination (Wright, 2005: 34). He aimed to acknowledge the complexities in allocating individuals to particular sets of class locations, including temporal issues of careers (where an individual is at a single point in

Table 4.1. Description of Wright's class locations

Non-owners	Owners
1. Managers	7. Petty bourgeoisie
2. Supervisors	8. Employers
3. Expert-managers	
4. Experts	
5. Skilled workers	
6. Workers	
All workers = 5 + 6	

Source: Based on Wright (1997)

time may not be a good representation of their lifetime relations), and the ways in which jobs may feature aspects of both capitalist and working class elements of power and relation to the means of production. He therefore argues that it is necessary to disentangle the different elements of what a job actually entails, rather than, for example, simply using the job title to classify people. Wright argues that the number of class locations identified should be that suitable for the subject of analysis. One example is that provided in *Class Counts*, which distinguished owners from non-owners but within non-owners then provided further gradation. See Table 4.1.

4.3.3 *Prestige Scales*

Prestige scales derive from the perspective that status is key to social relations (Ganzeboom and Treiman, 1996), and therefore rank occupations in relation to the 'prestige' associated with them. A large number (85 studies carried out in 55 countries) were integrated into a single Standard International Occupational Prestige Scale (SIOPS) (Treiman, 1977). The SIOPS has been criticized on the basis that it does not effectively distinguish those who truly have better life chances, since it is based on perceptions of the desirability of occupations rather than their material consequences. Nevertheless, there is a strong degree of cross-national consistency in the ways in which occupations are ranked (known as the Treiman constant).

4.3.4 *Socio-economic Indices (SEI)*

The International Socio-economic Index (ISEI), developed by Ganzeboom and Treiman (1996), is a socio-economic scale that was originally conceived as a way of generalizing prestige scales. However, it is differently constructed: position on the scale is based on education and income associated with a particular occupation. Results are scaled and lie in principle within a range from 10 to 90. It is able to translate occupational information from survey data in different countries to a common metric and is hence widely used for cross-national analysis. It is also not sex-specific: the translation accords both men and women with the same occupation the same ISEI rank. The ISEI has been extensively used for national and internationally comparative research.

4.3.5 *Categorical Scales: CASMIN, NS-SeC, E-SeC*

Also widely used for cross-national as well as within-country analysis is the EGP or CASMIN scale, developed by Erikson, Goldthorpe, and Portocarero (1979), and used in Erikson and Goldthorpe's (1993) influential account of continuities in social (im)mobility, *The Constant Flux*. CASMIN was a scale originally developed for harmonized cross-country analysis of fifteen countries (12 European countries plus Japan, the US, and Australia) (Erikson and Goldthorpe, 1993). It involved allocating occupations to a broad set of categories based on the expected economic rewards (and economic security of the job) and the nature of the employment relations and the levels of control or oversight. The labour contract—whether waged or salaried is seen as critical to the influence of occupation on life chances. Hence the salaried classes or 'salariat' were distinguished from wage earners, and self-employed (or petit bourgeoisie) from those in employment. The precise categories have been subject to some modification over time, as the scale has been used in a wide range of national and cross-national studies. For example, farmers are more relevant where agriculture is a more significant part of the overall economy; and certain categories are therefore sometimes collapsed. The full scale is not fully hierarchical, but it can be collapsed into a smaller, three-category class scheme.

More recently the NS-SeC for the UK and the E-SeC for Europe have been developed on very similar principles, but have incorporated more explicitly women's occupations and their employment relations into the scheme, since women were largely absent from early class and mobility analysis. The E-SeC categories are shown in Table 4.2. Agricultural workers can be distinguished, if needed, by splitting categories 8 and 9.

Like CASMIN, the E-SeC and NS-SeC have a similar basis for their claims of construct validity and criterion validity, validating against life expectancy and morbidity.

4.3.6 *The Cambridge Scale*

The Cambridge Scale (Prandy, 1990), or CAMSIS, while originally developed for the UK also has versions that cover other countries or that enable cross-national analysis as well versions for the analysis of different historical periods (see further http://www.camsis.stir.ac.uk/). This scale bases its measurement

Table 4.2. The European Socio-economic Classification (E-SeC) categories

	ESeC Class	Common term	Employment regulation
1	Large employers, higher grade professional, administrative, and managerial occupations	Higher salariat	Service Relationship
2	Lower grade professional, administrative, and managerial occupations and higher grade technician and supervisory occupations	Lower salariat	Service Relationship (modified)
3	Intermediate occupations	Higher grade white collar workers	Mixed
4	Small employer and self-employed occupations (excl. agriculture etc.)	Petit bourgeoisie or independents	–
5	Self-employed occupations (agriculture etc.)	Petit bourgeoisie or independents	–
6	Lower supervisory and lower technician occupations	Higher grade blue collar workers	Mixed
7	Lower services, sales and clerical occupations	Lower grade white collar workers	Labour Contract (modified)
8	Lower technical occupations	Skilled workers	Labour Contract (modified)
9	Routine occupations	Semi- and non-skilled workers	Labour Contract
10	Never worked and long-term unemployed	Unemployed	-

Source: Eric Harrison and David Rose (2006)

of class on the social relations, specifically marriage, that operate between classes. That is, classes are nearer or further from each other to the extent that individuals are more or less likely to marry people from those classes. The ranking of the scale (which class is at the top rather than which is at the bottom) is then intuitive. The continuity of the scale, ranging from 1 to 99 assumes, unlike the categorical CASMIN and E-SeC scales, that there are no clear breaks between classes, but instead a continuum of relative advantage and disadvantage, a position that is strongly debated between adherents of the two positions (Hout and DiPrete, 2006). It has good criterion validity, in that position on the scale is associated with outcomes that class would expect to be associated with, such as, for example, lower or higher life expectancy. Nevertheless, it has been criticized by proponents of the CASMIN scheme as having poor construct validity, because it is empirically driven by observed relationships and merges class with status.

4.3.7 Bourdieusian Class Schemas

Class and status are also meshed in operationalizations of Bourdieu's understanding of class. A recent example of a comprehensive attempt to produce a

set of class categories based on the three Bourdieusian dimensions of economic, social, and cultural capital is the 'Great British Class Survey' (Savage
et al., 2013). Measures of income and wealth, of cultural activity, and of the
characteristics (occupations) of social networks were collected from a wide
range of respondents. From their responses a set of seven 'classes' were
derived: elite, established middle class, technical middle class, new affluent
workers, traditional working class, emergent service workers, precariat. These
were defined in terms of variation across their levels of economic capital, their
social capital (both in status and number) and whether they had (strong)
highbrow or emerging cultural capital. It should be noted, however, that the
classes were linked quite closely to life cycle stages, with for example, those at
the beginning of their working lives having less economic capital, rather than
necessarily predicting life chances (see also http://www.bbc.co.uk/news/maga
zine-22000973).

4.3.8 *Class Fractions*

Finally, some have argued that current class categories are too broad for
effective explanatory purposes, while scales have been criticized because
they treat gradation equally. For example, Güveli, Need, and de Graaf
(2007) have suggested, at least for the Netherlands, that there is fractional-
ization within the 'top' classes between 'technocrats' and 'professionals',
and that splitting the classes on these lines allows them better to predict
other associations, such as voting patterns. Weeden and Grusky (2005;
2012) have argued that the 'big classes' of the CASMIN or E-SeC type cannot
properly explain patterns of social reproduction; and that better to understand the concrete processes driving intergenerational processes, we should
focus instead on finer grained 'microclasses', smaller class groupings that do
not follow a hierarchical ranking. It is in these micro-classes, Grusky argues,
that interactions and reproduction take place, since it is specific characteristics and behaviours that link the people in the micro-class. And it is the
aggregation of these more homogeneous micro-classes that explains how big
classes arise.

The measurement of class continues to provoke heated debate among analysts interested in processes of social stratification and social reproduction.
The use of different measures can produce some differences in associations at
the national or comparative level; but the persistent role of social origins in
influencing the outcomes of the subsequent generation are found to a lesser or
greater extent across all measures. The next section briefly reviews this fundamental issue of social reproduction and social mobility and some of the
international evidence on its patterns across time and space in developed
countries.

4.4 Class and Social Mobility: Some International Findings

Debate over the measurement of class is linked to differences in sociological understandings of the Western world. But there is wider agreement that the analysis of class and of class mobility specifically, that is, the (lack of) association between parents' and children's social class position, lies at the heart of the study of processes of continuity and change in advantage and disadvantage. This is also reflected in the concern and attention at policy level with the extent of social mobility. However, despite the widespread endorsement of social mobility and equality of opportunity (discussed further in Chapters 5 and 6) from a policy perspective, there is substantial confusion around the term, which can be used in different ways to represent different empirical realities.

Thus, before reviewing some of the international evidence on social mobility, this section first attempts to introduce some clarification. Intergenerational social mobility simply means that there is a lack of association between parents' social class position and their children's. Thus a society would be deemed to be more socially mobile than another if it had a lower correlation between, for example, parental ISEI and child's ISEI. This implies processes of both downward as well as upward mobility between generations. However, those concerned with equality of opportunity, or creating a level playing field are typically concerned with ensuring upward mobility of those from disadvantaged backgrounds rather than downward mobility of those from advantaged backgrounds (see also Aldridge et al., 2002). The confusion partly stems from the fact that it is possible to have absolute upward mobility (from the working class) while at the same time having relative immobility in terms of higher-class preservation of position.

The distinction between relative and absolute mobility is critical not only to how societies are characterized but also to how class change is experienced at the individual level. To the extent that the changing class structure creates more 'room at the top', it is possible for there to be substantial upward mobility from those with more disadvantaged backgrounds. Nevertheless this can still be accompanied by immobility in terms of relative chances. Figure 4.1 illustrates this point with a highly stylized description of change

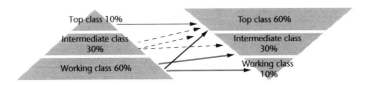

Figure 4.1. Stylized illustration of social mobility in a changing class structure

in class structure in a post-industrial society, as Western nations have moved to a high-skilled and more service-oriented economy.

Figure 4.1 shows that where there is substantial expansion at the top of the class structure there is *necessarily* absolute upward mobility from both the intermediate and the working class. However, if, as illustrated, those 10 per cent of the population with origins in the top class stay in the top class, 20 per cent of the 30 per cent with origins in the intermediate class move up and 10 per cent stay in the intermediate class, and 30 per cent of those 60 per cent with origins in the working class move into the top class, 20 per cent move into the intermediate class and 10 per cent stay in the working class, the relative and the absolute mobility experiences are quite different. Three times as many of the new top class would come from working class backgrounds as from top class backgrounds (30 per cent compared to 10 per cent), and these working-class-origin individuals would have far exceeded their parent's social class position. However, only 50 per cent (30 out of 60) of those with working-class backgrounds and two-thirds of those with intermediate backgrounds would be in the top class compared to 100 per cent of those with top-class backgrounds. At the same time, those with working-class origins would have a one-in-six chance (10/60) of ending up in the working class compared to a zero per cent chance among those from the top class. So their relative chances, expressed as the ratio between these two potential outcomes across the two classes, are a lot poorer. While not disputing the importance of absolute mobility, which has been a feature of many developed countries over the last few decades, most mobility analysts—and policymakers—concentrate on relative mobility chances, since relative mobility reflects the extent to which there is social fluidity (Erikson and Goldthorpe, 1993) compared to social reproduction.

Any account of class processes has to be able to incorporate an explanation of the ways in which absolute mobility can increase while relative advantage is still maintained. The overall picture of class patterning across OECD countries illustrates both of these regularities (Hout and DiPrete, 2006), though the continued expansion of managerial and professional social classes in post-industrial societies may be slowing. At the same time, while these general aspects of class structure show consistency across a large number of countries, there are clear differences in the openness of different societies that is, in the extent to which they enable movement between social classes or up and down social class ranks. Nevertheless, there is dispute over whether or not these can be called 'differences of degree but not of kind' (Hout and DiPrete, 2006: 5). The argument that there is a common pattern underpinning these differences was the premise of Erikson and Goldthorpe's study of twelve countries formulated as *The Constant Flux*. However, Breen's subsequent (2004) cross-national study of social mobility in eleven European countries, exploited multiple surveys from different time points within the same country better to disentangle temporal change, and challenged the earlier findings. This study suggested that there was no underlying trend in social fluidity, even while there was convergence across countries over time in terms of overall class structure, with a pattern of moves from agricultural to non-agricultural and from industrial to post-industrial economies (Breen and Luijkx, 2004). Countries were grouped into those with relatively high social fluidity, Sweden, Norway, Poland, Hungary, followed by those with, in descending order, lower levels of social fluidity, Britain, Ireland, France, and Italy. Germany had the strongest association between origins and destinations (immobility) and Israel was the most open in terms of social mobility.

Finally, they were able to show that in line with the modernization thesis and in contrast to Erikson and Goldthorpe's study there had been an increase in social fluidity over the period they had studied for most countries. That is, most countries had become more open over time. However, there were exceptions—Great Britain had not shared in this general trend towards greater openness. Studies on other countries suggested that Japan had also not shared in a move towards greater openness, though Australia had (Breen and Jonsson, 2005). The United States showed similar rates of class mobility to European countries, but this is often contrasted with a very different picture in relation to income mobility (Blanden, 2008; Jäntti and Jenkins, 2015).

A major contributing factor to differences in social mobility across countries has been argued to be education systems and the role of education in social mobility or social reproduction Breen and Jonsson (2005).

4.5 Understanding Class Reproduction and the Role of Education

As Hout and DiPrete (2006: 6) put it 'education is the main factor in both upward mobility and the reproduction of status from generation to generation'. While this may appear a contradictory claim, revisiting the stylized pattern shown in Figure 4.1 can reveal how education can account both for moves up from the bottom tier of the original distribution while also ensuring that those in the top tier remain there. Expanding education systems can help those from lower social class origins to reach the occupations available in an expanded service class, while those who have an interest in maintaining their privilege across generations will adapt in ways that aim to exploit the systems to their advantage and retain their social position (see also Chapters 5 and 6, this volume). While there are a number of ways of illustrating the role of education in social class outcomes, at their core is typically some variant on

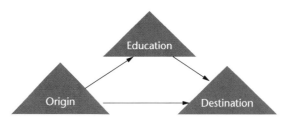

Figure 4.2. The OED model

the relationship between social (class) origins (O), (class) destinations (D), and the intervening role of education (E), as illustrated in Figure 4.2.

In Figure 4.2, the lines connecting origins to education demonstrate the influence of social class on educational attainment. The line connecting education to destinations represents the 'meritocratic' link between educational attainment and class outcomes; while the line connecting origins to destinations shows the impact of social class background that is not attributable to educational attainment. The stronger the OD line is the more the society represents a typical feudal society which is not dependent on education. The extent to which the ED line is strong and *not* strongly influenced by the OE line will demonstrate the independent role of educational attainment on subsequent life chances, and thus greater openness or meritocracy. The strength of the OE line demonstrates how far education is shaped by class origins, and hence how far education provides a route for maintenance of class advantage.

Blau and Duncan (1967) developed a highly influential account of the process of class advantage as a staged approach from father's education and occupation to child's (son's) education and hence to son's first job and then second job. This was an explicit attempt to trace the causal process of 'reproduction', by emphasizing the temporal ordering of different aspects of transmission of social origins. They distinguished indirect (i.e. through education) and direct (i.e. net of education) effects of social origins. They highlighted that both direct and indirect effects of class origins mattered, but that there was also much that was not driven by background. That is, education had a strong (though not total) effect on occupations and most of the effect of education was still independent of parental background.

This 'status attainment model' was further developed by Sewell, Haller, and Portes (1969), who brought social–psychological insights to the Blau and Duncan model. They aimed to identify 'mechanisms' driving the relationships. They focused on aspirations/expectations, both of young people themselves and of 'significant' others. They also aimed to adjust for cognitive ability, seen as an important route to educational outcomes, but also likely to differ with social class background. They found that socio-economic background (SES) affected educational expectations/aspirations both of others (e.g. parents) and young persons. These in turn affected educational attainment, though there was an additional remaining direct effect of SES on education (OE).

Their results were influential in providing one potential pathway between parental education and occupation and children's outcomes—that of aspirations, or more accurately expectations anchored in a particular view of the world. Subsequent research has continued to find a significant role for expectations on educational attainment (Goodman, Gregg, and Washbrook, 2011), but studies have also tended to identify a continuing independent effect of social background on subsequent occupational outcomes even net of education (OD) (Breen, 2004), though with substantial cross-national variation. Those countries that had lower inequalities in access to education were also those where the effect of class background net of education was lower. Breen (2004) also found an increased association between education and class position (ED) at the expense of that between origins and class position (OD).

4.5.1 Class and Relative Risks

The fact that education remains a critical route by which social advantage is reproduced, requires an attempt to explain the mechanisms by which that occurs. The attempts to disentangle these mechanisms can be divided broadly into cultural (or Bourdieusian) and materialist approaches, which are further elaborated in Chapter 6. Relative risk aversion proposed by Breen and Goldthorpe (1997), and extended and tested many times since, took its starting point from Boudon's (1974) insight, building on the status attainment model, that there is a spiral of aspirations and attainment that largely affects those in the middle of the attainment distribution. For those who are certain to do well or are protected by their strong class position, the risks of 'failure' are not a major consideration, and for those with very low educational attainment the issue does not arise. However, for those who face some uncertainty, a calculus is involved which offsets the benefits of continuing in education against the costs should it not work out.

Breen and Goldthorpe (1997) developed this theoretical argument and framed it as relative risk aversion. They argued that those starting from a higher social class position would need to obtain a higher level of qualifications in order to be sure of maintaining their position, and therefore the additional investment in time spent in education was worth making. They also suggested that those from different class backgrounds would be working with different subjective perspectives on their chances of success, which would be relatively inflated among those of higher social class position, and relatively deflated among those of lower social class origins. In combination, these factors would influence the relative chances of equally 'able' individuals continuing in education dependent on their social class origins. This theory allowed for both increasing levels of attainment across the board and for relatively constant class differentials in attainment, which are the patterns that are observed.

The potential for such accounts to help move closer to the mechanisms implied in social reproduction of class position have been welcomed, but it has also been highlighted that there is much more to be done adequately to explain both how social reproduction operates within countries, and differences in social fluidity between countries. The concluding section briefly reflects on some areas that have shown extensive development over recent years and have the potential to enhance our understanding further of these classic processes of class reproduction.

4.6 Conclusions and Reflections

Class position remains an enduring marker of life chances and the potential to transmit those life chances to subsequent generations. Class analysis can provide an effective description of stable life course positions and the advantages and disadvantages associated with them. Nevertheless, we still lack a complete understanding of both how advantage is perpetuated—but to a different degree in different societies—and what factors are implicated in the success of those from disadvantaged positions who are upwardly mobile.

Much of the classic early class analysis focused on early industrializing Western societies, as they have undergone transformations away from rural economies and to post-industrial societies, on the experience of majority populations, and primarily on men and father-to-son transmission, there are now extensive bodies of work that have developed research in all these areas. First, while the major cross-national studies outlined in this chapter focused on OECD countries, there is nevertheless a substantial and increasing strand of studies exploring how patterns of mobility are playing out in the particular conditions of developing countries and emerging economies (see e.g. Bian, 2002; Torche, 2005). These have shown how rapid or dramatic changes have altered the structure of stratification and the relevance of studies of class mobility to illuminating such changes.

The intersections of class with gender and ethnicity and the differences in mobility patterns by sex or ethnic group have the potential both to complicate but also to enhance our understanding of the pertinent factors in class mobility. There has been a long history of critique from a gender perspective of mobility analysis, which has focused on men and on father-to-son intergenerational transmission. See further the discussion in Crompton (2008). While women are now typically incorporated into class studies and measures, the issues that were linked to their original exclusion from analysis remain pertinent for effective analysis and interpretation. These include the fact that individuals are likely to share some aspects of the class position of others within the household, particularly their spouse. While marital homogamy is extensive, it is not a universal law and the class of one's husband or wife is likely to have a bearing on one's own life chances.

Individual-focused approaches to class analysis miss this important dimension of the role of household class on life chances. Moreover, the influence of mothers' as well as fathers' social class on both sons and daughters is an additional complicating factor in the appropriate analysis of class mobility; but can make a difference to observed patterns and how they are explained (see also Chapter 10).

Similarly, while ethnicity is still only rarely addressed in mobility studies, the different patterns of class mobility that pertain for minorities relative to the majority have the potential not only to problematize standard accounts of social mobility (Platt, 2005, 2007) but also to provide insight into what it is about advantaged social origins that helps perpetuate advantage. If not all groups experience the 'benefit' of advantaged origins to the same degree, then that indicates that we need to look for mechanisms which can incorporate such differences, perhaps articulating the relationship between class and 'status' further. (See further Chapters 12 and 13.)

Finally, one area that has been considered particularly fruitful for understanding in more detail the processes involved in intergenerational transmission is the early years. We know that class differences emerge early in childhood and that early educational transitions are more influenced by social origins than later transitions. Hence, to address both empirically and in policy the ways in which inequalities are perpetuated requires a better understanding of social (im)mobility as it plays out in the early years, a topic taken up in the next chapter.

References

Acheson, S. D. C. (1998). *Independent Inquiry into Inequalities in Health*. London: The Stationery Office.

Aldridge, S., Halpern, D., and Fitzpatrick, S. (2002). *Social Capital: A Discussion Paper*. London: Performance and Innovation Unit.

Bian, Y. (2002). 'Chinese Social Stratification and Social Mobility'. *Annual Review of Sociology*, 28: 91–116.

Björkland, A. and Jäntti, M. (2000). 'Intergenerational Mobility of Socio-economic Status in Comparative Perspective'. *Nordic Journal of Political Economy*, 26: 3–32.

Blanden, J. (2008). 'How Much Can We Learn from International Comparisons of Social Mobility?'. *Education and Social Mobility* (pp. 9–48). Carnegie Corporation of New York and the Sutton Trust.

Blau, P. and Duncan, O. D. (1967). *The American Occupational Structure*. New York: Wiley.

Boudon, R. (1974). *Education, Opportunity, and Social Inequality: Changing Prospects in Western Society*. New York: Wiley-Interscience.

Bourdieu, P. (1977). *Outline of a Theory of Practice*, tr. R. Nice. Cambridge: Cambridge University Press.

Bourdieu, P. (1989). *Distinction: A Social Critique of the Judgement of Taste*. London: Routledge.

Bourdieu, P. (1997). 'The Forms of Capital'. In A. Halsey, H. Lauder, P. Brown, and A. Stuart Wells (eds), *Education: Culture, Economy, Society* (pp. 46–58). Oxford: Oxford University Press.

Bourdieu, P. and Passeron, J.-C. (1977). *Reproduction in Education, Society and Culture*. London: Sage.

Breen, R. (ed.) (2004). *Social Mobility in Europe*. Oxford: Oxford University Press.

Breen, R. and Goldthorpe, J. H. (1997). 'Explaining Educational Differentials: Towards a Formal Rational Action Theory'. *Rationality and Society*, 9(3): 275–305.

Breen, R. and Jonsson, J. O. (2005). 'Inequality of Opportunity in Comparative Perspective: Recent Research on Educational Attainment and Social Mobility'. *Annual Review of Sociology*, 31(1): 223–43.

Breen, R. and Luijkx, R. (2004). 'Social Mobility in Europe between 1970 and 2000'. In R. Breen (ed.), *Social Mobility in Europe* (pp. 37–75). Oxford: Oxford University Press.

Cannadine, D. (1998). *Class in Britain*. London: New Haven.

Chan, T. W. and Goldthorpe, J. H. (2007a). 'Class and Status: The Conceptual Distinction and its Empirical Relevance'. *American Sociological Review*, 72(4): 512–32.

Chan, T. W. and Goldthorpe, J. H. (2007b). 'Social Stratification and Cultural Consumption: The Visual Arts in England'. *Poetics*, 35: 168–90.

Coleman, J. (1988). 'Social Capital in the Creation of Human Capital'. *American Journal of Sociology*, 94: S95-S120.

Collins, R. (1979). *The Credential Society: An Historical Sociology of Education and Stratification*. New York: Academic Press.

Crompton, R. (2008). *Class and Stratification*. 3rd edn. Cambridge: Polity Press.

Devine, F., Savage, M., Scott, J., and Crompton, R. (eds) (2005). *Rethinking Class: Cultures, Identities and Lifestyles*. London: Palgrave Macmillan.

Engels, F. (1969). *The Condition of the Working Class in England*. London: Panther.

Erikson, R. and Goldthorpe, J. (1993). *The Constant Flux: A Study of Class Mobility in Industrial Societies*. Oxford: Oxford University Press.

Erikson, R., Goldthorpe, J. H., and Portocarero, L. (1979). 'Intergenerational Class Mobility in Three Western European Societies'. *British Journal of Sociology*, 30: 415–41.

Fine, B. (2001). *Social Capital versus Social Theory: Political Economy at the Turn of the Millennium*. London: Routledge.

Fine, B. (2005). 'If Social Capital Is the Answer, We Have the Wrong Questions?'. *Social Capital, Civil Renewal and Ethnic Diversity, Proceedings of a Runnymede Trust Conference* (pp. 75–82). London: Central Books.

Ganzeboom, H. B. G. and Treiman, D. J. (1996). 'Internationally Comparable Measures of Occupational Status for the 1988 International Standard Classification of Occupations'. *Social Science Research*, 25: 201–39.

Goodman, A., Gregg, P., and Washbrook, E. (2011). 'Children's Educational Attainment and the Aspirations, Attitudes and Behaviours of Parents and Children through Childhood in the UK'. *Longitudinal and Life Course Studies*, 2(1): 1–18.

Granovetter, M. (1973). 'The Strength of Weak Ties'. *American Journal of Sociology*, 78: 1350–80.

Güveli, A., Need, A., and de Graaf, N. D. (2007). 'The Rise of "New" Social Classes within the Service Class in The Netherlands: Political Orientation of Social and Cultural Specialists and Technocrats between 1970 and 2003'. *Acta Sociologica*, 50(2): 129–46.

Halpern, D. (2005). *Social Capital*. Cambridge: Polity.

Harrison, E. and Rose, D. (2006). *The European Socio-economic Classification (ESeC) User Guide*. Colchester: Institute for Social and Economic Research, University of Essex. Available at: https://www.iser.essex.ac.uk/files/esec/guide/docs/UserGuide.pdf, accessed 1 September 2015.

Hout, M. and DiPrete, T. A. (2006). 'What Have We Learned? RC28's Contributions to Knowledge about Social Stratification'. *Research in Social Stratification and Mobility*, 24: 1–20.

Jäntti, M. and Jenkins, S. P. (2015). 'Income Mobility'. In A. B. Atkinson and F. Bourguignon (eds), *Handbook of Income Distribution. Volume 2* (pp. 807–935). Elsevier.

Johnston, G. and Percy-Smith, J. (2003). 'In Search of Social Capital'. *Policy & Politics*, 31(3): 321–34.

Lin, Nan (2001). *Social Capital: A Theory of Social Structure and Action*. Cambridge: Cambridge University Press.

Marmot, M. C. (2010). *Fair Society, Healthy Lives: Strategic Review of Health Inequalities in England post-2010*. London: The Marmot Review.

Marx, K. (1976). *Capital: Volume 1*. London: Penguin Books.

Platt, L. (2005). 'The Intergenerational Social Mobility of Minority Ethnic Groups'. *Sociology*, 39(3): 445–61.

Platt, L. (2007). 'Making Education Count: The Effects of Ethnicity and Qualifications on Intergenerational Social Class Mobility'. *The Sociological Review*, 55(3): 485–508.

Portes, A. (1998). 'Social Capital: Its Origins and Applications in Modern Sociology'. *Annual Review of Sociology*, 23: 1–24.

Portes, A. (2000). 'The Two Meanings of Social Capital'. *Sociological Forum*, 15(1): 1–12.

Prandy, K. (1990). 'The Revised Cambridge Scale of Occupations'. *Sociology*, 24: 629–55.

Putnam, R. D. (1995). 'Bowling Alone: America's Declining Social Capital'. *Journal of Democracy*, 61. 65–78.

Putnam, R. D. (2000). *Bowling Alone: The Collapse and Revival of American Community*. New York: Simon Schuster.

Putnam, R. D. (2007). 'E Pluribus Unum: Diversity and Community in the Twenty-first Century'. *Scandinavian Political Studies*, 30(2): 137–74.

Savage, M., Devine, F., Cunningham, N., Taylor, M., Li, Y., Hjellbrekke, J., Le Roux, B., Friedman, S., and Miles, A. (2013). 'A New Model of Social Class? Findings from the BBC's Great British Class Survey Experiment'. *Sociology*, 47(2): 219–50.

Schuller, T., Baron, S., and Field, J. (2000). 'Social Capital: A Review and Critique'. In S. Baron, J. Field, and T. Schuller (eds), *Social Capital: Critical Perspectives* (pp. 1–38). Oxford: Oxford University Press.

Scott, J. (1996). *Stratification and Power: Structures of Class, Status and Command*. Oxford: Blackwell.

Szreter, S. (1996). *Fertility, Class and Gender in Britain, 1860–1940*. Cambridge: Cambridge University Press.

Torche, F. (2005). 'Unequal but Fluid: Social Mobility in Chile in Comparative Perspective'. *American Sociological Review*, 70(3): 422–50.

Treiman, D. J. (1977). *Occupational Prestige in Comparative Perspective*. New York: Academic Press.

Weeden, K. A. and Grusky, D. B. (2005). 'The Case for a New Class Map'. *American Journal of Sociology*, 111(1): 141–212.

Weeden, K. A. and Grusky, D. B. (2012). 'The Three Worlds of Inequality'. *American Journal of Sociology*, 117(6): 1723–85.

Sewell, W. H., Haller, A., and Portes, A. (1969). 'The Educational and Early Occupational Attainment Process'. *American Sociological Review*, 34(1): 82–92.

Wright, E. O. (1997). *Class Counts: Comparative Studies in Class Analysis*. Cambridge: Cambridge University Press.

Wright, E. O. (2005). 'Foundations of a Neo-Marxist Class Analysis'. In E. O. Wright (ed.), *Approaches to Class Analysis* (pp. 6–41). Cambridge: Cambridge University Press.

Part II
Advantage and Disadvantage across the Life Course

5

The Family and Disadvantage

Kitty Stewart

If inequalities in health, wealth, and job quality resulted purely from hard work and effort, or even from the good fortune of natural talent, there might be less reason for concern about the extent of inequality in societies today. If life was a race with a fair starting point, unequal prizes for going further or faster might seem reasonable, even laudable, both as a just reward for the winners and as a positive incentive for all.

In practice, however, few societies have even come close to lining up the starting blocks, and the odds on an individual child taking one pathway or another are skewed well before he or she is even born. What is it about a child's circumstances that makes the difference? And what does this tell us about what we can do to make things fairer? This chapter considers these questions.[1] It begins by examining the relationship between family background and children's outcomes, and goes on to look at what is known about the factors that affect children's life chances, focusing in particular on what happens within the family. It then explores the implications for policy. The chapter draws primarily on data and illustrations from the UK and the US, but covers issues pertinent throughout higher- and middle-income countries.

5.1 Gaps in Child Development Emerge Early and Persist into Later Life

Differences in the life chances of children from different backgrounds are apparent straight after birth. Figure 5.1 shows data on low birthweight by

[1] The author thanks Sonia Exley, David Piachaud, and Lucinda Platt for helpful comments on an earlier draft, and Emily Grundy and Stephen Jenkins for suggestions on literature.

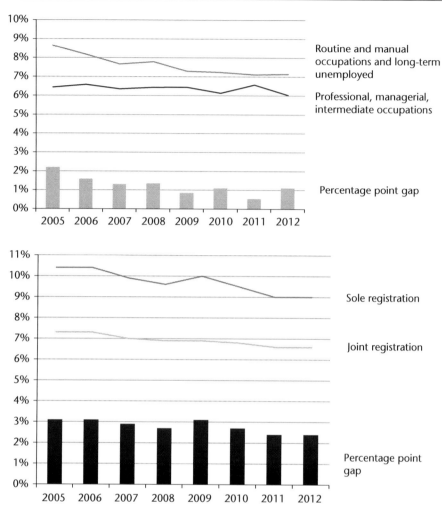

Figure 5.1. Percentage of babies born weighing less than 2,500g, by parents' occupational social class, and by registration (sole or joint registration), England and Wales 2005–12 (all live births)

Source: Stewart and Obolenskaya (2015) Figure 13

parents' social class in England and Wales (in the top panel) and by whether the birth was registered by one or both parents (in the panel below). Low birthweight matters in both the short- and the long-run: it is a key marker of mortality risk in a child's first year, and to a lesser extent also predicts developmental delays in childhood and health difficulties in adulthood (Kuh and Ben-Shlomo, 2006). Encouragingly, Figure 5.1 offers evidence that gaps can be narrowed: the social class gap in low birthweight halved in England and Wales in the first part of the period shown (Figure 5.1, upper panel) (see Stewart, 2013, for discussion). Nevertheless, babies born to parents working in routine or manual occupations or long-term unemployed remain one percentage point more likely to be born weighing less than 2.5kg than those born to parents in professional, managerial, or intermediate jobs. More strikingly, babies registered by one parent only are over two percentage points more likely to be born below this weight than babies registered by both parents, suggesting that a minority of children remain at particularly great disadvantage (Figure 5.1, lower panel). Back in 1999, explaining his pledge to eradicate child poverty in the UK in a generation, Prime Minister Tony Blair talked about the powerful symbol of seeing 'two babies side by side' in a maternity ward, equal at birth but with very different lives ahead of them (Blair, 1999). He imagined one baby returning to temporary accommodation with a mother on her own with no job or family support, and the other to a prosperous home and extended family. Figure 5.1 shows us that in practice pathways have diverged even before the babies leave hospital.

Within a few years of birth, differences by family background begin to emerge in indicators of early cognitive and behavioural development. Figures 5.2a and 5.2b draw on work by Jane Waldfogel and Elizabeth Washbrook (2011) to show early outcomes for young children in the UK and the US in the first part of the 2000s, grouped this time by quintile groups (or fifths) of family income. In both countries, three–five-year-olds in households in the bottom fifth of the distribution score considerably worse on a range of cognitive measures than their peers in middle-income households. Differences are also apparent, though somewhat less marked, in conduct problems and hyperactivity at age four or five. Note, however, that this is not a story of a simple distinction between poor families and non-poor ones: a gradient runs right across the distribution. In the US in particular, differences within the top half of the distribution are larger on most measures than those between the bottom and the middle.

These differences open up before children begin school, in a period when the family is not only the main but for many children the *only* influence on their daily experience. Among this particular cohort of children in the UK, less than one third attended any formal childcare before age three (and a lower share of children from lower income households) (Butt et al., 2007). We might expect that early disparities would narrow as children start to spend more of their day in formal education. In practice, differences appear to persist and even widen during the school years. Figure 5.3 presents data from analysis by Leon Feinstein (2003) of a cohort of British children born in 1970, tracking progress for children grouped by both social class at birth and early potential as measured by tests conducted at 22 months. The figure indicates that the children in this cohort with good early scores and from working-class backgrounds were less likely to translate this promise into successful outcomes in older childhood, and

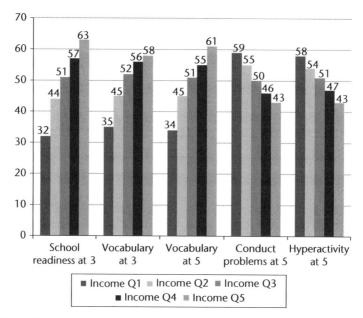

Figure 5.2a. Mean school readiness scores at age 3 and 5 in the UK Millennium Cohort Study (children born 2000–1)

Source: Waldfogel and Washbrook (2011) Figure 1
Notes: Income quintiles are based on family income averaged over the three waves of the survey. Scores are the average percentile for that income quintile; if there were no differences by income each quintile would show a score of 50.5. N= 10,476.

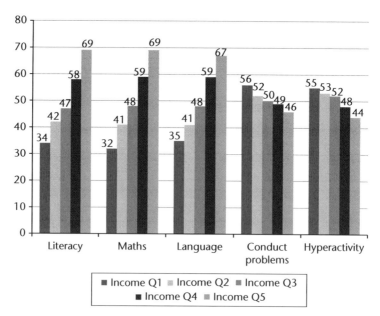

Figure 5.2b. Mean school readiness scores at age 4 in the US Early Childhood Longitudinal Study-Birth Cohort (children born 2001)

Source: Waldfogel and Washbrook (2011) Figure 2
Notes: Income quintiles are based on family income averaged over the three waves of the survey in each case. Scores are the average percentile for that income quintile; if there were no differences by income each quintile would show a score of 50.5. N=7,950.

indeed, were overtaken somewhere between age five and age ten by children from middle class backgrounds who performed less well early on.

Feinstein's figure sparked a debate about how far the observed pattern could be explained by the concept of 'regression to the mean', reflecting measurement error in the early test scores. All test scores to some extent reflect luck on the day, rather than being pure indicators of ability, and measures at age two are likely to be particularly 'noisy' both because of the nature of interaction with two-year-olds and because of the variation in the pace of development in these first few years. The 22-month tests included cube-stacking and grasp of language. In their critique of Feinstein's paper Jerrim and Vignoles (2011: 11) argue that the high-scoring children from working-class backgrounds 'have probably had a particularly large random positive error (i.e. a lot of luck) during the initial test', and that the big drop in their relative scores at the 44-month test reflects this, rather than indicating a genuine deterioration in performance. Feinstein's response is that it is the more subtle shift between ages five and ten, rather than the very early volatile scores, that should capture our interest (Feinstein, 2015). At age five there was a vocabulary test, a copying designs test, and a human figure drawing test. At age ten there were tests in maths and reading and the British ability scale test of IQ. Even if we dismiss the evidence of rankings at 22 and 42 months, Figure 5.3 shows that a group of working class children who were outperforming middle class peers at age five were failing to convert this into the same rate of success in more formal scholastic tests at age ten.

Wider evidence for both the US and the UK, including data from more recent cohorts, supports the idea that, at every stage of education, gaps persist or widen, with low-income children tending to progress more slowly on average than children from higher-income homes (e.g. Magnuson et al., 2012; Blanden et al., 2012).

Qualification levels are key drivers of employment opportunities, wages, and working conditions in OECD countries, so these disparities in educational performance at school cast a long shadow, driving differences in outcomes right across the life course. Using the 1958 National Child Development Study for the UK, Hobcraft and Kiernan (1998) find associations between childhood poverty and a range of adverse adult outcomes at age thirty-three, including no qualifications, a low household income, and low levels of satisfaction with life. Comparing this cohort of children to those born in the UK twelve years later (some of whom are represented in Figure 5.3), Blanden and Gibbons (2006) find an increase over time in the strength of the association between poverty at age sixteen and poverty in adulthood. Similarly, in the US, childhood poverty has been linked to lower success in education and the labour market and to higher risk of early childbearing, low income, benefit dependency, and homelessness (Duncan and Brooks-Gunn, 1997).

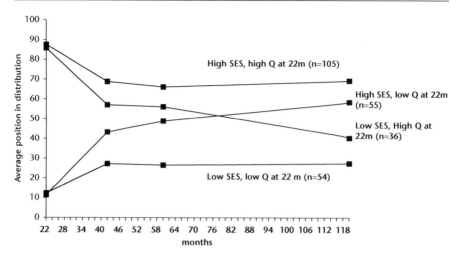

Figure 5.3. Average rank of test scores at 22, 42, 60, and 120 months in the 1970 British Cohort Study, by socio-economic status (SES) of parents and early rank position (Feinstein, 2003)

Source: Figure 2 in Feinstein (2003), using the British Cohort Study. Reproduced with permission by Leon Feinstein and John Wiley & Sons, Inc
Notes: Children were grouped into three SES ranks (high, middle, low) based on occupation of the adults in the household at birth. Middle group is not shown here. Father's occupation was used if mother not working; if two adults were working and in different groups the highest classification was used unless one adult was 'high' and one 'low' in which case child was classified as 'middle'. Test scores are all converted into rankings across all children.

Research into intergenerational earnings mobility adds to this picture by giving us comparative data across a larger set of countries, and by capturing associations not just between poverty and outcomes but across the wider income distribution. Figure 5.4 shows intergenerational earnings elasticities for a number of OECD countries, taken from work by Miles Corak (2006) and Anna Cristina d'Addio (2007). These elasticities tell us the extent to which children's earnings can be explained by the earnings of their parents: an elasticity of zero would mean that there was no association at all between the income of parents and children, while an elasticity of one would mean that the pattern of earnings inequality in the older generation was precisely reproduced among the children. (See also the discussion of relative social mobility in Chapter 4.) The elasticity of 0.5 for Great Britain indicates that, on average, 50 per cent of the relative difference in parental earnings is transmitted to children. This is more than three times the rate in Denmark, Austria, and Norway, showing that such a strong link between the circumstances of one generation and the next is not inevitable. Studies that have examined the way that earnings mobility varies across the distribution have come up with a range of results, but in many countries, including the UK,

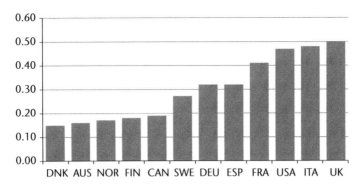

Figure 5.4. Intergenerational earnings elasticity estimates from various studies

Source: Reproduced from D'Addio (2007), 'Intergenerational Transmission of Disadvantage: Mobility or Immobility Across Generations?', OECD Social, Employment and Migration Working Papers, No. 52, OECD Publishing, http://dx.doi.org/10.1787/217730505550, drawing on Corak (2006) and other sources

mobility seems to be lower at the top and bottom than in the middle (d'Addio, 2007), indicating that there is an issue about the intergenerational transmission of poverty, but also one about middle-class parents cementing their children's position. Indeed, Jäntti et al. (2006) find the UK to be quite similar to the Nordic countries in the extent of mobility at the bottom of the distribution, but to show much less movement from the top to the bottom, while the US displays less mobility at both the bottom and the top.

Across countries, educational qualifications have been found to be key transmission mechanisms for social mobility (see Blanden and Gibbons, 2006; Blanden et al., 2007; d'Addio, 2007; see also Chapter 6): if we could break the link between family background and school results at eighteen, we would have gone a very long way towards ensuring equal life chances in these spheres. But two points are important. First, school qualifications explain a lot about later earnings but not everything. (See also the discussion in Chapter 4.) In the UK, Chowdry et al. (2013) find a small social class residual for entry to higher education even after controlling for all school exam results, while Macmillan et al. (2013) find higher wages for those who attended private school even after controlling for school and university performance.

Secondly, the long term markers set down by early health status are not well represented in the literature discussed so far, and may operate through entirely separate mechanisms. The Barker hypothesis (or foetal origins hypothesis) posits that maternal diet in late pregnancy and during breastfeeding induces adaptations in a baby which carry long-term consequences for the development of later diseases including coronary heart disease, hypertension, and diabetes. David Barker's research with colleagues in the 1980s indicated that geographical differences in deaths from heart disease in England and

Wales in the 1970s mirrored patterns of neonatal and postnatal mortality deaths sixty to seventy years earlier, and suggested that poor living standards at birth and in early childhood could have lasting effects (Barker and Osmond, 1986). Further work has built on this hypothesis, using animal studies to examine how nutrition in the womb may permanently programme the body's structure and metabolism (see Barker, 1998). Crucially, these mechanisms appear to operate without exerting any important effect on birth size, making low birthweight a central but not sufficient measure of health at birth. Thus some of the consequences of early disadvantage may lie dormant, and plausibly may never be compensated, even if the education link is broken.

5.2 The Family: What Do We Know?

It is clear that one of the most consistent and important predictors of children's outcomes across a range of domains is their parents' own levels of education (Gregg et al., 2008; Black and Devereux, 2011; Case and Paxson, 2002; Dickson et al., 2013). But while this is a helpful starting point, it leaves us with a circular argument, and it also begs the question about what it is about parental qualifications (or parents with qualifications) that matters.

5.2.1 What Parents Do

Sylva et al. (2008)'s study of developmental trajectories for 2,800 children in England from age three to age eleven points to the high correlation between parental qualifications and social class on the one hand and children's outcomes on the other. But the authors also argue that 'what parents do is more important than who they are' (p. 3). We can identify several aspects of what parents do that make a substantial difference to child development: their health behaviour, especially in pregnancy and after birth; their parenting style; the activities they engage in at home; and their aspirations and expectations for their children.

Parental health behaviour during pregnancy, including smoking, drinking, and nutrition are central risk factors for poor health at birth, and for later health outcomes (Case and Paxson, 2002). Meara (2001) finds that smoking alone explains up to half of the correlation between socioeconomic status and birthweight for white children in the US, and one third for black children. Smoking during pregnancy has also been implicated in cognitive and behavioural difficulties in older children, including lower IQ and attention deficit hyperactivity disorder (ADHD) (see Case and Paxson, 2002). The Barker hypothesis focuses in on maternal nutrition as a central driver of infant health, and of changes in a baby's body that raise the risk of disease in adulthood: the balance of protein and carbohydrate in a mother's diet in late pregnancy, and the amount of fat and protein in the diet, emerge as important influences on the later development of disease (Barker, 1998). After birth, it is well established that breastfeeding has a powerful protective effect on child health in the first year (NICE, 2008). Studies further present suggestive evidence that breastfeeding reduces the likelihood of obesity among children and improves their cognitive and behavioural outcomes, though these findings may in part reflect the influence of unobserved confounding factors (Borra et al., 2012; Heikkilä et al., 2011).

From the earliest stages, parenting style appears to exercise an important influence over child outcomes. Table 5.1 presents a typology of parenting styles, initially put forward by Diana Baumrind (1971) and subsequently developed by other authors. It combines the concept of parental responsiveness and sensitivity on one axis with that of consistent discipline and high expectations on the other. Baumrind argued that children of 'authoritative' parents—those who combined high levels of responsiveness and acceptance of their children with clear expectations and firm enforcement of rules—were more independent and had higher self-esteem and intrinsic motivation than children of 'authoritarian' or 'permissive' parents (see discussion in Maccoby and Martin, 1983). Many research studies since have looked at one or both of these dimensions of parenting, finding good evidence that both contribute to children's outcomes. For example, in seeking to explain the patterns documented in Figure 5.2b above, Waldfogel and Washbrook (2011) find that maternal sensitivity and responsiveness (assessed in their US dataset by observations of mothers interacting with their children) is the single largest explanation of the poorer cognitive performance of low-income relative to middle-income children. Using the UK Millennium Cohort Study Kelly et al. (2011) find that markers of family routines (bedtimes and mealtimes) and the psycho-social environment (including maternal warmth and responsiveness as well as discipline strategies) explained part of the income gap in

Table 5.1. A two-dimensional classification of parenting patterns

	Accepting Responsive Child-centred	Rejecting Unresponsive Parent-centred
Demanding Controlling	Authoritative	Authoritarian
Undemanding Low control	Permissive	Neglectful

Source: Based on Maccoby and Martin (1983), building on Baumrind (1971). Reproduction or translation of any part of this work beyond that permitted by Sections 107 and 108 of the 1976 United States Copyright Act without the permission of the copyright owner is unlawful. Reproduced with permission by John Wiley & Sons, Inc

children's emotional and behavioural difficulties at age three and five, though were less good at explaining the gap in cognitive scores. The evidence around routines such as bedtimes and mealtimes (as opposed to boundaries regarding behaviour) seems least well evidenced; Kelly et al. do not test separately for the effect of these variables, while using different data for England Sylva et al. (2008) find no evidence that measures of routines at age three (including eating meals with family and having a regular bedtime) predict children's outcomes at five.

The 'home learning environment' (HLE), encompassing activities such as being read to, singing songs and nursery rhymes, going to the library, playing with numbers and letters, as well as physical resources like books and computers also emerges consistently as an important influence. In Waldfogel and Washbrook's study the HLE is the second most important explanation for socioeconomic differences in children's cognitive performance after maternal responsiveness. Similarly, for England, Sylva et al. (2008: vii) find higher scores on an Early Years HLE index to be a strong predictor of why some children from disadvantaged backgrounds succeed 'against the odds'; the index trumps either social class or income in predicting child outcomes. Sylva et al. hypothesize that the impact may in part reflect the learning of particular skills such as letters and vocabulary which stand children in good stead when they start school, but that it may also be due to a more generalized effect: children exposed to these activities may be 'learning to learn' and may also be internalizing parental expectations and values, and coming to see themselves as learners.

5.2.2 Money Matters

A focus on what parents do may seem to push us towards individual behavioural explanations for the inequalities observed in the first part of this chapter, and away from more structural explanations. Yet clearly the two types of explanation are closely intertwined. In a systematic review of the literature, Kerris Cooper and I explored studies that have examined whether household income has a *causal* effect on children's outcomes in OECD countries (Cooper and Stewart, 2013). After reviewing thousands of potential studies, we ended up including only thirty-four, because these made use of techniques that lent us confidence that any effects identified did indeed reflect the impact of additional income and not other correlated factors such as parenting style. For example, some made use of experimental situations (where some families had received additional resources but other very similar ones had not), while others used longitudinal data that let researchers trace changes in both household income and children's outcomes over time. The results of our review indicated very strongly that additional financial resources do improve children's outcomes. The evidence was most convincing for cognitive outcomes and school achievement, and then for social and behavioural outcomes, with extra resources making most difference in households that had less income to start with.

To be having an effect on children's outcomes the additional money must be changing something about what happens within the household. Our study was able to reach some tentative conclusions about these mechanisms. For one thing, there is evidence that when low-income households with children receive additional resources they spend them on things that benefit child development—fruit and vegetables, books, and toys—and that the physical home environment improves (e.g. Gregg et al., 2006; Dearing and Taylor, 2007). A boost in income also seems to improve parental health behaviour, notably reducing parental smoking, including in pregnancy (e.g. Strully et al., 2010; Averett and Wang, 2013). The third mechanism has perhaps the largest body of evidence behind it: additional resources in low-income households change interactions in the households by reducing parental stress and anxiety and improving mental health. Several studies in our review pointed to the effect of extra resources on reducing maternal depression, which is one of the worst markers for child development (e.g. Evans and Garthwaite, 2010; Milligan and Stabile, 2011). Other studies found increases in parental supervision (Akee et al., 2010), or improvements in the emotional home environment, meaning parental warmth, stimulation, and lack of hostility (Dearing and Taylor, 2007). In short, income should not be set up in opposition to explanations that emphasize the importance of what parents do; a sufficient income is central to enabling parents to engage in the sort of parenting activities that we know make a difference.

5.2.3 *Employment*

The role played by household income suggests that having parents in work will be better for child development than having parents who are not working. Is parents' employment status relevant for other reasons, beyond any income effect? On the one hand, working parents may provide positive role models for children, raising aspirations, and modelling behaviour that is helpful in achieving school success. Work can also have positive effects on maternal mental health (Harkness and Skipp, 2013). On the other hand, having parents who work long hours, or when children are very young, might have a negative effect on the relationship between parent and child, or on the time parents have to supervise and engage with their children.

There is some evidence from UK and US studies that full-time maternal employment in the first year has small negative effects on both cognitive and socio-emotional outcomes, controlling for income; though the counter-balancing positive effect of income itself makes the impact negligible overall (see Waldfogel, 2006). For older pre-school children, there appear to be few risks, and maternal employment is if anything associated with fewer behavioural problems. Where negative effects do emerge they seem limited to children from more affluent backgrounds—as for child obesity and cognitive development in the US (Anderson et al., 2003; Ruhm, 2004).

For school-age children and adolescents, results are mixed, but a few points stand out. First, evidence from experimental studies of welfare-to-work programmes in the US indicates that increased employment is neutral or positive for child and adolescent health, but only where accompanied by an income increase; where employment is mandated without a corresponding rise in earnings, results are neutral or negative (Morris et al., 2001). This fits with the conclusion of D'Addio (2007: 20) who finds that from a child development perspective there is no difference between income from benefits and income from employment in studies that are able to control for selection effects.

Second, however, there may be some difference for girls and boys. US research has found that school-age girls have higher aspirations and do better in school when their mothers work, while school-age boys often do worse, suggesting that a role model effect may indeed operate for daughters (Smolensky and Gootman, 2003; and see discussion in Waldfogel, 2006).

Third, where risks of employment are identified for older children and teenagers, these appear to be mostly for those from lower-income households. This may be linked to the nature of alternative care arrangements or because of the additional responsibility placed on older children in these households. Research in the UK has found some positive effects on mental and physical health for teenagers whose mothers worked, but only in better-off households with more highly educated mothers. In less well-off households, more years in paid employment for mothers was linked to worse mental health for children as they reached adolescence (Pikhartova, 2012). Reviewing sixty-seven studies of welfare-to-work reforms for low-income US families, Grogger and Karoly (2005) find that mothers' increased work effort either had a negative effect on adolescent behaviour and academic achievement or no effect. Waldfogel (2006) reports that school outcomes were particularly poor in experimental studies of welfare-to-work programmes for adolescents with younger siblings: these teenagers were significantly more likely than the control group to be suspended or expelled or drop out of school, perhaps because additional responsibility at home interfered with school work (see Gennetian et al., 2002).

A separate literature examines the evidence for the intergenerational transmission of worklessness from father to son. Having a father who experienced unemployment appears to increase the likelihood of a son doing so in the UK

(Macmillan, 2014). However, there is little evidence that a culture of long-term welfare dependency is passed from one generation to the next (Shildrick et al., 2012): only 1 per cent of sons in Macmillan's (2011) analysis of three cohorts had never worked at all.

To sum up, these studies together highlight the potentially positive role of employment, but also raise clear notes of caution; positive effects are likely to depend on accompanying income gains, on parental working hours and flexibility, and on the nature of alternative care and supervision.

5.2.4 *The Structure of the Family*

One last essential element of children's life in the family must be considered: household structure. The most obvious aspect of this is whether a child lives with one or both parents. Children of lone parents have been found to be at greater risk of a range of worse health, cognitive, and social-behavioural outcomes (e.g. Baker et al., 2003). Children of step-parents have similar (or higher) risks to children of lone parents, while having parents who are cohabiting rather than married is also associated with poorer outcomes across a range of domains (Rodgers and Pryor, 1998; Crawford et al., 2011). However, it seems that many if not all of these effects are explained by associated characteristics and not by lone parenthood, cohabitation, or separation per se. Using British data, Walker and Zhu (2007) find only very limited evidence of a causal effect of lone parenthood once they include controls, in particular income, while Gregg et al. (2008) find no substantive effect of lone parenthood on any child outcome. Differences in relationship stability and outcomes for children of cohabiting/married couples are found by Crawford et al. (2013) to mainly or entirely reflect the fact that different types of people choose to get married. Outcomes for children whose parents separate are undeniably very poor, but differences in cognitive outcomes are not significant once controlling for education and socio-economic status, while differences in socio-emotional development also become insignificant once measures of relationship quality are controlled for (Crawford et al., 2011).

Thus while both low income and parental conflict make a difference to children's outcomes (and are associated with family structure), the structure itself does not appear to be very important. However, there is some evidence that children (and particularly teenagers) do not benefit (or in some cases do worse) when a parent repartners. Given the boost in household resources that usually accompanies repartnering, this suggests that adaptation to a new family structure may carry particular challenges, especially for older children (Rodgers and Pryor, 1998; MacKay, 2005).

5.3 So What Should We Do? The Family and Policy Dilemmas

Among the key messages that emerge from the previous section is that the way parents spend their time with their children is crucial to child development, and that household income is not just a proxy for better parenting but itself enables investment in books, toys, and nutritious food, lowers parental stress and anxiety, and reduces damaging behaviour such as smoking during pregnancy. What are the implications for policy? A series of questions arise.

5.3.1 *The Role of Early Education*

The first question is about how far policy can and should attempt to change what takes place inside the household, and how far it should seek instead to reduce the significance of different home environments by providing children with stimulating experiences outside the home. The failure of the school system to close gaps in achievement indicates that schools cannot do everything alone. But there is good evidence that high-quality early education and childcare can narrow gaps in children's readiness for starting school, understood as social and behavioural readiness as well as familiarity with books, letters, and numbers. The most influential evidence in favour of pre-school education comes from very small randomized controlled experiments such as the Perry Pre-School programme in the 1960s, which provided highly disadvantaged children in Michigan with very high quality (and high cost) early education, along with a programme of home visits (Karoly et al., 2005). Forty years later, the programme continues to identify long-term effects for those who received the intervention, in higher earnings, reduced welfare benefits and less engagement with the criminal justice system (Heckman et al., 2010).

Perry Pre-School and other experimental studies are powerful because of the randomized design and the long-term follow-up, but they do raise questions about generalizability, to other countries, to less intensive programmes, to less deeply disadvantaged groups of children, and to today's context, fifty years on. Evidence also exists from more standardized interventions, such as the roll-out of universal early education programmes in France and Denmark: these too find positive results which are consistently greater (or only exist) for children from more disadvantaged families, including those with less educated parents, lower incomes and/or immigrant status (see Ruhm and Waldfogel, 2012). These studies make use of differences in birthday cut-offs or regional availability to try to ensure that effects do not simply reflect unobserved differences in parental characteristics that are correlated with service take-up.

Increasingly, industrialized countries are investing in early years services, both to facilitate maternal employment and to further child development (OECD, 2006; OECD, 2011). In the European Union, good quality childcare is seen as central to a 'child-centred social investment strategy', enabling children to become 'lifelong learners and strong contributors to their societies' (Hemerijck, 2013: 382). However, despite steady improvements in many countries, few ensure that services reach all the children who stand to gain most from them, and very few invest sufficient funds to ensure that services are high quality (see Gambaro et al., 2014). In England, nearly all three- and four-year-olds now take up their right to free part-time early education; but the most disadvantaged children remain less likely to access the places (Speight and Smith, 2010), while the quality of some provision is still less than ideal. The weight of evidence underlines the importance of graduate trained staff in raising quality (Mathers et al., 2011; Mathers and Smees, 2014), but only two-thirds of three-year-olds attend a setting where a specialized graduate worked with them at any point during the week (DfE, 2014; Stewart and Obolenskaya, 2015). New research identifies fairly small and short-term effects of the initial roll-out of the free places in England; these disappointing results may well reflect the quality of the places created (Blanden et al., 2014).

5.3.2 Conditionality?

A related question is whether it is enough simply to provide high-quality services, or whether attendance needs to be mandatory, or be linked to cash benefits to incentivize parents to take services up. Evidence from the free places in England, and from other countries like France where nursery education is free though not compulsory, suggests that a universal free offer is an effective way to achieve near-universal take-up, though reaching the last families may require skilful local outreach and a good understanding of the reasons why some families do not enrol (Speight and Smith, 2010; Gambaro et al., 2014). But other countries have experimented with conditional approaches, which operate as either bribe or threat depending on design. The kindergarten allowance in Hungary offers parents with low income and low education cash incentives to send their children to kindergarten: eligible families receive roughly 79 Euro at first enrolment and a further 35 Euro each semester if children attend regularly (Medgyesi and Temesváry, 2013). In New Zealand, a more draconian approach has been introduced: in 2013 pre-school enrolment and regular attendance was made compulsory for all children aged between three and five in families in receipt of out-of-work or lone parent benefits (New Zealand Parliament, 2013).

Is conditionality of this kind an effective way for the state to improve outcomes? And even if effective is it morally justifiable? Used frequently in Latin American countries (and increasingly beyond them) to encourage take-up of health checks and school attendance, conditional cash transfers (CCTs) can be seen as a 'win-win', providing households with additional financial resources while ensuring they invest in their children's human capital. (See also the discussion in Chapter 11.) Fiszbein and Schady (2009) argue that they have successfully increased school enrolment, immunization rates, and health check-ups in country after country; the reduction of gender disparities in school enrolment in Bangladesh, Pakistan, and Turkey are notable successes. But Fiszbein and Schady also acknowledge that CCTs have been much less effective in improving health and educational *outcomes*—height-for-age (rather than growth monitoring); cognitive development and school achievement (rather than enrolment). This may flag up something about the quality of services on offer: not taking up low-quality services may be a rational decision for families for whom opportunity costs are high. If so, addressing quality rather than attaching conditions may be a more effective way to promote ultimate goals.

Aside from this instrumentalist concern, conditionality raises three further issues, more ethical in nature. The first is about the acceptability of mandating behaviour for some families but not others—making pre-school effectively compulsory for low-income children, when middle-class families might object to the state extending its reach in this way down into early childhood. There are many ways in which the state compels or rules out parental actions (corporal punishment in many countries; vaccinations in a few; schooling from age five or six nearly universally). Such action is frequently controversial and necessitates treading a delicate balance between the rights of the child and the sanctity of the family (and in some cases, such as compulsory vaccination, the wider interests of society). But introducing rules for some families but not others raises additional questions of its own.

Second, there are the consequences for children in families that do not follow the conditions. These are particularly worrying where pre-school enrolment (or other behaviour) is linked to the benefits on which families depend for survival, as in the New Zealand example, rather than to an additional supplement or incentive as in Hungary.

A last issue is highlighted by Sandel (2012), who argues that in introducing monetary incentives to behaviour that we would expect to be motivated by love, altruism, or moral conviction we risk crowding out intrinsic motivation and changing the nature of human relationships. A new scheme to promote breastfeeding in the UK highlights these tensions. Started by academics, the project offers mothers shopping vouchers in five instalments if they initiate and then persist in breastfeeding. A full trial is being developed after an initial pilot found the payments to be acceptable to mothers and midwives (Boseley, 2014; Relton et al., 2014), though the scheme was widely criticized in the press as being a 'bribe to breastfeed'. Much of the criticism stemmed from a belief that motivation is not the problem and therefore money not the solution: parents who had had difficulty breastfeeding argued that the approach showed a lack of understanding of the reasons mothers did not proceed. If the trial finds that the incentives *do* increase rates of breastfeeding, it will arguably answer this criticism and confirm that financial incentives can be effective, perhaps alongside other forms of support. But Sandel's concern about the potential crowding out of non-market motivation remains. Should we see this as squeamishness, with the ends (for the breastfed children) justifying the means ('bribing' mothers with shopping vouchers)? Or are the risks attached to commercializing this most intimate of maternal acts simply too high?

If not through compulsion and not through attaching conditions and financial incentives, what else can the state do to try to change parental behaviour? Influencing what takes place in the home is notoriously difficult to do. We discuss the potential of three ways the state can promote better parenting: by providing more time, more money, and more support.

5.3.3 *More Time*

The importance of sufficient maternity leave in the first year to enable mothers to bond and to breastfeed is now reflected in leave policies in many industrialized countries, though the US remains an exception (OECD, 2011). Maternity leave in the first year has been found to have positive effects on breastfeeding, not only in US studies that have looked at leave of up to three months (Berger et al., 2005; Ogbuanu et al., 2011), but also in studies examining the difference between leave entitlements of six months and a year (Baker and Milligan (2008) for Canada and Chuang et al. (2010) for Singapore). Effects of longer leave also show up in positive impacts on child health: examining data for eighteen OECD countries, Tanaka (2005) finds that the extension of paid maternity leave has significant effects on decreasing infant mortality rates, and posits that breastfeeding may be one mechanism. Longer leave has been linked to other outcomes too. Examining US states, Chatterji and Markowitz (2005) find that longer leave is associated with a significant drop in depressive symptoms in a context where the average leave taken was nine weeks after birth. Carneiro et al. (2010) trace the effects of an extension of maternity leave in Norway forward to the end of high school and find a significant drop in high-school dropout, especially large for lower-educated mothers.

There is less research on the impact of paternity leave and child development. In a study of the US, UK, Denmark, and Australia, Huerta et al. (2013) find that fathers who take at least two weeks leave are more involved in looking after their children when they are young, and that (except in Denmark) children with more involved fathers tend to do better in cognitive tests, though not in terms of behavioural development. There is also limited work on the effects of legislation enabling parents to work part-time or flexibly later in children's lives, but these policies seem likely to be key to enabling families to balance paid employment with the sort of active and engaged parenting discussed earlier.

5.3.4 More Money

Household income is not only a correlate but has a causal effect on children's outcomes, so eradicating income poverty must be central to policy attempts to ensure more equal starting points for children. Encouraging and facilitating parental employment will necessarily be a big part of this, but policy also needs to ensure that incomes are sufficient to keep children out of poverty whether or not their parents are in work. Increasing financial resources in low-income households helps to reduce maternal depression and improve parenting and the home environment, with positive effects on child development (Cooper and Stewart, 2013). In designing child benefits policymakers might also consider particularly vulnerable stages of life: the short-lived Health in Pregnancy Grant (child benefit paid in the last few months of pregnancy) was introduced in the UK with a view to improving nutrition in late pregnancy, fitting with the Barker Hypothesis emphasis on the vital importance of this pre-natal period. The grant was one of the first benefits to be cut under the 2010–15 Coalition Government's austerity regime.

5.3.5 More Support with Parenting

The evidence on the effectiveness of parenting classes and interventions is mixed, but a number of intensive programmes have been found to be effective when evaluated in randomized controlled trials, including the Incredible Years and Triple P Parenting programmes and the Nurse Family Partnership in the US, which works with young first-time parents during pregnancy and the first two years of life (Allen, 2011). There are two caveats, however. The first is that context matters. In the US, the Nurse Family Partnership was found to improve nutrition and reduce smoking during pregnancy and to improve parenting and the home environment; there were subsequent small effects on children's cognitive and behavioural outcomes, with larger effects for higher-risk children (Waldfogel and Washbrook, 2011). But evaluation results appear to have been withheld for the UK version of the programme, the Family Nurse Partnership, raising concern that the impact was less clear in the UK context.

The second point is that these programmes are expensive, and (in part for this reason) work with limited numbers of families. In Children's Centres in England, the Incredible Years and Triple P programmes were each found to be reaching on average twenty-two to twenty-three families a year in the centres that were offering them, compared to an average of 1,350 children under five in a centre's reach area (Goff et al., 2013; Smith et al., 2014). The relatively high costs (£1,600 per family) seemed to be the main reason the programmes were not used more widely (Goff et al., 2013). Programmes can of course pay back this investment many times in the future, but usually only under assumptions made for the most disadvantaged families. Thus the Nurse Family Partnership in the US costs $9,500 per family and has been calculated to result in net savings of over $17,000 (Aos et al., 2004), but much of the saving results from reduced spending on Medicaid (some of it not relevant in the context of a universal National Health Service) and savings to the child protection and criminal justice systems (Miller, 2010). These are of course fantastically important effects from the child's perspective, and they underline the importance of programmes that can successfully affect the family life of the children in most need. But they should be seen as operating on the tail of the distribution, not shifting the curve; and the income gradients presented in Figure 5.2 tell us that there is more driving inequality of life chances than a few highly disadvantaged families. This mirrors the dilemma summarized by Goodman and Gregg (2010) in relation to school interventions: intensive programmes that focus on helping small numbers of children most in need have the strongest evidence base behind them, but (less extreme) educational disadvantage affects a very large number of children from low-income families. Policymakers need to get the balance right in designing policy that works for the curve, with additional targeted support for the tail.

5.4 Policy and the Middle (and Upper) Classes

The discussion in this chapter has focused on the ways in which children can be disadvantaged by their family circumstances. It has argued that policies to ensure income security, high quality early education, and support with parenting all have a role to play in promoting more equal life chances, and that policymakers need to pay attention to the ways in which many low-income children face moderate levels of disadvantage, as well as the particularly high obstacles facing a few. But there are also ways in which children can be particularly *advantaged* by very high family income or wealth and by social contacts and networks. Figure 5.2 showed us social gradients that run right across the income distribution. Even within the top 20 per cent of incomes we know that life chances are not evenly distributed. In the UK, 7 per cent of children attend private schools but in 2014 the privately educated made up 33 per cent of Members of Parliament, 43 per cent of newspaper columnists, 53 per cent of senior diplomats and 71 per cent of senior judges (SMCP, 2014). Attending a private school even seems to boost one's chances of becoming a pop star—22 per cent of pop stars had a private education.

If our goal is to achieve more equal life chances, these inequalities also matter. How confident can we be that the policies proposed above will address them? Access to elite universities seems a key route to the top professions: the dominance of Oxford and Cambridge university graduates in the media, politics, and the justice system is even more disproportionate than that of the privately educated: they make up 75 per cent of senior judges, 47 per cent of newspaper columnists and 24 per cent of MPs, compared to just 1 per cent of the total population. Encouragingly, research shows that school attainment opens the doors to these universities, so policies that give children a fair chance of achieving their potential in school should in principle result in more open access to these institutions and in turn to top professions (Crawford et al., 2014). However, examining school results for recent cohorts of children in the UK, Blanden and Macmillan (2014) find that while income gaps have been closing at lower attainment levels (reaching the standard expected at age eleven; five 'good' passes in GCSE exams at age sixteen), there is no evidence so far of a narrowing of the gap at the highest levels (such as excellent results in 'A' levels at age eighteen). There is also little evidence of improvement in access to elite institutions, alongside signs that the increased numbers gaining a post-graduate qualification come predominantly from those from higher social classes. As Blanden and Macmillan point out, if education is a positional good (Goldthorpe, 2013), it is likely that more affluent parents will respond to improvements further down by pushing their children to higher levels of achievement.

In a society where levels of income and wealth inequality are high (see Chapters 7 and 8), it stands to reason that better-off parents will find it easier to do this, with the help of private education, the ability to buy housing in the catchment of the best state schools, and the resources to fund children through additional degrees and internships and to help them with housing costs in areas where well-paid jobs are concentrated. (See also the discussion in Chapter 6.) Furthermore, as John Hills (2015: 215) points out, where inequalities are high parents will also have extra *motivation* for doing these things: 'In a highly unequal society, many advantaged parents will do all they can to ensure that their children do not slip down the economic ladder—they know that it goes a long way down.'

How can policy prevent income and wealth from being used by better-off parents to cement their children's position? Only by what James Fishkin has argued to be a 'sacrifice of family autonomy' (Fishkin, 1987: 40). This might involve, for example, the abolition of private education and private tutors, lotteries for school places, an end to inheritance and to financial gifts to the next generation. These policies might help to create a society which ensures separation between what Michael Walzer calls 'spheres of justice' (Walzer, 1983), preventing the distribution of income from dominating the distribution of goods in other spheres, including the health, educational success, and job opportunities of children. If these policies are considered unrealistic it implies that we can only promote true equality of opportunity by limiting inequality of income and wealth.

Certainly, across countries, we see a broad correlation between lower levels of income inequality and higher levels of earnings mobility across generations: Miles Corak's figure showing this relationship, which has become known as the 'Great Gatsby Curve', is reproduced in Figure 5.5 (Corak, 2013). The correlation is far from perfect—countries such as Australia and Canada appear to be ensuring better levels of mobility than the UK even with similar levels of income inequality—and the extent to which the relationship is a causal one is not well understood. Nevertheless, the figure lends support to the hypothesis that boosting mobility will be harder where inequality is higher. If we wish to make children's starting points substantially more equal we therefore need to pay careful attention to the overall level of inequality in society, and to the disparities in returns to different jobs, as well as working to reduce the extent to which childhood disadvantage holds back children's development.

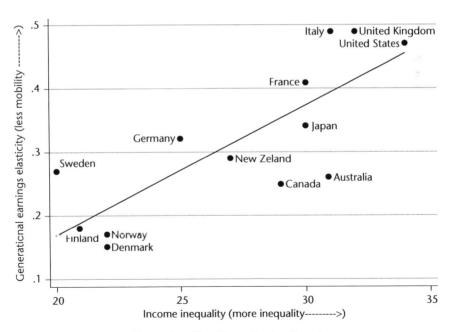

Figure 5.5. The 'Great Gatsby Curve'

Source: Corak (2013). Reproduced with permission by Miles Corak

References

Akee, R. K. Q., Copeland, W. E., Keeler, G., Angold, A., and Costello, E. J. (2010). 'Parents' Incomes and Children's Outcomes: A Quasi-experiment Using Transfer Payments from Casino Profits'. *American Economic Journal: Applied Economics,* 2(1): 86–115.

Allen, G. (2011). *Early Intervention: Smart Investment, Massive Savings.* London: The Cabinet Office.

Anderson, P., Butcher K., and Levine, P. (2003). 'Maternal Employment and Overweight Children'. *Journal of Health Economics,* 22(3): 477–504.

Aos, S., Lieb, R., Mayfield, J., Miller, M., and Pennucci, A. (2004). *Benefits and Costs of Prevention and Early Intervention Programs for Youth.* Washington, DC: Washington State Institute for Public Policy.

Averett, S. and Wang, Y. (2013). 'The Effects of Earned Income Tax Credit Payment Expansion on Maternal Smoking'. *Health Economics,* 22(11): 1344–59.

Baker, M. and Milligan, K. (2008). 'Maternal Employment, Breastfeeding and Health: Evidence from Maternity Leave Mandates'. *Journal of Health Economics,* 27(4): 871–87.

Baker, M., Pryor, J., Millar, J., and Shirley, I. (2003). *Lone Parenthood and Outcomes for Children: A Review of the Literature.* Prepared for the Ministry of Social Development, Wellington, New Zealand.

Barker, D. J. P. (1998). *Mothers, Babies and Health in Later Life.* Edinburgh: Churchill Livingstone.

Barker, D. J. P. and Osmond, C. (1986). 'Infant Mortality, Childhood Nutrition and Ischaemic Heart Disease in England and Wales'. *Lancet,* 1(8489): 1077–81.

Baumrind, D. (1971). 'Current Patterns of Parental Authority'. *Developmental Psychology Monographs,* 4(1): 1–103.

Berger, L., Hill J., and Waldfogel, J. (2005). 'Maternity Leave, Early Maternal Employment and Child Health and Development in the US'. *The Economic Journal,* 115(501): F29–F47.

Black, S. E. and Devereux, P. J. (2011). 'Recent Developments in Intergenerational Mobility'. Dublin: University College Dublin, Geary Institute.

Blair, T. (1999). Speech to the 1999 Labour Party Conference, 28 September 1999.

Blanden, J. and Gibbons, S. (2006). *The Persistence of Poverty across Generations: A View from Two British Cohorts.* Bristol: The Policy Press.

Blanden, J., Gregg, P., and Macmillan, L. (2007). 'Accounting for Intergenerational Income Persistence: Noncognitive Skills, Ability and Education'. *Economic Journal,* 117(519): C43–C60.

Blanden, J., Katz, I., and Redmond, G. (2012). 'Family Background and Child Outcomes'. In J. Ermisch, M. Jantti, and T. Smeeding (eds), *From Parents to Children: The Intergenerational Transmission of Disadvantage.* New York: Russell Sage Foundation.

Blanden, J., Del Bono, E., Hansen, K., McNally, S., and Rabe, B. (2014). 'Evaluating a Demand-side Approach to Expanding Free Pre-school Education'. https://www.iser.essex.ac.uk/files/projects/the-effect-of-free-childcare-on-maternal-labour-supply-and-child-development/childoutcomes.pdf, last accessed 29 July 2015.

Blanden, J. and Macmillan, L. (2014). 'Education and Intergenerational Mobility: Help or Hindrance?' Social Policy in a Cold Climate Working Paper No. 8. CASE, LSE.

Borra, C., Iacovou, M., and Sevilla, A. (2012). 'The Effect of Breastfeeding on Children's Cognitive and Non-cognitive Development'. *Labour Economics*, 19(4): 496–515.

Boseley, S. (2014). 'Scheme Offering Shopping Vouchers to Mothers Who Breastfeed to be Extended'. *The Guardian*, 20 November 2014.

Butt, S., Goddard, K., La Valle, I., and Hill, M. (2007). *Childcare Nation? Progress on the Childcare Strategy and Priorities for the Future*. London: Daycare Trust.

Carneiro, P., Loken, K., and Salvenes, K. (2010). 'A Flying Start? Long Term Consequences of Maternal Time Investments in Children During their First Year of Life'. IZA Discussion Paper No 5362.

Case, A. and Paxson, C. (2002). 'Parental Behaviour and Child Health'. *Health Affairs*, 21(2): 164–78.

Chatterji, P. and Markowitz, S. (2005). 'Does the Length of Maternity Leave Affect Maternal Health?' *Southern Economic Journal*, 72(1): 16–41.

Chowdry, H., Crawford, C., Dearden, D., Goodman, A., and Vignoles, A. (2013). 'Widening Participation in Higher Education: Analysis Using Linked Administrative Data'. *Journal of the Royal Statistical Society A*, 176(2): 431–57.

Chuang, C., Chang, P., Chen, Y., Hsieh, W., Hurng, B., Lin, S., and Chen, P. (2010). 'Maternal Return to Work and Breastfeeding: A Population-based Cohort Study'. *International Journal of Nursing Studies*, 47(4): 461–74.

Cooper, K. and Stewart, K. (2013). *Does Money Affect Children's Outcomes? A Systematic Review*. York: Joseph Rowntree Foundation.

Corak, M. (2006). 'Do Poor Children Become Poor Adults? Lessons from a Cross-country Comparison of Generational Earnings Mobility'. IZA Discussion Paper No. 1993.

Corak, M. (2013). 'Income Inequality, Equality of Opportunity and Intergenerational Mobility'. *Journal of Economic Perspectives*, 27(3): 79–102.

Crawford, C., Goodman, A., and Greaves, E. (2013). 'Cohabitation, Marriage, Relationship Stability and Child Outcomes: Final Report'. IFS Report R87.

Crawford, C., Goodman, A., Greaves, E., and Joyce, R. (2011). 'Cohabitation, Marriage, Relationship Stability and Child Outcomes: An Update'. IFS Commentary C120.

Crawford, C., Macmillan, L., and Vignoles, A. (2014). 'Progress Made by High-attaining Children from Disadvantaged Backgrounds'. Social Mobility and Child Poverty Commission Research Report June 2014.

D'Addio, A. C. (2007). 'Intergenerational Transmission of Disadvantage: Mobility or Immobility across Generations? A Review of the Evidence for OECD Countries'. OECD Social, Employment and Migration Working Paper No 52.

Dearing, E. and Taylor, B. A. (2007). 'Home Improvements: Within-family Associations between Income and the Quality of Children's Home Environments'. *Journal of Applied Developmental Psychology*, 28(5–6). 427–44.

DfE [Department for Education] (2014). 'Provision of Services for Children under Five Years of Age in England: January 2014'. Statistical First Release.

Dickson, M., Gregg, P., and Robinson, H. (2013). 'Early, Late or Never? When Does Parental Education Impact Child Outcomes?' Bristol: Centre for Market and Public Organisation (Working Paper No. 13/298).

Duncan, G. and Brooks-Gunn, J. (1997). *The Consequences of Growing Up Poor*. New York: Russell Sage Foundation.

Evans, W. N. and Garthwaite, C. L. (2010). 'Giving Mom a Break: The Impact of Higher EITC Payments on Maternal Health'. National Bureau of Economic Research, NBER Working Paper No. 16296.

Feinstein, L. (2003). 'Inequality in the Early Cognitive Development of British Children in the 1970 Cohort'. *Economica*, 70(277): 73–98.

Feinstein, L. (2015). 'Social Class Differences in Early Cognitive Development and Regression to the Mean'. *Longitudinal and Life Course Studies*, 6(3): 331–43.

Fishkin, J. (1987). 'Liberty versus Equal Opportunity'. *Social Philosophy and Policy*, 5(1): 32–48.

Fiszbein, A. and Schady, N. (2009). *Conditional Cash Transfers: Reducing Present and Future Poverty*. Washington, DC: The World Bank.

Gambaro, L., Stewart, K., and Waldfogel, J. (eds) (2014). *An Equal Start? Providing Quality Early Education and Care to Disadvantaged Children*. Bristol: The Policy Press.

Gennetian, L., Duncan, G., Knox, V., Vargas, W., Clark-Kauffman, E., and London, A. (2002). *How Welfare and Work Policies for Parents Affect Adolescents: A Synthesis of Research*. New York: Manpower Demonstration Research Corporation.

Goff, J., Hall, J., Sylva, K., Smith, T., Smith, G., Eisenstadt, N., Sammons, P., Evangelou, M., Smees, R., and Chu, K. (2013). *Evaluation of Children's Centres in England (ECCE) Strand 3: Delivery of Family Services by Children's Centres*. Research Report. July 2013. London: Department for Education.

Goldthorpe, J. (2013). 'Understanding—and Misunderstanding—Social Mobility in Britain: The Entry of Economists, the Confusion of Politicians and the Limits of Educational Policy'. *Journal of Social Policy*, 42(3): 431–50.

Goodman, A. and Gregg, P. (eds) (2010). *Poorer Children's Educational Attainment: How Important Are Attitudes and Behaviour?* York: Joseph Rowntree Foundation.

Gregg, P., Propper, C., and Washbrook, E. (2008). 'Understanding the Relationship between Parental Income and Multiple Child Outcomes: Decomposition Analysis'. Bristol: The Centre for Market and Public Organisation, Working Paper No. 08/193.

Gregg, P., Waldfogel, J., and Washbrook, E. (2006). 'Family Expenditures Post-welfare Reform in the UK: Are Low-income Families Starting to Catch up?' *Labour Economics*, 13(6): 721–46.

Grogger, J. and Karoly, L.A. (2005). *Welfare Reform: Effects of a Decade of Change*. Cambridge: Harvard University Press.

Harkness, S. and Skipp, A. (2013). *Lone Mothers, Work and Depression*. London: The Nuffield Foundation.

Heckman, J., Moon, S., Pinto, R., and Savelyev, R. (2010). 'The Rate of Return to the High Scope Perry Pre-School Program'. *The Journal of Public Economics*, 94(1–2): 114–28.

Heikkila, K., Sacker, A. Y., Kelly, Y., Renfrew, M., and Quigley, M., (2011). 'Breastfeeding and Child Behaviour in the Millennium Cohort Study'. *Archives of Disease in Childhood*, 96(7): 635–42.

Hemerijck, A. (2013). *Changing Welfare States*. Oxford: Oxford University Press.

Hills, J. (2015). *Good Times, Bad Times: The Welfare Myth of Them and Us*. Bristol: The Policy Press.

Hobcraft, J. and Kiernan, K. (1998). 'Childhood Poverty, Early Motherhood and Adult Social Exclusion'. *British Journal of Sociology*, 52(3): 495–517.

Huerta, M. C., Adema, W., Baxter, J., Han, W.-J., Lausten, M., Lee, R., and Waldfogel, J. (2013). 'Fathers' Leave, Fathers' Involvement and Child Development: Are They Related? Evidence from four OECD countries'. OECD Social, Employment and Migration Working Papers No 140.

Jäntti, M., Bratsberg, B., Røed, K., Raaum, O., Naylor, R., Österbacka, E., Björklund, A., and Eriksson, T., (2006). 'American Exceptionalism in a New Light: A Comparison of Intergenerational Earnings Mobility in the Nordic Countries, the United Kingdom and the United States'. IZA Discussion Paper No. 1938.

Jerrim, J. and Vignoles, A. (2011). 'The Use (and Misuse) of Statistics in Understanding Social Mobility: Regression to the Mean and the Cognitive Development of High Ability Children from Disadvantaged Homes'. DoQSS Working Paper 11-01. London: Institute of Education.

Karoly, L. A., Kilburn, M. R., and Cannon, J. S. (2005). *Early Childhood Interventions: Proven Results, Future Promise.* Santa Monica, CA: RAND Distribution Services.

Kelly, Y., Sacker, A., Del Bono, E., Francesconi, M., and Marmot, M. (2011). 'What Role for the Home Learning Environment and Parenting in Reducing the Socioeconomic Gradient in Child Development? Findings from the Millennium Cohort Study'. *Archives of Disease in Childhood.* doi:10.1136/adc.2010.195917.

Kuh D. and Ben-Shlomo, Y. (2004). *A Life Course Approach to Chronic Disease Epidemiology.* 2nd edn. Oxford: Oxford University Press.

Maccoby, E. E. and Martin, J. A. (1983). 'Socialization in the Context of the Family: Parent–child Interaction'. In P. Mussen and E. Hetherington (eds), *Handbook of Child Psychology, Volume 4: Socialization, Personality, and Social Development.* 4th edn. New York: Wiley.

MacKay, R. (2005). 'The Impact of Family Structure and Family Change on Child Outcomes: A Personal Reading of the Research Literature'. *Social Policy Journal of New Zealand*, 24: 111–33.

Macmillan, L. (2011). 'Measuring the Intergenerational Correlation of Worklessness'. CMPO Working Paper No. 11/278. December 2011. University of Bristol: Centre for Market and Public Organisation.

Macmillan, L. (2014). 'Intergenerational Worklessness in the UK and the Role of Local Labour Markets'. *Oxford Economic Papers*, 66(3): 871–89.

Macmillan, L., Tyler, C., and Vignoles, A. (2013). 'Who Gets the Best Jobs? The Role of Family Background and Networks in Recent Graduates' Access to High Status Professions'. Department of Quantitative Social Science Working Paper 13–15. London: Institute of Education.

Magnuson, K., Waldfogel, J., and Washbrook, E. (2012). 'SES Gradients in Skills During the School Years'. In J. Ermisch, M. Jantti, and T. Smeeding (eds), *From Parents to Children: The Intergenerational Transmission of Disadvantage.* New York: Russell Sage Foundation.

Mathers, S., Ranns, H., Karemaker, A., Moody, A., Sylva, K., Graham, J., and Siraj-Blatchford, I. (2011). 'Evaluation of the Graduate Leader Fund: Final Report'. DfE Research Report DfE-RR144. London: Department for Education.

Mathers, S. and Smees, R. (2014). *Quality and Inequality: Do Three- and Four-year-olds in Deprived Areas Experience Lower Quality Provision.* London: Nuffield Foundation.

Meara, E. (2001). 'Why Is Health Related to Socioeconomic Status? The Case of Pregnancy and Low Birthweight'. NBER Working Paper No. 8231.

Medgyesi M. and Temesváry, Z. (2013). 'Conditional Cash Transfers in High-income OECD Countries and their Effects on Human Capital Accumulation'. AIAS, GINI Discussion Paper 84, August 2013.

Miller, T. (2010). 'Societal Return on Investment in Nurse-Family Partnership Services in California: A Factsheet for the Pacific Institute for Research and Evaluation (PIRE)'. http://wwwr.nursefamilypartnership.org/assets/PDF/Communities/CA-Documents/ROI-California.aspx, last accessed 29 July 2015.

Milligan, K. and Stabile, M. (2011). 'Do Child Tax Benefits Affect the Well-being of Children? Evidence from Canadian Child Benefit Expansions'. *American Economic Journal: Economic Policy,* 3(3): 175–205.

Morris, P., Huston, A., Duncan, G., Crosby, D., and Bos, J. (2001). *How Welfare and Work Policies Affect Children: A Synthesis of Research*. New York: Manpower Demonstration Research Corporation.

New Zealand Parliament (2013). *Social Security (Benefit Categories and Work Focus) Amendment Act 2013*. Section 60RA, Social obligations of certain beneficiaries with dependent children.

NICE (2008). *Maternal and Child Nutrition*. NICE Public Health Guidance 11. London: National Institute for Health and Care Excellence.

OECD (2006). *Starting Strong II*. Paris: Organisation for Economic Co-operation and Development.

OECD (2011). *Doing Better for Families*. Paris: Organisation for Economic Co-operation and Development.

Ogbuanu, C., Glover, S., Probst, J., Liu, J., and Hussey, J., (2011). 'The Effect of Maternity Leave Length and Time of Return to Work on Breastfeeding'. *Pediatrics*, 127: e1414–27.

Pikhartova, J. (2012). 'The Relationship between Maternal Employment in Childhood and Health-related Outcomes in Adolescence: Findings from the BHPS'. Doctoral thesis, University College London.

Relton, C., Whelan, B., Strong, M., Thomas, K., Whitford, H., Scott, E., and van Cleemput, P. (2014). 'Are Financial Incentives for Breastfeeding Feasible in the UK? A Mixed Methods Field Study'. *The Lancet*, 384(S5), 19 November 2014.

Rodgers, B. and Pryor, J. (1998). *Divorce and Separation: The Outcomes for Children*. York: Joseph Rowntree Foundation.

Ruhm, C. (2004). 'Parental Employment and Child Cognitive Development'. *Journal of Human Resources*, 39(1): 155–92.

Ruhm, C. and Waldfogel, J. (2012). 'Long-term Effects of Early Childhood Care and Education'. *Nordic Economic Policy Review*, 1(1): 23–51.

Sandel, M. (2012). *What Money Can't Buy: The Moral Limits of Markets*. New York: Farrar, Straus and Giroux.

Shildrick, T., MacDonald, R., Furlong, A., Roden, J., and Crow, R. (2012). *Are 'Cultures of Worklessness' Passed Down the Generations?* London: The Joseph Rowntree Foundation.

SMCP [Social Mobility and Child Poverty Commission] (2014). *Elitist Britain?* London: The Stationery Office.

Smith, G., Field, K., Smith, T., Noble, S., Smith, T. and Plunkett, E. (2014). 'Evaluation of Children's Centres in England (ECCE): The Extent to Which Centres "Reach" Eligible Families, their Neighbourhood Characteristics and Levels of Use'. Research Report June 2014. London: Department for Education.

Smolensky, E. and Gootman, J. (eds) (2003). *Working Families and Growing Kids: Caring for Children and Adolescents*. Washington, DC: National Academy Press.

Speight, S. and Smith, S. (2010). *Towards Universal Early Years Provision: Analysis of Take-up by Disadvantaged Families from Recent Annual Childcare Surveys*. London: Department for Education.

Stewart, K. (2013). 'Labour's Record on the Under-fives: Policy, Spending and Outcomes 1997–2010'. Social Policy in a Cold Climate Working Paper No. 4. CASE, LSE.

Stewart, K. and Obolenskaya, P. (2015). 'The Coalition's Record on the Under-fives: Policy, Spending and Outcomes 2010–2015'. Social Policy in a Cold Climate Working Paper No. 12. CASE, LSE.

Strully, K., Rehkopf, D., and Xuan, Z. (2010). 'Effects of Prenatal Poverty on Infant Health: State Earned Income Tax Credits and Birth Weight'. *American Sociological Review*, 75(4): 534–62.

Sylva, K., Melhuish, E., Sammons, P., Siraj-Blatchford, I., and Taggart, B. (2008). 'Final Report from the Primary Phase: Pre-School, School and Family Influences on Children's Development During Key Stage 2 (Age 7–11)'. Research Report DCSF-RR061. London: Department for Children, Schools and Families.

Tanaka, S. (2005). 'Parental Leave and Child Health across OECD Countries'. *Economic Journal*, 115(501): F7–F28.

Waldfogel, J. (2006). *What Children Need*. New York: Russell Sage Foundation.

Waldfogel, J. and Washbrook, E. (2011). 'Early Years Policy'. *Child Development Research*, 2011, 1–12.

Walker, I. and Zhu, Y. (2007). 'Do Dads Matter? Or Is It just their Money that Matters? Unpicking the Effects of Separation on Educational Outcomes'. UCD Geary Institute Discussion Paper Series WP2007/22. Dublin: University College Dublin.

Walzer, M. (1983). *Spheres of Justice*. New York: Basic Books.

6

Education and Learning

Sonia Exley

The notion of 'educational advantage' and its converse, 'educational disadvantage', can be described in sum as being the relative possession or otherwise for individuals of the knowledge and skills required within society and the labour market for their own enlightenment, empowerment, and participation. The relationship between *educational* (dis)advantage and wider *social* (dis)advantage is an intimate one. To be educated in life is to be afforded the odds of better employment opportunities, greater economic activity, and higher earnings. To be uneducated is to be more susceptible than others to the risks of unemployment, low wages, poverty, and social exclusion. Being poorly educated increases one's likelihood of experiencing social disadvantage; but being socially disadvantaged also implies a greater likelihood of experiencing poor education.

International policy discourses focus heavily on the importance of education for ameliorating social disadvantage and for promoting individuals' upward social mobility (as discussed in Chapter 4). At the same time, however, critical perspectives on education challenge the notion that national state systems of teaching and learning, as part of elite-controlled government infrastructures, could ever possess sufficient autonomy to engender significant social change. Instead, they are argued to reinforce and sometimes exacerbate intergenerational transmission of advantage and disadvantage.

Educational inequalities between individuals are typically measured using indicators such as student attainment levels in national—and sometimes international—tests and examinations. This chapter will begin with an outline of key current gaps in educational performance among students across the OECD, according to family origins. The chapter will then move on to considering key factors which are associated with and which may go some way to explaining both advantage and disadvantage in education, covering issues relating both to material and cultural inequalities between families, and issues relating both to life outside and inside formal education. It will also explore the possible impact of wider macro-level factors relating to the organization of education systems. The focus will be primarily on compulsory (school) education, rather than tertiary education; and while the broader context is international, many of the explicit examples will be from the UK. Drawing on the existing research base, the chapter will conclude by pointing to a number of important considerations for contemporary education policy.

6.1 Educational Divisions across the OECD

Gaps in educational attainment between the highest and lowest achieving social groups are wide across the global north. Table 6.1 below shows results from the 2012 Programme for International Student Assessment (PISA), undertaken by thirty-four OECD countries and testing students in reading, mathematics, and science at age fifteen. In 2012, overall, among fifteen-year-olds 8 per cent and 13 per cent demonstrated high proficiency (Level 5 or above) in reading and mathematics respectively, while nearly a fifth of all students (18 per cent) scored below 'baseline proficiency' for 'participating effectively and productively in life' (below Level 2) in reading and more than a fifth (23 per cent) scored below baseline proficiency in mathematics. However, there were substantial variations in these overall distributions according to the student's family backgrounds: reporting on associations between PISA scores and students' socio-economic status (SES), one OECD report (2013) notes that students from low SES backgrounds were, both in reading and mathematics, more than twice as likely as those from high SES backgrounds to score in the bottom quarter of the PISA performance distribution. Across the OECD, students from low SES backgrounds are, at age fifteen, on average more than

Table 6.1. Programme for International Student Assessment (PISA) 2012—OECD proportions of students attaining different proficiency levels in reading and mathematics aged 15

	Below level 2 %	Levels 2–4 %	Levels 5–6 %	Total %
Reading	18	74	8	100
Mathematics	23	64	13	100
Reading by gender				
Male	24	70	6	100
Female	12	77	11	100
Mathematics by gender				
Male	22	63	15	100
Female	24	65	11	100

Source: Based on OECD (2014a)

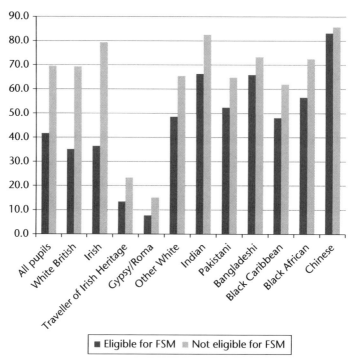

Figure 6.1. General Certificate of Secondary Education (GCSE) in England, 2013/14—percentage attaining five or more 'good' passes (A*–C) including English and Mathematics, by Free School Meal (FSM) eligibility and ethnicity
Source: Based on Department for Education (2014)

two years behind their high SES counterparts in terms of educational progress (OECD, 2013).

Such findings at the international level on differences in attainment by SES are corroborated by evidence from individual countries. Figure 6.1 shows the proportions of students in England achieving five or more 'good' examination passes (including English and Mathematics) in the 2014 General Certificate of Secondary Education (GCSE), undertaken at the end of compulsory education (age sixteen). Here, while just four in ten (42 per cent) of all students eligible for Free School Meals (FSM—a means-tested benefit indicating that students live in low-income households) in England achieved five such passes, the comparable figure for students not eligible for FSM was seven in ten (70 per cent). Polarization in educational attainment between young people who are advantaged and disadvantaged in terms of SES is known to begin early in life and to continue or even widen across their educational careers (see Chapter 5; also Sullivan et al., 2013). Moreover, significant educational transitions are not only dependent on differences in attainment but are also shaped by family background, over and above the influence on achievement. Not only do predicted and actual levels of achievement in examinations at the end of compulsory schooling play a major role in students deciding whether or not they will apply to university, both parental income and parental occupation constitute significant predictors of whether or not a student of a given level of attainment will stay on in formal education. This is particularly the case where a student has experienced below-average educational attainment (Payne, 2003). Attainment at school additionally impacts on applicants' access to universities and indeed partly determines *which* universities or other programmes of academic or vocational further or higher education students will attend.

Educational inequalities however do not only relate to students' SES. Rather, they are mediated in complex ways by factors such as students' gender and ethnicity. Referring back to Table 6.1, we can see that across the OECD, almost a quarter of all boys (24 per cent) score below baseline proficiency in reading at age fifteen, compared with just 12 per cent of girls. At the same time, the proportions achieving below basic proficiency in mathematics are broadly even between boys and girls.

Greater disparities in attainment exist across all OECD countries along lines of ethnicity and students with migrant backgrounds. The OECD in its PISA reports uses 'immigrant background', either first or second generation, as a proxy for ethnic minority status in the absence of a more differentiated indicator of student ethnicity (see discussions in Chapters 12 and 13). While a fifth (21 per cent) of all students across the OECD who do not have 'immigrant backgrounds' fail to attain basic proficiency in mathematics at age fifteen, the comparable proportions for first and second generation immigrant students are 40 and 34 per cent respectively (OECD, 2013). Care must be taken, however, not to assume a simple story of ethnic minority disadvantage in education (see also the discussion in Chapter 12). Referring back to Figure 6.1 which reports educational achievement in England for students of different ethnic origins by eligibility for FSM, it can be seen that the highest achieving ethnic groups at GCSE level are not those who are White British, but rather those who are of Chinese, Indian, and Irish origin. Moreover, ethnicity interacts with disadvantage in complex ways, such that the gap between those on FSM and those not is typically smaller for minority groups than it is for the White British majority. Recent research by Burgess (2014) has highlighted strong performance of schools in London relative to the rest of England as being explained partly by London schools' having above-average ethnic diversity, combined with the general insensitivity of high-performing minority groups' performance to levels of deprivation. Nevertheless, this is not simply an 'immigrant success story'—relatively low GCSE attainment in England for students from Black Caribbean, Pakistani, and, particularly, Gypsy/Roma and Traveller of Irish Heritage backgrounds remains a matter for concern.

Moreover, students from Black Caribbean backgrounds in England are more than twice as likely as students from White British backgrounds to be excluded from school. They are also more than twice as likely as students from White British backgrounds to be classified formally as experiencing emotional, social, and behavioural difficulties (Parsons, 2009; Strand, 2011).

6.2 Explaining Educational Advantage and Disadvantage

What factors might explain such clear divisions between those who achieve 'success' in formal schooling and those who do not? Over the course of the second half of the twentieth century, academic researchers in the field of education have sought through quantitative and qualitative analysis in a vast number of studies to identify a wide range of factors which may predict individuals' and groups' high or low educational achievement. At this point, it is crucial to emphasize that statistical inferences and conclusions emerging from all such research can never be treated as definitive proof that certain factors have *caused* particular patterns of high or low achievement. Nevertheless, some important patterns and associations have been identified.

Early academic discussions across many countries about unequal educational attainment during the 1950s and 1960s traditionally focused heavily on notions of individuals' 'natural' ability, with an emphasis on the extent to which educational success might be attributed to people's *innate heritable characteristics*, as captured by methods such as IQ testing (see for example Jensen, 1969; also later Hernstein and Murray, 1994). Over time, however, the fierce contesting of eugenics as a helpful branch of academic inquiry and indeed the widespread challenges to past studies purporting not only to be able to identify fixed heritable intelligence within individuals but then also link this causally to educational attainment (see for example Fraser, 1995), has led to a gradual broadening of focus in educational research towards considering *environmental factors* which might explain educational inequalities.

Central to studies exploring aspects of individuals' environmental circumstances which may impact on educational achievement have been considerations of the importance of material wealth and deprivation. Possessing greater material affluence within society enables parents to gain significant educational advantage for their children, investing in, for example:

- Private schools offering facilities beyond those available to children in the state sector and affording long-term benefits to those who attend (Green et al., 2009);
- Houses within the close vicinity of 'better' state schools (Allen et al., 2010);

- Educational resources at home such as books and toys (Melhuish, 2010);
- Private tutors and the purchasing of commercially available educational packages online and in private study centres (often referred to as supplementary or, in East Asia, 'shadow' education—see Bray and Kwo, 2013; Ball, 2010).

Beyond the clear importance of straightforward material advantage in education, however, social science debates in recent decades have also explored the notion that there exist cultural and social 'capitals' (as discussed extensively in Chapter 4) underpinning social advantage and disadvantage, and these are believed additionally to impact on children's educational development. 'Cultural capital', as developed by Pierre Bourdieu (1986; Bourdieu and Passeron, 1990), is believed to be distributed unequally between families. Parents in socially advantaged families transmit dominant cultural characteristics to their children—knowledges, tastes, and dispositions—and these characteristics hold power because they are deemed within society—but importantly for this chapter in particular *within formal systems of education*—to be more 'legitimate' than are other, less advantaged families' cultural characteristics. Parents with extensive cultural capital possess 'valued' knowledge within society, enabling them to influence both heavily and beneficially their children's learning. First, having themselves higher levels of educational qualifications, they are more able than others to engage in activities such as bedtime reading and helping with homework. Second, they are more able to cultivate in their children ambitious future educational and labour market aspirations (for example the aspiration to attend higher education) and to possess the knowledge necessary to explain what achieving such goals would require. Finally they are more able than others to select the most highly culturally valued resources within society—particular sorts of books, toys and crafts, particular films and TV programmes, visits to museums, libraries, and places of interest—in order to support their children's educational success.

The notion of parents engaging strategically in all such activities outlined above has been described by Lareau (1987) as 'concerted cultivation'. Ideas about the boosting of young people's educational advantage relating not only to families' economic resources but also to their social and cultural forms of capital have fed into a growing number of studies over time researching—and indeed a growing number of policy discourses emphasizing—the importance of parental attitudes towards education and the importance of parents' aspirations for their children (Sewell et al., 1969; Boudon, 1974; Goodman and Gregg, 2010; Kintrea et al., 2011; Freeney and O'Connell, 2012; St Clair et al., 2013).

Policy emphasizing the importance of aspirations and attitudes in education must, however, take care to maintain a simultaneous focus on the reality that economic and material resources are known to mediate family cultural capital (van Otter, 2013). Museum visits require parents to have both time and sufficient income to pay for entry fees and transport fares. Books, computers, and study space at home require a certain level of household income and engaging fully in children's education requires not only manageable and flexible working hours, but also good health overall and a relative absence of mental stress relating to financial hardship (West, 2007a). Work by Sullivan (2001) on children's educational attainment has highlighted that even after a family's cultural capital is taken into account, large effects remain relating to social class in its more material respects. Work by Rennison et al. (2005) has additionally reported that pressure to earn often constitutes a key reason why young people leave school and do not continue on to post-compulsory education. Research studies by authors such as Goodman and Gregg (2010) and Kintrea et al. (2011) emphasize an important theme emerging from qualitative research on aspirations, which is that, in emphasizing the importance of parents' aspirations for their children in ensuring children's educational success, it should also be noted that, among socially disadvantaged parents, aspirations often at least start out high, with parents understanding and expressing significant anxiety regarding the importance of their children's education. Aspirations are found to relate strongly, however, to parents' own social and environmental circumstances; they are situated in space, time, and in the context of wider external structures of economic reality. Parents may adapt to the reality of patterns of attainment that are themselves structured by socio-economic status; and the costs and benefits of staying on in education for those who achieve only moderate levels of success differ across social groups (Breen and Goldthorpe, 1997). Hence, as noted above, poorer performing students from advantaged backgrounds are substantially more likely to go to university than their disadvantaged peers. On the other hand, ethnic minority students often hold high educational aspirations that are less sensitive to their attainment than those of their majority counterparts (Kao and Tienda, 1998; Strand, 2011).

6.3 Home Learning Environments and Family–School Relationships

Taken together, cultural and material resources within socially advantaged families enable the fostering of what is often termed a positive 'home learning environment'. The importance of such an environment outside of formal schooling for boosting children's educational success has been emphasized a great deal in educational research (for recent examples see: Sylva et al., 2010; Siraj Blatchford, 2010; Hartas, 2012; Gershenson, 2013; see also discussion in Chapter 5). Academic work exploring and attempting to quantify the impact of home background 'effects' on how well children do at school relative to the contribution made by formal institutions has for many years shown that the effects of the former are markedly greater in size than the effects of the latter (Jencks, 1972; Rutter et al., 1979; Mortimore, 1997).

Parental engagement also matters—but is also unequal between social groups—outside the home and in the realm of family–school relationships. Disadvantaged parents are less likely than others to know the details of their children's schoolwork day-to-day and they are less likely to know the extent to which their children are attending school. They tend less than others to be on close or familiar terms with their children's teachers, to volunteer to take part in school activities, to attend parents' evenings, and overall to know how well or otherwise their children are progressing educationally (Lareau, 1987). The explanation for such patterns among more disadvantaged parents does not, however, relate to how much or how little these parents value their children's education and view it as important. Research has shown that among working-class and disadvantaged parents there is, in addition to a clear valuing of education, also simply a stronger tendency than is the case in middle-class households towards believing and trusting in the idea that the 'teacher knows best'. Deference to the superior expertise of school staff and keeping home and school distinctly separate in a context of not knowing the best strategies for helpful involvement in children's education is often viewed as being the most appropriate course of action among less advantaged families (Lareau, 1987).

Schools can also play a role in the exclusion and alienation of more disadvantaged families, and consequently the success of more advantaged families. Work carried out by Lareau (1987), Carvalho (2001), and Casanova (1996) has emphasized issues arising within formal education regarding normative middle-class assumptions made by school staff about the material and cultural resources with which parents will be endowed (for example cars, computing facilities at home, affordable childcare), enabling their involvement in their children's education and also in school events and activities. Research on the relationships between schools and parents carried out by Crozier and Davies (2007) has highlighted not only that cultural assumptions made by school staff are hegemonic and middle class, but also that they are white. Pakistani and Bangladeshi parents in England were, for example, deemed by teachers and others in one research study as being 'hard to reach', 'impenetrable', and obstructive. A study by Lareau and McNamara Horvat (1999) reported similarly on the way in which Black parents in one Midwestern US case study school were perceived by teachers as being hostile and 'negative' even though this was largely on account of their being openly critical and expressing genuine concerns regarding historical legacies of discrimination against black families in education.

119

6.4 The Role of Schooling

Beyond their relationships with parents, schools matter more widely in the reinforcing or challenging of educational inequalities. Processes inside formal systems of education are considered often to reward white middle-class cultures over working-class cultures and the cultures of ethnic minorities, drawing differentially via a 'hidden curriculum' on the skills and knowledges possessed by different groups (Apple, 1979) and enabling easier transitions into schooling for some children more than others.

Middle-class parents' and pupils' relationships to formal education have often been described in research as being characterized by less formality, by frequent contact, and by shared references and understandings between teachers, students, and parents (for a critical review see Power et al., 2003). Working-class families' relationships to education are by contrast characterized by greater distance and detachment (as indicated above) and by more formal, hierarchical, and authoritarian relationships between teachers and students/parents, 'corresponding' with social class structures and social relationships in the labour market and in wider society (Bowles and Gintis, 1976). During the 1970s, the work of educationalist Basil Bernstein made famous the notion that working class families' communication experiences were based on a 'restricted' linguistic code, but that an 'elaborate code' was the linguistic basis for communication both among middle-class families and inside formal schooling, putting working-class pupils at a disadvantage (Bernstein, 1975).

Building on these ideas, challenges faced by more disadvantaged pupils at school are often said to become compounded by the role schools and teachers play in subjectifying students and in constructing or reinforcing specific aspects of their identity (Althusser, 1971; Youdell, 2011). Hegemonic 'cultures of masculinity' reinforced inside schooling are often considered to impact on boys' learner identities, contributing to disparities in boys' and girls' educational attainment and to a 'laddish' resistance to education, particularly among those who are working class (Epstein et al., 1998; Francis, 2000). Socially advantaged students, with a pre-existing cultural and economic 'head start' in education, have historically been more likely at school to become labelled as 'able' and rewarded accordingly, whereas disadvantaged students have historically been more likely to be classified as having lower ability (Hallam and Parsons, 2013), as well as having 'special educational needs' and social and behavioural problems, with consequences for their esteem and self-perception, as well as access to learning opportunities. In 2008–10, data from the Department for Education in England indicated that socially disadvantaged students (as measured by their eligibility for Free School Meals) were notably under-represented on a national programme set up for 'gifted and talented' students (DfE, 2010). Earlier reports from the same programme suggested that White students in England were in 2005 more than twice as likely as Black Caribbean or Black African students to be identified as gifted and talented (DfES, 2005). Related to this, and building on findings reported above regarding the exclusion of Black Caribbean students from schools in England and their disproportionate designation as having emotional, social, and behavioural issues, it has been found in a number of research studies that teachers in England, after taking students' prior attainment into account, are disproportionately likely to place Black Caribbean students into classes for those of lower ability (Gillborn, 2008; Strand, 2011).

Nevertheless, formal education can in many respects also be crucial in limiting the conversion of social inequalities into educational inequalities. One key finding consistently emphasized within educational research and in particular emphasized by international organizations such as UNESCO and the World Bank (UNESCO, 2007, 2010; World Bank, 2006) has been the importance of preschool or 'Early Years' education in boosting the cognitive development of children and in particular the importance of Early Years education for ameliorating the negative effects of a poor home learning environment (Sylva et al., 2010; Heckman, 2011; Kilburn and Karoly, 2008; OECD, 2006; Magnuson et al., 2004; Zoritch et al., 2000—see Chapter 5 for further discussion). Across the global north, however, access to good quality preschool education for children is by no means universal; rather it is partly dependent on parents' ability to pay. Governments across many OECD countries are believed to underspend on early years provision as a proportion of GDP (though Nordic countries are a notable exception here—see OECD, 2006); and it is consequently the case that children most in need of such provision as a result of social disadvantage are at the same time those least likely to gain sufficient access. Disadvantaged children are also found to benefit most from Early Years education settings which have a socially balanced mix of children overall, where positive 'peer effects' from more cognitively advanced children are spread to the wider group. However, segregation of children along lines of social advantage and disadvantage in the early years is marked, partly on account of parents' differential ability to pay, but also partly on account of residential inequalities between neighbourhoods and their local provisions.

Although the contribution schools can make either to challenging or reinforcing educational inequalities is found to be limited (schools account statistically for only around one tenth of variable attainment between students, Mortimore, 1997) there are nevertheless important ways they can mitigate or exacerbate inequalities. These relate to how effective different schools and school types are—the quality of institutional facilities, leadership and organizational structures, the quality and number of teachers employed and the nature of school social composition, which can lead to positive or negative 'peer effects' for pupils (Mortimore, 1997, 1998; Mortimore and Whitty, 2000).

6.5 Segregation Matters

Schooling that is socially segregated by neighbourhood is found to concentrate educational advantage in terms of positive pupil peer effects—and the positive effects generated by the presence within a school of assertive and socially advantaged parents rich in economic, social, and cultural capitals—in more affluent neighbourhoods. Concentrated pupil deprivation, by contrast, and a lack of such capital in segregated schools in more disadvantaged neighbourhoods is found to impact on educational quality, for example presenting constraints on teachers' ability to adopt particular pedagogical approaches (see for example Lupton and Hempel-Jorgensen, 2012) and disruptions in classrooms relating to pupil behaviour, hampering school effectiveness, and depressing outcomes for pupils attending those schools (Palardy, 2013).

Segregated pupil intakes within schools along lines of socio-economic status, beneficial in certain respects for those attending more affluent schools, but detrimental in terms of outcomes to those attending schools with more disadvantaged pupil intakes, are produced by systems of local neighbourhood schooling in combination with macro-level social inequalities which produce disparities in wealth and income between neighbourhoods. They are however exacerbated by further macro-level factors including the existence of private schools within societies, which educate only a 'creamy layer' of the most socially advantaged students, the presence of religious schools which are known also disproportionately to admit socially advantaged students (Allen and West, 2009) and the presence of academically selective schools, which select pupils on the basis of 'ability' but suffer from the problem (as indicated above) that measured ability determined through tests of achievement is known to correlate with students' socio-economic status.

'Tracking' of students into different schools on the basis of measured prior achievement, particularly where this happens earlier in students' educational lives, is believed to contribute in many countries to those countries' wider than average disparities in educational attainment (Hanushek and Woessmann, 2005; West and Nikolai, 2013; OECD, 2014b; Schleicher, 2014). Selective academic systems as seen in many Continental European countries, for example Austria, Belgium, Germany, and the Netherlands (Green et al., 2006), also England's past selective system of 'grammar schools' (though there remain 164 grammar schools in England today), while considered to have had some mild benefits for higher achieving students from disadvantaged backgrounds selected into more prestigious schools, are also considered to have contributed to unequal outcomes between individuals and to have hampered progress for students not selected into more prestigious schools (Boliver and Swift, 2011; Harris and Rose, 2013; Burgess et al., 2014). Social segregation of advantaged and disadvantaged pupils with resultant positive and negative 'peer effects' on educational outcomes takes place *between schools*, but also *inside schools*. 'Streaming' and 'setting' of pupils into different 'ability' tiers for teaching purposes is found to impact positively on educational outcomes and to accelerate achievement inside schools for higher achieving pupils. However, for lower achieving students placed in large numbers of separate classes without the presence of higher achieving peers, there are found to be detrimental effects on attainment (Slavin, 1990). Highlighting the 'problems of meritocracy', Goldthorpe (1996) points to a fundamental critique of systems which search for and reward 'talent', 'ability', or indeed 'motivation' inside formal education, which is that perceptions of 'merit' are ultimately highly subjective, rendering an unequal distribution of educational opportunities on the basis of such perceptions problematic.

With regard to school segregation and the problems it poses for educational equity, one further matter of major contention in education policy literature in recent decades has been the introduction of 'quasi-market' mechanisms inside state education across many countries, aiming to liberalize both school supply (i.e. the autonomy given to individual institutions) and school demand (opening up the possibility of school choice for parents as market actors). In a context of school 'choice and diversity', instead of children simply being allocated to their nearest state school, parents as proxy 'consumers' of education are granted the opportunity to express a preference for alternative schools for their children, with schools in turn competing for families' 'business' and being given autonomy to diversify and transform in order to appeal to the greatest number of parents (securing the greatest amount of government funding). Examples of such measures across the world include the rise of Magnet and Charter Schools in the USA, open enrolment and the rise of 'Academies' in England, 'Free Schools' and parental choice reforms in Sweden (Wiborg 2010), 'Self Governing' schools in New Zealand, decentralization initiatives in Canada, school voucher reforms in Chile and indeed state aid for non-government schools in a further wide range of countries, including Australia, Argentina, and India (for a review see Forsey et al., 2008).

Advocates of quasi-market mechanisms in education (see for example Le Grand, 2007) argue that, for disadvantaged families, systems of 'open enrolment' enable parents to exercise agency and a preference for schools outside their local area, escaping problems of segregated schooling and the clear educational challenges present in more deprived neighbourhood schools. Critics, however, argue that in a context of wider social inequalities, structural limits to parental choice are significant, because schools in socially

123

desirable areas with more advantaged pupil intakes will only ever have limited spaces. Processes of school 'choice' in such a context, then, it is argued, lead to a situation where parents, unequally endowed as they are with economic, social, and cultural capital, compete strategically for spaces in the most socially advantaged schools (Gewirtz et al., 1995; Ball, 2003). Oversubscribed schools enjoying enhanced autonomy furthermore tend often towards 'cream-skimming' the most able and advantaged students (West et al., 2006) for the purposes of further boosting their success and popularity. Ultimately, it is argued, a context arises in which middle-class families are more likely to succeed in securing access to the 'best' schools while others remain segregated in schools which become more disadvantaged than was previously the case. Reliable studies on the social and educational segregation implications of school choice policies in different countries are, however, so far mixed and inconclusive (see Allen and Burgess, 2010, for a review of evidence from England, the US, Sweden, and Chile). Recent research by Burgess et al. (2007) has highlighted associations in England between areas of urban density with greater levels of competition between schools/parents and areas which have higher levels of socio-economic segregation between schools. However, it must be noted here that associations do not prove any causal link between quasi-market reforms and heightened school segregation.

6.6 Policy—Challenging or Reinforcing Educational (Dis)advantage?

Within government policy, education seems ever-increasingly viewed as constituting a powerful vehicle for promoting social change and for challenging divisions between those experiencing social advantage and disadvantage. Upon election to government in 1997, UK Prime Minister Tony Blair famously declared that his Labour government would focus on 'education, education, education', and contemporary international policy discourses increasingly emphasize the importance of formal education for breaking intergenerational transmissions of disadvantage, enabling children to become socially mobile, to develop 'resilience' against poverty, and to succeed 'against the odds' (see, for example, OECD, 2013; Field, 2010; Allen, 2011; HM Government, 2011). Education systems across the world are heavily emphasized as having the power to promote fairness in society and equalize opportunities (World Bank, 2006), helping to create a 'level playing field' and promoting equality of opportunity for individuals across different socio-economic backgrounds. Fair allocations of government 'social investment' in the early years, in school, and in further and higher education, are viewed as imperative in ensuring all have a fair chance to succeed.

From a radical perspective, it can be noted here in the first instance that many left-wing theorists writing on education have historically emphasized the fact that formal education systems constitute 'ideological state apparatuses' (Althusser, 1971). Being produced by existing society and being part of government-controlled infrastructures, state schools arguably do not possess the required autonomy from national capitalist states to engender true empowerment within society for those who are socially disadvantaged. Even from a less radical perspective, however, questions can be raised over the extent to which formal systems of education might be able to engender significant social change in a context where dominant themes emerging in government education policies are in many senses contradictory.

Problematizing the notion of 'equal educational opportunities', Christopher Jencks in 1988 argued that markedly different understandings of this notion among educational practitioners and policymakers alike point to diverse and frequently conflicting implications for the distribution of educational resources. While some see promoting equal opportunities in education somewhat extensively as providing 'compensatory' resources to students who are systematically disadvantaged within society (by poverty or indeed by a lack of 'natural' ability), others see equal opportunities simply as ensuring that 'natural' ability and capacity for excellence are always supported regardless of students' socio-economic backgrounds, or indeed alternatively as ensuring that hard work is always rewarded in the form of additional resources, regardless of students' socio-economic background or their high/low achievement. Education policy regimes across the world can be considered typically as comprising contradictory amalgams of measures, with different sorts of initiatives having different implications for the allocation of resources.

'Compensatory' funding efforts in education policy, which aim to provide, through various types of initiative, extra resources to disadvantaged students, families, schools, and neighbourhoods, in the English context have recently included:

- Targeted early years provision in the form of 'Sure Start'—an area-based initiative announced in 1998 which at its outset had some similarities to 'Head Start' in the United States and Australia; (see also the discussion in Chapter 5);

- A 'Pupil Premium' for schools announced in 2010, allocating extra funding per capita for each pupil admitted from a low-income household (Chowdry et al., 2010);

- 'Education Action Zones' (a targeted area-based scheme introduced under New Labour in 1998, though now abolished);

- An 'Educational Maintenance Allowance' granting financial support to socially disadvantaged students over the age of 16 who wish to continue in full-time education.

Compensatory measures on the whole—in England and elsewhere—have been shown to generate some success in boosting educational achievement for socially disadvantaged groups (see for example a recent evaluation of New Labour's 'record' on education in England from 1997 to 2010—Lupton and Obolenskaya, 2013; also Lupton and Glennerster, 2009; Lupton, 2010). In light of the positive evidence on the importance of Early Years education provision for helping disadvantaged children to succeed, it is encouraging to note that across many countries within Europe such as Belgium, France, Sweden, Norway, Italy, Spain, and the UK, participation in early years education and care for children aged three and four is near universal (Eurydice and Eurostat, 2014). Quality of provision on offer is, however, variable across countries (OECD, 2006, 2012; Gambaro et al., 2014) and countries such as the US and Ireland lag behind in terms of access to and affordability of good quality early years provision (Penn, 2011; West et al., 2010). Recent work by Morabito et al. (2013) has provided a critical perspective regarding international institutions' particularly strong focus on investment in early years education (UNESCO, 2007, 2010; World Bank, 2006) as constituting an incontrovertible panacea for combating social disadvantage. Factors influencing our success or otherwise in life are, after all, highly complex, existing outside and continuing long after we leave early years education.

Considering compensatory measures in schools, the effects of straightforward additional funding, though beneficial, are also found to be both limited and dependent on how funding is spent (Hanushek, 1986; Levacic and Vignoles, 2002). Additional funding must, if equity is a key goal for society, definitively 'reach' those who are most disadvantaged. It must also be utilized in ways which have been shown in high quality pedagogical research to be beneficial for narrowing educational inequalities (Cassen et al., 2015; West, 2007b). By contrast, numerous policy regimes and ways of organizing education prevalent across the global north—tracking and selection from an early age, the continued existence of private schools, encouraging parents to engage strategically in market practices for competitive advantage, and a failure to tackle fully significant inequalities between neighbourhood schools—can all be considered as contributing to a reinforcing, rather than a narrowing, of educational divisions, ultimately damaging progress towards the key goal for society of there being 'the completest possible educational equality' (Tawney, 1934, quoted in Reay, 2012).

In light of research highlighting the importance of home learning environments and also on the limited difference formal institutions can make to challenging social disadvantage, an increasing policy focus on the role parents can play in aiding their children's educational development, may represent a positive direction. Policy agendas often focus narrowly on schools and indeed there is frequently an excessively narrow contemporary focus on *teachers'* capacity to 'make the difference' in education (Skourdoumbis, 2014). Looking beyond formal schooling at home circumstances, Siraj-Blatchford (2010) has demonstrated that, while structural constraints to involvement in education and the cultivation of strong home learning environments certainly exist for working-class and disadvantaged parents, there is also room for disadvantaged parents' agency in the realm of education, helping children to succeed 'against the odds' and generating significant positive benefits for their intellectual and social development.

This highlights the importance of avoiding generalized 'culture of poverty' assumptions about socially disadvantaged parents and 'deficit models' of working class parenting (Gewirtz, 2001) based on stereotypes of less affluent parents as being somehow incomplete and in need of 'improvement' (Reay, 2001). At the same time, policy discourses emphasizing the notion that social deprivation should be considered 'no excuse' for educational underachievement (see, for example, Strauss, 2012) give cause for concern because they risk putting excessive responsibility for children's success or failure on to parents, promoting a dominant message that sending children to school is not 'enough' and shifting significant onus for delivering educational quality away from the state and on to individual families—particularly mothers— who may be in vulnerable circumstances (see Vincent, 2012; Vincent et al., 2010). Concerns have been raised in particular over recent trends towards an increasing 'management' of disadvantaged parents in the realm of education and a growing juridification of relations between parents and schools, with parents increasingly expected to sign and adhere to formal lists of obligations such as 'home school agreements' (Gibson, 2013; see also discussions on mandated behaviour for low-income parents in Chapter 5 of this volume).

Questions might finally be raised over the extent to which 'concerted cultivation' of children (Lareau, 1987) and middle-class and affluent parents' practices for gaining positional advantage in education are necessarily always desirable, or even acceptable—a point also made in Chapter 5. Authors such as Vincent and Ball (2007; see also Ball, 2010) have, for example, highlighted problems for educational equality which are arguably inherent in activities on the part of more advantaged parents feeding into a culture of instrumental and competitive 'hyper-developmentalism'. In a context of: 1) persistent wider social inequalities, where marked disparities in families' cultural capital and capacity to spend due to unequal wages and household income show no immediate signs of abating; and 2) increased global marketing of new ways to invest in children educationally, for example the exponential growth of commercial 'edutainment' products for purchase, practices of advantage will arguably tend increasingly to 'ratchet' to new and ever-more intensive levels. Some young people will experience constant and perhaps increasingly frantic educational stimulation, while at the same time, disadvantaged families will find themselves 'catching up' only to discover they are still falling behind.

6.7 Conclusion

Educational inequalities within society both produce and are produced by wider social divisions. Gaps in educational achievement which can be seen in every country in the world—between rich and poor, between boys and girls, and between different ethnic groups—have been shown in research to be caused by multiple complex factors. Material inequalities in income and wealth affect families' capacity to invest in key resources for supporting their children's educational development. At the same time, however, inequalities in cultural capital between families mean that socially disadvantaged parents are frequently ill-equipped with the 'legitimate' and socially valued knowledge and skills they need to engage fully and properly in their children's education, while advantaged parents can benefit from these to capitalize on educational opportunities. Exclusionary practices on the part of schools impact both on the possibilities for parental involvement which do exist and on the esteem and identity of different groups of students.

Policy regimes seeking to narrow the gap between those educationally advantaged and those educationally disadvantaged by their background must place at their heart the question of resources. Increased 'compensatory' funding for those who are experiencing disadvantage, however, needs to be well targeted to be effective, not only in the early years and at school but also crucially *outside* of schools. At the same time, compensatory agendas can be undermined by initiatives within education and ways of organizing institutions which exacerbate problems such as the hierarchical segregation of different pupils into different sorts of schools. With the overwhelming emphasis on the significance of education for life chances and in a competitive liberal market economy, parents are likely to continue on the whole to try in multiple ways to maximize their own children's chances of success relative to others'.

Finally, attempts to foster greater social mobility or any more egalitarian vision for society *through education systems* need to remain mindful of what are fundamentally inherent limits to these attempts. Without broader redistribution and political change *outside* the realm of education (see further discussion in Chapters 7 and 8), formal systems of schools, nurseries, colleges, and universities across the world, created as they are by unequal societies, will forever to some degree reflect those societies.

References

Allen G. (2011). *Early Intervention: The Next Steps*. London: Department for Work and Pensions.

Allen, R. and Burgess, S. (2010). *The Future of Competition and Accountability in Education*, available at http://www.2020publicservicetrust.org/publications/, accessed 20 August 2015.

Allen, R., Burgess, S., and Key, T. (2010). *Choosing Secondary Schools by Moving House: School Quality and the Formation of Neighbourhoods*. Bristol: Centre for Market and Public Organisation.

Allen, R. and West, A. (2009). 'Religious Schools in London: School Admissions, Religious Composition and Selectivity'. *Oxford Review of Education*, 35(4): 471–94.

Althusser, L. (1971). 'Ideology and Ideological State Apparatuses'. In *Lenin and Philosophy and other Essays*. New York: Monthly Review Press.

Apple, M. (1979). *Ideology and Curriculum*. London: Routledge and Kegan Paul.

Ball, S. J. (2003). *Class Strategies and the Education Market: The Middle Classes and Social Advantage*. London: Routledge.

Ball, S. J. (2010). 'New Class Inequalities in Education: Why Education Policy May Be Looking in the Wrong Place'. *International Journal of Sociology and Social Policy*, 30(4): 155–66.

Bernstein, B. (1975). *Class, Codes and Control*. London: Routledge and Kegan Paul.

Boliver, V. and Swift, A. (2011). 'Do Comprehensive Schools Reduce Social Mobility?' *British Journal of Sociology*, 62(1): 89–110.

Boudon, R. (1974). *Education, Opportunity, and Social Inequality*. New York: John Wiley and Sons.

Bourdieu, P. (1986). 'The Forms of Capital'. In H. Lauder, P. Brown, and A. Stuart Wells (eds) *Education: Culture, Economy and Society*, pp. 46–58. Oxford: Oxford University Press.

Bourdieu, P. and Passeron, J.-C. (1990). *Reproduction in Education, Society and Culture*. 2nd edn. London: Sage.

Bowles, S. and Gintis, H. (1976). *Schooling in Capitalist America: Educational Reform and the Contradictions of Economic Life*. New York: Basic Books.

Bray, M. and Kwo, O. (2013). 'Behind the Façade of Fee-free Education: Shadow Education and its Implications for Social Justice'. *Oxford Review of Education*, 39(4): 480–97.

Breen, R. and Goldthorpe, J. H. (1997). 'Explaining Educational Differentials: Towards a Formal Rational Action Theory'. *Rationality and Society*, 9: 275–305.

Burgess, S. (2014). *Understanding the Success of London's Schools*. Bristol: CMPO.

Burgess, S., Dickson, M., and MacMillan, L. (2014). *Do Grammar Schools Increase or Reduce Inequality?* Bristol: CMPO.

Burgess, S., McConnell, B., Propper, C., and Wilson, D. (2007). 'The Impact of School Choice on Sorting by Ability and Socio-economic Factors in English Secondary Education'. In L. Woessmann and P. Peterson (eds) *Schools and the Equal Opportunity Problem*, pp. 273–92. Cambridge, MA: MIT Press.

Carvalho, M. E. (2001). *Rethinking Family-School Relations: A Critique of Parental Involvement in Schooling*. New York: Psychology Press.

Casanova, U. (1996). 'Parent Involvement: A Call for Prudence'. *Educational Researcher*, 25(8): 30–46.

Cassen, R., McNally, S., and Vignoles, A. (2015). *Making a Difference in Education: What the Evidence Says*. Abingdon: Routledge.

Chowdry, H., Greaves, E., and Sibieta, L. (2010). *The Pupil Premium: Assessing the Options*. London: Institute for Fiscal Studies.

Crozier, G. and Davies, J. (2007). 'Hard to Reach Parents or Hard to Reach Schools? A Discussion of Home–School Relations, with Particular Reference to Bangladeshi and Pakistani Parents'. *British Educational Research Journal*, 33(3): 295–313.

Department for Education (2010). *Schools, Pupils and their Characteristics, January 2010*. Statistical First Release, available at https://www.gov.uk/government/uploads/system/uploads/attachment_data/file/218952/main_20text_20sfr092010.pdf, accessed 30 July 2015.

Department for Education (2014). *GCSE and Equivalent Attainment by Pupil Characteristics: 2012 to 2013*, available at https://www.gov.uk/government/statistics/gcse-and-equivalent-attainment-by-pupil-characteristics-2012-to-2013, accessed 30 July 2015.

Department for Education and Skills (2005). *Ethnicity and Education: The Evidence on Minority Ethnic Pupils*. London: DfES.

Epstein, D., Elwood, J., Hey, V., and Maw, J. (1998). *Failing Boys?* Buckingham: Open University Press.

Eurydice and Eurostat (2014). *Key Data on Early Childhood, 2014 Edition*. Brussels: Education, Audiovisual and Culture Executive Agency.

Field, F. (2010). 'The Foundation Years: Preventing Poor Children Becoming Poor Adults', The report of the Independent Review on Poverty and Life Chances. London: HM Government.

Forsey, M., Davies, S., and Walford, G. (eds) (2008). *The Globalisation of School Choice?* Oxford: Symposium.

Francis, B. (2000). *Boys, Girls and Achievement: Addressing the Classroom Issues*. London: Routledge.

Fraser, S. (ed.) (1995). *The Bell Curve Wars: Race, Intelligence, and the Future of America*. New York: Basic Books.

Freeney, Y. and O'Connell, M. (2012). 'The Predictors of the Intention to Leave School Early among a Representative Sample of Irish Second-level Students'. *British Educational Research Journal*, 38(4): 557–74.

Gambaro, L., Stewart, K., and Waldfogel, J. (eds) (2014). *An Equal Start? Providing Quality Early Education and Care for Disadvantaged Children*. Bristol: The Policy Press.

Gershenson, S. (2013). 'Do Summer Time-use Gaps Vary by Socioeconomic Status?' *American Educational Research Journal*, 50(6): 1219–48.

Gewirtz, S. (2001). 'Cloning the Blairs: New Labour's Programme for the Re-socialization of Working-class Parents'. *Journal of Education Policy*, 16: 365–78.

Gewirtz, S., Ball, S. J., and Bowe, R. (1995). *Markets, Choice and Equity in Education*. Buckingham: Open University Press.

Gibson, H. (2013). 'Home–school Agreements: Explaining the Growth of 'Juridification' and Contractualism in Schools. *Oxford Review of Education*, 39(6): 780–96.

Gillborn, D. (2008). *Racism and Education: Coincidence or Conspiracy?* London: Routledge.

Goldthorpe, J. H. (1996). 'Problems of "Meritocracy"'. In R. Erikson and J. O. Jonsson (eds) *Can Education Be Equalised? The Swedish Case in Comparative Perspective*, pp. 255–87. Boulder, CO: Westview Press.

Goodman, A. and Gregg, P. (eds) (2010). *Poorer Children's Educational Attainment: How Important Are Attitudes and Behaviour?* London: Institute for Fiscal Studies.

Green, A., Preston, J., and Janmaat, G. (2006). *Education, Equality and Social Cohesion: A Comparative Analysis*. London: Palgrave.

Green, F., Machin, S., Murphy, R., and Zhu, Y. (2009). 'What Have Private Schools Done for (Some of) Us?, *Significance*, 6(2): 63–7.

Hallam, S. and Parsons, S. (2013). 'Prevalence of Streaming in UK Primary Schools: Evidence from the Millennium Cohort Study'. *British Educational Research Journal*, 39(3): 514–44.

Hanushek, E. (1986). 'The Economics of Schooling: Production and Efficiency in Public Schools'. *Journal of Economic Literature*, 24(3): 1141–77.

Hanushek, E. and Woessmann, L. (2005). 'Does Educational Tracking Affect Performance and Inequality? Differences-in-differences Evidence across Countries'. NBER Working Paper No. 11124.

Harris, R. and Rose, S. (2013). 'Who Benefits from Grammar Schools? A Case Study of Buckinghamshire, England'. *Oxford Review of Education*, 39(2): 151–71.

Hartas, D. (2012). 'Inequality and the Home Learning Environment: Predictions about Seven-year-olds' Language and Literacy'. *British Educational Research Journal*, 38(5): 859–79.

Heckman, J. (2011). 'The Economics of Inequality: The Value of Early Childhood Education'. *American Educator*, Spring 2011: 31–5, 47.

Hernstein, R. J. and Murray, C. A. (1994). *The Bell Curve: Intelligence and Class Structure in American Life*. New York: Free Press.

HM Government (2011). *Opening Doors, Breaking Barriers: A Strategy for Social Mobility*. London: Cabinet Office.

Jencks, C. (1972). *Inequality: A Reassessment of the Effect of Family and Schooling in America*. New York: Basic Books.

Jencks, C. (1988). 'Whom Must We Treat equally for Educational Opportunity to Be Equal?' *Ethics*, 98: 518–33.

Jensen, A. (1969). 'How Much Can We Boost IQ and Scholastic Achievement?' *Harvard Educational Review*, 39(1): 1–123.

Kao, G. and Tienda, M. (1998). 'Educational Aspirations of Minority Youth'. *American Journal of Education* 106: 349–84.

Kilburn, M. R. and Karoly, L. (2008). *The Economics of Early Childhood Policy: What the Dismal Science Has to Say about Investing in Children*. Santa Monica, CA: Rand Corporation.

Kintrea, K., St Clair, R., and Houston, M. (2011). *The Influences of Parents, Places and Poverty on Educational Attitudes and Aspirations*. York: Joseph Rowntree Foundation.

Lareau, A. (1987). 'Social Class Differences in Family–School Relationships: The Importance of Cultural Capital. In H. Lauder, P. Brown, and A. Stuart Wells (eds) *Education: Culture, Economy, and Society*. Oxford: Oxford University Press.

Lareau, A. and McNamara-Horvat, E. (1999). 'Moments of Social Inclusion and Exclusion: Race, Class, and Cultural Capital in Family–School Relationships'. *Sociology of Education*, 72(1): 37–53.

Le Grand, J. (2007). *The Other Invisible Hand: Delivering Public Services through Choice and Competition*. New York: Princeton University Press.

Levacic, R. and Vignoles, A. (2002). 'Researching the Links between School Resources and Student Outcomes in the UK: A Review of Issues and Evidence'. *Education Economics*, 10(3): 313–31.

Lupton, R. (2010). 'Area-based Initiatives in English Education: What Place for Place and Space?' In C. Raffo, A. Dyson, H. Gunter, D. Hall, L. Jones, and A. Kalambouka (eds) *Education and Poverty in Affluent Countries*, pp. 111–23. New York: Routledge.

Lupton, R. and Glennerster, H. (2009). 'Tacking Ignorance: Education Policy 1948–2008'. *Social Policy Review 21: Analysis and Debate in Social Policy*, pp. 49–66. Bristol: The Policy Press.

Lupton, R. and Hempel-Jorgensen, A. (2012). 'The Importance of Teaching: Pedagogical Constraints and Possibilities in Working-class Schools'. *Journal of Education Policy*, 27(5): 601–20.

Lupton, R. and Obolenskaya, P. (2013). 'Labour's Record on Education: Policy, Spending and Outcomes 1997–2010'. CASE Paper SPCCWP03. London: Centre for the Analysis of Social Exclusion, LSE.

Magnuson, K. A., Myers, M. K., Ruhm, C. J., and Waldfogel, J. (2004). 'Inequality in Preschool Education and School Readiness'. *American Educational Research Journal*, 41(1): 115–57.

Melhuish, E. (2010). 'Why Children, Parents and Home Learning Are Important'. In K. Sylva, E. Melhuish, P. Sammons, I. Siraj-Blatchford, and B. Taggart (eds) *Early Childhood Matters: Evidence from the Effective Pre-school and Primary Education Project*, pp. 44–69. Oxford: Routledge.

Morabito, C., Vandenbroeck, M., and Roose, R. (2013). '"The Greatest of Equalisers": A Critical Review of International Organisations' Views on Early Childhood Care and Education'. *Journal of Social Policy*, 42(3): 451–67.

Mortimore, P. (1997). 'Can Effective Schools Compensate for Society?' In H. Lauder, P. Brown, and A. Stuart Wells (eds) *Education: Culture, Economy, and Society*, pp. 476–88. Oxford: Oxford University Press.

Mortimore, P. (1998). *The Road to Improvement: Reflections on School Effectiveness*. Abingdon: Swets and Zeitlinger.

Mortimore, P. and Whitty, G. (2000). *Can School Improvement Overcome the Effects of Disadvantage?* Revised edn. London: Institute of Education.

OECD (2006). *Starting Strong II: Early Childhood Education and Care*. Paris: OECD.

OECD (2012). *Starting Strong III: A Quality Toolbox for Early Childhood Education and Care*. Paris: OECD.

OECD (2013). *PISA 2012 Results: Excellence through Equity (Volume II)*. Paris: OECD.

OECD (2014a). *PISA 2012 Results: What Students Know and Can Do (Volume I)*. Paris: OECD.

OECD (2014b). *PISA 2012 Results: What Makes Schools Successful? Resources, Policies and Practices (Volume IV)*. Paris: OECD.

Palardy, G. (2013). 'High School Socioeconomic Segregation and Student Attainment'. *American Educational Research Journal*, 50(4): 714–54.

Parsons, C. (2009). 'Explaining Sustained Inequalities in Ethnic Minority School Exclusions in England—Passive Racism in a Neoliberal Grip'. *Oxford Review of Education*, 35(2): 249–65.

Payne, J. (2003). 'Choice at the End of Compulsory Schooling: A Research Review'. DfES Research Report 414. London: Department for Education and Skills.

Penn, H. (2011). *Quality in Early Childhood Services: An International Perspective*. Buckingham: Open University Press.

Power, S., Edwards, T., Whitty, G., and Whigfall, V. (2003). *Education and the Middle Class*. Buckingham: Open University Press.

Reay, D. (2001). 'Finding or Losing Yourself? Working Class Relationships to Education'. *Journal of Education Policy*, 16(4): 333–46.

Reay, D. (2012). 'What Would a Socially Just Education System Look Like? Saving the Minnows from the Pike'. *Journal of Education Policy*, 27(5): 587–99.

Rennison, J., Maguire, S., Middleton, S., and Ashworth, K. (2005). 'Young People Not in Education, Employment or Training'. Research Report RR628. London: DfES.

Rutter, M., Maughn, B., Mortimore, P., and Ouston, J. (1979). *Fifteen Thousand Hours*. London: Open Books.

Schleicher, A. (2014). *Equity, Excellence and Inclusiveness in Education Policy Lessons from around the World*. Paris: OECD.

Sewell, W., Haller, A., and Portes, A. (1969). 'The Educational and Early Occupational Attainment Process'. *American Sociological Review*, 34(1): 82–92.

Siraj-Blatchford, I. (2010). 'Learning in the Home and at School: How Working Class Children "Succeed against the Odds"'. *British Educational Research Journal*, 36(3): 463–82.

Skourdoumbis, A. (2014). 'Teacher Effectiveness: Making the Difference to Student Achievement?' *British Journal of Educational Studies*, 62(2): 111–26.

Slavin, R. E. (1990). 'Achievement Effects of Ability Grouping in Secondary Schools: A Best-evidence Synthesis'. *Review of Educational Research*, 60(3): 471–99.

St. Clair, R., Kintrea, K., and Houston, M. (2013). 'Silver Bullet or Red Herring? New Evidence on the Place of Aspirations in Education'. *Oxford Review of Education*, 39(6): 719–38.

Strand, S. (2011). 'The White British–Black Caribbean Achievement Gap: Tests, Tiers and Teacher Expectations'. *British Educational Research Journal*, 38(1): 75–101.

Strauss, V. (2012). 'The Bottom Line on "No Excuses" and Poverty in School Reform'. *Washington Post*, 29 September.

Sullivan, A. (2001). 'Cultural Capital and Educational Attainment'. *Sociology*, 35(4): 893–912.

Sullivan, A., Ketende, S., and Joshi, H. (2013). 'Social Class and Inequalities in Early Cognitive Scores'. *Sociology*, 47(6): 1187–206.

Sylva, K., Melhuish, E., Sammons, P., Siraj-Blatchford, I., and Taggart, B. (2010). *Early Childhood Matters: Evidence from the Effective Pre-school and Primary Education Project*. Oxford: Routledge.

Tawney, R. H. (1934). 'Lecture to the New Educational Fellowship'. London: British Political and Economic Library.

United Nations Educational, Scientific and Cultural Organisation (UNESCO) (2007). *Education for All Global Monitoring Report 2007: Strong Foundations—Early Childhood Care and Education.* Paris: UNESCO.

United Nations Educational, Scientific and Cultural Organisation (UNESCO) (2010). *Education for All Global Monitoring Report 2010: Reaching the Marginalised.* Paris: UNESCO.

Van Otter, C. (2013). 'Family Resources and Mid-life Level of Education: A Longitudinal Study of the Mediating Influence of Childhood Parental Involvement'. *British Educational Research Journal*, 40(3): 555–74.

Vincent, C. (2012). *Parenting: Responsibilities, Risks and Respect.* London: Institute of Education.

Vincent, C. and Ball, S. J. (2007). '"Making up" the Middle-class Child: Families, Activities and Class Dispositions'. *Sociology*, 41(6): 1061–77.

Vincent, C., Braun, A., and Ball, S. J. (2010). 'Between the Estate and the State: Struggling to Be a "Good" Mother'. *British Journal of Sociology of Education*, 31(2): 123–38.

West, A. (2007a). 'Poverty and Educational Achievement: Why Do Children from Low Income Families Tend to Do Less Well at School?' *Benefits: The Journal of Poverty and Social Justice*, 15(3): 283–97.

West, A. (2007b). 'Schools, Financing and Educational Standards'. In J. Hills, J. Le Grand, and D. Piachaud (eds) *Making Social Policy Work: Essays in Honour of Howard Glennerster*, pp. 85–108. London: Policy Press.

West, A., Ingram, D., and Hind, A. (2006). '"Skimming the cream"? Admissions to Charter Schools in the US and Autonomous Schools in England'. *Educational Policy*, 20(4): 615–39.

West, A. and Nikolai, R. (2013). 'Welfare Regimes and Education Regimes: Equality of Opportunity and Expenditure in the EU (and US)'. *Journal of Social Policy*, 42: 469–93.

West, A., Roberts, J., and Noden, P. (2010). 'Funding Early Years Education and Care: Can a Mixed Economy of Providers Deliver Universal High Quality Provision?' *British Journal of Educational Studies*, 58(2): 155–79.

Wiborg, S. (2010). *Swedish Free Schools: Do They Work?* LLAKES Research Paper 18. London: Centre for Learning and Life Chances in Knowledge Economies and Societies available at http://www.llakes.org, accessed 20 August 2015.

World Bank (2006). *World Development Report: Equity and Development.* Washington DC: The World Bank.

Youdell, D. (2011). *School Trouble: Identity, Power and Politics in Education.* London: Routledge.

Zoritch, B., Roberts, I., and Oakley, A. (2000). 'Day Care for Pre-school Children'. *Cochrane Database of Systematic Reviews*, 3. Art No.: CD000564.

7

The Income Distribution in the UK

A Picture of Advantage and Disadvantage

Stephen P. Jenkins

This chapter presents a picture of advantage and disadvantage in Britain using the lens provided by the most commonly used measure of individuals' material well-being, the income of the household to which they belong. Income is not the only indicator that may be used to characterize whether an individual is badly off or well off or to summarize the extent of poverty and affluence in a country overall. Complementary perspectives are provided by information about social inclusion and exclusion measured by a set of material deprivation indicators (Chapter 1), individuals' capabilities and functionings (Chapter 2), whether their human rights are realized (Chapter 3), or their social class (Chapter 4). Nonetheless, income-based measures are particularly important. In a modern-day mixed economy such as the UK's, individuals' money income (and their wealth, treated in Chapter 8) is the preeminent measure of their command over resources. For this reason, income is the principal focus of the statistics used to assess social progress in the UK and other rich countries. The strengths and weaknesses of using income to measure material living standards are not reviewed here. Instead, the aim of this chapter is to describe the distribution of income in the UK today, documenting how it has changed over the last fifty years and how it compares with those of international comparators such as other European and OECD countries.[1]

The chapter provides multiple perspectives on the income distribution. I discuss evidence about real income levels and inequality, as well as the

[1] I wish to thank Tony Atkinson, John Hills, Rob Joyce, Lucinda Platt, and other contributors to the volume for their comments and suggestions on a preliminary draft. For comments and advice on my use of HBAI and SPI data, I thank Nancy Singh and Peter Matejic (DWP) and Jeremy Reuben (HMRC).

prevalence of poverty and of affluence. In the concluding section, I reflect on some of the issues raised by the evidence. First, however, I explain the definitions and sources used in the chapter.

7.1 Definitions and Sources

Throughout the chapter (with an exception discussed below), an individual's 'income' is the *equivalized net income of the household* to which he or she belongs. This is equal to the total money income received by all household members from all sources minus income taxes and national insurance contributions paid and some other deductions, deflated by an equivalence scale factor that adjusts for differences in household size and composition, and adjusted using a price index to take account of inflation. A household is a 'single person or group of people living at the same address as their only or main residence, who either share one meal a day together or share the living accommodation (i.e. living room)' (Department for Work and Pensions, 2014a: 227).

The specific money income sources included in the net income definition are those used by the Department for Work and Pensions' (DWP's) *Households Below Average Income (HBAI)* statistics, and are shown in Table 7.1. (These statistics are the UK's official statistics about the income distribution among persons.) Incomes are reported on a weekly basis. If someone reports earnings or other receipts over a longer period (e.g. an annual or monthly salary), the amount is converted to a weekly-equivalent amount pro rata.

There is an important distinction between net income before the deduction of housing costs (net income BHC) and net income after the deduction of housing costs (net income AHC). The HBAI statistics report income distribution estimates based on both definitions; the BHC definition is the one that is used by international organizations such as Eurostat and the OECD, and international data providers such as the Luxembourg Income Study, and is consistent with the recommendations of bodies such as the Expert Group on Household Income Statistics (2001). For this reason, my discussion focuses on distributions based on the net income BHC definition, but I also refer to AHC distributions measures where they lead to different conclusions about distributional trends. Observe that an increase in someone's Housing Benefit to cover an increase in their rent would be counted as an increase in their income according to the BHC measure even though the household's net spending power would be unchanged. Also, BHC measures do not take account of variations in housing costs, and a given amount of income will go less far in areas with high housing costs. On the other hand, AHC measures do not reflect the fact that housing costs represent choices made by households

Table 7.1. The definition and sources of net household income: receipts and deductions

		Income sources: receipts and deductions:
	(a)	usual gross earnings from employment
+	(b)	earnings from subsidiary employment
+	(c)	profit or loss from self-employment
+	(d)	income from social security benefits and tax credits
+	(e)	private and occupational pensions
+	(f)	income from investments and savings
+	(g)	private transfers and other income
−	(h)	income tax paid (employees and self-employed)
−	(i)	local tax paid (Council Tax)
−	(j)	National Insurance contributions (employee and self-employed)
−	(k)	contributions to occupational pension schemes
=		*Net household income before the deduction of housing costs ('BHC')*
−	(l)	Housing costs: rent (gross of housing benefits), mortgage interest payments, water rates and other water charges, structural insurance payments (owner-occupiers), and ground rent and service charges
=		*Net household income after the deduction of housing costs ('AHC')*

Notes: Equivalized net household income is equal to net household income divided by an equivalence scale (to adjust for differences in household size and composition). Incomes in different years are adjusted by a year-specific price index to express them in constant purchasing power terms. See main text for further details.

about how they live. Among households with the same BHC income, those choosing to spend a higher share of their income on higher quality housing will be counted as having a worse AHC standard of living than those living in cheap, poor quality housing. For further discussion of BHC and AHC measures, see Johnson and Webb (1992).

In order to compare real living standards over time in constant purchasing power terms, taking account of the fact that £1 in 1990 is worth more than £1 in 2000 because of inflation, all incomes are adjusted using a price index and expressed in the prices of a particular year (financial year 2012–13 below). This assumes that all groups in society experience the same rate of price inflation. Evidence about differences in experience of inflation is provided by Flower and Wales (2014).

Equivalization produces a measure of real living standards that is comparable across households in a given year. A money income of £500 per week (say) leads to higher living standards for a single householder than a childless married couple or a family of four. Looking at per capita income (total income divided by household size) would be one way of taking account of this issue, but this adjustment would not take account of potential economies of scale in the provision of household goods and services such as space, heat, and light, food preparation and purchase, and so on. According to HBAI definitions, a net household income (BHC) of £500 per week for a married couple is equivalent in living standards terms to £750 pounds per week for a single householder (£500 is two-thirds not one-half of £750). Children add to household needs, of course, but not as much as an additional adult. According to HBAI definitions, a net household income of £500 per week corresponds to £417 per week in living standards' terms for a married couple with one child (aged less than fourteen years), or £357 per week if there are two children. These adjustments are characterized as the so-called modified-OECD equivalence scale: see DWP (2014b) for further details and note the slightly different adjustment applied to AHC incomes.

The final step in defining the income distribution is the assumption that the household income total is shared equally within each household, so that each individual is attributed the equivalized income of the household to which he or she belongs. Individuals without income of their own, such as children, are assumed to benefit from income transfers by other individuals within the household. Supposing that complete income sharing is the universal rule is undoubtedly inaccurate, but it is also difficult to imagine what other assumptions would be more appropriate as a general rule. The equal-sharing assumption is widely adopted by analysts and statistical agencies around the world, not only in the UK. The assumption and alternatives are analysed by Jenkins (1991). There is also the issue of whether the aggregate 'income unit' should be taken to be the household, or the more narrowly defined nuclear family. The National Equality Panel (2010) additionally provides information about the distribution of 'individual incomes'—the distribution arising were each adult to benefit only from the income that he or she received and be unaffected by that of other household members.

Estimates of income distributions using these definitions are derived in the UK using data from the Family Resources Survey, a large household survey that has been running since the early 1990s. Data for earlier years (back to 1961) come from the Family Expenditure Survey. At several points in this chapter, I supplement the survey-based estimates with information derived from income tax data from Her Majesty's Revenue and Customs (HMRC). For assessing economic advantage (rather than poverty), tax data have benefits compared with household surveys because there is better coverage of the top of the income distribution and, arguably, measurement error may be less. In addition, sample sizes are much larger and some data series go back to the beginning of last century. On the other hand, the distributional definitions are less satisfactory because 'income' for tax purposes differs from the more comprehensive measures discussed earlier. The tax data definitions refer to gross taxable (or after-tax) income of tax units (which in the UK refer to individuals since 1990). Moreover, the most detailed data (from the Survey of Personal Incomes) refer to taxpayers rather than to the full population, thereby excluding all those in receipt of low (below tax) or zero incomes.

The final point to note about definitions is that this chapter is about income. Income is not the same as 'consumption', which refers to the resources actually enjoyed by households (measured in terms of their spending) rather than their potential command over resources. Income is arguably a better indicator of someone's economic power, and not dependent on choices about how they spend their money. (For comparisons of distributions of consumption expenditure and income in the UK, see Brewer and O'Dea (2012).) Also, income and consumption each refer to flows per period, and should be distinguished from the stock of financial assets at a particular point in time, that is, wealth. The distribution of wealth is the subject of Chapter 8.

7.2 The UK Income Distribution, 2012–13

The UK's income distribution in 2012–13 (BHC definition) is pictured in Figure 7.1. The chart shows the numbers of individuals with (equivalized) incomes in each £10 band between zero and £1,000 per week. The stripes classify individuals according to where they stand in the income parade that orders them from poorest to richest. The poorest tenth (decile group 1) are on the left and the richest tenth (decile group 10) on the right, with the other eight decile groups in between. The frequency distribution is not bell-shaped

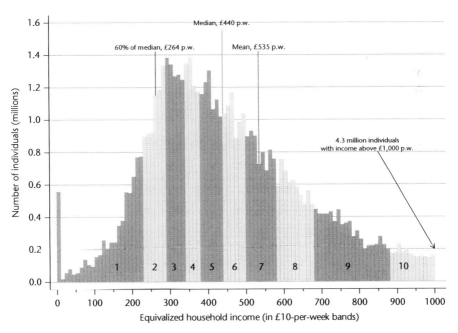

Figure 7.1. The UK income distribution, 2012–13

Notes: Graph drawn by the author using data from the spreadsheet accompanying Chart 2.4 (BHC) in DWP (2014a).

as with a normal distribution; rather, it is skewed with a long right-hand tail. Not all of the very richest individuals can be shown on the chart: the income of the person in the middle of richest tenth (the 95th percentile) is £1,117 per week, and there are around 2.93 million people with incomes above this amount.

The greatest concentration of individuals along the income range is between about £250 and £400 per week (the frequencies are greatest, and the stripes narrowest). The middle income (the median or 50th percentile) is £440 per week, which is only 82 per cent of the average (mean) income of £535 per week. The person with average income is found some two-thirds of the way along the income parade (i.e. between the 60th and the 70th percentile) and hence not particularly representative of 'middle incomes'. Also shown in Figure 7.1 is the value of the most-commonly used poverty line in the UK and Europe (60 per cent of median income). The threshold was £264 per week in 2012–13, and it can be seen that around 15 per cent of individuals were income-poor in 2012–13. I provide more detail about the prevalence of disadvantage later in the chapter.

Finally, observe the perhaps surprisingly large number of individuals with an income between £0 and £10 per week. Although this refers to fewer than 1 per cent of the UK population, the number raises questions about the accuracy of measurement of very low incomes. On this, see Brewer et al. (2009).

The HBAI data also tell us *who* the poorest and richest individuals were in 2012–13. Table 7.2 shows the composition of the poorest tenth and the richest tenth, using a range of subgroup definitions that classify individuals according to their or their family's characteristics.

Table 7.2 shows, for example, that adult men and women and children are represented in the poorest tenth in proportion to their numbers in the population as a whole, but men are over-represented in the richest tenth (45 per cent compared to 38 per cent) and children are under-represented (16 per cent compared with 21 per cent).

Individuals from pensioner couples, and couples with and without children, are under-represented in the poorest tenth relative to their numbers in the population as a whole (see *Family type*). Over-represented are single female pensioners, individuals in lone parent families, and childless singles. In the richest tenth, almost all groups are under-represented, with one striking exception. Childless couples are substantially over-represented, and account for more than one-third of the richest tenth though they comprise only 18 per cent of the population.

Looking at *Economic status,* Table 7.2 shows that over- and under-representation at the top and bottom is closely associated with participation in paid employment. For example, individuals in benefit units in which all adults are in full-time work are substantially under-represented in the poorest

Table 7.2. Composition of the poorest and richest tenths of the 2012–13 income distribution, by subgroup

Subgroup	Subgroup share (%) of		
	Poorest tenth	Richest tenth	Population
Sex and adulthood			
Adult man	38.6	45.0	38.3
Adult woman	39.5	39.6	40.5
Child	21.9	15.5	21.2
Family type			
Pensioner couple	10.3	12.3	13.6
Single male pensioner	1.9	1.3	1.9
Single female pensioner	7.5	1.7	5.2
Couple with children	32.4	32.6	34.9
Single with children	10.1	1.0	8.0
Couple without children	13.1	35.3	18.4
Single male without children	16.0	10.9	10.8
Single female without children	8.6	5.1	7.2
Economic status			
One or more self-employed	14.8	18.1	9.8
Single/couple all in full-time work	4.9	45.7	26.2
Couple/one in full-time, one part-time	2.6	13.2	13.1
Couple, one full-time, one not working	8.3	8.2	10.5
No full-time, one or more part-time worker	15.0	5.2	10.1
Workless, head or spouse aged 60 or over	20.7	6.7	17.3
Workless head or spouse unemployed	14.6	0.7	3.8
Workless, other inactive	19.2	2.3	9.3
Region			
Rest of the UK	75.3	55.4	73.2
London and South East	24.7	44.6	26.8

Notes: Author's estimates using data from the public-use file of unit-record HBAI data (accompanying DWP 2014a). *Reading note*: 38.6% of the poorest tenth and 45.0% of the richest tenth in 2012–13 were adult men; 38.3% of the total population were adult men.

tenth (5 per cent compared with their population proportion of 26 per cent) and substantially over-represented in the richest tenth (46 per cent compared to 26 per cent). The situation is reversed for non-pensioner families in which the head or spouse is unemployed: individuals in this group comprise almost 4 per cent of the population, but nearly 15 per cent of the poorest tenth and less than 1 per cent of the richest tenth. By contrast, individuals belonging to a family with self-employment income are over-represented in both the poorest and the richest tenths. The *Region* panel illustrates that, although there is no difference in the composition of the poorest tenth, people living in London and the South East form a substantially greater fraction of the richest tenth than would be expected from their relative numbers in the country as a whole (45 per cent compared to 27 per cent).

The range of incomes within each of the various subgroups is summarized in Figure 7.2 using boxplots. The left- and right-hand ends of the box for each group show the 25th and 75th percentiles for that group (half the group have incomes within this range). The end of the 'whisker' extending left from the box shows the 10th percentile for the subgroup, whereas the end of the right whisker shows the 90th percentile (80 per cent of the subgroup have incomes within the range spanned by the box and whiskers). Subgroup median income (50th percentile) is shown by the black bar within the box. The vertical dashed lines show the 10th, 50th, and 90th percentiles for the population as a whole ('all individuals'; as also shown in Figure 7.1), and hence demarcate the thresholds used to define the poorest and richest income groups in Table 7.2. When the whisker crosses the horizontal lines, the sub-group is over-represented in the top or bottom decile group, as we saw in Table 7.2.

The boxplots, therefore, illustrate both subgroup income levels and the range of subgroup incomes. Individuals in families with children, and dependent

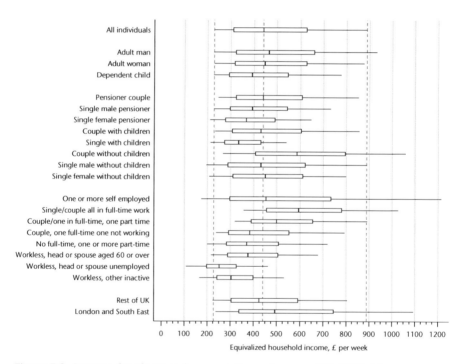

Figure 7.2. Income distributions for population subgroups, UK, 2012–13

Notes: Each subgroup's boxplot shows the 10th, 25th, 50th, 75th, and 90th percentiles for the relevant subgroup: see the main text. The vertical dashed lines show the 10th, 50th, and 90th percentiles for the population as a whole ('all individuals'). Graph drawn by the author using data from the spreadsheet accompanying Belfield et al. (2014) for 'all individuals' and his calculations using data from the public-use file of unit-record HBAI data (accompanying DWP 2014a) for all other groups. Incomes in the public-use HBAI file are rounded to the nearest pound.

children in particular, tend to have lower incomes than other groups. Although the distribution among all women closely mimics that of the population as a whole, there are groups of women who are clearly worse off: look at the plots for single female pensioners and the 'single with children' group (most of whom are in families headed by lone mothers). In contrast, childless couples have relatively high incomes: almost three-quarters of this group have an income above the population median.

Figure 7.2 highlights again the importance of paid employment for income, with distributions further to the left (lower) as the degree of participation falls. For example, contrast individuals in benefit units in which all individuals are in full-time work (more than 75 per cent have an income above the population median) with individuals in a family with an unemployed head or spouse (almost 90 per cent have an income below the population median). Families with self-employed members are a distinctive case because of the relatively high prevalence of both low incomes and (especially) very high incomes. Substantially more than one-tenth of this group have an income placing them in the richest five per cent of the population as a whole.

The bottom of Figure 7.2 highlights the relative affluence of most individuals living in London and the South East. The person at the 75th percentile for this region's distribution is clearly within the richest twentieth of the population ranked by income (see Figure 7.1), whereas the corresponding person in the distribution for the rest of the UK is on the borders of the richest seventh and eighth tenths nationally. More than 10 per cent of individuals living in London and the South East are in the richest 5 per cent of the population.

7.3 Trends in Real Income Levels since 1961

Having looked at the contemporary distribution of income, I now consider how the distribution has changed over time. Conclusions about the extent to which real incomes have been rising depend a lot on how long one looks back and which part of the income distribution one considers. See Figure 7.3, which shows income levels at the 10th, 50th, and 90th percentiles, as well as the mean. Grey stripes demarcate recessions. Appendix Table A1 summarizes the trends shown in the graph, providing income growth rates for the period as a whole and subperiods within it. (All the Appendix tables and figures cited in this chapter are available at http://sticerd.lse.ac.uk/dps/case/cp/casepaper186.pdf.)

Looking at the fifty-year period since 1961, the general picture is of rising incomes for all, punctuated by short periods of slow or negative growth accompanying recessions. The sharpest deviation from trend is the period after 2007, that is, following the most recent recession, though it should be noted that a slowing in income growth is also apparent earlier—from the

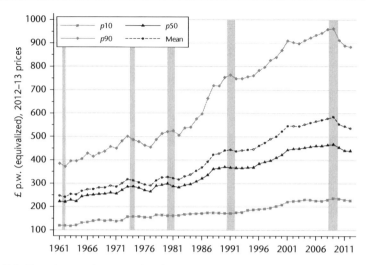

Figure 7.3. Trends in real income levels since 1961

Notes: Graph drawn by the author using data from spreadsheet accompanying Belfield et al. (2014). The grey strips identify periods with at least two consecutive quarters of negative real GDP growth. *p*10, *p*50, and *p*90 are the 10th percentile, 50th percentile (median), and 90th percentile, respectively. The data refer to financial years from 1994 onwards, and the estimates to the UK from 2002–03 and Great Britain in earlier years. See Jenkins (2015) Appendix Table A1 for numerical estimates of growth rates for the period as a whole as well as sub-periods.

beginning of the 2000s—and there was also a period of little growth in the early 1990s.

Also striking is the differential income growth across the income range: growth has been greatest at the top and small at the bottom. Over the five decades between 1961 and 2012, the 90th percentile grew by 130 per cent (equivalent to a rate of around 1.6 per cent per year), the median grew by 97 per cent and the 10th percentile by 89 per cent (equivalent to 1.3 per cent per year in both cases). Although income falls were greatest for the richest groups between 2007 and 2012 (the 90th percentile fell by 6.2 per cent per year; the 10th percentile by 0.2 per cent per year), this reversal of fortunes is small if compared with the longer-term trend of growing real incomes at the top.

The fall in real incomes across the income distribution after the most recent recession is not as dramatic as the squeeze on real wages reported by Gregg, Machin, and Fernández-Salgado (2014), particularly at the bottom of the distribution. Several factors are likely to explain this. For example, a fall in real wages of one household member might be offset by more work hours by another household member. Household composition may itself change: for example, young people may be more likely to live with their parents or share with others. And the safety-net income provided by benefits and tax credits has continued to provide a real income floor.

7.4 Inequality

The growing gap between top and bottom incomes shown in Figure 7.3 implies growth in income inequality. Inequality is summarized directly in Figure 7.4, in terms of the ratio of the 90th to the 10th percentile ($p90/p10$) and the Gini coefficient. Regardless of which index is used, the rise in inequality over the last fifty years has been substantial: between 1961 and 2012, the Gini rose by almost one-third and $p90/p10$ by around one half. Most of that inequality growth occurred in the 1980s. Clearly this is an exceptional period: within both the preceding two decades and the subsequent two, the two inequality series are relatively flat, with relatively small year-on-year changes. Nonetheless, there is a small but distinct decline in $p90/p10$ after 1991 that is not apparent in the Gini coefficient. This reflects changes in the distribution of incomes below the median to which the Gini is not as sensitive.

Inequality declined during the most recent recession, reflecting the larger income falls for those at the top compared to those at the bottom, but even this inequality decline is relatively small and a bit smaller than the decline in the early to mid 1970s (when inequality was much lower).

The level and trend in inequality in the UK is compared with those of twenty other OECD countries in Figure 7.5 (the distributional definitions are similar to those employed in previous figures). Countries are grouped according to whether inequality fell, increased, or remained much the same, between the mid 1980s and 2011–12, with inequality measured using the

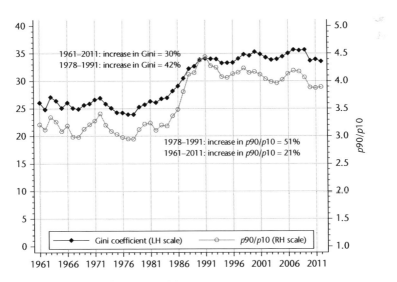

Figure 7.4. Income inequality since 1961

Notes: Graph drawn by the author using data from IFS (2014). The data refer to financial years from 1994 onwards, and the estimates to the UK from 2002–3 and Great Britain in earlier years.

Gini coefficient. The UK's estimate for 2011–12, around 0.34, places it just above the average in the twenty-one-country ranking (the OECD Gini was around 0.32) but, if middle-income countries such as Mexico and Turkey are excluded, the UK shows up more clearly as a high-inequality country relative to other rich countries. Inequality in the UK is not as great as in the USA, however.

Figure 7.5 also shows that the majority of OECD countries experienced inequality growth over the last quarter century; it was not only the UK. Moreover, the magnitude of the increase was greater in a number of other countries besides the UK, several of which were relatively low-inequality countries in the mid 1980s (Finland, Sweden, and Germany). Be aware, however, that the inequality-increase rankings are contingent on the period considered: the increase in the UK during the 1980s, shown earlier, was substantial by cross-national standards; and is only partly reflected in the change measured in Figure 7.5 since the mid 1980s. None the less, we can also see that an increase in inequality is not inevitable: inequality changed hardly at all in France, the Netherlands, and Belgium.

If the comparison is with the EU-15 as a whole, income inequality in the UK has been greater for most of the last decade but in 2013 was about the same. At the beginning of the 2000s, the UK Gini was around four percentage points

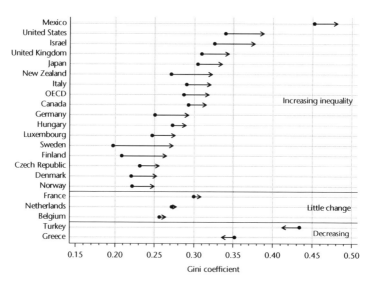

Figure 7.5. Income inequality in twenty-one OECD countries: mid 1980s and 2011/12

Notes: Graph drawn by the author using data in the spreadsheet accompanying OECD (2014, Figure 1). This source provides details of the actual years compared for each country. 'Little change' in inequality refers to changes of less than 1.5 percentage points. Countries are ordered within each panel by their Gini coefficient for 2011/12. Income is household disposable income adjusted for household size.

greater than the EU-15 Gini, but the former subsequently declined and the latter increased (see Jenkins, 2015, Appendix Figure A2).

Much of the trend in UK inequality has been driven by what happens to top incomes and yet estimates derived from household surveys (such as shown in Figure 7.3) may miss what is going on at the very top of the income distribution. In contrast, income tax data have better coverage of the richest incomes and provide estimates for a much longer period.

Estimates of top income shares derived from tax data are shown in Figure 7.6 and go back almost a century. The series shown in black shows trends in the share of total income held by the richest 10 per cent, 1 per cent, and 0.1 per cent. The share of the top 10 per cent in 2011, around 40 per cent of total income, is much the same as it was just after the First World War. Over the subsequent six decades, the share declined by around 10 percentage points, but increased steadily thereafter, albeit with a pause associated with the most recent recession. A U-shaped trend is also apparent for the shares of the top 1 per cent and top 0.1 per cent, though the inequality increases since the late 1970s have not taken the shares back to First World War levels. Also shown are trends in the shares of nearly top groups variously defined (the series in grey) and, intriguingly, there is no distinct U-shape to these series to the extent that there is for the others. This implies that the U-shape trends for top income shares are mostly being driven by what is happening to the very richest group (the richest 0.1 per cent in this case).

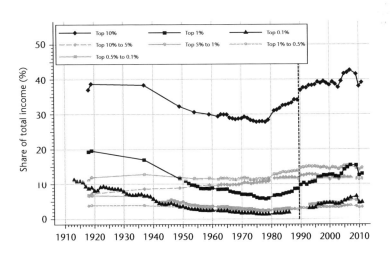

Figure 7.6. Top income shares (%) in the UK over the last 100 years

Notes: Graph drawn by the author using data from the World Top Incomes Database (Alvaredo et al., 2014). The vertical dashed line marks the change in the definition of the tax unit from the family to the individual in 1990.

Thus, even though inequality in the UK has not grown much over the last two decades according to HBAI-based measures (Figure 7.4), the evidence from tax data about top income shares suggests a continuing and substantial rise in inequality over this period. Put differently, recent inequality trends are a story of greater differentials that are driven by increasing advantage of the best off. The UK experience is similar to that of other 'Anglo' countries such as the USA, but is less apparent in other countries such as Germany, and especially France where the long inequality decline has not been followed by a large inequality rise. See Jenkins (2015) Appendix Figure A3 and, for more extensive cross-national comparisons, Atkinson, Piketty, and Saez (2011).

7.5 The Prevalence of Poverty

Historically, social policy has been particularly concerned with the prevalence of poverty rather than other aspects of income distribution (see Chapter 1). As this volume makes clear, one should think of the organization of society along a continuum of advantage and disadvantage, and looking at the whole of the income distribution reflects this position. Nonetheless, the situation of the worse-off people in society is often of pressing interest because of individual welfare considerations. Trends in income poverty are therefore the subject of this section.

A fundamental issue is how the income cut-off that differentiates poor people from non-poor people should be defined. The threshold most commonly employed by the European Union, and the UK as well, is 60 per cent of contemporary national median income. The 'contemporary national' tag means that the poverty line varies from one year to the next (as median income changes), and differs in real terms across countries: UK median income is substantially greater than Romanian median income, for instance.

This 'relative poverty' definition implements—in a particular way—the idea that '[p]eople are said to be living in poverty if their income and resources are so inadequate as to preclude them from having a standard of living considered acceptable in the society in which they live' (Council of the European Union, 2004: 8). Although a relative poverty definition has many conceptual attractions, it can lead to implausible estimates in times of economic boom or sharp recession when the median income itself can change substantially (Jenkins et al., 2013: ch. 1).

This suggests that more 'absolute' poverty threshold definitions be employed in tandem with relative ones. However, few would seriously argue that a fully absolute definition—a real income cut-off that is fixed over time and the same for all countries—is appropriate for rich countries such as the UK. More commonly used for assessing trends are 'anchored' poverty lines.

The idea is that poverty in the current year and previous years be assessed using a threshold that is fixed at the value of the relative poverty line for an earlier (but relatively recent) year. Thus, DWP HBAI publications supplement estimates based on a cut-off of 60 per cent of contemporary national median income with estimates based on a threshold equal to 60 per cent of 2010–11 median income or (previously) the 1998–99 median. The Institute for Fiscal Studies has provided data on anchored poverty rates using the 1996–97 median, which I use here alongside those for the 2010–11 median. Estimates of poverty rates for the last fifty years based on the relative and two anchored thresholds are shown in Figure 7.7.

Clearly, the choice of low-income cut-off makes a substantial difference to estimates of both the prevalence of poverty in recent years, and its trend over time. Using the relative poverty line based on contemporary medians, the poverty rate fluctuated between around 12 per cent and 15 per cent in the twenty years after 1961, then increased sharply to reach more than 20 per cent in the late 1980s, and has been gradually declining since the early 1990s. In particular, the poverty rate continued to decline during the recent recession— because the median also fell (Figure 7.3). According to the relative poverty line definition, the UK poverty rate in 2012–13 was 15.4 per cent, corresponding to around 9.7 million poor people.

The poverty experience differs for particular subgroups. Of particular relevance for policy in recent years has been child poverty and pensioner poverty. At the beginning of the 1990s, the child poverty rate was nearly 10 percentage

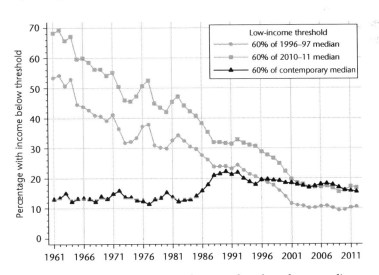

Figure 7.7. Poverty rates (%) since 1961: relative and anchored poverty lines

Notes: Graph drawn by the author using data from spreadsheet accompanying Belfield et al. (2014). The data refer to financial years from 1994 onwards, and the estimates to the UK from 2002–3 and Great Britain in earlier years. The BHC income definition is used (see text).

points higher than the all-persons rate, but it has declined at a faster pace and was only two percentage points larger in 2012–13. The decline in pensioner poverty rates has been substantial, from around 40 per cent in the 1960s to the same as the all-persons rate in 2012–13, albeit with large increases and declines in between. See Jenkins (2015) Appendix Figure A4 for details. For more extended discussion of long-run trends, see Cribb et al. (2013: ch. 5).

These estimates are based on a BHC income definition. If, instead, an AHC income definition is used, the picture of poverty levels and trends is different, especially since the 1990s. In 1990, the AHC relative poverty rate was 24 per cent (compared to a BHC rate of 21 per cent) but did not decline at the same rate thereafter. In 2012–13, the AHC relative poverty rate was 21 per cent (13.2million people), that is, around six percentage points greater than the BHC rate for that year. See Jenkins (2015) Appendix Figure A5 for details.

The BHC series based on anchored poverty lines show a substantial decline in poverty rates over the last five decades. For example, according to the relative poverty standards of the mid 1990s, more than half of the UK population was poor in the early 1960s, but only one-tenth five decades later. The rate of decline in both anchored series slows noticeably from around 2000 onwards—which is unsurprising given the slowing of income growth rates at the bottom of the distribution around that time (Figure 7.3). Observe as well, and by contrast with the relative poverty series, that both anchored poverty series show a rise in the poverty rate with the recent recession (albeit a relatively small one).

The UK had a relative poverty rate two or three percentage points higher than the EU-15 average from 1995 until around 2009, after which the rates converged: the UK rate declined (reflecting the falling UK median) and the EU-15 rate increased slightly. See Figure 7.8. Again, using anchored poverty lines for each country (60 per cent of national medians in 2008) reveals a different picture for the post-recession period. In particular, both the UK and EU-15 poverty rates are estimated to increase by around two percentage points in the following four years, and so the differential is maintained.

7.6 The Prevalence of Affluence

The prevalence of affluence can also be assessed in terms of relative and anchored thresholds and, again, the specific choice is somewhat arbitrary. (The few researchers who have looked at the prevalence of affluence have used a range of definitions; there are no commonly used precedents as in the poverty case. There is also the problem that the higher the threshold, the more statistically unreliable the estimates may be.) For the purposes of this chapter, I use twice the contemporary median as a relative threshold, and a fixed real income threshold equal to £1,000 per week in 2012–13 prices.

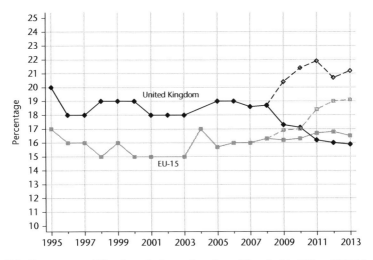

Figure 7.8. Poverty rates (%) using relative and anchored thresholds: UK and EU-15 average

Notes: Graph drawn by author using EU-SILC-based estimates reported in Eurostat (2014, series ilc_li02 and ilc_li22b). The solid lines show poverty rates calculated using a relative threshold (60% of contemporary national median income); the dashed lines show poverty rates calculated using an anchored threshold (60% of national median income in 2008). Estimates of anchored poverty rates are available only from 2008 onwards.

Estimates using these two thresholds are shown in Figure 7.9, and derived from the same data that are used to compile the DWP's HBAI statistics. The proportion of persons with an income greater than twice the contemporary median has remained remarkably stable since the mid 1990s, at around 11 per cent. (Remember that the median, and hence the value of twice-median threshold also rose over this period: Figure 7.3.) The figure also highlights substantial differences in the prevalence of affluence in London and the South East (a rate of around 17 per cent over the last two decades) compared with its prevalence in the rest of the UK (a rate of around 8 per cent).

With the fixed £1,000-per-week threshold, the prevalence of affluence steadily increased, more than doubling from around 4 per cent in the mid 1990s to around 9 per cent in 2009, after which the rate fell by several percentage points. Again, individuals living in London and the South East had higher rates than those in the rest of the UK throughout the period, but the trends for each group mimicked the national picture.

The advantage of summaries such as Figure 7.9 is that they use the definitions of income and income-receiving unit routinely used to assess the income distribution in the UK. However, as discussed earlier, the coverage of the very top incomes in the underlying household survey data is not as good as that in income tax data.

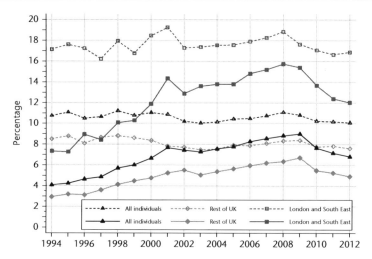

Figure 7.9. Percentages of individuals with an equivalized income greater than twice the contemporary median (dotted lines) or greater than £1,000 per week (2012–13 prices) (solid lines)

Notes: Graph drawn by the author using public-use files of HBAI unit record data accompanying DWP (2014a). The income definition is the same as the BHC definition used in Figures 7.1–7.4. The data refer to financial years from 1994 onwards, and the estimates to the UK from 2002–03 and Great Britain in earlier years.

Changes in the prevalence of affluence in the UK between 1995–96 and 2010–11 estimated from income tax data are summarized in Figure 7.10 using two absolute thresholds: £500,000 per year and £1,000,000 per year of after-tax income in 2012–13 prices. (These thresholds are substantially higher than the £1,000 (equivalized) per week used for Figure 7.9.) By HBAI standards, an income above these cut-offs would place a person well into the top 1 per cent of the income distribution. These estimates refer to proportions of all tax-payers, not to proportions of the population as a whole (or to proportions of all adults as in the top income shares discussion). Most non-taxpayers have little or no income. (In 2010–11, there were around 31.3 million taxpayers, but the UK population was around 60 million, so to be expressed as fractions of the population or all adults, the percentages shown in the figure would need to be adjusted downwards.)

Figure 7.10 shows that the proportion of taxpayers with an after-tax income of more than £500,000 per year rose fivefold between the mid 1990s and the late 2000s, from around 0.02 per cent to nearly 0.10 per cent. The growth in the prevalence of taxpayers with an after-tax income of more than £1 million per year is more muted. The proportion remained at around 0.01 per cent from the mid 1990s until the early 2000s, but increased thereafter and by 2009–10 it was some three times higher. (The numbers of taxpayers involved is still only a few thousand.)

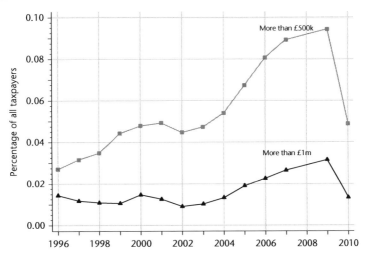

Figure 7.10. Percentages of taxpayers with an after-tax income greater than £500,000 and greater than £1 million per year (2012–13 prices)

Notes: Years shown are financial years, e.g. 2010 refers to 2010–11. The data refer to taxpayers only, and are not available for 2008–9. Data for 1995–6 are not used because of a series discontinuity (introduction of self-assessment and changes to the SPI methodology). Graph drawn by the author using data from the public-use files of the *Survey of Personal Incomes* (various years). Incomes converted to 2012–13 prices using within-year averages of the monthly Consumer Price Index for each financial year.

The marked rise in the prevalence of affluence appears to go into reverse after 2009–10, with both series showing much lower rates for 2010–11, with the fraction of millionaire taxpayers roughly halving for example. One obvious explanation for this reversal of fortunes is the recent recession. However, other more subtle changes mean that one has to be cautious about interpreting the 2010–11 estimates. In particular, a 50 per cent marginal rate of income tax was introduced in April 2010, and the announcement and introduction of this tax rate provided incentives for high income tax payers to bring forward income to 2009–10 that would otherwise have been reported in 2010–11 income tax returns or possibly later years.

This is the process of 'forestalling', discussed in more detail by HM Revenue and Customs (2012) and Cribb et al. (2012, 2013). Reverse forestalling in reaction to the reduction of the top marginal tax rate to 45 per cent (from April 2013) is also likely to affect reporting for later years. These issues make assessment of recent trends in the income distribution problematic for any summary measure that is calculated using top incomes, including the Gini inequality index (Cribb et al., 2013). However, the effects on the Gini (cf. Figure 7.4) are likely to be minor compared to their effects on estimates of the prevalence of affluence based on fixed real income thresholds as in Figure 7.9 and especially Figure 7.10.

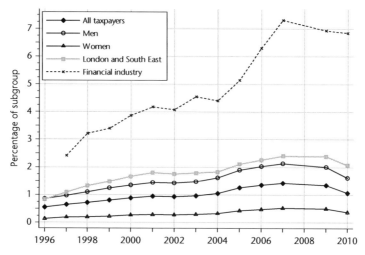

Figure 7.11. Percentages of taxpayers with an after-tax income greater than £100,000 per year (2012–13 prices), by subgroup

Notes: Years shown are financial years, e.g. 2010 refers to 2010–11. The data refer to taxpayers only, and are not available for 2008–9. Data for 1995–6 are not used because of a series discontinuity (introduction of self-assessment and changes to the SPI methodology). Graph drawn by the author using data from the public-use files of the *Survey of Personal Incomes* (various years). Incomes converted to 2012–13 prices using within-year averages of the monthly Consumer Price Index for each financial year.

Reading note: 7% of taxpayers working in the financial industry had an after-tax income of more than £100,000 in financial year 2009–10.

The growth in affluence is shown for selected subgroups in Figure 7.11 using a threshold of £100,000 per year (2012–13 prices). The chart shows that such high after-tax incomes are much more prevalent among male taxpayers than female taxpayers, and among taxpayers in London and the South East than among all taxpayers. Prevalence rates rose for all groups between the mid 1990s and the onset of the late 2000s recession. Figure 7.11 also highlights the relatively large prevalence of high incomes among taxpayers working in the financial industry: in 1997–98 about 2.5 per cent of this group had after-tax incomes over the £100,000 threshold; in 2009–10, the proportion was 7 per cent.

For further discussion of top incomes through to the mid 2000s, the income tax data, and comparisons with HBAI series, see Brewer, Sibieta, and Wren-Lewis (2008). On recent trends in top-wage income, see Bell and Van Reenen (2013).

7.7 Income Mobility and Poverty Dynamics

The perspectives on distributional trends employed so far do not take account of the fact that someone who is poor in one year may be non-poor in the

Table 7.3. Where in the income distribution individuals spent the majority of their time over the nine-year period, 2000–8

	Quintile group in 2000					
	Bottom (poorest)	Second	Third	Fourth	Top (richest)	All individuals
All years in the same quintile group as 2000	14	3	2	4	26	10
Majority of years in same quintile group as 2000	41	36	32	36	34	36
Majority of years above 2000 quintile group	45	31	25	16	–	23
Majority of years below 2000 quintile group	–	14	25	29	40	22
None of the above	–	17	15	16	–	9
All individuals	100	100	100	100	100	100

Notes: 'Majority of years in same quintile group' row: five or more years out of nine in the same quintile group as in base-year but does not include the individuals in the 'All years in same quintile' row. 'None of the above' implies that the individual has neither remained in the same quintile group as the base-year, nor been in a higher or lower quintile group for five of the nine years. '–': no estimate (not logically possible given definitions of groups).
Source: Department for Work and Pensions (2010, Tables 3.2 (BHC) and 3.3 (BHC)), derived from British Household Panel Survey data. See Jenkins (2015) Appendix Table A2 for corresponding estimates for the 1990s.

following year (or vice versa). Similarly, there is mobility into and out of middle- and top-income groups. The group of people that is poor—or rich—is not fixed over time.

Evidence about income mobility throughout the income range is displayed in Table 7.3. Individuals are classified by their quintile group origins in 2000 and their income group membership is tracked over the following eight years. The table shows that mobility is common but most of it is relatively short-distance. Only around one-seventh of individuals in the poorest fifth in 2000 remained in the poorest fifth in all nine years, though nearly one half spent all or the majority of years in that group. But this also means that 45 per cent spent the majority of years in the period in a higher income group. At first glance, downward mobility among those who were in the richest fifth in 2000 is less common than upward mobility from the poorest fifth, since just over a quarter of individuals with richest fifth origins remained there all years, but around 40 per cent spent the majority of years in a lower income group. There is more scope for both upward and downward mobility for those starting in the middle: around two-thirds of those in the middle fifth in 2000 spent significant periods in a different income group.

Despite the changes in the income distribution during the 1990s and 2000s shown earlier, the patterns of mobility were very similar in the two decades. See Jenkins (2015) Appendix Table A3 which provides estimates for the two

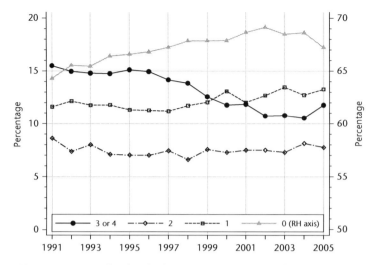

Figure 7.12. Percentages of individuals poor once, twice, or three or more times in a four-year period, by year

Notes: Author's calculations from British Household Panel Survey data (Levy and Jenkins, 2012). Year labels refer to the first year of each four-year period, e.g. '1991' refers to the years 1991–4. The poverty line for each year is 60% of median net household income (BHC). Poverty counts refer to poverty status around the date of the annual BHPS interview.

periods in the same format as Table 7.3. The no-change conclusion is also reported by Jenkins (2011) using an extensive portfolio of mobility measures.

The experience of poverty is likely to be more detrimental the longer that it is experienced; thus, there is particular interest in the extent of poverty persistence. Information about trends in poverty persistence is provided by Figure 7.12. This shows the distribution of the number of times that individuals are poor within successive four-year periods. (The first calculation is for 1991–94 and then the observation window is moved along a year at a time; the latest period is 2005–08. The BHPS ended in 2008.) Using DWP (2010) definitions, an individual is persistently poor if he or she is poor three or four times in the four-year period. Figure 7.12 shows that since the mid 1990s, the persistent poverty rate has declined substantially, by around one-third from 15 per cent to nearly 10 per cent, between the first four-year period and the one beginning in 2004. Over the same period, the number of people experiencing occasional poverty (one or two years poor in a four-year period) increased slightly, and the proportion never poor increased from 65 per cent to 70 per cent. As the recession hit, however, the earlier trends reversed somewhat. For example, for the 2005–08 period, the proportion persistently poor was around two percentage points higher than for the previous four-year period, and the proportion never poor fell by roughly the same amount.

The downward trend in persistent poverty prior to the late-2000s recession reflects improvements that were greatest for families with children, especially lone parent families, and also single pensioners. See Jenkins (2011: ch. 8) for details.

7.8 Concluding Remarks

Although social policy has often treated poverty as the main feature of the income distribution of interest, recent distributional trends in the UK suggest that other features demand as much attention and analysis. This chapter has drawn attention to the stagnation in real income growth for those at the bottom while at the same time incomes at the top have been growing, particularly at the very top. Issues for the UK of contemporary concern are as much the growth in the prevalence of advantage rather than disadvantage— growing inequality as much as poverty.

The reasons why the growth in economic inequality is an important social issue nowadays are threefold: there are views that greater inequality may have deleterious consequences for economic growth, that greater income inequality is associated with greater inequalities in many other spheres, and that the higher incomes are not fairly achieved.

The relationship between inequality and economic growth has long been controversial but recent research concludes that, among OECD countries, 'when income inequality rises, economic growth falls. One reason is that poorer members of society are less able to invest in their education. Tackling inequality can make our societies fairer and our economies stronger' (OECD, 2014: 1). Others have emphasized that stagnation in incomes at the bottom has been accompanied by unsustainable growth in household debt that may have led to the recent financial crisis or at least hindered recovery from it. For a review of evidence, see Lucchino and Morelli (2012).

There is a growing literature arguing that income inequality growth is harmful because it weakens the fabric of our society and social cohesion in its broadest sense. The fabric is represented by a shared experience of a common education system, health service, and pensions, as well as fundamental democratic principles such as one person one-vote and equality before the law. The problem is that the very rich may increasingly opt out of, or be less willing to contribute to, the collective pot that finances benefits and services, or deploy their resources to secure outcomes that are favourable to their own interests via politics, media, or the law. (This is the idea of top incomes reflecting 'rent-seeking' behaviour rather than fairly reflecting talents, or skills.) To date, the literature on this topic has mostly been about the US, no doubt reflecting the fact that inequality levels and inequality growth have been greater there than in the UK. (See, for example, Bartels, 2008; Hacker and Pierson, 2010; and Stiglitz, 2012.) Given the distributional trends in the UK that have been described in this chapter, analysis of their consequences is clearly an important topic on this side of the Atlantic as well. Extensive discussion of what can be done about economic inequality is provided by Atkinson (2015). These issues are also picked up in Chapter 17.

References

Alvaredo, F., Atkinson, A. B., Piketty, T., and Saez, E. (2014). The World Top Incomes Database, online database. http://topincomes.g-mond.parisschoolofeconomics.eu/, last accessed 14 October 2014.

Atkinson, A. B. (2015). *Inequality: What Can Be Done?* Cambridge, MA: Harvard University Press.

Atkinson, A. B., Piketty, T., and Saez, E. (2011). 'Top Incomes in the Long Run of History'. *Journal of Economic Literature*, 49(1): 3–71.

Bartels, L. M. (2008). *Unequal Democracy: The Political Economy of the New Gilded Age.* Princeton, NJ: Princeton University Press.

Belfield, C., Cribb, J., Hood, A., and Joyce, R. (2014). 'Living Standards, Poverty and Inequality in the UK: 2014'. Report R96. London: Institute for Fiscal Studies. http://www.ifs.org.ukr/publications/7274 (accessed 29 November 2014).

Bell, B. and Van Reenen, J. (2013). 'Extreme Wage Inequality: Pay at the Very Top'. *American Economic Review, Papers and Proceedings*, 103(3): 153–57.

Brewer, M. and O'Dea, C. (2012). 'Measuring Living Standards with Income and Consumption: Evidence from the UK'. Working Paper W12/12. London: Institute for Fiscal Studies. http://www.ifs.org.uk/wps/wp1212.pdf (accessed 29 November 2014).

Brewer, M., O'Dea, C., Paull, G., and Sibieta, L. (2009). 'The Living Standards of Families with Children Reporting Low Incomes'. DWP Research Report No 577. London: Department for Work and Pensions. http://eprints.ucl.ac.uk/18312/1/18312.pdf (accessed 29 November 2014).

Brewer, M., Sibieta, L., and Wren-Lewis, S. (2008). 'Racing Away? Income Inequality and the Evolution of High Incomes'. Briefing Note 76. London: Institute for Fiscal Studies. http://www.ifs.org.uk/bns/bn76.pdf (accessed 29 November 2014).

Council of the European Union (2004). Joint report by the Commission and the Council on Social Inclusion. Brussels. Council of the European Union. http://ec.europa.eu/employment_social/soc-prot/soc-incl/final_joint_inclusion_report_2003_en.pdf (accessed 29 November 2014).

Cribb, J., Hood, A., Joyce, R., and Phillips, D. (2013). 'Living Standards, Poverty and Inequality in the UK: 2013'. Report R81. London: Institute for Fiscal Studies. http://www.ifs.org.uk/comms/r81.pdf (accessed 29 November 2014).

Cribb, J., Joyce, R., and Philip, D. (2012). 'Living Standards, Poverty and Inequality in the UK: 2012'. Commentary C214. London: Institute for Fiscal Studies. http://www.ifs.org.uk/comms/comm124.pdf (accessed 29 November 2014).

Department for Work and Pensions (2010). 'Low Income Dynamics'. London: Department for Work and Pensions. https://www.gov.uk/government/publications/low-income-dynamics-1991-to-1998 (accessed 29 November 2014).

Department for Work and Pensions (2014a). 'Households Below Average Income 1994/5–2012/13'. London: Department for Work and Pensions. https://www.gov.uk/government/statistics/households-below-average-income-19941995-to-20132014 (accessed 9 August 2015).

Department for Work and Pensions (2014b). 'Quality and Methodology Information Report'. London: Department for Work and Pensions. https://www.gov.uk/government/statistics/households-below-average-income-19941995-to-20132014 (accessed 9 August 2015).

Eurostat (2014). Online statistical database. http://ec.europa.eu/eurostat/ (accessed 19 October 2014).

Expert Group on Household Income Statistics (The Canberra Group) (2001). 'Final Report and Recommendations'. Ottawa: Statistics Canada. http://www.lisdatacenter.org/books/the-canberra-group-expert-group-on-household-income-statistics-final-report-and-recommendations/ (accessed 29 November 2014).

Flower, T. and Wales, P. (2014). 'Variation in the Inflation Experience of UK Households: 2003–2014'. London: Office for National Statistics. http://www.ons.gov.uk/ons/guide-method/user-guidance/prices/cpi-and-rpi/variation-in-the-inflation-experience-of-uk-households–2003-2014.pdf (accessed 15 January 2015).

Gregg, P., Machin, S., and Fernández-Salgado, M. (2014). 'The Squeeze on Real Wages—and What It Might Take to End It'. *National Institute Economic Review*, 228: R3–R16.

Hacker, J. S. and Pierson, P. (2010). *Winner-Take-All Politics: How Washington Made the Rich Richer—and Turned its Back on the Middle Class*. New York: Simon and Schuster.

HM Revenue and Customs (2012). 'The Exchequer Effect of the 50 Per Cent Additional Rate of Income Tax'. London: HMRC.

Jenkins, S. P. (1991). 'Poverty Measurement and the Within-household Distribution: Agenda for Action'. *Journal of Social Policy*, 20(4): 457–83.

Jenkins, S. P. (2011). *Changing Fortunes: Income Mobility and Poverty Dynamics in Britain*. Oxford: Oxford University Press.

Jenkins, S. P. (2015). 'The Income Distribution in the UK: A Picture of Advantage and Disadvantage'. CASE Paper 186. London: Centre for Analysis of Social Exclusion (CASE), London School of Economics and Political Science.

Jenkins, S. P., Brandolini, A., Micklewright, J., and Nolan, B. (eds) (2013). *The Great Recession and the Distribution of Household Income*. Oxford: Oxford University Press.

Johnson, P. and Webb, S. (1992). 'The Treatment of Housing in Official Low Income Statistics'. *Journal of the Royal Statistical Society. Series A*, 155(2): 273–90.

Levy, H. and Jenkins, S. P. (2012). 'Derived Net Current and Annual Income Variables to Accompany BHPS Waves 1–18'. Study SN3909. Colchester: UK Data Service.

Lucchino, P. and Morelli, S. (2012). 'Inequality, Debt and Growth'. London: Resolution Foundation. http://www.resolutionfoundation.org/wp-content/uploads/2014/08/Final-Inequality-debt-and-growth.pdf (accessed 29 November 2014).

National Equality Panel (J. Hills, Chair). (2010). 'An Anatomy of Economic Inequality in the UK'. Report of the National Equality Panel. London: Government Inequalities Office. http://eprints.lse.ac.uk/28344/1/CASEreport60.pdf (accessed 29 November 2014).

OECD (2014). *Focus on Inequality and Growth—December 2014*. Paris: OECD. http://www.oecd.org/els/soc/Focus-Inequality-and-Growth-2014.pdf (accessed 15 January 2015).

Stiglitz, J. E. (2012). *The Price of Inequality: How Today's Divided Society Endangers Our Future*. London: Allen Lane.

8

Accumulated Advantage and Disadvantage

The Role of Wealth

John Hills and Jack Cunliffe

Much discussion of people's advantages and disadvantages is dominated by comparisons of the immediate—the flows of income of one kind or another out of which they normally meet their weekly or monthly shopping bills or spending of other kinds.[1] But to get a fuller understanding of people's relative economic positions we also need to know about their stocks of assets. How much money do they have in the bank out of which they could meet the costs of a sudden emergency? What savings and investments do they have that will give them a continuing flow of interest or dividends to augment their income from earnings or state pensions or benefits? Do they own a home which they can live in rent-free, and do they have rights to a future pension after they retire?

Two families may have the same incomes coming in this year, but if the first are tenants with no savings and no pension rights beyond those from the state they will be much less advantaged than the second, if they are owner-occupiers with accumulated financial assets and the right to good pensions after they retire. A third family may have the same income but have accumulated debts

[1] Chapter 8 was written as part of the 'Social Policy in a Cold Climate' programme at the Centre for Analysis of Social Exclusion supported by the Joseph Rowntree Foundation, the Nuffield Foundation, and the Trust for London. It draws on other work carried out within the programme, in particular the research reported in Hills, Cunliffe, Obolenskaya, and Karagiannaki (2015). It also draws on work carried out within the research programme on the changing distribution of wealth supported by the Nuffield Foundation and reported in Hills et al. (2013). The authors are very grateful to Alan Newman and Elaine Chamberlain from the UK Office for National Statistics for their great assistance with the analysis of the ONS Wealth and Assets Survey reported in it, and to Tony Atkinson for permission to reproduce Figure 8.2 from his 2015 book, *Inequality: What Can Be Done?*

that outweigh the value of any assets or possessions they have. Many of the most disadvantaged not only have very low incomes, but also have high-interest debts to repay, and money owed for rent, gas and electricity bills, or local taxes. They have 'negative wealth'.

The attention given to wealth and wealth inequalities has recently been greatly increased by the worldwide impact of the French economist Thomas Piketty's book, *Capital in the Twenty-First Century*, particularly after its publication in English in 2014. That emphasized two features: the way in which wealth is (and always has been) much more unequally distributed than earnings or other measures of income; and the rise in recent decades in many countries (including the UK) in the value of personal wealth in relation to national income. Put together these mean that some people have the security of accumulated assets that are equivalent to many years of average household incomes, and right at the top fortunes are much greater than even the most successful could envisage accumulating from regular earnings.

Piketty's central argument is that the industrialized world has been reverting to a relationship between wealth and income that prevailed through the nineteenth century—with all the social consequences of that, such as the relative importance of what career people follow compared to the wealth they marry into. It has changed from what had come to be seen as 'normal' in the thirty years after the Second World War, during which accumulated wealth and inheritance played a much smaller role. We may now, he argues, have left what was in effect an historical aberration, during which high growth rates and low post-tax rates of return on wealth had reduced the comparative importance of personal wealth in setting patterns of advantage and disadvantage within Western societies.

Further, and as importantly for differences in people's life chances, much of that wealth will be transmitted on to (some of) the next generation either as an inheritance or through lifetime gifts of one kind or another. As the data for Great Britain described later in this chapter suggests, there will be a huge difference in the amounts that a small number of grandchildren stand to inherit eventually from professional grandparents who are owner-occupiers in high value parts of the country (such as London or the South East of England) and the expectations of a larger number of grandchildren of working-class tenants living in regions with low house prices (such as the North of England). The difference can easily equate to assets equivalent to half a typical lifetime's earnings.

Wealth and the dynamics of its accumulation can therefore be seen in two ways. First, it represents the solidification of economic advantage across the life cycle. Those with the highest incomes and those hit by the lowest demands have the most opportunity to save, to avoid expensive debts, and to secure high pension incomes in retirement.

Within all of this, age differences play a prominent role. One reason for household wealth being unequal is that its accumulation has a pronounced life-cycle pattern. Differences in wealth-holdings are an important part of the age-related inequalities discussed in Chapter 10. Apart from inheritances and gifts, most people start their working careers with little by way of savings and assets. But then through their working lives they may be able to buy a house, pay off any mortgage involved, build up pension rights or savings, and then enter retirement with assets some of which (explicitly in the case of pension rights) they run down through the rest of their lives. In some countries (including the UK in recent years), those who have been students may start their working life with negative wealth—student debt—which they pay off during their careers or is written off after a number of years.

We would therefore expect to see older people, especially those near the point of retirement, to have higher wealth than younger people. But as we explore below, such life-cycle patterns of saving and dis-saving only explain a small part of overall wealth inequalities. In addition, the opportunities open to generations born at different dates have varied widely and look set to continue to do so.

In all of this, whatever those currently at the top of the wealth pile may argue, there is clearly a huge amount of brute luck involved. British people who were able to become owner-occupiers during house price dips such as in the early 1980s and early 1990s have had to pay far less for their housing than someone would have to pay after the long house price boom since then, especially if they bought in London or the South East of England. The more fortunate members of the generation promised the most generous occupational pensions or who have been the biggest beneficiaries of the now discontinued 'state earnings related pension scheme' (SERPS) in the UK can look forward to a much better-financed retirement than most of their children's generation. Those with cash savings in banks and building societies in years when inflation was high saw their wealth fall in real terms, but those who had mortgages or other loans at the same time gained from the way inflation eroded the value of their debt. A small part of the differences that have emerged within and between generations will reflect who made the greatest sacrifices of current consumption or who made the best-informed investment decisions. But most of it will have been the luck of the draw.

That draw is not, and increasingly will not be, one in which everyone has an equal chance of success. The second aspect of wealth is, as we discuss below, that it acts as a key mechanism for the transmission of advantage, and the lack of it, from generation to generation. As we shall see, the distribution of wealth reinforces other patterns of advantage and disadvantage—not just by location, family background, and social class (see Chapters 5 and 6, this volume), but also by housing tenure and ethnicity. We illustrate this using data from

Britain, but similar patterns apply and similar issues arise in other countries, as Piketty (2014) has shown.

8.1 The Current Distribution of Wealth in Great Britain

As far as the bulk of the population is concerned, the clearest picture of the distribution of household wealth is shown by the Office for National Statistics' Wealth and Assets Survey (WAS). This is now available for three two-year periods starting in July 2006, July 2008, and July 2010. The latest therefore covers the period July 2010 to June 2012 (ONS, 2014). This survey is likely, however, to under-represent the very top incomes, for which we can draw on inheritance tax data; see further Figure 8.2 and related discussion (and see Chapter 7 for related discussion of the use of tax data to examine top incomes). Note that the WAS covers Great Britain (excluding Northern Ireland) rather than the whole of the UK.

There are different ways of defining 'wealth', depending on what kinds of asset are included. Some people may only be interested in assets that can be easily sold and used for other purposes, such as bank accounts and financial investments. But for other purposes we will be interested in property assets, such as the value of the home people live in that they own (net of any outstanding mortgage debt). We may also want to include somewhat less tangible assets—a promise of a future flow of income from a pension over many years of retirement can have an equivalent value to a large amount of savings, which could be run down in retirement to support the same consumption. The ONS statistics on household wealth use three definitions:

- Financial and physical wealth (net financial assets plus other personal possessions, excluding housing)

- Non-pension wealth (which also includes the value of housing and other property, net of mortgages)

- Total wealth (which also includes an estimated value of *non-state* pension rights, based on what sum of money would be needed in cash to generate an equivalent flow through someone's expected life after retirement).

Note that all three of these definitions therefore include personal physical possessions such as furniture, clothing, consumer durables, and cars. As most households have some of these possessions, this makes the distribution look more equal than it would do if we looked only at financial and housing assets that many have little or none of. But on the other hand, even the 'total wealth' definition excludes people's *state* pension rights, which are much more equal than those from private or occupational pensions.

(a) Financial and physical wealth

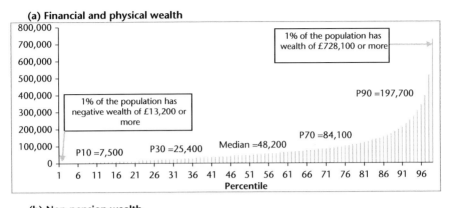

(b) Non-pension wealth

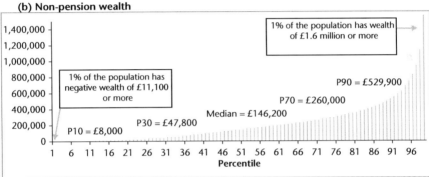

(c) Total wealth

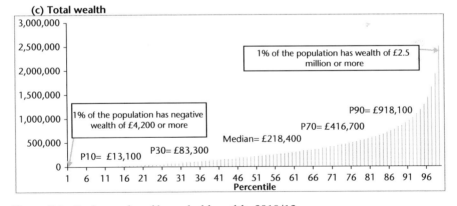

Figure 8.1. Pen's parades of household wealth, 2010/12

Source: Hills et al. (2015), Figure 2.10 based on ONS/CASE analysis of the Wealth and Assets Survey

Figure 8.1 shows the overall distributions of wealth in 2010/12 using all three definitions in what is sometimes called the 'Pen's parade' format with each bar showing the level of wealth at the 'percentile' points that divide households into one hundred groups, with the least wealthy on the left, and the cut-off point marking the bottom of the top one per cent on the right. The top panel shows, for instance that more than 2 per cent of households had zero or negative wealth on the narrowest ONS definition, but 1 per cent had financial and physical wealth of more than £728,000. Half of households had wealth on this basis of £48,200 or less. In some ways this is already remarkable. On ONS's estimates total net financial assets were £1.3 trillion and 'physical' wealth a further £1.1 trillion, so *mean* wealth was £99,000 per household. Fully three-quarters of households had less wealth than this average.

Adding in property wealth (net of mortgages) the aggregate for non-pension wealth rises to £5.9 trillion, or £245,000 per household. But, as the middle panel shows, median non-pension wealth was only £146,000. Two-thirds of households had wealth below the mean level. One tenth had less than £8,000, but a tenth had more than £530,000. The ratio between the two gives the '90:10' ratio, one measure of how unequally wealth is distributed—in this case a ratio of 66:1. Chapter 7 revealed substantial inequalities in income in the UK. But wealth (in all countries) is *far* more unequally distributed than wages or incomes. For example, the 90:10 ratio for household net incomes in the UK (adjusted for household size and composition) was 3.9:1 in 2012–13 (Figure 7.4), while for hourly wages in 2013 it was 4.0:1 (Hills et al., 2015: Figures 2.3 and 2.7). While Chapter 7 (Figure 7.4) shows a Gini Coefficient of 34 per cent for income inequality in 2012–13, the Gini coefficient for non-pension wealth in the 2010/12 WAS was 59 per cent. Even though the survey used does not fully cover the very highest wealth-holders, the figure shows that 1 per cent of households had non-pension wealth of £1.6 million or more in 2010/12 (accounting for 11 per cent of the total).

The third panel adds in estimated private pension rights. This takes aggregate household wealth to £9.5 trillion and mean total wealth to £393,000. To give an idea of just how big this was, it was equivalent to around six times the annual Gross Domestic Product (GDP) at the time (compared to four times, if pension rights were not included). In this case a tenth of households had under £13,000 and half less than £218,000, but a tenth had more than £918,000, so the 90:10 ratio was seventy to one. One per cent had over £2.5 million.

The top tenth of households had 44 per cent of the national total of personal wealth, £4.2 trillion (ONS, 2014: Figure 2.3). The average total wealth within the top 1 per cent of just under £5 million each gave them 12 per cent of the total. This may well, however, be an underestimate of the share of the very top: the very wealthiest are rather unlikely to respond to surveys of this kind. An alternative is to use tax records relating to the estates of those dying each year to show the wealth of (deceased) *individual adults* rather than households, and then adjust these to match the composition of the whole population. One would expect individual wealth to be more unequal than that of households taken together, as wealth ownership will not always be shared between the adults in a household. Such records suggest that the top

1 per cent of adults accounted for 21 per cent of 'marketable' wealth in 2005, the latest year for which consistent statistics are available (Hills and Bastagli, 2013, Table 2.3, based on HM Revenue and Customs 'Series C' estimates for the UK). On that measure wealth inequality was the same as it had been in 1976, when the HMRC series started. However, it was considerably lower than it had been before the Second World War, when Atkinson, Gordon, and Harrison's (1986: Table 1) estimates put the top 1 per cent share at 55 per cent in 1938 (in Great Britain) and 61 per cent in 1923 (in England and Wales). Wealth may still be highly unequal, but it is not as unequal as it was in the Britain before the Second World War.

Figure 8.2, reproduced from Atkinson (2015), uses this series to show the combined effects of two different trends—the fall in wealth inequality (as measured by the top 1 per cent's share) up to 1975, and the decline but then recovery of the overall total of personal wealth in relation to national income (national income is lower than GDP, as it deducts capital consumption). Wealth in this series excludes pension rights. Note also that this series would omit assets that people had already passed on before they died.

Back in 1923 the top 1 per cent had between them wealth totalling more than two years of total national income; the other 99 per cent had wealth of three years of national income. Fifty years later the wealth of the top 1 per cent was down to a little over half a year of national income, while that of the rest of the population was down to 2.3 years. The effects of war and high top income tax and inheritance tax rates, as well as the growing importance of 'middle wealth' in the form of owner-occupation, had taken their toll on the relative value of wealth at the top. But by 2000, the wealth of the top 1 per cent had already rebounded to a year's worth of national income, within a

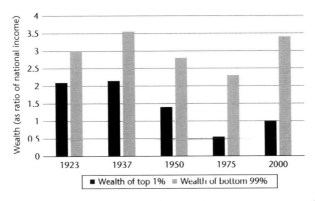

Figure 8.2. Wealth of top 1 per cent and bottom 99 per cent compared to national income, UK, 1923–2000

Source: Atkinson (2015), Figure 6.1B. Reprinted by permission of the publisher from INEQUALITY: WHAT CAN BE DONE? by Anthony Atkinson, p. 157, Cambridge, Mass.: Harvard University Press. Copyright © 2015 by the President and Fellows of Harvard College.

total now equivalent to 4.4 years, reflecting the growing scale of wealth in relation to income which Piketty draws attention to.

8.2 Wealth and Age

If wealth differences were simply about the kind of life-cycle saving and dis-saving discussed in the introduction to the chapter, we would expect to see a peak in assets close to retirement, but with them run down to near zero for the oldest groups. We would also expect to see differences *within* age groups that were no greater than those in incomes or earnings. Looking at median total wealth in 2010/12 by age shown in Figure 8.3 this kind of pattern can be seen to some extent. Households aged under 25 typically have little or no wealth. Those now nearing retirement have the greatest median wealth—£425,000 for those aged 55–64. The oldest surviving households have less—just under £200,000 at the median for those aged 85 or more. But the figure also shows that life-cycle differences actually explain only a small part of wealth inequality, even when pension rights are included as they are here. First, the oldest households do not run their savings down to zero, even though their expected future pensions may not be worth very much. Many owner-occupiers continue to own their house, with few selling it off (or taking out a 'reverse mortgage') and living off the proceeds. Even financial assets are run down only slowly—median financial and physical wealth still exceeded £44,000 for households aged 85 or over in 2010/12 compared to £70,000 for those aged

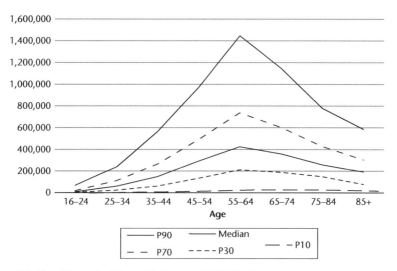

Figure 8.3. Total household wealth by age, 2010/12, £

Source: CASE/ONS analysis of Wealth and Assets Survey. Age is that of household reference person

Table 8.1. Changes in median non-pension wealth, 2006/08 to 2010/12 and wealth levels in 2010/12, by age group

	16–24	25–34	35–44	45–54	55–64	65–74	75–84	85+
Percentage changes 2006/08 to 2010/12	–31.7	–10.1	–16.9	–8.8	–5.0	+8.9	+12.5	+15.4
Absolute changes 2006/08 to 2010/12 (£000s, nominal)	–3.8	–4.8	–20.6	–16.3	–12.2	+19.0	+23.1	+24.0
Median non-pension wealth in 2010/12 (£000s)	8.2	42.8	101.5	169.3	232.8	233.5	207.2	180.0
90:10 ratio within age group in 2010/12	Na[1]	61	57	55	48	43	34	32

Note: [1] Tenth percentile wealth is minus £6,200 and ninetieth percentile is £61,400.
Source: ONS/CASE analysis of Wealth and Assets Survey

55–64, despite the older group coming from a generation who had lower lifetime earnings out of which to save.

The figure also shows that there is considerable inequality *within* each age group. Looking at the wealthiest age group, those aged 55–64, 10 per cent had more than £1.4 million (shown by the 'P90' line), but 10 per cent had less than £27,000 (shown by the P10 line). The 90:10 ratio of fifty-three to one for total wealth may not be as large as the seventy to one across all households, but was still very considerable. There are comparable inequalities within the other age groups.

In the recent past, these age-related differences have increased. The percentage and absolute changes in median non-pension wealth between the first wave of the Wealth and Assets Survey (from July 2006 to June 2008), and the most recent round (from July 2010 to June 2012) are shown in Table 8.1 (not adjusted for inflation). There has been a strong tilt against younger households, taking place over what is just a four-year period.

Looking at both proportionate and absolute changes in nominal wealth the biggest gains were for the older age groups, while wealth fell for those aged below 55 across the distribution (with the exception of the tenth percentile for those aged 25–34, which grew by 23 per cent, although that was only a rise of £600; see Hills et al., 2015, Figure 3.10 and Table 3.5 for more detail of these changes). For the households aged 65 and over, median non-pension wealth grew by around £20,000, but for those aged 35–44, it fell by £20,000. By 2010–12, median non-pension wealth for those aged 55–64 had reached £232,800 (or £424,500 including ONS's assessment of pension rights), while that for those aged 25–34 was only £42,800 (£59,700 including pension rights).

As with other aspects of their ecomomic situation, the relative position of young adults, now in their twenties and early thirties, has deteriorated since the start of the economic crisis, suggesting that part of the pattern shown in

Figure 8.2 reflects difference between generations born at different ages, not simply life-cycle patterns that will continue to the reproduced. For the generation approaching retirement or recently retired, rising wealth levels are an advantage, although as we have seen, very unequally distributed. At the other end of working lives, wealth fell for those in their twenties and early thirties. As a result, the generational wealth divide is now immense in relation to annual incomes. Median total wealth (including pension rights) of those aged around 60 reached £425,000 in 2010/12 (Figure 8.3). For those aged around 30 it was £60,000.

For the younger generation to bridge the gap between the two would require them to find £365,000. To do this through their own savings, would mean saving and/or pension contributions of £33 each and every day for the next thirty years. This is unlikely to happen as a typical experience. Indeed, the generations born in the 1970s have been spending greater amounts than their incomes—running up debts—even in their twenties and thirties, unlike previous generations (Hood and Joyce, 2013, Figures 3.12 and 3.9). Instead, what will matter most will be what happens to the wealth of the older generations, and to whom it is passed on. As we discuss below, that is also likely to be very unequally distributed. The younger generation is one where the 'luck of the draw' has gone against them taken as a whole, but where some members will be compensated by their luck of another draw, who they happen to be related to.

8.3 Wealth Differences and Other Characteristics

Wealth differences are affected by—and compound—other dimensions of difference associated with advantage and disadvantage. Data based on the total wealth of households are not well suited to exploring differences by gender, of the kind discussed in Chapter 11, as they assume pooled ownership and do not tell us who within a household would retain ownership of an asset after a divorce, for instance. Looking at the wealth of the household of which they were members, there was virtually no difference between the overall distributions of men and women between bands of wealth in 2010/12, for instance (ONS, 2014: Table 2.13). However, household data can be used to look at other socio-economic differences.

8.3.1 Occupational Social Class

First, Table 8.2 shows how strongly the wealth people had accumulated by the time they had reached age 55–64 in 2010/12 relates to their occupational social class. The differences driven by lifetime differences in the benefits that

Table 8.2. Household wealth for 55–64 year-olds by household occupational social class, 2010–12 (£000s)

	Median financial and physical wealth	Median financial, physical, and property wealth	Total household wealth			Proportion of households aged 55–64 (%)
			10th percentile	Median	90th percentile	
Large employers/ higher managerial	131	425	278	1,055	2,227	5
Higher professional	156	467	304	983	2,381	9
Lower managerial/ professional	99	323	120	669	1,670	26
Intermediate	71	248	73	443	1,053	11
Small employers/own-account workers	71	258	35	383	1,207	10
Lower supervisory/ technical	54	188	32	328	826	9
Semi-routine	39	120	12	206	736	15
Routine	33	91	9	162	577	13
Never worked/long-term unemployed	17	47	na	125	na	2
All	71	233	27	425	1,445	100

Source: Hills et al. (2013), Table 2.1 updated using CASE/ONS analysis of the Wealth and Assets Survey restricted to those where household reference person is aged 55–64. Proportions of households in each social class group from unweighted sample numbers

flow from their occupation are considerable, even focusing just on one cohort at a particular age, and so abstracting from life-cycle effects. At the median, the total wealth of the top two groups was more than £980,000, but for the bottom three groups it was less than £210,000—a five-fold difference, depending on how people's working lives had evolved. For the top two groups, private pension rights contributed more than £500,000 to this total; for the bottom three groups they contributed less than £90,000. If one focused just on financial and physical assets, the top two groups had more than £130,000, but the bottom two groups less than £40,000.

While this shows how powerfully people's career paths (with the implied differences in lifetime earnings) determine their accumulated pre-retirement assets, there are considerable differences *within* each of the social class groupings. There are considerable differences in trajectories within these relatively broad occupational groupings (see, for instance, Lauriston and Friedman, 2015). A tenth of those in the top two groups had wealth of more than £2.2 million (ninety years' worth of median pre-tax full-time earnings, to set it in context). But a tenth of higher professionals had less than £300,000. A tenth of those who had been in routine occupations had more than £580,000, but a tenth were facing retirement with household assets of less than £9,000.

8.3.2 Housing Tenure

Given how dominant housing wealth is within non-pension wealth, it is unsurprising that the wealth differences between tenures are so large. These differences widened considerably in absolute terms between 2006–08 and 2010–12 (see Table 8.3). By 2010–12 median non-pension wealth of outright owners had increased by £21,000 to £307,000, twenty times that of social tenants (£16,000). More detailed analysis (see Hills et al., 2015, Table 5.4 and Figure 5.10) shows that the greatest fall for mortgagors was for those who were least wealthy, while a very large percentage fall meant that the poorest tenth of private tenants had virtually no net assets at all by 2010–12 (just £300 or less), despite the inclusion of personal possessions, after allowing for their debts.

If one looks only at financial and physical wealth, before allowing for housing, social tenants had median wealth of only £16,000 and this rose only to £25,000 even when non-state pension rights were allowed for. By contrast, those owning their homes outright had median financial and physical wealth of £88,000, rising to £472,000 including housing and private pension rights. A tenth of outright owners had total wealth of more than £1.3 million, but a tenth of social tenants had total wealth of less than £3,000 (although a tenth had more than £138,000). Even if one looks only at social tenants aged 55–64, a tenth had total wealth of less than £3,300.

Tenure divides therefore do not just translate into differences in housing wealth, as one would expect, but are also associated with very large differences in the other forms of wealth that people can accumulate at the same time. Both matter in terms of what may be passed on to the next generation, as we discuss below.

Table 8.3. Changes in median non-pension wealth, 2006/08 to 2010/12, and wealth levels in 2010/12, by housing tenure

	Social tenant	Private tenant	Own main residence outright	Buying with mortgage/loan
Percentage changes 2006/08 to 2010/12	+6.1	+7.1	+7.3	−5.5
Absolute changes 2006/08 to 2010/12 (£000s, nominal)	0.9	1.2	21.0	−9.7
Median non-pension wealth in 2010/12 (£000s)	15.7	18.2	306.8	167.3
90:10 ratio	22	358	5	10

Source: ONS/CASE analysis of Wealth and Assets Survey

8.3.3 *Region*

Differences in housing tenure combine with regional differences in house prices to create very large wealth differences across the country, and these have widened in various ways since the start of the economic crisis, as Table 8.4 shows (for more detail, see Hills et al., 2015, Table 6.4 and Figure 6.10). Most notably, the fastest rise in median non-pension wealth over the period from 2006/08 to 2010/12 was in London—by more than a quarter in nominal terms, and by £32,000 in absolute terms. It also grew by more than a quarter for the wealthiest Londoners, reaching £750,000. However, net non-pension wealth at the 10th percentile, £4,500 in London in 2010/12, was the *lowest* in the country. Inequalities in wealth remained far greater in London than elsewhere, with a 90:10 ratio of 167 (compared to 66 nationally), while median households in London had less non-pension wealth than those in the South East, South West, and East of England. If ONS's estimated value of pension wealth was included, the richest tenth of London households had nearly £1.1 million in assets, but the poorest tenth less than £6,300 (after debts but including personal possessions)—a 90:10 ratio of 173 to 1 (compared to 70 to 1 nationally).

While people continue to live in the same house, it may matter comparatively little to them that the paper value of their house has increased by hundreds of thousands of pounds. But if they were to downsize, move to a cheaper region, or when they die, these differences can translate into cash that will have huge effects on their own or their heirs' lives.

Table 8.4. Changes in median non-pension wealth, 2006/08 to 2010/12, and wealth levels in 2010/12, by region (£, nominal terms)

	Percentage change 2008/10 to 2010/12	Absolute change 2006/08 to 2010/12 (£000s)	Median non-pension wealth, 2010/12 (£000s)	90:10 ratio
South East	+4.6	9.7	218.8	49
South West	+2.6	5	198.9	45
Eastern	+2.5	4.6	187.4	41
London	26.1	31.5	150.9	167
E Midlands	−7.4	−11.4	142.6	42
W Midlands	−7.0	−10	132	59
Yorkshire & Humberside	−2.4	−3	121.6	47
North West	+0.1	0.1	118.2	65
North East	−18.9	−22	94.7	47
England	−0.1	−0.1	152.3	68
Scotland	+0.9	1	107.9	50
Wales	−3.8	−5.4	137.1	56

Source: ONS/CASE analysis of Wealth and Assets Survey

8.3.4 Ethnicity

Using sample surveys such as the Wealth and Assets Survey, sample sizes can be too small to analyse changes over time or differences within groups, but Table 8.5 gives an indication of how non-pension wealth varied by ethnicity (of household reference person) in 2010/12 (see Hills et al., 2015, section 4 for more detail, and Chapter 12 for more general discussion of 'race' and ethnicity). Median non-pension wealth for Indian and Chinese households was around £200,000, more than the £155,000 for White households. Given their similar levels of disadvantage in many aspects of labour market and income outcomes, the contrast between the median wealth of £129,000 for Pakistani households but only £21,000 for Bangladeshi households suggests an important difference in fortunes (reflecting tenure patterns) which is not seen in other dimensions. Inequality within 'White British' households is somewhat less than within the population as a whole, a 90:10 ratio of 57 to 1 for non-pension wealth, compared to 66 to 1 overall. The inequalities within the 'Other White' group are striking, perhaps reflecting the large differences between particular groups of immigrants (see Chapter 13 for more discussion).

8.3.5 Disability Status

If one looks simply at median non-pension wealth, that of households with a disabled member was £124,000 in 2010/12, compared to £157,000 for non-disabled households. This difference does not initially appear to be so large, but wealth differentials between those who are disabled and those who are not are strongly affected by their age differences (with disabled people tending to be older). The onset of disability interrupts people's ability to earn and to save, however. Abigail McKnight (2014) therefore looked in detail at the effects of disability on wealth accumulation, separating out the effects of disability from those of ageing and other characteristics. She compared the non-pension wealth of those who had been disabled five to ten years earlier with those

Table 8.5. Median non-pension wealth in 2010/12, by ethnic group (£000s)

	White British	Other White	White and Black Caribbean	Indian	Pakistani	Bangladeshi	Other Asian	Black Caribbean	Black African	Chinese
Median	155.2	68.8	15.9	194.7	129	21.3	52	34.4	20.9	201.5
90:10 ratio	57	170		73						

Source: ONS/CASE analysis of Wealth and Assets Survey. 90:10 ratio cannot be calculated for many ethnic groups because of small sample sizes

who had not been, finding for instance a 'disability penalty' of £133,000 for 45–54 year-olds in 2005. Again, disadvantage in the labour market at one point in time can compound into very substantial wealth differences.

8.4 Inheritance and the Transmission of Wealth

Wealth, and the security (and sometimes power) that it brings is one aspect of advantage for the generation that owns it. The patterns described above show how its inequality adds to the other aspects of advantage and disadvantage discussed in this book. But we have also stressed a second role—that of transmission of advantage between generations. Because those with even moderate levels of wealth tend not to run it all down to zero before they die, considerable amounts are passed on to the next generation, sometimes on death, through inheritance, but also through lifetime gifts.

Tony Atkinson has used inheritance tax data, adjusted for under-reporting and avoidance, to estimate the scale of wealth transmitted between generations (through lifetime gifts as well as inheritance) in the UK since 1896 (Atkinson, 2013: Figure G). He suggests that at the start of the twentieth century, wealth transmission was running at an annual rate equivalent to around 20 per cent of net national income. This fell in the inter-war period to 15 per cent, and again after the Second World War to 10 per cent, falling again to a low point of around 5 per cent in the late 1970s. Living off inherited wealth had gone out of fashion. Since then, it has, however, been rising again as wealth has grown in value relative to income, reaching more than 8 per cent of net national income by 2006. One would expect this to continue to grow in future, particularly as the generation of owner-occupiers who gained most from the house price boom reach the ends of their lives over the next thirty years.

In France, this process is further advanced. Piketty (2014: Figure 11.1) calculates that through the nineteenth century up to the First World War, the annual flow of inheritance was also equivalent to 20 per cent or more of national income in France, falling to 5 per cent or less after the Second World War. But the rebound in its relative value started earlier, and the annual flow had already reached 12–15 per cent (depending on the data source used) by 2010. At this rate, inheritance is again material by comparison with other sources of people's economic resources.

If such flows came to all, they would not reinforce inequality. Indeed, if they came literally as an equal lump sum endowment to all citizens when they reached adulthood they could be a powerful force for greater equality, as advocated originally by Tom Paine two hundred years ago (and most recently by Atkinson, 2015: 170–2). But they do not. Between 1995 and 2005, the

British Household Panel Study suggests that about 2.4 per cent of adults received an inheritance each year, but for only around 1.4 per cent was the value more than £2,000 (at 2005 prices). Among the fifth of adults who inherited anything between 1996 and 2005, around half of the total of all inheritances went to the top tenth of inheritors, that is, to around 2 per cent of all adults (Hills and Karagiannaki, 2013: Tables 5.1 and 5.2).

All sorts of people inherit, including some who have low incomes or who previously had little wealth. But those who are already economically more advantaged are both more likely to inherit, and inherit more when they do. Allowing for other factors (such as age), the chances of receiving an inheritance are greatest for those with degrees and least for those with no qualifications, and are much higher for homeowners and those who already have financial wealth. In each case, the amount that inheritors receive is also greater for the better qualified and for homeowners and those with financial wealth (Karagiannaki, 2011).

This is borne out in what people currently expect for the future. Using data from the 2006–08 Wealth and Assets Survey, Andrew Hood and Robert Joyce (2013: Figures 4.3 and 4.4) have looked at how people's expectations that they would inherit related to how much wealth they already had. The most telling differences are for those in their early thirties, when they had already started to build their own savings (if they could), but would not yet have received most of their likely inheritances. They found that 78 per cent of the already wealthiest third expected a future inheritance, and that 35 per cent of them expected that it would be above £100,000. For those in the least wealthy third, only 45 per cent expected any inheritance, and only 12 per cent that it would be over £100,000. These figures are just for individuals; they are compounded when looking at partners' expectations. For all those in their thirties who expected to inherit more than £100,000, nearly all (87 per cent) of partners expected an inheritance, and more than half of their partners (52 per cent) an inheritance of more than £100,000.

Inheritance and lifetime gifts of cash—for instance, for education or towards a deposit for a house—are only part of the way in which advantage is passed from generation to generation (see Chapter 5, this volume), but they are already an important one, and set to become even more important.

8.5 Conclusions

Writing a generation ago, wealth might have played a more minor role in the discussion of advantage and disadvantage than it would have done in the first half of the twentieth century, let alone in the nineteenth century. But wealth is back. This is not because wealth inequality in itself has increased, but because its *scale* compared with annual income flows has increased, and it remains much more unequally distributed than the annual incomes discussed in the last chapter. Its role in determining current opportunities and the life chances of the next generation is not just a matter of the extremes, such as the billionaires covered by publications such as the *Sunday Times Rich List* or Oxfam's calculation that 80 billionaires now have the same wealth as the bottom half of the world's population combined (Oxfam, 2015, based on data from *Forbes* and Credit Suisse).

'Everyday' wealth differences now matter as well. A British household just on the edge of the top tenth—not necessarily one that would think itself particularly 'wealthy'—now has total assets, including accumulated pension rights, of more than £900,000. Looking just at those aged 55–64, a tenth have more than £1.4 million. This is more than most people could expect to earn, even before tax, in a whole lifetime. But a tenth of those of the same age have less than £27,000, even including all their personal possessions. These kinds of difference do not just affect the lives and choices people can expect in retirement themselves, but also what they can do to help their children and grandchildren (or others, if they choose). This puts wealth—and policies towards it—at the centre of any debate about 'equality of opportunity', as well as about patterns of inequality today.

References

Atkinson, A. B. (2013). 'Wealth and Inheritance in Britain from 1896 to the Present'. CASE paper 178. London: London School of Economics.

Atkinson, A. B. (2015). *Inequality: What Can Be Done?* Cambridge, MA: Harvard University Press.

Atkinson, A. B., Gordon, J., and Harrison, A. J. (1986). 'Trends in the Distribution of Wealth in Britain, 1923–1981'. TIDI Discussion Paper 70. London: London School of Economics.

Hills, J. and Bastagli, F. (2013). 'Trends in the Distribution of Wealth in Britain'. In J. Hills, F. Bastagli, F. Cowell, H. Glennerster, E. Karagiannaki, and A. McKnight, *Wealth in the UK: Distribution, Accumulation and Policy* (pp. 10–34). Oxford: Oxford University Press.

Hills, J., Cunliffe, J., Oboloenskaya, P., and Karagiannaki, E. (2015). 'Falling Behind, Getting Ahead: The Changing Structure of Inequality in the UK, 2007–2013'. Social Policy in a Cold Climate Research Report 5. London: London School of Economics.

Hood, A. and Joyce, R. (2013). 'The Economic Circumstances of Cohorts Born between the 1940s and the 1970s'. IFS Report 89. London: Institute for Fiscal Studies.

Karagiannaki, E. (2011). 'Recent Trends in the Size and Distribution of Inherited Wealth in the UK'. CASE paper 146. London: London School of Economics.

Karagiannaki, E. and Hills, J. (2013). 'Inheritance, Transfers, and the Distribution of Wealth'. In J. Hills, F. Bastagli, F. Cowell, H. Glennerster, E. Karagiannaki, and A. McKnight, *Wealth in the UK: Distribution, Accumulation and Policy* (pp. 92–118). Oxford: Oxford University Press.

Lauriston, D. and Friedman, S. (2015). 'Introducing the Class Ceiling: Social Mobility and Britain's Elite Occupations'. LSE Sociology Working Paper Series. London: London School of Economics.

Office for National Statistics (ONS) (2014). *Wealth in Great Britain Wave 3, 2010–12*. London: Office for National Statistics.

Oxfam (2015). 'Wealth: Having it All and Wanting More'. Oxfam Issue Briefing, January 2015. Available at <https://www.oxfam.org/sites/www.oxfam.org/files/file_attachments/ib-wealth-having-all-wanting-more-190115-en.pdf> (accessed 10 August 2015).

McKnight, A. (2014). 'Disabled People's Financial Histories: Uncovering the Disability Wealth-penalty'. CASE paper 181. London: London School of Economics.

Piketty, T. (2014). *Capital in the 21st Century*. Cambridge, MA: Harvard University Press.

9

Divisions of Labour and Work

Hartley Dean

A key determinant of the advantages and disadvantages that people experience in the course of their lives is their access to work, whether as a means of livelihood or as a means of social engagement, identity, and fulfilment. Like 'poverty', which was discussed in Chapter 1, 'work' is an everyday word imbued with an array of meanings; meanings that have evolved over time. Just as poverty became peculiarly visible and acquired particular meaning as a result of the social dislocations associated with the rise of industrial capitalism, so the meaning of work was substantially reshaped by the emergence of the modern wage labour system. Work was rendered largely synonymous with productive economic activity; a particular form of *labour* that could be bought and sold as a commodity (Polanyi, 1944). The development of formal labour markets provided the basis for social divisions between those at different locations within the labour market and fostered particular disadvantages for those excluded from the labour market.

In this chapter we firstly reflect on the meanings of work as an essential human activity, the central role of wage labour as the dominant form of work throughout much of the world, and the implications for relative advantage and disadvantage. We consider the changing nature of labour markets, which has resulted during the post-industrial era from changes in the character of the labour process and from the effects of economic globalization. Secondly, the chapter will develop our discussion in Chapter 4 regarding class and the relationship between socio-economic status and relative advantage. It will focus on the changing nature of socio-economic divisions and the emergence of socio-economic fault-lines between relatively privileged core workers and relatively disadvantaged peripheral workers. The drivers of these evolving axes of advantage and disadvantage and their social consequences relate not only to changing class structures, but also to secular trends relating to gender relations, population ageing, migration, and ethnicity which will be considered in later chapters in this volume. For now, however, we examine more generally issues of wage inequality; the problem of precarious or vulnerable and under-remunerated forms of work; and the significance of skills differentials. Finally, the chapter will address, on the one hand, the implications of labour market exclusion and the problems of unemployment and worklessness in developed economies; and on the other, the disadvantages associated with informality and the exclusion from regulated forms of labour that may be experienced in emerging economies. Though the principal emphasis will be on trends within the post-industrial economies of the global north, attention will be paid to the relevance for the global south.

9.1 Formalization and Wage Labour under Capitalism

The story this chapter tells revolves around the way that wage labour as a specific form of work has been socially and historically constituted.

9.1.1 *Work and Labour*

In their different ways, Aristotle (*c.*350 BCE), Karl Marx (1844), and Hannah Arendt (1958) attempted, respectively, to encapsulate a notion of work as *praxis* (active engagement), as *stoffwechsel* (metabolism with nature), or as *vita activa* (active life); as something constitutive of 'a good life', of the essence of our 'species being', or of 'the human condition'; as activity undertaken for its own sake and/or that has intrinsic rather than market value. Socially reproductive work—caring for others, creative endeavour, studying, civic engagement—may be valued at least as highly as necessary productive activity, or labour. The patrician elites and ruling orders of pre-modern eras prized creativity and public participation above the kinds of onerous but indispensable physical labour that could be imposed upon disadvantaged slaves or serfs. The rise of industrial capitalism portended, supposedly, an eventual end to slavery and serfdom through the *commodification* of labour. It should be noted, however, that there are still throughout the world approaching 36 million people who are subject to 'modern' slavery—a concept encompassing such practices as human trafficking, debt bondage, servile marriage, and forced labour (Global Slavery Index, 2014).

Though Polanyi (1944) declared that labour was but a 'fictitious' commodity and the ILO (1944) insisted it was not a commodity at all, the formal essence of the wage relationship is that the worker freely contracts to sell her or his labour as if it were a commodity, albeit under market conditions that will most often be to the advantage of the employer rather than the employee and that may disproportionately disadvantage some workers more than others. With the incorporation of human activity into formal market processes and the burgeoning and diversification of industrial production, the compass and significance of 'labour'—both manual and non-manual—expanded, albeit at the expense of socially reproductive activity, which, if it could not itself be commodified, was no longer constituted or acknowledged as 'work'. The embedding of the capitalist market economy into the fabric of social life had far-reaching implications, especially for gender divisions, as will be discussed in Chapter 11.

There is evidence that people around the world regard 'work' as a moral obligation; and as one of life's central life activities—alongside, but nonetheless *distinct* from, familial, community, religious, and leisure activities (MOW International Research Team, 1987). For some workers wage labour does indeed bring a range of advantages. Most obviously it provides income. It can also be a source of identity, self-esteem, and social networks. It provides or represents the organizational framework for our daily lives (Glucksmann, 1995; Jahoda, 1982). But it is also the case, as we shall see, that the income work provides may not be sufficient; some forms of work may be degrading, socially isolating, stressful, or dangerous; work can encroach upon and disrupt family life and other forms of social engagement (Mooney, 2004; Noon and Blyton, 2007). Paid labour can be inherently alienating when it instils or foments a sense of social *anomie* (Durkheim, 1893) or when it alienates the worker from the product of her labour and/or from 'work' in the wider and deeper senses variously implied, as we have seen, by Aristotle, Marx, and Arendt.

9.1.2 *Labour Market Change*

Since industrial capitalism shaped our understanding of work as a form of paid labour, the world of work has been changing. At its height, industrial capitalism conformed to what has been described as the Fordist paradigm (Gilbert et al., 1992). This represented the apogee of the factory system and of mass production for mass markets. It brought a modicum of relative affluence to elements within the traditional working class (Goldthorpe et al., 1968). However, the transition from industrial to post-industrial capitalism that followed entailed a number of intersecting components. Centralized production of standardized products gave way to decentralized forms of production of diverse products for a variety of markets. At the same time there was a concerted shift away from manufacturing towards 'tertiary' service sector industries; and, by the end of the twentieth century, the burgeoning of new information technologies and the growth of the 'knowledge economy'. Such change was accelerated by economic globalization, increased capital mobility, and the ascendancy of powerful transnational corporations able to invest selectively wherever labour is cheap or most adaptable (Held and McGrew, 2007).

For workers in the global north, these processes have had a number of effects bearing on the distribution of advantage and disadvantage. The relative advantage that once accrued to many non-manual 'lower middle-class' workers was eroded as routine non-manual service sector labour become increasingly routinized or 'proletarianized' (Braverman, 1974). Simultaneously, the relatively privileged socio-economic stratum once represented by the professional 'upper middle-class' salariat began to be augmented as new high-tech and financial service occupations emerged, creating a relatively privileged service or 'profician' class (Standing, 2009). The distinction that mattered was no longer between manual and non-manual labour, but between routinized and relatively poorly rewarded jobs—sometimes caricatured as 'McJobs' and 'MacJobs': the former supposedly typified by the working environment in the McDonalds restaurant chain (Ritzer, 2004); the latter by working environments in which the latest Apple Macintosh computers are designed, developed, and used (Goos and Manning, 2003). The 'New Capitalism' thereby ushered in has been driven, according to some commentators, by neo-liberal orthodoxies favouring financialization, deregulation, and new modes of corporate management (Doogan, 2009). Changes in the ways that workplaces are managed have, according to critics, transformed the nature of the work ethic and the culture of the workplace, corroding the very 'character' of work (Sennett, 1998). Central to this 'corrosion' has been a trend towards 'flexibilization'; a term that captures the way in which the costs of accommodating the labour process to fluctuations in market conditions began to shift the balance of power and rewards between capital and labour (Gough, 2000). In the Fordist era the consequences of short-term fluctuations in demand could be accommodated by maintaining a degree of slack within established workforce levels. But in the post-Fordist and information eras enterprises have been accommodating to ever more rapid shifts in market conditions by reserving a capacity to hire and fire at short notice; to stand-down expendable workers, but to develop and re-deploy the skills of essential workers; to incentivize workers using performance-maximizing techniques, so as to manage returns from 'human capital' (see Chapter 4, this volume).

For workers in the global south, the era of post-colonial global capitalism has fuelled new inequalities both between and within nation states. The key to capitalist economic development is the evolution of formal labour markets; the emergence of paid labour as the dominant medium for the maintenance of human livelihoods. Critics maintain that in some instances this has amounted to a damaging or distorted form of 'development' (Escobar, 2012; Midgley, 2013). Competitive global markets can exacerbate the relative advantages and disadvantages in the labour market conditions experienced by workers in different parts of the world. And *within* developing countries, a dysfunctional divide can be created between workers in the formal and informal economies; between urban and rural areas; between relative privilege enjoyed by those with access to a formal labour market and the chronically unstable livelihoods for those without.

9.2 Advantage and Disadvantage within the Labour Market

We turn now to consider issues affecting the relative advantages and disadvantages experienced by workers engaged *within* the formal labour market: their security and status; the terms and conditions of their employment; and the skills required of them.

9.2.1 *Security and Status*

We have already alluded to the ways in which the changing nature of labour markets affected the basis of class divisions. But it also affected workers' fundamental expectations of what it means to have a 'job'. In the post-Second-World-War Western world, the imaginary 'standard' job was something men did for forty hours a week, for forty years—working to maintain their wives and families, and probably working for the same employer throughout their working lives. Women, it was imagined, in between home-making and child-rearing, might take 'non-standard' or 'atypical' jobs, that would be part-time and/or temporary. The real world even then was different, albeit not so different as it has now become (Lewis, 2000, 2002). During the second half of the twentieth century labour markets not only opened their doors to women, but the norm of the 'standard' job receded, along with the classic demarcations between manual and non-manual labour and the idea that anybody could expect a job for life. The gradual emergence within post-industrial capitalist economies of dual 'core and peripheral' labour markets was captured in the popular vernacular as a distinction between 'career jobs and crap jobs' (Lloyd, 1999).

The reality is more complex. Insofar as the trends in question have global implications, Guy Standing (2011) presents a primarily heuristic analysis wherein he detects the advent of a new global class, the 'precariat': a systemically disadvantaged class increasingly distanced from, above them, a rapidly shrinking traditional unionized working class, the emerging 'proficians' and the established professional salariat, and the tiny but all-powerful global elite at the top of the class order; and yet distinguishable from, below them, the permanently unemployed and an underclass he characterizes as the 'detached'. We might question Standing's theoretical conceptualizations of class and whether the real significance of job insecurity has more to with people's manufactured fears and uncertainties than with substantive trends (Doogan, 2009). Nevertheless, there is a chronically precarious stratum of workers within some post-industrial labour markets, with restricted skills and opportunities and dwindling rights; a stratum amongst whom many are likely to experience a succession of low paid short-term jobs at the labour market periphery, interspersed with spells of unemployment and who are thereby vulnerable to entrapment in a 'low pay/no pay cycle' (Capellari and Jenkins, 2008; McKnight, 2002; Shildrick et al., 2012).

If we take the incidence of short-term job tenure as a measure of vulnerability or *precarité*, it may be seen from the illustrative data in Table 9.1 that this varies quite widely between countries, but would appear to be especially marked in the US on the one hand and in certain emerging economies—Mexico and Turkey—on the other. In Britain, a report by a Commission on Vulnerable Employment established by the Trades Union Congress, defined vulnerable employment as 'Precarious work that places people at risk of continuing poverty and injustice resulting from an imbalance of power in the employer-worker relationship' (TUC Commission on Vulnerable Employment, 2008: 11). Though well-rewarded jobs can also be insecure (Pahl, 1995), insecurity in the labour market is most often associated with other disadvantages relating to terms and conditions of employment.

9.2.2 Terms and Conditions

The first of these disadvantages is low pay. An earlier report for the TUC had estimated, controversially, that around one in five UK workers could be described as 'vulnerable' insofar as their pay was in the bottom third of the hourly income distribution and was not determined by union agreement (Policy Studies Institute, 2006; and see Pollert and Charlwood, 2009). Low pay is most commonly relatively defined as a wage level falling beneath some set proportion of average wages (see Table 9.2). Relatively defined, low pay may be regarded as an ordinary feature of any labour market. What is more, wages need not be the only source of income for an individual or a household. Nevertheless, paid employment is a substantial contributor to general household income levels (e.g. ONS, 2014), and wage inequality contributes to the income inequalities discussed in Chapter 7 of this volume; inequalities that have increasingly well recognized consequences for general social well-being (Dorling, 2010; Wilkinson and Pickett, 2009).

The illustrative dispersion of earnings data shown in Table 9.1 demonstrate differing degrees of wage inequality in different countries, but it appears to be higher in the Anglophone countries (US and UK) and emerging economies

Table 9.1. Selected comparative labour market data

	Employment rate % (2013)	Unemployment rate % (2013)	Youth unemployment rate % (2013)	Long-term unemployment rate % (2013)	Incidence of job-tenure of less than 1 Year % (2013)	Earnings dispersion: 9th to 1st decile ratio (2012)	Quality of working environment ranking/32 countries (2005)
Germany	73.3	5.4	7.9	44.7	13.6	3.26	19th
Japan	71.7	4.3	6.9	41.2	no data	2.99	20th
UK	71.3	7.8	20.9	36.3	15.1	3.55	9th
USA	67.4	7.5	15.5	25.9	21.7 (2012 data)	5.22	13th
France	64.1	9.9	23.9	40.4	12.3	2.97	23rd
Mexico	61.0	5.2	9.2	1.5	21.4	3.67	15th
Italy	56.4	12.4	40.0	56.9	9.1	2.32	21st
Turkey	49.5	9.9	18.7	24.4	25.6	3.80	32nd

Source: OECD Employment Outlook (2014)

Table 9.2. Low Pay in Britain

	Definition	Level in 2012 £ per hour	Percentage of employees 2012
Extreme low pay	Hourly wages below one-half of gross median hourly pay for all employees	5.58	2
Low Pay	Wages below two-thirds of gross median hourly pay for all employees (This threshold approximates to the 'decency threshold' set by the Council of Europe before the definition was changed in 2004)	7.44	21
Non-Living Wage	Wages below: • the living wage level set for London by the Greater London Authority, *or*	8.30	20
	• the living wage set for the rest of the UK by Centre for Research in Social Policy, University of Loughborough	7.20	

Source: Based on analysis from ONS data by Whittaker and Hurrell (2013)

(Mexico and Turkey) than in others. Generally speaking, earnings dispersion has been widening at an accelerating rate since around the 1980s (e.g. Hills, 2004: ch. 4) partly, it is supposed, because of increasing skill differentials (see Section 9.2.3); partly, as a consequence of economic globalization and the trends we have already discussed. The longer-term trend towards widening wage dispersion has also been associated on the one hand with the declining power of trade unions (Weeks, 2005) and on the other with dramatic increases in rewards claimed by the highest paid earners. In the UK, for example, between 1986 and 2011, the average equivalent hourly pay of the top 1 per cent of earners rose by 117 per cent (to £61.10 per hour); two and a half times faster than the average hourly pay of the bottom 10 per cent of earners, which rose only 47 per cent (to just £7.01 per hour) (ONS, 2013).

Most recently, during the global recession of 2008–13, real wages for the lowest paid—that is the net purchasing power of their earnings—actually fell throughout much of the developed world (Blanchflower and Machin, 2014; OECD, 2014). The implications at the very bottom of the earnings distribution could be dire as in countries like Britain numbers of the working poor were driven to resort to the use of food banks run by charities (Lambie-Mumford, 2013; O'Hara, 2014). However, the phenomenon of in-work poverty in affluent countries is hardly new (Ehrenreich, 2002; Marx and Nolan, 2012; Toynbee, 2003). The question of how low wages must be to constitute 'poverty wages' takes us back to debates we considered in Chapter 1. An alternative to relative definitions of low pay are definitions based on estimations of what might constitute a 'living wage'. Such an approach has been attempted, for example, by campaigns in Britain (Bennett and Lister, 2010), where the

Greater London Assembly has promoted a London-wide voluntary scheme whereby employers are encouraged to pay a minimum 'living wage'. There is a campaign for a similar nationwide scheme (http://www.livingwage.org.uk; and see Table 9.2). Such schemes are only voluntary. Governments, however, by regulatory intervention can and do play a role in determining the extent to which labour markets create relative advantage and disadvantage. Policy-makers were originally motivated—in the words of Winston Churchill, when President of the British Government's Board of Trade in 1909—by concerns that otherwise 'the good employers are undercut by the bad, and the bad are undercut by the worst' (cited in Howell, 2005: 69).

The British government, abandoned its system of wage regulation in the 1980s, but reinstated a statutory minimum wage in 1999. By 2012 this stood at £6.99 per hour for adults (with lower rates for young people) (Whittaker and Hurrell, 2013). As may be seen from Table 9.2, though this was above the 'extreme low pay' level, it was beneath the level of the so called European Decency Threshold and both the London and the UK living wage thresholds. Worldwide, over 190 countries fix minimum wages (ILO, 2012), though the rates set and methods of enforcement are highly variable. Opponents of statutory minimum wages assert either that such schemes increase unemploy-ment, or else that they inhibit wage growth. Their actual effects are more complex (e.g. Coates, 2007). There are at least a dozen countries that address low wages by means of state-funded wage top-up schemes for low paid workers (Dean, 2012). These may range from means-tested in-work cash transfer schemes to refundable tax credits. They provide an incentive to workers to take low-paid jobs, but in the process may perpetuate low-waged peripheral labour markets and the disadvantage with which these are associated.

In less developed countries low wages are even more likely to be directly associated with disadvantage, as may be seen from the working poverty indicators shown later in this chapter in Table 9.3. In regions such as South Asia and sub-Saharan Africa more than half of those who are able to engage in paid labour are still living on less than $2 a day.

Disadvantage in the labour market may be associated not only with low pay, but low job quality. The ILO (1999) upholds the importance of 'decent work', premised on rights and international standards (see Dean, 2015: ch. 6). There is legal provision—dating back in some instances to the nineteenth century in more than 120 countries worldwide (ILO, 2009) for the regulation of health and safety at work, though enforcement may be lax and provision generally addresses risks only to physical health, rather than the hazards occasioned by work that is mentally or emotionally stressful. Nevertheless, there are some restrictions in over 100 countries on working hours (Lee et al., 2007). The European Union Working Time Directive provides for a maximum 48-hour week, from which individual employees may opt out—as they may often be

Table 9.3. Vulnerable employment and in-work poverty in global perspective

	Vulnerable employment shares (%)			Working poor indicators (share in employment, %)	
	2013 estimate			2013 estimate	
	Total	Male	Female	Less than $1.25 a day	Less than $2 a day
Developed economies	10.0	11.3	8.3	–	–
Central/SE Europe and CIS	19.2	19.1	19.3	1.0	3.6
East Asia	45.8	42.3	50.3	5.2	13.5
SE Asia and Pacific	59.0	56.0	63.1	11.2	30.5
South Asia	76.1	74.4	80.9	24.6	61.5
Latin America and Caribbean	31.6	31.6	31.6	3.0	6.7
Middle East	25.2	23.7	33.2	1.1	7.4
North Africa	35.6	30.2	54.7	3.0	14.2
Sub-Saharan Africa	77.4	70.5	85.5	39.2	62.8

Source: ILO *Global Employment Trends* (2014)

implicitly or explicitly required to do by their employers. The issue here is the extent to which workers have choice or control over the hours they work. While some workers may be subject to an exhausting long-hours culture, others as we shall shortly see may be prevented from working as many hours as they might wish. Critical to the quality of work is the quality of the working environment (OECD, 2014: 102–14). Occupational health is affected on the one hand by 'job *demands*' (e.g. work load, time pressures, etc.) and on the other by 'job *resources*' (e.g. the degree of autonomy and amount of support workers have). These can—up to a point—be measured and used to compile a job strain index. The illustrative data presented in Table 9.1 include country rankings relating to scores using one such index, according to which the UK and US appear to outrank France, Germany, Italy, and Japan. But this conceals different patterns in the contribution made by different components of the index. The UK and US ranking on the job resources component is more favourable than on the job demands component, whereas the French, German, Italian, and Japanese ranking on the demands component is more favourable than on the resources component. There is evidence that allowing workers greater autonomy enables them better to cope with high levels of work intensity (Gallie and Zhou, 2013) and such an assumption may perhaps specifically inform Anglophone management cultures.

As important (perhaps more important) to the well-being of workers than the strain of their jobs when they are at work is the relationship between their jobs and the rest of their lives; between paid work and unpaid work; between labour and social reproduction. The changes in the functioning and character of labour markets that have occurred in the past few decades have altered the dynamics of the interface between 'work', family, and recreational activity. It has been suggested that it is changes in the household economy that may hold the key to the future shape of post-industrial society (Esping-Andersen, 1999), though in many ways it may be seen that household survival strategies have necessarily been adapting to the flexibilization of labour markets (Dean and Shah, 2002). Since the 1990s, policymakers in the global north have been driven to facilitate some mutual accommodation between labour markets and household living and earning strategies, by introducing extended parental leave schemes, the enhancement of childcare and the promotion of 'family friendly' employment practices (Kröger and Yeandle, 2014; Lewis, 2006; and see Chapter 11, this volume). What is clear, however, is that so far as employers are concerned, there may be a business case for work-life balance or work-family reconciliation policies and practices where these assist the retention of valued professional and skilled workers, but none at all when it comes to expendable low-skilled workers (Dean, 2002). In practice flexible employment arrangements can work to the advantage of some workers, but to the disadvantage of others.

9.2.3 *Skills*

The changing structure of labour markets is directly reflected in changes in the nature of the skills required of workers and the relative advantage or disadvantages experienced by workers with different skills. Polarization is directly related to skills; with high knowledge-based skills dominating the core of the labour market and low routine-based skills dominating the extensive labour market periphery (Gallie, 1991). An alternative to the core-periphery metaphor is the 'hour glass' metaphor illustrated in Figure 9.1. Middle-range and craft-based skills declined in significance and it might be argued that just as the meaning of 'work' has narrowed over time so has our appreciation of skills. It is narrowly defined technical skills that are valued and, according to Standing (2009), the idea of workers being defined by their 'occupation' has been eclipsed by the narrower idea of them simply holding a *job*.

Chapter 6 has already addressed the role that education systems play in the development and distribution of skills, including the skills required for labour market participation. Historically, vocational training had been achieved through apprenticeship systems, some of which dated back to the time of the mediaeval guilds. In the industrial era these evolved into self-regulated systems administered by employers, in consultation with trades unions. Apprenticeship entailed a process of occupational socialization in addition to practical training and the acquisition of technical knowledge and skills. In the post-industrial era, however, there has been a tendency for the state to become increasingly involved in regulating and subsidizing vocational

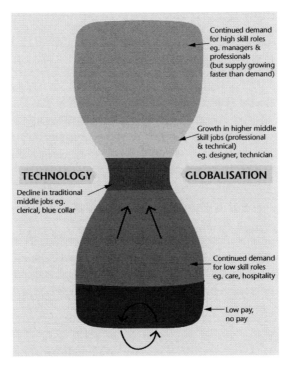

Within the figure:

Continued demand for high skill roles eg. managers & professionals (but supply growing faster than demand)

Growth in higher middle skill jobs (professional & technical) eg. designer, technician

TECHNOLOGY

GLOBALISATION

Decline in traditional middle jobs eg. clerical, blue collar

Continued demand for low skill roles eg. care, hospitality

Low pay, no pay

Figure 9.1. The future shape of the labour market

Source: UKCES (2014) *The Labour Market Story: An Overview*. UK Commission for Employment and Skills, Wath-upon-Dearne. Reproduced with the kind permission of the UKCES. Available at <https://www.gov.uk/government/publications/skills-and-employment-in-the-uk-the-labour-market-story>

training schemes; schemes structured around prescribed qualifications frameworks; but which generally entail far shorter training periods and the acquisition of lower-level skills than under traditional apprenticeship models (Ainley, 1999; Steedman, 2011). An emerging interest in the concept of 'lifelong learning' (see http://www.uil.unesco.org) reflects the extent to which the boundaries between governmental and employer responsibilities, between education and training, and between academic and vocational skills acquisition are being redrawn. The concept chimes with an emphasis on the responsibility of individuals to foster appropriate skills and promote their own 'employability' (McQuaid and Lindsay, 2005).

The preoccupation of policymakers in an era of supply-side economics has been to facilitate the 'upskilling' of key segments within the labour force in order to meet the demands of the labour market. However, a recent report based on a Survey of Adult Skills (OECD, 2013), conducted in twenty-four developed countries, concluded that:

- In most countries—including some with well-developed education systems—there were significant proportions of adults who scored at the lowest level of proficiency on literacy and numeracy scales.
- In nearly all countries at least 10 per cent of adults lacked the most elementary computer skills, while low proportions (between 3 and 9 per cent) of adults demonstrated the highest levels of proficiency on the problem-solving in a technology-rich environment scale.
- Overall, 21 per cent of workers were over-qualified and 13 per cent were underqualified for their jobs.
- Skills have a major impact on individual life chances, and inequality in skills is associated with inequality in income.

The OECD suggests that the removal of regulatory obstacles to labour market flexibility, improved career guidance services, and more transparent qualifications frameworks might better enable workers' skills to be aligned with employers' requirements. This is to an extent already consistent with a trend identified by Standing, who controversially suggests that responsibility for training is being transferred to the market 'leaving the state to play a passive facilitating or legitimating role . . . [while] removing a worker's control over skills' (2009: 135). In the meantime, according to one European employers' organization (VOB/FEB cited in Hancké, 2012), although three-quarters of employers agree that more investment in skills is needed, 9 out of 10 are themselves no longer investing in skills training. In some instances, employers may recruit appropriately skilled migrants rather than invest in skills training (see Chapter 13, this volume). Other recent evidence, however, suggests that skills training in Europe may in fact have survived the recent recession, with some attention being paid to the development of both low-skill and high-skill workers (Dieckhoff, 2013), albeit in the context of a continuing destruction of intermediary level jobs (Gallie, 2013).

9.3 Labour Market Exclusion

Insofar as 'work' equates with paid labour, 'worklessness' for people of 'working age' is likely to be associated with disadvantage and, in the UK, for example, workless households are twice as likely as other households to be in poverty (DWP, 2014: 62). Children and older people adjudged not to be of 'working age' may be disadvantaged because they are excluded from paid labour. Childhood and retirement are socially constructed concepts. In different eras children in the global north might well have been expected to contribute their labour from an early age (Gittens, 1993) and in parts of the global south they still are (Edmonds and Pavcnik, 2005). Similarly the concept of retirement as a 'kind of mass redundancy' (Townsend, 1991: 6) is a relatively modern invention. But children can be disadvantaged by their parents' worklessness, while older people who lack either family support or a decent pension can similarly be disadvantaged (see Chapters 5 and 10, this volume).

'Worklessness' is therefore a term reserved for those whom society might otherwise expect to work, but are either 'economically inactive' or unemployed. To be a student, a full-time parent or carer, or a long-term sick or disabled person who does not or cannot undertake paid labour is to be counted as economically inactive. The category might also encompass so-called 'discouraged workers', who are not otherwise counted as unemployed because they are not seeking paid work. To be classified as unemployed—by the widely used ILO definition—a person of working age must be available to start paid work within two weeks and have been actively looking for paid work within the past four weeks. It will be seen in later chapters that exclusion from paid work may compound the disadvantages associated with a range of other inequalities. At the same time, those who are unpaid or working unseen in the informal economy though they are not workless by these definitions, may nonetheless suffer the disadvantages of worklessness.

9.3.1 *Employment and Unemployment*

Insofar as paid employment is regarded as good for adult members of society and unemployment as bad, employment and unemployment rates are widely regarded as measures of economic health or weakness. If we return to Table 9.1 above, it may be seen that employment rates—the proportion of people of working age who are engaged in paid labour vary, even between countries within the OECD, from approaching three-quarters, to around half. Unemployment rates—based on the ILO definition—vary between a level around 5 or 6 per cent, which some economists would regard as the 'natural' rate of unemployment (e.g. Friedman, 1968) to over 12 per cent. The data in Table 9.1 are from 2013 when developed countries were recovering from the global recession that had begun in 2008 and the economies in Germany and Japan appear to have been resilient; the UK and US, though employment appeared reasonably resilient were suffering higher rates of unemployment; France and Italy, though they are both high-income countries, remained badly affected; Mexico and Turkey—both middle-income countries with significant informal sectors—fared differently, though Mexico appears to have had a more resilient formal sector.

Certain workers are at particular risk of unemployment: those with lower-level skills, as we have seen; disabled people (Roulstone and Barnes, 2005); certain minority ethnic groups (see Chapter 12, this volume). Of particular significance in terms of the disadvantages that may result from labour market exclusion are youth unemployment on the one hand, and long-term unemployment (which may disproportionately affect older workers) on the other. Youth unemployment rates (generally measured in terms of the proportion of 16–24 year olds, excluding students, who are unemployed) have tended in recent times to run as much as twice the level of adult unemployment rates. This is a consequence of labour market restructuring. Whereas in developed countries in the 1970s the majority of young people leaving school would go straight into a job, this began to change as traditional entry-level jobs declined and as competition for peripheral labour market jobs increased. The transition from school to work, for many young people, became more protracted or complex (Coles, 1995; O'Higgins, 2001), not least because a significant minority could become trapped in the status that has become widely defined at NEET—not in employment, education, or training (e.g. ILO, 2013).

Long-term unemployment (the rate of which is generally measured in terms of the proportion of unemployed people who have been out of work for more than 12 months) tends to be somewhat lower in countries with the most flexible labour markets, such as the UK and the US, but appears intransigently high in some established economies (see illustrative data in Table 9.1). The enduring disadvantages attributed to long-term unemployment are 'scarring' (Arulampalam et al., 2001), on the one hand, and 'welfare dependency' (Mead, 1997; Murray, 1994; Social Justice Policy Group, 2006) on the other. The term 'scarring' refers to the long-term effects of unemployment, not only in terms of workers' own loss of motivation, skills, and confidence, but also in terms of employers' perceptions of, and prejudices towards, people who have been out of the labour market for an extended period. Welfare dependency is a term used by a variety of commentators who fear that the provision of unemployment benefits acts as a disincentive to work and adds to workers' demotivation, so compounding their disadvantage. The evidence that generous unemployment benefits adversely affect employment incentives has been questioned (Atkinson and Micklewright, 1991; Dean and Taylor-Gooby, 1992), but the issue of incentives continues to dominate the debate about labour market flexibilization.

9.3.2 Underemployment

While flexibilization may effectively increase labour market participation and so minimize unemployment, it may do so by promoting underemployment. Underemployment can take several forms, including involuntary part-time work, self-employment, or zero-hours contract work. Such employment patterns may suit many workers, depending on their life-styles and living arrangements, but for others they represent the only alternative to unemployment: they are in effect partially excluded from the labour market. Currently, in the UK for example:

- Around 27 per cent of the labour force works part-time, of whom a quarter would like to work more hours (ONS, 2012).

- Around 1 in 7 of the labour force is formally self-employed, of whom, research suggests, 27 per cent have taken on self-employment for lack of an alternative. Self-employed workers earn 40 per cent less than those working for an employer (D'Arcy and Gardiner, 2014).

- Around 19 per cent of employers make some use of zero-hours contracts (under which employees do not have fixed or guaranteed working hours). Of the employees working under such contracts, research suggests that 75 per cent were working variable hours and 25 per cent said they would like to work more hours (Brinkley, 2013).

Underemployment can affect not only individuals, but households. Not only do workless households face a high risk of poverty, but increasingly the risk of poverty in households in which there is only one adult member in paid employment is greater than for households with more than one (e.g. DWP, 2014). Research on household survival strategies suggests that in some communities, in households in which one adult member is connected with the labour market it is more likely that through the social networks and local knowledge this generates, other adult members will find paid work, thus generating a degree of polarization between 'work-rich' and 'work-poor' households within a local neighbourhood (Pahl, 1988). Long-term trends in labour market participation have tended to exacerbate this polarization as in many post-industrial economies dual and one-and-a-half earner households have become the social norm, compounding the relative disadvantage attaching to labour market detachment in households whose adult members are excluded from paid employment, for example, through lack of affordable childcare, disability, or poor skills (Berthoud, 2007; Lewis, 2002; and see Chapter 11, this volume).

9.3.3 Precarité *and Vulnerability*

Precarité (Bordieu, 1998) or risk (Beck, 1992) are, supposedly, the defining features of the prevailing era and this plays out in the ways that advantage and disadvantage accrue in the world of work, albeit differently in different contexts. In the global north, it might be argued, policy intervention is calculated to sustain a degree of *precarité*, while in much of the global south it is an absence of effective intervention that ensures the survival of *precarité* or particular vulnerabilities to risk.

Mention was made in Chapter 1 in this volume of a hegemonic social inclusion discourse (SID) identified by Ruth Levitas (1996, 1998). This is a discourse that equates social inclusion with labour market inclusion; not simply in the sense that wage labour is central to the social relations of production under capitalism, but in the sense that in the post-industrial era it is labour supply, not labour demand, that must be managed. Supply-side labour market policies have emerged under a variety of labels: workfare, welfare-to-work, labour market activation, flexicurity (Lødemel and Trickey, 2000; Peck, 2001; Serrano and Keune, 2014). It has already been suggested that the function—whether immanent or explicitly intended—was to accommodate labour to the competitive risks and requirements associated with a new and dynamic form of capitalism: a capitalism that needed not only flexibly skilled workers to meet the technical challenges of the information age, but cheap and flexibly motivated workers to provide the abundant lower-tech goods and services upon which the new capitalism also depends. A raft of policies can serve such ends, including policies that fuel competition for lower-skill, low-paid peripheral labour market jobs: policies that entail not only carrots, such as low-wage top-ups and child-care subsidies; but sticks, such as benefits sanctions and compulsory work or training placements. The effect for the least advantaged workers can be to make life perennially risky and precarious.

In the global south, risk and disadvantage stem from informality, including the absence of social protection. Though social assistance provision through various forms of conditional cash transfer schemes are developing (Leisering and Barrientos, 2013) in a range of emerging and lower-income economies, the extent of social insurance for formally employed workers remains limited in many countries. Unemployment protection is available to only 38 per cent of the labour force across Latin America, 21 per cent in the Middle East, 17 per cent in Asia Pacific, and 8 per cent in Africa (ILO, 2014b). This and other forms of protection are not available to people working in the informal sector; working on their own account or unpaid within their families. Using a different conception of 'vulnerability' to that of the TUC in the UK (see Section 9.2.1), the ILO define such work as vulnerable employment and estimate that over half of all workers in the developing world are trapped in such work (see Table 9.3).

9.4 Conclusion

This chapter, in common with others in this book, has sought to locate disadvantage in the context of advantage. In the case of divisions of labour and work, this has firstly entailed a discussion of the distinction between labour and work. If work is regarded as something that is an essential and inherently life-affirming human activity, it is *more* than labour. The wage labourer may in this sense be systemically disadvantaged if she is alienated from her work. However, the capitalist wage labour system can undoubtedly bestow advantages on workers. In the process of harnessing material resources and human skills it provides a mechanism—for the distribution of incomes and rewards; for the organization of social relations; for the realization of human potential and, for the more fortunate, human fulfilment. But it can disadvantage people, on the one hand, by restricting access to or, alternatively, devaluing or disrupting useful or morally meaningful forms of work; and on the other, through the manner of its exploitation of labour. Though social policy can mitigate such effects, the rewards that labour markets offer are not necessarily proportionate; their organization of social relations can be sometimes oppressive; and they often fail optimally to realize human potential.

The chapter has considered how it is that people who are engaged with labour markets can experience relative disadvantage in respect of pay and conditions of employment and how they may be vulnerable because they lack social protection. The chapter has also considered how in a world where wage labour is the dominant form of work, those who are excluded from wage labour may be systematically disadvantaged.

References

Ainley, P. (1999). *Learning Policy: Towards the Certified Society*. Basingstoke: Macmillan.

Arendt, H. (1958). *The Human Condition*. Chicago: Chicago University Press.

Aristotle. (*c.*350 BCE). *Eudemian Ethics,* Books I, II, and VIII (1982 edn. translated by M. Woods). Oxford: Clarendon Press.

Arulampalam, W., Gregg, P., and Gregory, M. (2001). 'Unemployment Scarring'. *Economic Journal*, 111(November): F577–84.

Atkinson, A. and Micklewright, J. (1991). 'Unemployment Compensation and Labour Market Transitions: A Critical Review'. *Journal of Economic Literature*, 29(1): 679–727.

Beck, U. (1992). *Risk Society: Towards a New Modernity*. London: Sage.

Bennett, F. and Lister, R. (2010). *The 'Living Wage': The Right Answer to Low Pay?* London: The Fabian Society.

Berthoud, R. (2007). *Work-rich and Work-poor: Three Decades of Change*. Bristol: The Policy Press/Joseph Rowntree Foundation.

Blanchflower, D. and Machin, S. (2014). 'Falling Real Wages'. *CentrePiece* (Spring): 19–21.

Bordieu, P. (1998). 'La precarité est ajourd'hui partout'. In P. Bordieu (ed.), *Contre-feux*. Paris: Raisons d'agir.

Braverman, H. (1974). *Labor and Monopoly Capital*. New York: Monthly Review Press.

Brinkley, I. (2013). *Flexibility or Insecurity? Exploring the Rise in Zero-hours Contracts.* London: The Work Foundation.

Capellari, L. and Jenkins, S. (2008). 'Transitions between Unemployment and Low Pay'. In S. Polachek and C. Tatsiramos (eds), *Work, Earnings and Other Aspects of the Employment Relation—Research in Labor Economics.* Vol. 28 (pp. 57–79). Bingley, UK: Emerald Group Publishing.

Coates, D. (2007). *The National Minimum Wage: Retrospective and Prospect.* London: The Work Foundation.

Coles, B. (1995). *Youth and Social Policy.* London: UCL Press.

D'Arcy, C. and Gardiner, L. (2014). *Just the Job—or a Working Compromise? The Changing Nature of Self-employment in the UK.* London: The Resolution Foundation.

Dean, H. (2002). 'Business versus Families: Whose Side Is New Labour on?' *Social Policy and Society*, 1(1): 3–10.

Dean, H. (2012). 'Welcome Relief or Indecent Subsidy? The Implications of Wage Top-up Schemes'. *Policy and Politics*, 40(3): 305–21.

Dean, H. (2015). *Social Rights and Human Welfare.* Abingdon: Routledge.

Dean, H. and Shah, A. (2002). 'Insecure Families and Low-paying Labour Markets: Comments on the British Experience'. *Journal of Social Policy*, 31(1): 61–80.

Dean, H. and Taylor-Gooby, P. (1992). *Dependency Culture: The Explosion of a Myth.* Hemel Hempstead: Harvester Wheatsheaf.

Department for Work and Pensions (DWP). (2014). *Households Below Average Income: An analysis of the income distribution 1994/95–2012/13.* London: DWP.

Dieckhoff, M. (2013). 'Continuing Training in Times of Economic Crisis'. In D. Gallie (ed.), *Economic Crisis, Quality of Work, and Social Integration.* Oxford: Oxford University Press.

Doogan, K. (2009). *New Capitalism? The Transformation of Work.* Cambridge: Polity.

Dorling, D. (2010). *Injustice: Why Social Inequality Persists.* Bristol: The Policy Press.

Durkheim, E. (1893). *The Social Division of Labour* (1964 edn.). New York: Free Press.

Edmonds, E. and Pavcnik, N. (2005). 'Child Labor in the Global Economy'. *Journal of Economic Perspectives*, 19(1): 199–220.

Ehrenreich, B. (2002). *Nickel and Dimed: Undercover in Low-wage USA.* London: Bloomsbury.

Escobar, A. (2012). *Encountering Development: The Making and Unmaking of the Third World.* 2nd edn. Princeton, NJ: Princeton University Press.

Esping-Andersen, G. (1999). *The Social Foundations of Post-Industrial Economies.* Oxford: Oxford University Press.

Friedman, M. (1968). 'The Role of Monetary Policy'. *American Economic Review*, 58(1): 1–17.

Gallie, D. (1991). 'Patterns of Skill Change: Upskilling, De-skilling or the Polarisation of Skills?' *Work, Employment and Society*, 5(3): 319–51.

Gallie, D. (2013). 'Economic Crisis, Country Variations and Institutional Structures'. In D. Gallie (ed.), *Economic Crisis, Quality of Work, and Social Integration.* Oxford: Oxford University Press.

Gallie, D. and Zhou, Y. (2013). 'Job Control, Work Intensity and Work Stress'. In D. Gallie (ed.), *Economic Crisis, Quality of Work and Social Integration.* Oxford: Oxford University Press.

Gilbert, N., Burrows, R., and Pollert, A. (eds) (1992). *Fordism and Flexibility: Divisions and Change*. Basingstoke: Macmillan.

Gittens, D. (1993). *The Family in Question*. 2nd edn. Basingstoke: Macmillan.

Global Slavery Index. (2014). *The Global Slavery Index 2014*. Claremont, Western Australia: Help for Children Organisation.

Glucksmann, M. (1995). 'Why "Work"? Gender and the "Total Social Organisation of Labour"'. *Gender, Work and Organisation*, 2(2): 63–75.

Goldthorpe, J., Lockwood, J., Bechoffer, F., and Platt, J. (1968). *The Affluent Worker: Industrial Attitudes and Behaviour*. Cambridge: Cambridge University Press.

Goos, M. and Manning, A. (2003). 'McJobs and MacJobs: The Growing Polarisation of Jobs in the UK'. In R. Dickens, P. Gregg, and J. Wadsworth (eds), *The Labour Market Under New Labour*. Basingstoke: Palgrave Macmillan.

Gough, I. (2000). *Global Capital, Human Needs and Social Policies*. Basingstoke: Palgrave.

Hancké, B. (2012). '9 out of 10 European Employers Are no longer Investing in Training', <http://eprints.lse.ac.uk/45902/1/blogs.lse.ac.uk-9_out_of_10_European_employers_are_no_longer_investing_in_training_Governments_need_to_encourage_them.pdf>, accessed 5 August 2015.

Held, D. and McGrew, A. (2007). *Globalization and Anti-Globalization*. 2nd edn. Cambridge: Polity.

Hills, J. (2004). *Inequality and the State*. Oxford: Oxford University Press.

Howell, C. (2005). *Trade Unions and the State*. Princeton, NJ: Princeton University Press.

International Labour Organisation (ILO). (1944). *Declaration Concerning the Aims and Purposes of the International Labour Organisation, adopted at the 26th session of the ILO*. Philadelphia, 10 May.

International Labour Organisation (ILO). (1999). *Report of ILO Director-General: Decent Work, International Labour Conference, 87th Session*. Geneva: ILO.

International Labour Organisation (ILO). (2009). *General Survey Concerning the Occupational Safety and Health Convention, 1981 (No. 155), the Occupational Safety and Health Recommendation, 1981 (No. 164), and the Protocol of 2002 to the Occupational Safety and Health Convention, 1981*. Geneva: ILO.

International Labour Organisation (ILO). (2012). *Global Wage Report 2012/13*. Geneva: ILO.

International Labour Organisation (ILO). (2013). *Global Employment Trends for Youth: A Generation at Risk*. Geneva: ILO.

International Labour Organisation (ILO). (2014a). *Global Employment Trends 2014*. Geneva: ILO.

International Labour Organisation (ILO). (2014b). *World Social Protection Report 2014/ 15*. Geneva: ILO.

Jahoda, M. (1982). *Employment and Unemployment: A Social Psychological Analysis*. Cambridge: Cambridge University Press.

Kröger, T. and Yeandle, S. (eds) (2014). *Combining Paid Work and Family Care: Policies and Experiences in International Perspective*. Bristol: The Policy Press.

Lambie-Mumford, H. (2013). '"Every Town Should Have One": Emergency Food Banking in the UK'. *Journal of Social Policy*, 42(1): 73–89.

Lee, S., McCann, D., and Messenger, J. (2007). *Working Time around the World: Trends in Working Hours, Laws and Policies in a Global Comparative Perspective.* London: Routledge.

Leisering, L. and Barrientos, A. (2013). 'Social Citizenship for the Global Poor? The Worldwide Spread of Social Assistance'. *International Journal of Social Welfare*, 22 (Supplement 1): S50–S67.

Levitas, R. (1996). 'The Concept of Social Exclusion and the New Durkheimian Hegemony'. *Critical Social Policy*, 16(2): 5–20.

Levitas, R. (1998). *The Inclusive Society? Social Exclusion and New Labour.* Basingstoke: Macmillan.

Lewis, J. (2000). 'Work and Care'. In H. Dean, R. Sykes, and R. Woods (eds), *Social Policy Review 12*. Newcastle: Social Policy Association.

Lewis, J. (2002). 'Gender and Welfare State Change'. *European Societies*, 4(4): 331–57.

Lewis, J. (2006). 'Work/family Reconciliation, Equal Opportunities and Social Policies: The Interpretation of Policy Trajectories at the EU Level and the Meaning of Gender Equality'. *Journal of European Public Policy*, 13(3): 420–37.

Lloyd, T. (1999). *Young Men's Attitudes to Gender and Work.* York: Joseph Rowntree Foundation.

Lødemel, I. and Trickey, H. (eds) (2000). *'An Offer You Can't Refuse': Workfare in International Perspective.* Bristol: The Policy Press.

Marx, I. and Nolan, B. (2012). 'In Work Poverty'. Gini Discussion Paper 51. Amsterdam: AIAS.

Marx, K. (1844). 'Economic and Philosophical Manuscripts'. In L. Colletti (ed.), *Early Writings* (1975 edn.). Harmondsworth: Penguin.

McKnight, A. (2002). 'Low-paid Work: Drip-feeding the Poor'. In J. Hills, J. Le Grand, and D. Piachaud (eds), *Understanding Social Exclusion*. Oxford: Oxford University Press.

McQuaid, R. and Lindsay, C. (2005). 'The Concept of Employability'. *Urban Studies*, 42(2): 197–291.

Mead, L. (1997). *From Welfare to Work: Lessons from America.* London: IEA Health & Welfare Unit.

Midgley, J. (2013). *Social Development: Theory and Practice.* London: Sage Publications.

Mooney, G. (ed.) (2004). *Work: Personal Lives and Social Policy.* Bristol: The Policy Press.

MOW International Research Team. (1987). *The Meaning of Working.* London: Academic Press.

Murray, C. (1994). *Underclass: The Crisis Deepens.* London: IEA.

Noon, M. and Blyton, P. (2007). *The Realities of Work.* 3rd. edn. Basingstoke: Palgrave Macmillan.

O'Hara, M. (2014). *Austerity Bites.* Bristol: The Policy Press.

O'Higgins, N. (2001). *Youth Unemployment and Employment Policy.* Geneva. International Labour Office.

Office for National Statistics (ONS). (2012). 'Underemployed Workers in the UK', http://www.ons.gov.uk/ons/rel/lmac/underemployed-workers-in-the-uk/2012/index. html, accessed 5 August 2015.

Office for National Statistics (ONS). (2013). 'Earnings Have Risen by 62% (after Adjusting for Inflation) since 1986. <http://www.ons.gov.uk/ons/rel/lmac/earnings-in-the-

uk-over-the-past-25-years/2012/rpt-earnings-in-the-uk-over-the-past-25-years.html>, accessed 5 August 2015.

Office for National Statistics (ONS). (2014). 'Wealth and Income, 2010–12'. <http://www.ons.gov.uk/ons/dcp171778_368612.pdf>, accessed 5 August 2015.

Organisation for Economic Co-operation and Development (OECD). (2013). *OECD Skills Outlook: First Results from the Survey of Adult Skills*. Paris: OECD.

Organisation for Economic Co-operation and Development (OECD). (2014). *OECD Employment Outlook 2014*. Paris: OECD.

Pahl, R. (1988). 'Some Remarks on Informal Work, Social Polarization and the Social Structure'. *International Journal of Urban and Regional Research*, 12(2): 247–67.

Pahl, R. (1995). *After Success: Fin-de-siècle Anxiety and Identity*. Cambridge: Polity Press.

Peck, J. (2001). *Workfare States*. New York: Guilford Press.

Polanyi, K. (1944). *The Great Transformation*. New York: Rinehart.

Policy Studies Institute. (2006). *The Hidden One-in-Five: Winning a Fair Deal for Britain's Vulnerable Workers*. London: TUC.

Pollert, A. and Charlwood, A. (2009). 'The Vulnerable Worker in Britain and Problems at Work'. *Work, Employment and Society*, 23(2): 343–62.

Ritzer, G. (2004). *The McDonaldization of Society*. Revised edn. Thousand Oaks, CA: Pine Forge Press.

Roulstone, A. and Barnes, C. (eds) (2005). *Working Futures? Disabled People, Policy and Social Inclusion*. Bristol: The Policy Press.

Sennett, R. (1998). *The Corrosion of Character: The Personal Consequences of Work in the New Capitalism*. New York: Norton.

Serrano, A. and Keune, M. (eds) (2014). *Alternatives to Flexicurity: New concepts and approaches*. London: Routledge.

Shildrick, T., MacDonald, R., Webster, C., and Garthwaite, K. (2012). *Poverty and Insecurity: Life in Low-pay, No-pay Britain*. Bristol: The Policy Press.

Social Justice Policy Group. (2006). *Breakdown Britain*. London: Centre for Social Justice.

Standing, G. (2009). *Work after Globalization: Building Occupational Citizenship*. Cheltenham: Edward Elgar.

Standing, G. (2011). *The Precariat: The New Dangerous Class*. London: Bloomsbury.

Steedman, H. (2011). *Apprenticeship Policy in England: Increasing Skills versus Boosting Young People's Job Prospects*. London: Centre for Economic Performance, London School of Economics.

Townsend, P. (1991). 'The Structured Dependency of the Elderly: A Creation of Social Policy in the Twentieth Century'. *Ageing and Society*, 1(1): 5–28.

Toynbee, P. (2003). *Hard Work: Life in Low-pay Britain*. London: Bloomsbury.

TUC Commission on Vulnerable Employment. (2008). *Hard Work, Hidden Lives*. London: Trades Union Congress.

Weeks, J. (2005). 'Inequality Trends in Some Developed OECD Countries'. Working Paper 6. New York: UN Department of Economic and Social Affairs.

Whittaker, M. and Hurrell, A. (2013). *Low Pay in Britain 2013*. London: Resolution Foundation.

Wilkinson, R. and Pickett, K. (2009). *The Spirit Level: Why More Equal Societies almost always Do Better*. London: Allen Lane.

10

Ageing and Disadvantage

Emily Grundy

Robert Butler (1975) in his seminal Pulitzer Prizewinning book, *Why Survive? Being Old in America,* noted that multitudes of people became poor only after growing older and drew attention to a range of discriminatory practices, policies, and attitudes which impacted negatively on the lives of all older Americans. Some more recent commentaries suggest that, far from being disadvantaged, older people may now be unduly privileged. UK Cabinet Minister David Willetts' much publicized book, *The Pinch* (2010) was subtitled *How the Baby Boomers Took their Children's Future—and Why They Should Give It Back.*

This chapter reviews the evidence on the extent to which ageing is associated with disadvantage in contemporary societies with a focus on which sections of the older population are most at risk of various disadvantages. The chapter starts with an overview of population ageing and a brief introduction to processes associated with ageing that may lead to disadvantage. Later sections consider dimensions of advantage and disadvantage in the domains of life identified by older people and agencies representing them as the most important. These are material circumstances, including income and wealth (see also Chapters 7 and 8, this volume); health and disability; social and family contacts and support (see also Chapter 6, this volume), including opportunities for social participation and engagement. The main focus is on the UK and other European countries.

The advantages and disadvantages associated with ageing are now a hugely important issue both for individuals and societies as population ageing is a predominant demographic feature in all richer, and an increasing proportion of poorer, countries. In the European Union 18 per cent of the population in 2010 was aged 65 and over and by 2050 this proportion is expected to exceed 25 per cent (Eurostat, 2014). Moreover the older population is itself ageing with large increases in both the number and proportion of older old people, the group most likely to experience disadvantages of various kinds. By 2050 it is highly probable that those aged 80 and over will constitute at least one in ten of the population in the European Union (Eurostat, 2014).

This ageing of populations is widely perceived to present a major policy challenge (Longman, 2004; OECD, 2006). Policy concerns arise from associations between age and participation in activities deemed productive, notably paid work (see also Chapter 9, this volume), and in needs for various forms of assistance including income support and health and long-term care. Reductions in the ratio of 'workers' to 'pensioners' mean reduced government income while increases in support needs imply pressure for greater expenditure.

Both of these dimensions of policy concern about ageing—labour market participation and needs for care and support—are to an extent contingent on health and so related to, although by no means wholly determined by, biological ageing processes. However, ageing is also a social process and it has been argued that many of the disadvantages that older people may experience, and indeed the whole idea of old age as a separate phase of life, are socially constructed (Townsend, 1981; Phillipson, 1982; 1998). Moreover, there is increasing recognition that there is considerable variation between individuals—and between social groups—in their experience of the ageing process. The extent to which senescent change impacts on function and quality of life also depends on interactions with environmental factors many of which are strongly influenced by policy. Ageing, at both the individual and the population level, is thus a core concern of social policy and the need to compensate for possible disadvantages attendant on ageing has been an important motivation for policy developments stretching back to the establishment of the Elizabethan Poor Law in England in 1601 and even earlier (Grundy, 1997).

10.1 Population Ageing

The demographic determinants of population size and age structure are fertility, mortality, and migration. Fertility (the child-bearing performance of an individual, couple, or population) has historically been of much greater importance than either mortality (death) or migration. This is because every birth represents not just an addition to the current generation of children, but also potentially an exponentially increasing augmentation in the size of future generations. The predominant demographic change underlying a primary shift to an older age structure is a long-term fall in fertility rates. Sustained falling fertility reduces the proportionate share of children and young people in the population—and the number of potential future parents—which means that older people, who are the survivors of earlier larger birth cohorts, account for a larger share of the total population. In most European countries this process, which together with mortality declines which occurred at much the same time, is termed the demographic transition, started in the late nineteenth or early twentieth centuries. Change generally came earlier in Northern and Western Europe and occurred later—but at faster pace—in Southern and Eastern European countries. In England and Wales, for example, the Total Fertility Rate (a measure of how many children a woman would have if she experienced current age-specific fertility rates throughout her reproductive life) dropped from 4.8 to 2.8 between 1871–5 and 1911–15 and by the early 1930s was below 'replacement level'—(the level needed to maintain the population at its current size; in low mortality populations this is slightly over two births per woman on average). In much of Europe, and in other regions of the world, there was an increase in fertility during the post-Second-World-War 'baby boom' but no return to pre-transition levels. The baby boom was succeeded in many countries by a 'birth dearth' in the 1970s. Since then fertility rates in much of Northern Europe, including the UK, and also in the US and Canada have tended to fluctuate at levels between 1.5 and 2 while falling to lower levels in Southern and Eastern Europe, and also in South East Asia. Fluctuations in numbers of births result in corresponding bulges in the numbers of older people sixty-five years later and the ageing of the baby-boom cohorts has added to concern about structural changes in the age of populations. This is particularly the case in the US where the baby boom lasted for the whole period 1946–66 and the Total Fertility Rate (TFR) peaked at 3.8 in 1957. In Britain, there was a brief 'reunification' bulge in births following demobilization at the end of the Second World War but the baby-boom proper did not start until 1956 and the highest birth rate reached was 2.9 (Morgan, 2003).

10.1.1 Mortality Change

Historically, and apparently paradoxically, initial improvements in mortality in those European populations which now have high proportions of old people initially served to *offset* the trend towards population ageing, as they chiefly benefited the young—and led to increases in the proportions surviving to have children themselves. However, many populations in richer countries now have fertility at or below replacement level, life expectancies at birth around eighty years and near universal survival to the end of the (female) reproductive span. The official Government Actuary's Department period mortality schedule for the UK in 2011–13, for example, implies survivorship to age 65 for 87 per cent of boys and 91 per cent of girls born then, even in the absence of any further improvement throughout their lifetimes (Office for National Statistics, 2014). In these conditions, further improvements in mortality have the greatest impact at old ages and mortality changes are now the main motor of the further ageing of populations with already old age structures (Preston and Stokes, 2012). The distribution of the older population by sex is also driven by mortality. In virtually all populations women have lower mortality than men and the population becomes progressively more female dominated in older age groups. Throughout much of the twentieth century this female advantage in mortality increased for reasons including the greater exposure of men to unhealthy behaviours, particularly smoking, and hazardous working conditions. Recently this trend has reversed with some narrowing of differentials, although still a female advantage in terms of mortality.

In most European countries (other than for men in some of the former Eastern bloc countries) survival to at least age 65 is the normal expectation and mortality before age 75 is defined as premature. Moreover, in recent decades improvements in later age mortality, as well as in survival to age 65, have been considerable (Oeppen and Vaupel, 2002).

Table 10.1 presents summary demographic information for the ten largest European countries in 2010 and for the European Union (post 2004) as a whole. In Germany and Italy 20 per cent of the population were aged 65 and over and this proportion exceeded 15 per cent in all the other countries shown except Poland. All these countries have Total Fertility Rates below 2 and life expectancies at birth of seventy years or more. (Life expectancy indicates how many years a newborn would live if he or she experienced current age-specific mortality rates throughout his or her life). Further life expectancy at age 65 (remaining years of life at current levels of older age mortality for people aged 65) was twenty-one for women and seventeen for men for the European Union as a whole with the highest levels in France, Spain, and Italy and the lowest in the Ukraine, Romania, and Poland.

Table 10.1. Proportion of the population aged 65 and over, Total Fertility Rate and life expectancy at birth and at age 65, selected European countries 2010

	% 65+	TFR	Life expectancy at birth			Further life expectancy at age 65		
			Persons	Males	Females	Persons	Males	Females
Belgium	17.2	1.8	80.3	77.5	83.0	19.6	17.6	21.3
France	16.8	1.9	82.0	78.4	85.4	21.5	19.0	23.5
Germany	20.6	1.4	80.6	78.1	83.1	19.6	18.0	21.1
Italy	20.3	1.4	82.5	79.8	85.0	20.8	18.7	22.5
Netherlands	15.5	1.8	81.2	79.1	83.1	19.6	17.9	21.2
Poland	13.5	1.4	76.6	72.3	80.8	17.7	15.2	19.6
Romania	14.9	1.3	73.8	70.2	77.6	15.6	14.1	17.3
Spain	17.0	1.4	82.3	79.2	85.4	20.9	18.7	22.9
Ukraine	15.5	1.4	70.3	65.2	75.3	14.5	12.2	16.7
UK	16.6	1.9	80.8	78.8	82.7	19.8	18.4	21.0
European Union	17.5	1.6	80.2	77.2	83.1	19.6	17.6	21.2

Source: WHO European Health for All databases (April 2015). (TFR for Italy and UK from national sources.)

10.2 Ageing Processes at the Individual Level

There is no biological reason for choosing any particular chronological age as marking the onset of 'old age' and the demarcation line of sixty or sixty-five often used to distinguish older from other mature adults is largely a convention following common ages of eligibility for pension receipt. Ageing as a process involves greater risks of being exposed to certain specific challenges and, crucially, of reduced capacity to respond to them. From a biological perspective ageing (or senescence) in the individual is associated with decrements in the homeostatic mechanisms that bring about adaptive responses to environmental challenges and so maintain an optimum internal balance through a dynamic equilibrium (for example, humans maintain a constant body temperature by responding to decreases or increases in external temperature by shivering or sweating and cues to behavioural responses such as adjusting clothing). Senescence reduces the efficiency of the regulatory mechanisms needed to maintain homeostasis, this results in an unstable internal environment which increases the risk of disease (Ferucci et al., 2010). The near exponential increase in probability of death from late adolescence until advanced old age is a powerful indicator of this process, although it is worth noting that in the oldest age groups rates of increase in risks of death flatten out.

Depictions of later life as a period of unremitting and unmodifiable decline have been challenged by social scientists and others who have pointed to evidence of large social variation in this process and evidence of continuing plasticity which makes it possible to modify or partially reverse decrements associated with ageing (Estes et al., 2001). For example, age-associated conditions such as high blood pressure can be treated and modified with drugs and changes in diet and lifestyle; rehabilitative physical therapy may help people regain function after an accident or acute illness; cataract or hip-replacement surgery may reverse or reduce disability; and exercise programmes and social interventions may improve mental health (Forsman et al., 2011; Heaven et al., 2013; Windle et al., 2010). Bowling and Dieppe (2005) have also pointed out that many older people enjoy happy and fulfilled lives even in the presence of disease and disability. Nevertheless, although experiences of ageing are varied and to some extent modifiable, there are limits to plasticity and particularly among the older old levels of impairment and disability are high, as considered in more detail in the section of this chapter focused on health.

The model of homeostasis is also useful in considering associations between ageing processes and disadvantage or vulnerability to disadvantage more generally (Grundy, 2006). Older people's needs in a range of spheres depend on their lifetime accumulation and depletion of resources and skills which determine the 'reserve' they bring to later life. Important dimensions of reserve include mental and physical health status; family relationships and social networks; coping strategies; personality and social skills; wealth and other material resources; and legal or moral rights to various forms of collective support. The level of these reserves may in some cases be largely determined by life-course factors. However, this does not mean that *current* environmental influences, including those determined by policy, are unimportant. A powerful example of this was demonstrated following the reunification of Germany when the earlier gap between East and West Germany in mortality at older ages narrowed considerably (Gjonca et al., 2000).

Older people face various challenges which may deplete the reserves they bring to later life such as loss of income on retirement, erosion of social networks through bereavement, and deterioration in health. This may lead to disadvantage unless offset by the provision of compensatory supports such as replacement income sources and opportunities to forge new relationships and activities. Policies to reduce disadvantage at older ages may focus on increasing the reserve people bring *to* later life, for example by encouraging asset accumulation and healthy life styles, or by providing compensating supports *in* later life, such as provision of services and income supplements, or a combination of both.

10.3 Poverty, Income, and Wealth

In the absence of pension schemes older people unable to support themselves through work are reliant on savings, transfers from family members, or various forms of charitable or public assistance and until relatively recently poverty (see Chapter 1, this volume) and old age were considered virtually synonymous. Bismarck is widely credited with the introduction of the first pension scheme in Germany in 1889 under which workers were eligible for a pension annuity at the age of seventy. However in some countries forms of rudimentary income support for older people predate this innovation. In England and Wales older people had some recourse to assistance under arrangements dating from the seventeenth century. These became more restrictive in the latter part of the nineteenth century but as documented by the 1895 *Royal Commission on the Aged Deserving Poor* some 15 per cent of those aged 65 and over were in receipt of 'Medical Out Relief' (which could take the form of money payments and food as well as rudimentary medications) and a further 10 per cent were in various forms of institutional 'care' (Grundy, 1997). The Old Age Pensions Act of 1908 introduced a non-contributory pension at age 70; contributory pensions payable at age 65 were introduced in 1925 and in 1940 the age of eligibility reduced to 60 for women on the grounds that wives were usually four years younger than their husbands and should be able to retire at the same time. However, levels of payments were low and even after the introduction of means-tested supplementary pensions in 1925, poverty in old age was common. Rowntree in his enquiry into poverty in York in 1936 (which informed the Beveridge report) concluded that 'the poverty of old age is more acute than that due to any other single cause' (Rowntree, 1941: 66; McNicol, 1998). Further reforms were introduced as part of the new welfare state arrangements of the 1940s but Townsend and Wedderburn's (1965) survey of '*The Aged in the Welfare State*' conducted in 1962–3 nevertheless found that a quarter of the nationally representative sample of people aged 65 and over included had minimal assets and very low incomes. They concluded that older people 'have income levels a half or more below the levels of the population generally' (p. 95).

During the 1970s and 1980s older people continued to be at a higher risk of poverty than those in younger age groups but this situation has now changed. As shown in Figure 10.1, in many European countries in 2010 the proportion of people aged 65 and over with less than half of median incomes was no higher, or even lower, than in the population as a whole, although the older old still were disadvantaged compared to those aged 66–74. In the European Union, the proportion at risk of poverty is now higher among children (27 per cent) than among those 65 and over (23 per cent) (Vilaplana, 2013). A similar conclusion has been reached in UK studies in which incomes delivered through social security payments are compared with Minimum Income Standards derived by asking focus groups and experts to define how much

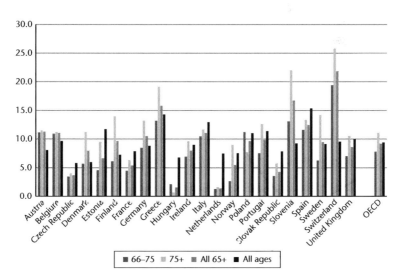

Figure 10.1. Percent of the population aged 66–74, 75+, 65+ and all ages with incomes less than 50% of median, selected European countries 2010
Source: OECD, *Pensions at a Glance*, 2013. Derived from Table 5.4, version 1

money certain types of household would need to maintain a minimal socially acceptable standard of living. Results for 2014 showed that for pensioners benefit levels (Pension Credit) would meet 95 per cent of this minimum income standard. However, out-of-work benefits for younger adults with no children would meet only 39 per cent of the Minimum Income Standard, and those for families with children 60 per cent (Davis, Hirsch, and Padley 2014).

These changes in the distribution of poverty risks do not mean that no older people are disadvantaged by poverty—rather that poverty risks are now as great or greater at younger ages. Groups of older people at higher risk of poverty include the very old, widowed, and divorced women, those with lifetime low incomes and members of some minority ethnic groups (Emmerson and Muriel, 2008).

Many Europeans now enter retirement with far more material resources than previous generations. However, older individuals' assets and incomes almost invariably diminish as they age and opportunities to replenish resources are limited. The importance of state sources of income is illustrated for Britain in Figure 10.2 which shows the distribution of sources of income in households headed by a person over age 65. Pension sources of income predominate in all age groups and even among households headed by a person aged 65–74 (which may include younger members), only 15 per cent of income was derived from earnings. In households headed by a person aged

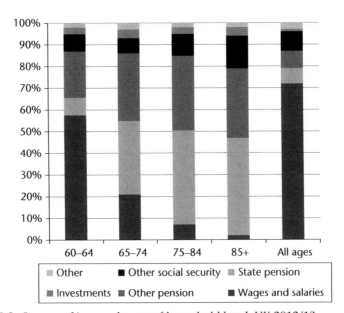

Figure 10.2. Sources of income by age of household head, UK 2012/13

Source: Dept. Work and Pensions, Family Resources Survey UK 2012/13
National Statistics, 2014

75 and over, more than 80 per cent of household income was drawn from pensions and other state benefits. The reliance of older people on transfers and returns on investments means that they depend on decisions made by others (governments, pension fund managers) and may be affected by shocks or trends, such as political change, mismanagement, inflation, or stock market performance, over which they have no direct control. This is a particular disadvantage in countries such as the UK in which returns on pension investments are poor partly because of the high fees charged by fund managers (McKee and Stuckler, 2013). Importantly, too, it is not possible for older adults to 'go back' and take different decisions about asset accumulation in the light of present-day knowledge about longevity or costs of living.

Older people's reliance on transfers to sustain income is an outcome of reduced activity in the labour market and policies such as mandatory retirement were identified in seminal gerontological texts as a key element in the 'structured dependency' of older people (Townsend, 1981). More recently the imperative of age structure change has led to an emphasis on 'active ageing' including encouragement to postpone retirement (Walker and Maltby, 2012). Many governments have moved towards delaying entitlements to state pensions and removing mandatory retirement ages and the trend towards earlier retirement which marked the 1970s and 1980s seems to have halted (Kunemund and Kolland, 2007). Even so high proportions of people leave the labour market earlier than 'official' pensionable ages, particularly in Southern Europe (Rechel et al., 2013). Moreover, older workers face barriers such as lack of access to training and difficulties in re-entering the labour market after gaps arising from, for example, episodes of ill health, caring commitments, or unemployment. Crucially a sizeable proportion of people, particularly those from less advantaged groups in manual or routine occupations have health problems which make work difficult even before reaching state pension age and potential working environments that may be unattractive, unsuitable, and stressful (Phillipson, 2014). For these groups restrictions on welfare supports, such as unemployment and disability payments, that have often been used as 'bridges' between withdrawal from the labour market and eligibility for pensions together with the raising of pension ages and actuarial penalties for early retirement have led to increasing disadvantage (Naegele and Walker, 2007).

10.4 Health and Disability

Indicators of health show a strong association with age with a high prevalence of chronic diseases in older age groups; multimorbidity (having more than one chronic condition) is also common (Ornstein et al., 2013). Many chronic diseases are also strongly socially patterned with common conditions, such as heart disease, stroke, and arthritis being more prevalent among those with a lower socio-economic position (Dalstra et al., 2005). Although relative differences between socio-economic groups tend to slightly weaken with older age (partly because those at most risk will have already died) differences in absolute risk tend to be greater (because of the overall higher prevalence rates in older age groups). A recent systematic review of socio-economic differences in mortality rates at older ages in Europe (Huisman et al., 2013) found that a low socio-economic position continued to be associated with increased risks of death relative to more advantaged groups even among the oldest old. A further review of European research on indicators of subjective well-being (self-rated health and measures of quality of life) similarly showed continuing differentials at older ages by indicators of socio-economic status and resources such as education, past occupation, housing tenure, and deprivation level of the locality (Read et al., 2015). Differences between ethnic groups have also been identified with South Asian and Black Caribbean groups in the UK tending to have worse health profiles in later life and higher rates of depressive symptoms which, particularly for the Black Caribbean group, are related to socio-economic disadvantage (Williams et al., 2015). These inequalities reflect the cumulative effect of differential exposures to harmful or salutogenic influences over the life course including socio-economic disadvantage in childhood and earlier adult life, differences in exposures to stress and differences in health-related behaviours and access to and use of health services (Herd, 2009).

Chronic conditions and impairments (such as visual or hearing impairment) may lead to functional limitation or disability—restrictions in the ability to perform usual everyday functions such as self-care or housework. Functional limitations are strongly associated with age, and with gender as well as with socio-economic position. Although women have lower mortality than men they are more at risk of disability in later life, especially from musculo-skeletal impairments and overall they spend a larger proportion of their later life with some functional limitation (Van Oyen et al., 2013). Table 10.2 presents recent data from England on the proportions who needed help with key activities of daily living and instrumental activities of daily living, and mobility. It can be seen that in the oldest groups—particularly the oldest groups of women—the proportions needing help with household tasks like shopping and laundry are high and 40 per cent of women aged 85 and over (and 27 per cent of men of the same age) need help with having a bath or a shower. Moreover the data set on which this table is based does not include people resident in nursing or care homes so the true proportion will be higher. The table also shows the proportions who reported receiving help—these are considerably lower than reported need even for essential daily

Table 10.2. Proportion of older men and women needing and receiving help (in past month) with various tasks, England, 2011

Activity	%	Men						Women					
		65–69	70–74	75–79	80–84	85+	65+	65–69	70–74	75–79	80–84	85+	65+
Getting up and down stairs	Needed help	13	15	16	38	38	20	15	23	32	50	55	31
	Received help	3	5	5	11	8	5	4	6	9	9	14	7
Having a bath or shower	Needed help	10	9	14	25	27	14	9	15	21	26	40	19
	Received help	7	5	8	12	12	7	5	8	9	9	20	9
Dressing or undressing	Needed help	11	9	12	17	23	13	8	12	16	17	27	14
	Received help	6	6	8	9	13	8	4	6	7	7	17	7
Getting in and out of bed	Needed help	8	11	10	14	19	11	7	11	17	16	18	13
	Received help	5	7	7	7	8	6	4	6	8	5	14	6
Shopping for food	Needed help	12	15	17	36	48	21	14	23	32	54	70	33
	Received help	8	9	12	26	40	14	11	20	30	46	55	28
Housework or laundry	Needed help	12	17	20	33	44	21	15	20	29	44	57	29
	Received help	6	10	12	23	31	13	10	16	26	33	45	22

Source: Health Survey for England 2011, Table 5.7

activities like getting in out of bed and dressing. The implication is that people either manage their best even if it involves pain or discomfort and somehow have to manage perhaps by, for example, not getting properly dressed or washed. Most help needed by older people with functional limitations is provided by close family members, particularly spouses and children (Pickard et al., 2012). Older people who lack these sources of help and are unable to pay for care privately need to rely on state-provided resources (Larsson and Silverstein, 2004). In many countries access to these state-provided sources of help were becoming more restricted even before the current economic crisis (Sundström, Malmberg, and Johansson, 2006). Disadvantages associated with unmet needs for assistance may therefore have increased.

Disability is a consequence of interactions between the person and his or her environment and may be modified, prevented, or even caused by some aspect of the environment as well as by personal factors, a dynamic incorporated into the World Health Organisation International Classification of Functioning, Disability and Health (WHO, 2001). For example, an older person with osteoarthritis might be unable to get in or out of a bathtub but fully able to use a walk-in shower—access to the latter would therefore reduce the extent of their activity limitation. Step-free access, accommodating public transport, and helpful store staff may enable some older people to carry on going out to shop while barriers such as poorly placed street furniture, uneven paving stones, and fear of crime may have the opposite effect. Older people may suffer disadvantage not only because chronic conditions and impairments increase with age, but also because sometimes their environments may be less, rather than more, accommodating than those of younger age groups—for example they may live in older housing with fewer amenities. In Ireland, for example, the National Survey of Housing Quality 2001–2 showed that older people living alone were the group most likely to lack central heating (Watson and Williams, 2003).

10.5 Family and Social Support

Families, friends, and neighbours are important not just as a potential source of practical help if needed, but also because social contacts, and social support drawn from them, are positively associated with health and quality of life at older ages (Netuveli and Blane, 2008; Seeman, 2000); a lack of social ties and involvement is associated with higher risks of depression, loneliness (the perception of having less contact than desired), and death (Holt-Lunstad et al., 2015).

Later life brings various challenges to people's social environments, particularly bereavement. Gender differences in mortality rates mean that women are more likely to survive their partner but the consequences of becoming widowed seem to be worse for men, possibly because women have stronger links with friends and other relatives and so are less reliant on spouses for emotional support. Similarly never-married and divorced men in Britain are less likely to join organizations and clubs than married men (Perren, Arber, and Davidson, 2003) whereas other studies have found that never-married childless women are often more actively engaged in social networks, organizations, and voluntary work than their married counterparts with children (Cwikel, Gramotnev, and Lee, 2006). Friends and other relatives are also lost through death and, although older people form new friendships and may gain family members (such as grandchildren), the size of people's social networks tends to diminish with older age and do so to a greater extent in groups experiencing other disadvantages (Cornwell, 2015).

Adult children are an important element of the networks of older parents and many studies have shown frequent contacts and exchanges of support between them, although there is some variation in intensity by country, gender, and socio-economic status (Attias-Donfut, Ogg, and Wolff, 2005; Buber and Engelhardt, 2008; Tomassini et al., 2004; Zunzunegui, Béland, and Otero, 2001). A synthesis of studies from a range of high-income countries concluded that childless older people were more likely to have social networks with limited support potential than older parents (Dykstra and Hagestad, 2007) but there is some evidence of 'compensation' in that childless women (but not childless men) have more frequent contacts with friends than older mothers (Dykstra, 2006; Gray, 2009; Wenger, Dykstra, Melkas, and Knipsheer, 2007; Wenger, Scott, and Petterson, 2000). A recent study using data from the English Longitudinal Survey of Ageing (ELSA) found that childless older people had lower rates of regular social interaction than parents and among parents those with larger families were more likely to receive help if needed (Grundy and Read, 2012). Parents also have lower risks of admission to nursing and residential care facilities, although it is not clear whether having more than two children further reduces the risk (Hays, Pieper, and Purser, 2003; Grundy and Jitlal, 2007).

Currently the proportions of childless people in European populations are at a historic low point (Murphy, Martikainen, and Pennec, 2006) as those who are now old include the parents of the baby boom who had higher rates of marriage and parenthood than earlier cohorts (and less depletion of their children through premature mortality). However those born after around 1955 include larger proportions of people who have not had children, and also more with disrupted partnerships, which has implications for their support in later life.

There are also differences between socio-economic groups in patterns of intergenerational exchange. Contacts with family are more frequent among less well educated groups, partly associated with greater geographical proximity, (see Gray, 2009; Grundy and Murphy, 2006) and the less well educated are more likely to name family members as their closest friends (Pahl and Pevalin, 2005) and have social networks including a larger proportion of relatives (Gray, 2009). These socio-economic differences are more important in Northern than in Southern Europe where levels of intergenerational contact and interaction are high in all social groups (Tomassini et al., 2004).

Some older people may experience social exclusion or detachment (not being able to participate fully in society). Tomaszewski and Barnes (2008) analysed data from the English Longitudinal Study of Ageing to investigate factors associated with this. They defined social exclusion (see also, Chapter 1, this volume) using six indicators of participation relating to societal involvement (for example, church membership); participation in social or recreational activities; frequent contact with others; social support (perceived support from a close other); participation in cultural activities, and leisure (holiday or day trip). They found that about half of the sample of people aged 50 and over experienced disadvantage on one or more of these domains at least once over three waves of the survey but only 5 per cent experienced three or more disadvantages in every wave. This group had a lower quality of life and were more likely to report being unhappy and feeling socially isolated. Factors associated with higher risks of detachment included not living with a partner, having no children alive, material deprivation, low education, and living in an unsafe or unfriendly neighbourhood. Other studies which have examined disadvantages in several domains of life have also found that although sources of disadvantage tend to cluster together (for example, low education is associated with material disadvantage and living in deprived neighbourhoods), the proportions with multiple disadvantages is relatively low (Grundy and Bowling, 1999).

10.6 Discussion

Gerontologists have long emphasized the heterogeneity of the older population and the ageing experience and argued against aspects of social organization and attitudes which stigmatize and marginalize older people. Robert Butler coined the term 'ageism' to describe these features of modern societies drawing attention to the exclusion of older people from work and other socially valued activities and the abundant negative images of older people in advertisements and greeting cards, as well as the poverty often accompanying later life. Forty years on from the publication of *Why Survive*, many aspects of the lives of older people in Western societies have improved immeasurably. Positive developments include substantial falls in mortality and improved material circumstances (although growing inequalities). Moreover international and national policymakers now emphasize the promotion of 'active ageing' and measures to promote social integration across the generations (UNECE/European Commission, 2015). Most older people are not seriously disabled or isolated and levels of happiness are higher among older people than the middle-aged (Blanchflower and Oswald, 2008). Less positively, there are groups within the older population who experience serious disadvantage in terms of their material or social circumstances and most people will experience several years of disability before death. For those with serious disabilities, both the quality and quantity of support provided may be deficient. Moreover current policy and popular rhetoric often attributes pressure on resources to population ageing (rather than to the increasing cost of medical procedures and poor organization of services) and ageist attitudes still abound. Policies to reduce disadvantages experienced in later life need to address inequalities over the life course, recognize both the diversity and dynamic nature of ageing, help people still healthy and active in old age, and improve the robustness of health, long-term care, and welfare systems in Europe (Rechel et al., 2013).

References

Attias-Donfut, C., Ogg, J., and Wolff, F. C. (2005). 'European Patterns of Intergenerational and Financial Time Transfers'. *European Journal of Ageing*, 2: 161–73.

Blanchflower, D. and Oswald, A. (2008). 'Is Well-being U-shaped over the Life Cycle? *Social Science & Medicine*, 66(8): 1733–49.

Bowling, A. and Dieppe, P. (2005). 'What Is Successful Ageing and Who Should Define It?' *BMJ*, 331(7531): 1548–51.

Buber, I. and Engelhardt, H. (2008). 'Children's Impact on the Mental Health of their Older Mothers and Fathers: Findings from the Survey of Health, Ageing and Retirement in Europe. *European Journal of Ageing*, 5: 31–45.

Butler, R. (1975). *Why Survive? Being Old in America*. New York: Harper and Row.

Cornwell, B. (2015). 'Social Disadvantage and Network Turnover'. *Journals of Gerontology, Series B: Psychological Sciences and Social Sciences*, 70(1): 132–42.

Cwikel, J., Gramotnev, H., and Lee, C. (2006). 'Never-married Childless Women in Australia: Health and Social Circumstances in Old Age'. *Social Science & Medicine*, 62: 191–2001.

Dalstra, J. A., Kunst, A. E., Borrell, C., Breeze, E., Cambois, E., Costa, G., Geurts, J. J., Lahelma, E., Van Oyen, H., Rasmussen, N. K., Rgidor, E., Spadea, T., and Mackenbach, J. P. (2005). 'Socioeconomic Differences in the Prevalence of Common Chronic Diseases: An Overview in Eight European Countries'. *International Journal of Epidemiology*, 34: 316–26.

Davis, A., Hirsch, D., and Padley, M. (2014). *A Minimum Income Standard for the UK in 2014*. York: Joseph Rowntree Foundation.

Dykstra, P. A. (2006). 'Off the Beaten Track: Childlessness and Social Integration in Late Life'. *Research on Aging*, 28: 749–67.

Dykstra, P. and Hagestad, G. (2007). 'Childlessness and Parenthood in Two Centuries: Different Roads—Different Maps?' *Journal of Family Issues*, 28: 1518–32.

Estes, C. L., Wallace, S., Linkins, K. W., and Binney, E. A. (2001). 'The Medicalization and Commodification of Aging and the Privatization and Rationalization of Old Age Policy'. In C. L. Estes and Associates (eds), *Social Policy and Aging: A Critical Perspective* (pp. 45–59). Newbury Park, CA: Sage.

Emmerson, C., and Muriel, A. (2008). 'Financial Resources and Well-being'. In J. Banks, E. Breeze, C. Lessof, and J. Nazroo (eds), *Living in the 21st Century: Older People in England; the 2006 English Longitudinal Study of Ageing* (pp. 118–49). London: Institute for Fiscal Studies.

Eurostat (2014). 'Statistics Explained: Population Structure and Ageing', <http://ec.eur opa.eu/eurostat/statistics-explained/index.php/Population_structure_and_ageing#Past_ and_future_population_ageing_trends_in_the_EU>, accessed 3 September 2015.

Ferrucci, L., Hesdorffer, C., Bandinelli, S., and Simonsick, E. M. (2010). 'Frailty as a Nexus between the Biology of Aging, Environmental Conditions and Clinical Geriatrics'. *Public Health Reviews*, 32: 475–88.

Forsman, A. K., Nordmyr, J., and Wahlbeck, K. (2011). 'Psychosocial Interventions for the Promotion of Mental Health and the Prevention of Depression among Older Adults. *Health Promotion International*, 26, Issue suppl. 1: i85–i107.

Gjonca, A., Brockman, H., and Heiner, M. (2000). 'Old-age Mortality in Germany prior to and after Reunification'. *Demographic Research*, 3(1): ISSN 1435–9871.

Gray, A. (2009). 'The Social Capital of Older People'. *Ageing and Society*, 29: 5–31.

Grundy, E. (1997). 'The Health of Older Adults 1841–1994'. In J. Charlton and M. Murphy (eds), *The Health of Adult Britain 1841–1994*, Volume II (pp. 183–204). London: The Stationery Office.

Grundy, E (2006). 'Ageing and Vulnerable Elderly People: European Perspectives'. *Ageing & Society*, 26: 1–30.

Grundy, E. and Bowling, A. (1999). 'Enhancing the Quality of Extended Life Years: Identification of the Oldest Old with a Very Good and Very Poor Quality of Life'. *Aging and Mental Health*, 3: 199–212.

Grundy, E. and Jitlal, M. (2007). 'Socio-demographic Variations in Moves to Institutional Care 1991–2001: A Record Linkage Study from England and Wales'. *Age and Ageing*, 36: 1–7.

Grundy, E. and Murphy, M. (2006). 'Kin Availability, Contact and Support Exchanges between Adult Children and their Parents in Great Britain'. In F. Ebtehaj, B. Lindley, and M. Richards (eds), *Kinship Matters* (pp. 217–35). Oxford: Hart.

Grundy, E. and Read, S. (2012). 'Social Contacts and Receipt of Help among Older People in England: Are There Benefits from Having More Children?' *Journal of Gerontology: Social Sciences*, 67(6): 742–54.

Hays, J. C., Pieper, C. F., and Purser, J. L. (2003). 'Competing Risk of Household Expansion or Institutionalization in Late Life'. *Journals of Gerontology*, 58b: S11–S20.

Heaven, B., Brown, L. J., Errington, L., Mathers, J. C., and Moffatt, S. (2013). 'Supporting Well-being in Retirement through Meaningful Social Roles: Systematic Review of Intervention Studies'. *Millbank Quarterly*, 91(2): 222–87.

Herd, P. (2009). 'Social Class, Health and Longevity'. In P. Uhlenberg (ed.), *International Handbook of Population Ageing* (pp. 583–604). Dordrecht: Springer.

Holt-Lunstad, J. H., Smith, T. B., Baker, M., Harris, T., and Stephenson, D. (2015). 'Loneliness and Social Isolation as Risk Factors for Mortality, a Meta-analytic Review'. *Perspectives on Psychological Science*, 10: 250–64.

Huisman, M., Read, S., Towriss, C., Deeg, D., and Grundy, E. (2013). 'Socioeconomic Inequalities in Mortality in Old Age in the WHO Europe Region'. *Epidemiologic Reviews*, 35(1): 84–97.

Kunemund, H. and Kolland, F. (2007). 'Work and Retirement'. In J. Bond, S. Peace, F. Dittman-Kohli, and G. Westerhof (eds), *Ageing Society: European Perspectives on Gerontology* (pp. 167–85). 3rd edition. London: Sage.

Larsson, K. and Silverstein, M. (2004). 'The Effects of Marital and Parental Status on Informal Support and Service Utilization: A Study of Older Swedes Living Alone'. *Journal of Aging Studies*, 18: 231–44.

Longman, P. (2004). *The Empty Cradle: How Falling Birthrates Threaten World Prosperity [and What to Do about It]*. New York: Basic Books.

McKee, M. and Stuckler, D. (2013). 'Older People in the UK: Under Attack from all Directions'. *Age & Ageing*, 42: 11–13.

McNicol, J. (1998). *The Politics of Retirement in Britain, 1878–1948*. Cambridge: Cambridge University Press.

Morgan, P. S. (2003). 'Is Low Fertility a 21st Century Demographic Crisis?' *Demography*, 40(4): 589–603.

Murphy, M. J., Martikainen, P., and Pennec, S. (2006). 'Demographic Change and the Supply of Potential Family Supporters in Britain, Finland and France in the Period 1911–2050'. *European Journal of Population*, 22: 219–40.

Naegele, G. and Walker, A. (2007). 'Social Protection: Incomes, Poverty and the Reform of Pension Systems'. In J. Bond, S. Peace, F. Dittman-Kohli, and G. Westerhof (eds), *Ageing Society: European Perspectives on Gerontology* (pp. 142–66). 3rd edition. London: Sage.

Netuveli, G. and Blane, D. (2008). 'Quality of Life in Older Ages'. *British Medical Bulletin*, 85: 113–26.

OECD, (2006). *Live Longer, Work Longer*. Paris: OECD Publishing.

OECD, (2013). 'Old-age Income Poverty'. In *Pensions at a Glance 2013*: OECD and G20 Indicators, Paris: OECD Publishing.

Oeppen, J. and Vaupel, J. (2002). 'Broken Limits to Life Expectancy'. *Science*, 296 (1126): 1029–31.

Office for National Statistics (2014). *National Life Tables, United Kingdom 2011–2013*. Office for National Statistics, <http://www.ons.gov.uk/ons/rel/lifetables/national-life-tables/2011-2013/stb-uk-2011-2013.html>, accessed 3 September 2015.

Ornstein, S. M., Nietert, P. J., Jenkins, R. G., and Litvi, C. B. (2013). 'The Prevalence of Chronic Diseases and Multimorbidity in Primary Care Practice: A PPRNet Report'. *Journal of the American Board of Family Medicine*, 26: 518–24.

Pahl, R. and Pevalin, D. J. (2005). 'Between Family and Friends: A Longitudinal Study of Friendship Choice'. *British Journal of Sociology*, 52: 199–221.

Perren, K., Arber, S., and Davidson, K. (2003). 'Men's Organizational Affiliations in Later Life: The Influence of Social Class and Marital Status on Informal Group Membership'. *Ageing and Society*, 23: 69–82.

Phillipson, C. (1982). *Capitalism and the Construction of Old Age*. London: Macmillan.

Phillipson, C. (1998). *Reconstructing Old Age*. London: Sage.

Phillipson, C. (2014). ' "Fuller" or "Extended" Working Lives: A Critical Commentary'. *Quality in Ageing and Older Adults,* 15: 237–40.

Pickard, L., Wittenberg, R., Comas-Herrera, A., King, D., and Malley, J. (2012). 'Mapping the Future of Family Care: Receipt of Informal Care by Older People with Disabilities in England to 2032'. *Social Policy and Society*, 11(4): 533–45.

Preston, S. H. and Stokes, A. (2012). 'Sources of Aging in More Developed and Less Developed Countries'. *Population and Development Review*, 38: 221–36.

Read, S., Grundy, E., and Foverskov, E. (2015). 'Socio-economic Position and Subjective Health and Well-being among Older People in Europe: A Systematic Narrative Review'. *Aging & Mental Health*, doi: 10.1080/13607863.2015.1023766.

Rechel, B., Grundy, E., Robine, J. M., Cylus, J., Mackenbach, J. P., Knai, C., and McKee, M. (2013). 'Ageing in the European Union'. *Lancet*, 381(9874): 1312–22.

Rowntree, B. S. (1941). *Poverty and Progress: A Second Social Survey of York*. London: Longmans.

Seeman, T. E. (2000). 'Health Promoting Effects of Friends and Family on Health Outcomes in Older Adults'. *American Journal of Health Promotion*, 14: 362–70.

Sundström, G., Malmberg, B., and Johansson, L. (2006). 'Balancing Family and State Care: Neither, Either or Both? The Case of Sweden'. *Ageing & Society*, 26: 767–82.

Tomassini, C., Kalogirou, S., Grundy, E., Fokkema, T., Martikainen, P., Broese van Groenou, M., and Karisto, A. (2004). 'Contacts between Elderly parents and their Children in Four European Countries: Current Prospects and Future Patterns'. *European Journal of Ageing,* 1:54–63.

Tomaszewski, W. and Barnes, M. (2008). 'Investigating the Dynamics of Social Detachment in Older Age'. In J. Banks, E. Breeze, C. Lessof, and J. Nazroo (eds), *Living in the 21st Century: Older People in England; the 2006 English Longitudinal Study of Ageing* (pp. 150–85). London: Institute for Fiscal Studies.

Townsend, P. (1981). 'The Structured Dependency of the Elderly: A Creation of Social Policy in the Twentieth Century'. *Ageing and Society*, 1: 5–28.

Townsend, P. and Wedderburn, D. (1965). *The Aged in the Welfare State*. London: G. Bell and Sons.

UNECE/European Commission, (2015). *Active Ageing Index 2014: Analytical Report*. Report prepared by A. Zaidi and D. Stanton. Geneva: United Nations Economic Commission for Europe.

Van Oyen, H., Nusselder, W., Jagger, C., Kolip, P., Cambois, E., and Robine, J.-M. (2013). 'Gender Differences in Health Life Years within the EU: An Exploration of the "Health-survival" Paradox'. *International Journal of Public Health*, 58: 143–55.

Vilaplana, C. L. (2013). 'Children Were the Age Group at the Highest Risk of Poverty or Social Exclusion'. *Statistics in Focus*, Eurostat 4/2013.

Walker, A. and Maltby, T. (2012). 'Active Ageing: A Strategic Policy Solution to Demographic Ageing in the European Union'. *International Journal of Social Welfare*, 21: S117–30.

Watson, D. and Williams, J. (2003). *Irish National Survey of Housing Quality, 2001–2002*. Dublin: The Economic and Social Research Institute.

Wenger, G. C., Dykstra, P. A., Melkas, T., and Knipsheer, K. C. P. M. (2007). 'Social Embeddedness and Late-life Parenthood—Community Activity, Close Ties, and Support Networks'. *Journal of Family Issues*, 28: 1419–56.

Wenger, G. C., Scott, A., and Patterson, N. (2000). 'How Important Is Parenthood? Childlessness and Support in Old Age in England'. *Ageing and Society*, 20: 161–82.

Willetts, D. (2010). *The Pinch*. London: Atlantic Books.

Williams, E. D., Tillin, T., Richards, M., Tuson, C., Chaturvedi, N., Hughes, A. D., and Stewart, R. (2015). 'Depressive Symptoms Are Doubled in Older British South Asian and Black Caribbean People Compared with Europeans: Associations with Excess Co-morbidity and Socio-economic Disadvantage'. *Psychological Medicine,* doi:10.1017/S0033291714002967.

Windle, G., Hughes, D., Linck, P., Russell, I., and Woods, B. (2010). 'Is Exercise Effective in Promoting Mental Well-being in Older Age? A Systematic Review'. *Aging & Mental Health*, 14(6): 652–69.

World Health Organisation, (2001). *The International Classification of Functioning, Disability and Health*. Geneva: The World Health Organisation.

Zunzunegui, M. V., Béland, F., and Otero, A. (2001). 'Support from Children, Living Arrangements, Self-rated Health and Depressive Symptoms of Older People in Spain'. *International Journal of Epidemiology*, 30: 1090–9.

Part III
Cross-cutting Themes

11

Gender and (Dis)advantage

Margarita León

Much water has flowed under the bridge since Simone de Beauvoir famously claimed that one is not *born* a woman but rather *becomes* a woman. After decades of feminist work and activism, most people would agree that behavioural differences between women and men are socially acquired rather than biologically set. Some might still find it tempting to keep the myth of biological determinism alive by explaining men's more violent behaviour, girls' underperformance in maths, or women's greater inability to read maps on the basis of different brain compositions and hormone fluctuations (see Fausto-Sterling, 1992). However, by and large, the fact that gender constitutes 'one of the most fundamental divisions of society' (West and Zimmerman, 1987: 126) is today hard to dispute even if gender, as indeed class (see Chapter 4, this volume) is a highly contested term. If biological facts are not dictating inequalities between the sexes to perform and access resources, if we agree that our behaviours are the consequence of a complex array of social factors that operate even before we are born, then the quest becomes unveiling the social roots of gender (dis)advantage. This chapter is committed to such endeavour.[1] Women are not systematically paid less because by nature they cannot access better paid occupations; men are not more likely to be in positions of economic or political power because they have a natural impulse for domination, children are not overwhelmingly cared for by their mothers because fathers lack the instinct to do so. The list is endless. The point is clear: anatomy or evolutionary theory offer little help to understand processes of gender advantage and disadvantage. We need the explanations that the social sciences can offer and even here, the road has been long.

---

[1] The work of Lara Maestripieri as research assistant is gratefully acknowledged.

Sociological theory has traditionally concentrated on social divisions based on class remaining oblivious to other forms of subordination. Likewise, political theory has anchored notions of political rights to 'the male citizen' (Lister, 1995). Feminist theory of the 1960s and 1970s stressed the need to understand the ways in which dividing lines around productive and reproductive work result in a series of disadvantages for women. At least in Western societies, gender differences in life chances have primarily been explained from the perspective of the interplay between the public and the private spheres. A set of dichotomies pivoting around the public–private divide shape the formation of gender identities, the subordination of women by men and the division of labour between paid and unpaid work. The way in which emotional labour is encapsulated as reproductive work has already determined its subordinated nature within the division of work. Domestic labour in the household is not counted as economic activity, although it takes up a large part of women's (and also men's) everyday lives. To overcome this distinction between the outside world of paid employment and the private world of unpaid work, Glucksmann developed the concept of the *total social organization of labour* referring to the 'manner by which all the labour in a society is divided up between and allocated to different structures, institutions and activities' (Glucksmann, 1995: 67). This gendered division deeply affects women's access to employment and social rights as well as men's responsibilities towards care.

This chapter considers gender as an inherent and intersecting dimension of advantage and disadvantage. It examines the processes by which gender relations are implicated in the construction of (dis)advantage. The study of disadvantage demands a multidimensional approach where gender intersects with other dimensions such as social class, ethnicity, age, and so on (McCall, 2005; Davis, 2008). The reciprocal inequalities which arise from the gendered division of work will be addressed in the first section of this chapter together with a consideration of gender gaps in a series of social spheres worldwide. The following section goes beyond the gendered division of labour to consider issues of culture and agency. The concluding section considers new manifestations of gender disadvantage deeply entrenched with in processes of global social inequality.

11.1 Understanding Gender Disadvantage

Throughout the globe, the disadvantages that women (and girls) face are a major source of inequality. The United Nations' Gender Inequality Index (GII) looks across different indicators of sex inequality in health, education, politics, and employment to identify the presence and degrees of systematic differences between men and women. These differences are not just a relevant

Table 11.1. UN Gender Inequality Index (2013)

	Gender Inequality Index		Share of seats in parliament	Population with at least some secondary education (% aged 25 and above)	Labour Force Participation rate (% aged 15 and above)	Human Development Ranking
	Value	Rank	(% held by women)	Female	Female	
Switzerland	0.030	2	27.2	95.0	61.2	3
Germany	0.046	3	32.4	96.3	53.5	6
Sweden	0.054	4	44.7	86.5	60.2	12
Denmark	0.056	5	39.1	95.5	59.1	10
France	0.080	12	25.1	78.0	50.9	20
Spain	0.100	16	35.2	66.8	52.6	27
Poland	0.139	26	21.8	79.4	48.9	35
United Kingdom	0.193	35	22.6	99.8	55.7	14
Australia	0.113	19	29.2	94.3	58.8	2
Japan	0.138	25	10.8	87.0	48.1	17
United States	0.262	47	18.2	95.1	56.8	5
Argentina	0.381	74	37.7	57.0	47.3	49
Regions						
Arab States	0.546	–	13.8	32.9	24.7	–
East Asia and the Pacific	0.331	–	18.7	54.6	62.8	–
Europe and Central Asia	0.317	–	18.2	70.4	45.5	–
Latin America and the Caribbean	0.416	–	25.3	53.3	53.7	–
South Asia	0.539	–	17.8	28.4	30.7	–
Sub-Saharan Africa	0.578	–	21.7	21.9	63.6	–

Note: The Gender Inequality Index (GII) is a statistical indicator which measures inequalities between genders in three dimensions considered relevant for human development: reproductive health (maternal mortality ratio and adolescent birth rates), empowerment (rate of parliamentary seats occupied by women and share of secondary education in the population above 25 years old) and economic status (expressed as labour market participation). The higher is the value of GII, the greater are the disparities among men and women.

Source: For Gender Inequality Index: UN statistics (2013), for share of seats: IPU (2013), for education: UNESCO (2013), for labour market: ILO (2013). Denmark data for labour market refers to population 25–74, Australia data for labour market refers to population 25–64, Argentina data for labour market are estimations

concern from a social justice viewpoint. As the UN's synthetic indicators show, there is a close link between gender (in)equality and human development: high levels of gender inequality are associated with a more unequal distribution of human development. In other words, societies where women encounter systematic differences in accessing education, health care, the labour market, or health care are those which do not create the necessary conditions for the general enhancement of human abilities. The UN's human development approach stems from Amartya Sen's work on human capabilities which will be explained later in the chapter.

As Table 11.1 shows, significant differences exist between and within regions. There is a sharp cross-regional contrast between Western and non-Western countries. In certain parts of the world as for example in Latin America and Caribbean, South Asia, Arab States, and sub-Saharan Africa, women have a much lower representation in politics compared to men, more difficulties in accessing education, and consequently a lower labour force participation rate. A recurrent question in the literature is the extent to which policies and instruments widely used in the developed world are in any way useful when prescribed to developing contexts. Indeed, in Western countries, the gender gap with regards participation in employment, access to education, and political representation has narrowed considerably over the last decades. In all countries the percentage of women elected to national parliaments has increased, partly because of the spread of the practice of quotas (Dahlerup, 2006). In addition, the gender gap with regard to educational attainment has in some countries been reduced to zero. In fact, in many countries educational attainment of women now outstrips that of men. Buchmann for instance has investigated on the causes for the gender gap in college completion in the US which has reversed from favouring men to favouring women (see Buchmann and DiPrete, 2006). Furthermore, the participation of women in the labour market is no longer the exception, but the rule. In advanced industrialized countries, general trends in education, health, and also the labour force have contributed towards reducing the gender gap in these general indicators. The introduction of gender issues in the political agenda and the creation of gender-specific social policies have also contributed, even if only partially, to these improvements in the life chances of women.

There are nevertheless significant differences that can still be observed between countries. In Europe, the distance between the North and the South is mainly attributed to the lack of specific policies supporting women. Comparative social policy research tends to agree on the role of the welfare state, through for instance the expansion of childcare services, as enabling the participation of women in paid employment. The presence of social-democratic governments is also positively associated with the presence of women-friendly social policies (Esping-Andersen, 1990; Huber and Stephens, 2000). Still, even in countries where gender gaps in employment, education, or politics have been reduced, notable levels of gender disadvantage prevail when we take a closer look. Systematic differences between men and women persist despite 'social' and 'economic' development. In fact a twofold effect seems to take place: on the one hand welfare states promote the participation of women in the labour force whilst on the other, levels of occupational segregation increase since women concentrate in welfare-related jobs in the public sector (Mandel and Semyonov, 2006).

With regard to the participation of women in the labour market, at the beginning of the 1970s, only a few Western countries had female employment rates above 50 per cent. For all countries there has been an upward trend. Since

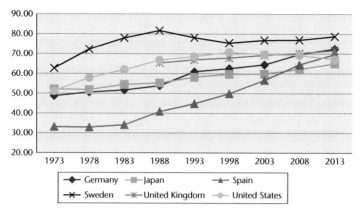

Figure 11.1. Female activity rate (15–64 years old), 1973/2013, selected countries
Source: OECD statistics database

Table 11.2. Female integration in the European labour market (2012)

	Employment rates (% aged 15–64)	Unemployment rates (% aged 15– 64)	Part-time employment (% aged 15–64)	Gender pay gap
	Female	Female	Female	
Denmark	70.0	7.7	35.8	14.9
Germany	68.0	5.3	45.0	22.4
Spain	51.2	25.2	23.9	17.8
France	60.0	10.0	30.0	15.4
Italy	47.1	12.0	31.0	6.7
Austria	67.3	4.4	44.4	–
Poland	53.1	11.0	10.6	6.4
Sweden	71.8	7.8	38.6	15.9
United Kingdom	65.1	7.5	42.3	19.1
Switzerland	73.6	4.6	60.1	–

Source: Eurostat database

the end of the 1990s Western countries have converged in rates of female employment above 60 per cent (see Figure 11.1). But as Table 11.2 shows, despite increasing participation of women in the labour market, gender disadvantage remains present in a number of ways.

Countries such as Denmark, Germany, Sweden, and Switzerland have rates of female employment close to or above 70 per cent. However, a large percentage of women who participate in the labour market in these countries work part-time (with the highest peak in Switzerland where the majority of women are part-time workers). Lower female employment levels in Southern and Eastern European countries are also linked to the low presence of part-time employment. Part-time work has customarily become an efficient way to increase levels of female employment. At the same time it operates as a contradictory way of integrating women into the labour market since it usually brings lower hourly wage and limited opportunities for advancement. It also increases the risk of female segregation in the labour market, because part-time employment is more frequently available in feminized occupations such as education and care, or in the lowest level of organizational hierarchies (Maestripieri, 2015). In countries where part-time employment is a common option for women (especially for those with caring responsibilities) the pay gap between men and women tends to be high. Therefore, part-time work does not equalize the position of women vis-à-vis full-time workers but becomes an option for households' additional income which maintains families' sexual division of labour (Blossfeld and Hakim, 1997). The decline of the so-called 'male breadwinner model' has been replaced by a 'one and a half earner model' rather than by a more balanced arrangement where both men and women work and care (Lewis, 2001). In this respect, and as will be later discussed, with the exception of a few Nordic countries, the support for women's equal employment opportunities has not been matched by considerations of men's sharing of childcare and household responsibilities or attempts to transform organizational structures (i.e. long hours at work) that hinder the reconciliation of work and family life (Haas et al., 2002).

Changes in employment have undoubtedly challenged the rationale of the gendered division of work. In general terms, the division of labour as it has been typically set up does not any longer cater for the great complexity and diversification we today find in the world of work. In gender terms, women have massively entered the labour market and men's employment is in decline. It is clear that as the participation of women in the world of paid employment increases, the boundaries around which productive and reproductive work are placed have become more blurred. Still, two important points are worth making. First, the existence of gender disadvantage in the world of paid employment signals the presence of institutional/structural barriers to equality between men and women. Second, even in countries with high proportions of female labour force participation, housework is still heavily gendered.

With regard to the first point, the concept of a glass ceiling refers to the gender pay gap (see Table 11.2) across the wage distribution and (difficulties for) promotions to top managerial position of female professionals. In all Western countries, despite mass incorporation of women in the labour market, a general increase in the levels of education of women, and the introduction of equal pay and sex equality legislation, women are still in a disadvantaged position for promotion to jobs of higher responsibility and pay. Research carried out in several countries shows that hidden gender-specific mechanisms are at play in the ways in which corporations hinder women from reaching top positions. Albrecht and colleagues (2001) for instance used micro data to explain the gender gap at the top of the wage distribution in Sweden, which accounted for the large majority of the overall gender wage gap in this country during the 1990s. Controlling for other variables such as occupation, age, or education, the authors conclude that gender differences in rewards are the primary factor responsible for the observed gap. In this sense, they argue, the way in which policies in Sweden support the role of women as workers and carers might be part of the explanation: 'women may have strong incentives to participate in the labour force but not to do so very intensively' (2001: 20). In sum, an understanding of women's underrepresentation and underpay in top managerial positions requires analysing the context in which women make career choices including procedural discrimination, the set up of policies for the reconciliation of work and family life, women's own preferences, and the work culture (such as, long hours and the personal characteristics which are linked with professional success) (Liff and Ward, 2001).

Considering household work, in 1992 Gershuny argued that a process of 'lagged adaptation' was taking place between women taking on paid work and households adapting to change. He based his argument on data that showed that the longer a woman had been in paid employment, the more equal the division of household work with her partner had become. Some years later, Sullivan also analysed time use data which in general terms supported Gershuny's hypothesis. In the UK, by the end of the 1990s women were doing less housework than in previous decades although they were still doing more housework than men. Recent studies show, however, that the 'lagged adaptation' explanation only worked up to a point. Despite women's increasing labour force participation, men's share of household work and childcare has been rather modest (Blossfeld and Drobnic, 2001): see Table 11.3. So, in Beck's terms, couples continue to 'do' gender despite mass incorporation of women to the labour force. According to Breen and Cooke (2005) progress in gender material equality needs to be paired with an evolution in men's gender ideology.

The contentious question of who takes responsibility for reproductive work has in many countries been solved not through a more equal distribution of domestic and care work within a couple but by externalizing tasks that used to belong to the exclusive realm of the family. The commodification of care work through informal channels has given way to what Hochschild (2000) has called the *Global Care Chain*: women from the South migrating to the North to care for children and the elderly leaving behind their own children, who are in turn looked after by female relatives or even migrant women from even poorer countries. In the most affluent societies, the percentage of migrant female workers employed as care workers or household employees in both

Table 11.3. Female to male ratio devoted to unpaid care work (2014)

	Unpaid care work
Denmark	1.30
Sweden	1.49
Switzerland	1.75
Germany	1.79
United Kingdom	1.85
France	1.90
Austria	1.95
Poland	2.01
Spain	3.04
Italy	3.37
Argentina	2.88
United States	1.61
Australia	1.81
Japan	4.83

Source: OECD Statistics Database

institutional and non-institutional settings is on the rise (Van Hooren, 2014; Anderson and Shutes, 2013). And everywhere paid domestic/care work is among the poorest paid and most precarious jobs (León et al., 2014). Thus, as women's employment patterns become more like those of men the division of reproductive labour becomes increasingly international and still heavily gendered (Anderson, 2000, Parrenas, 2001; Williams, 2012). This together with a global increase in income inequalities (Krugman, 2008; Piketty, 2014) warns us against too linear interpretations of gender advantage and disadvantage. Many women are relatively advantaged compared to other women (and men). So the notion of gender (dis)advantage needs to be seen in relative terms. In this sense, what becomes relevant is not so much whether some women (Western upper- to middle-class professionals) have 'escaped' the tyranny of domestic and routine care work by paying other women to do it but the fact that work linked to the world of reproduction continues to be undervalued and underpaid (cf. Chapter 9, this volume). Moreover, some professions decline in prestige and working conditions when they become increasingly feminized—primary school teachers and general practitioners for instance (León, 2014). So the question is not only (or not so much) women's economic disadvantage given prevailing gendered divisions of work but the fact that productive models determine some occupational categories as less productive and competitive, which translates into low salaries and less security (Chang, 2000). The dichotomy of unpaid *versus* paid employment is too limited to understand the complexity of gender disadvantage because it does not necessarily challenge the undervaluing of unpaid work.

Feminist economics, today a well-established sub-discipline within economics, looks precisely at alternative measurement of economic growth and national accounts to include the monetary value of unpaid domestic and care work. The seminal work of Marilyn Waring *If Women Counted: A New Feminist Economics* (1988) gave way to a prolific field of research preoccupied with finding accurate measurement of the value of non-market household labour for national incomes and product accounts. In many ways, issues embedded in feminist economics connect with wider debates on human progress and to issues of ecological sustainability. The neglect of non-monetary values is a concern common to these. Criticisms of neo-liberal models of economic growth stress the need to concentrate not just in women's engagement with the world of production but in the improvement of working conditions worldwide. To the extent that growth strategies come with a deterioration of job quality, the tensions between economic growth and gender equality are self-evident (Fraser, 2009).

11.2 Politics and Policy: Addressing Gender Disadvantage

In policy and in politics there is much greater awareness of gender disadvantage today than there was in the past. Labour shortages, demographic disequilibrium, and the perseverance of gender inequalities have led modern welfare states to abandon the prescription of the male breadwinner model and engage, with varying degrees of success, with the implementation of policy mechanisms that support women in their double role as workers and carers (Daly, 2011; Orloff, 2005). These new policies addressing new needs imply a recasting of the concept of family in terms of roles, functions, and relations vis-à-vis other institutions (Daly, 2011). Current new social policy paradigms place gender prominently on the agenda not only to grasp the nature of the transformation of contemporary welfare states but also to propose new ways forward. Addressing gender disadvantage has also become a fundamental component in global agendas to combat poverty and enhance social and economic development. The link that has been established at the level of policy rhetoric between empowering women and effective poverty alleviation has resulted in programmes targeting women specifically and giving additional resources to women instead of men.

The introduction of gender in the political agenda at different levels has been achieved thanks to the embedding of feminism and feminist causes in institutions, just as women's entry into politics has also been central to the transformation of public policy paradigms (Orloff and Palier, 2009: 407). Feminist research and women's movements of the 1960s and 1970s managed to unveil the gender-blindness of public policies (Walby, 2011; Jenson, 2009). Progressively, women's advocacy groups were able to place their demands within the structures of the state, giving rise to the concept of 'state feminism'

(Hernes, 1987; Stetson and Mazur, 1995). Of course, as Walby (2011: 57) notes, changes in the form of feminism from protest to engagement have implications for the effectiveness of feminist projects. A stronger coordination of feminist activities at organizational, national, European, and international level increases their influence, although concerns have been raised as to the weakening of radical demands and being drawn into dominant perspectives. Action on the part of institutions on mechanisms targeting gender disadvantage cannot be disassociated from this process of institutionalization of the feminist movement and the incorporation of women's policy agencies within the state apparatus.

In Europe, the Nordic countries have been clear pioneers on gender equality legislation, playing also an active role in enforcing gender equality policies at EU level. That said, sex discrimination in the workplace has been an item on the agenda of the European Community since the inception of the Treaty of Rome in 1957 which introduced the principle of Equal Pay for Equal Work. The requirement to reward equal work by men and women with equal pay was designed to enhance the functioning of the internal market, and so was motivated by considerations of economy and competition rather than gender justice. Nevertheless, the pursuit of equal treatment between men and women has rapidly developed into a social policy objective in its own right. Compliance with EU legislation has become in many countries the main force behind the introduction of gender equality norms and policies at national level (León, 2011). However, despite a common EU legal framework, benchmarks, and policy recommendations to address gender inequalities, differences between member states led to a variety of 'EU gender equality regimes' (Krizsan and Squires, 2014; Siim, 2014; Kennett and Lendvai, 2014). Outside the EU, other international agencies such as the United Nations and the World Bank have since the 1990s been introducing gender equality and gender mainstreaming policies as strategic instruments to tackle discrimination against women, and poverty and disadvantage more generally. A key turning point was the 1995 Fourth World Conference on Women in Beijing when strong pressure from feminist activists at national and transnational levels served to put gender justice in the political agenda of global actors (Kennett and Payne, 2014).

But, how far have we gone? Certainly, there have been clear advances in the position of women around the world and greater awareness of the causes and consequences of gender disadvantage, but inequalities between the genders persist and as Kennet and Payne note, 'there has been a failure to translate the global policy paradigm of gender equality in the everyday lives of many men and women'. In many countries, progress in procedural equality might actually hide obstacles and barriers placed at the level of institutions as well as individuals. As we know too well, the ideal world of the policy paradigm might encounter all sorts of mutations when ideas and discourses end up in different places (Béland and Cox, 2010; Jenson, 2010). There are two main shortcomings of gender equality policies. Firstly, it has become increasingly hard to interpret gender inequality without understanding divisions among women in terms of class, ethnicity, levels of education, or age. At EU level for example, the most recent Treaties indicate a policy shift away from discursive approaches solely addressing gender inequalities towards a more comprehensive intersectional approach on multiple inequalities addressing all grounds of discrimination (Lombardo et al., 2009). Secondly, in some instances, gender equality has been instrumentally used to target wider social problems resulting in a narrower understanding of the term. Two clear examples are the emerging social investment (SI) paradigm to recalibrate welfare states and the feminization of poverty agenda. In the first case, social investment is an approach to social policy that emphasizes equalizing life opportunities rather than life outcomes (Morel et al., 2012; and see Chapters 5 and 6, this volume). Most of our contemporary welfare states offer insufficient institutional support for the reconciliation of work and family life, which usually works as a deterrent to the participation of women in the labour market and to having children. Women who anticipate a high conflict between the sphere of employment and family life are either less likely to be employed or to 'resolve' the conflict by not having children and so, what Hobson and Ólah (2006) have called 'birth striking effects' are likely to be found in countries with weak reconciliation policies, including childcare (Brewster and Rindfuss, 2000; Gauthier, 2007; Esping-Andersen, 2009; Kamerman and Moss, 2009; Boje and Ejnraes, 2011; Drobnic and León, 2013). The SI perspective thus argues that enabling women to reconcile their family life with being active in the labour market has positive returns in fertility and economic productivity more generally.

In the case of the feminization of poverty agenda, targeting women as recipients of anti-poverty programmes also has positive returns in the rates of success of these programmes. However, the predominance of 'investment' and economic rationales often reveals an understanding of gender equality as an instrumental means to productive gains through high returns on investment and/or development. Some apparently win–win scenarios, that is, addressing simultaneously gender equality and economic growth or poverty reduction and development, can in fact exacerbate, rather than reduce, gender differences. Policy measures addressing the work/family conflict often rely on specific arrangements especially designed for women: low hours of part-time work when children are small or long maternity leaves, for instance. Very few countries make enough effort to make these arrangements for men as well. Likewise, poor women often become overburdened in targeted programmes by increasing their responsibilities (in working outside the home while continuing with their household tasks). So, while there are positive aspects to having gender figuring so prominently in the overarching goals of the social Investment and poverty and development agendas, more comprehensive approaches to address gender disadvantage are still needed. As Chant (2008: 182–3) points out, 'the emphasis on alleviating gender inequality and poverty simultaneously is misguided when these are distinct, albeit overlapping forms of disadvantage'. In these policy directions in high-income countries as well as low- to middle-income countries what has been lacking (with some honourable exceptions) is a consideration of gender relations. Somewhat paradoxically, these 'gender aware' policy agendas (poverty reduction in the global south and welfare adaptation in the global north) have ended up hijacking a more comprehensive understanding of gender equality and disadvantage. In sum, while the introduction of gender in certain policy fields is at first sight encouraging, the way in which gender disadvantage has been framed calls for a cautionary view. As Jenson has put it referring to social investment:

> At first blush, this gender awareness seems to represent a victory for decades of feminist mobilization and analysis. Closer attention reveals, however, that something has been lost in the translation of egalitarian feminism into the gender awareness that infuses the social investment perspective.   (Jenson, 2009: 472)

Of course, policies and politics can only to a limited extent intervene in modifying pre-existing gender cultures. Culture certainly intervenes in the way in which institutions regulate and shape family life and gender relations, and the way in which gender disadvantage is reproduced in a society. Besides institutional constraints, shared social norms, values, and beliefs also interact with institutions and are also crucial in understanding gender divisions in society (Pfau-Effinger, 2005; Kremer, 2007). A particular culture or normative frame might either encourage or discourage the participation of women in paid employment, might welcome or not the involvement of fathers in childbearing, might justify or denounce unequal social mobility for men and women, might facilitate or hinder the participation of women in politics, and so on. Thus, the 'acceptability' of various forms of balancing care work and employment given cultural and social values and norms plays a major role in shaping these different care models (Crompton et al., 2007; Lister et al., 2007; Pfau-Effinger, 2005). Understanding how norms, beliefs, social practices, and traditions intervene in (re)producing social disadvantage is also key to explaining certain patterns of gender disadvantage in the labour market. One of the problems of dealing with cultural traditions that perpetuate gender disadvantage is that it would require dealing with unequal power relations in the private sphere of the home and it does not seem easy to make this subject to policy intervention. One exception though is programmes to combat domestic violence where private relations are subject to public interventions.

11.3 Beyond 'Structure': Issues of Agency

Our capacity to make decisions, to choose between different options, to take 'risks', in sum our capacity for autonomous agency is bound to depend on the economic, social, and political environments in which we live. The open-ended debate within the social sciences between structure and agency is also mirrored in debates about gender (dis)advantage. Although classical social theorists tended to see structure as dominating agency, modern social theorists have come to understand the capacity of agents to also modify and shape the structure. This is the case of Giddens' structuration theory (1984) or Bourdieu's 'habitus' concept. For the latter, we are socialized in a 'field' with a set of roles and relations, we position ourselves in relation to such a field but at the same time with our actions we modify such relationships and expectations. Contemporary feminist theory has increasingly reflected on Giddens and Bourdieu's sociological concepts to develop further the relationship between structure and agency from a gender perspective (see for instance Adkins and Skeggs, 2004).

The capabilities approach originally developed by Sen in the early 1990s has incorporated a new perspective on the relationship between agency and structure. The capabilities approach offers an integrated understanding of the complex ways in which our capacity to make decisions and to choose freely is intertwined with the opportunities we actually have to make those decisions and choices. In other words, the capabilities approach asks us what the opportunities are to exercise 'real' choice (Hobson, 2014). It is intrinsically multidimensional in the sense that inequalities between men and women are not reducible to inequalities in income and means. Martha Nussbaum further developed the analytical implications of moving beyond income inequalities to integrate issues such as time autonomy, reproductive work, or household labour. Sen and Nussbaum's work has been highly influential in the development of the United Nations' Gender Empowerment Index and Gender Inequality Index discussed earlier (see Table 11.1). Disadvantage in health, education, political representation, or participation in the labour market has negative repercussions for women's capabilities and freedom of choice. Benería (2008) for instance claims that the capabilities approach might provide a useful framework for designing reconciliation policies for non-Western countries in ways which can expand the individual capabilities of women. The relevance of subjective dimensions of poverty and a capability approach that gives the possibility of moving beyond lack of income as the primary indicator of poverty has also been vindicated by scholars who criticize the instrumentalization of gender and development (GAD) in poverty reduction programmes (Jackson, 1996; Chant, 2008).

However, as Burchardt and Hick argue (Chapter 2, this volume) the very complex and subjective component of the concept can be an obstacle for its implementation and analytical research. The fact that we do not have an agreed capability list means that we do not yet have a precise under-standing of how to measure these, and so the ordering of advantage and disadvantage becomes problematic. As the authors argue the multidimen-sional and open-ended nature of the capabilities which might be included has led to some questions about whether the approach can be successfully operationalized. In her edited collection, Hobson (2014) shows ways in which the capability approach can be applied to issues of work–life bal-ance. The starting point is that whilst rights and entitlements for the reconciliation of work and family life, such as reduced working time, parental leaves, and childcare have been introduced in Europe following EU legislation and benchmarks, there still is an agency gap in the actual possibilities for using these entitlements. The ways in which firms and workplaces interpret entitlements and how these adapt to individuals' circumstances are two elements which might account for this agency gap. Research showing the interactions between welfare state policies and socio-economic positions also call for differentiated approaches to the reconcili-ation of work and family life rather than addressing universal work–family tensions (Mandel, 2012).

11.4 Further Reflections: New Manifestations of Gender Disadvantage

How is gender disadvantage placed within the changing nature of eco-nomic and social structures in late-capitalist societies? Societies are chan-ging and the changing role of women is probably one of the strongest triggers for this transformation. Whilst some old cleavages of gender (dis)advantage have disappeared and others have remained, new manifest-ations of gender tensions arise, creating new sources of conflict and also new possibilities for action. These new cleavages are often embedded within a global context and are strongly associated with multiple forms of disadvantage. The global dimension of some of these problems justifies the intervention of international organizations which attempt to operate beyond the nation state. One example is the United Nations' work on violence against women:

> Violence against women is a problem worldwide, occurring, to a greater or lesser degree, in all regions, countries, societies and cultures, and affecting women irrespective of income, class, race or ethnicity. All these forms of violence . . . are

not examples of random victimization, but are associated with inequality between women and men, and strategies to perpetuate or entrench that inequality.
(http://www.un.org/womenwatch/daw/news/unwvaw.html)

Political mobilization and public intervention in issues such as gender violence, forced migration, or sex trafficking have taken several decades to crystallize thanks to the work of grass-root and non-governmental organizations. In this sense, the space of mobilization has also gone global to a large extent. As Fraser (2005) proposes, nation states are very limited in dealing with transnational problems connected with women's rights and therefore a transnational solution is needed. Fraser's theory of post-national justice comes as a response to the global nature of struggles for economic and social redistribution that need to be dealt with at a supra-national level. This global dimension to gender disadvantage is translated with more or less success into a global policy paradigm on gender equality with gender mainstreaming being the most accepted policy instrument. However, doubts exist as to the real effectiveness of this goal at different scales and geographical locations. Furthermore, the apparent consensus behind political discourses and policy paradigms hides a whole array of contradictory views. This is the case of the highly contentious feminist debate around the legal status of sex workers and the state regulation of sexual commerce—the criminalization versus legalization debate (see Bernstein, 2014). All in all, while there have been noticeable improvements in the status of women around the world, forms of disadvantage between men and women remain. The global policy paradigm of gender equality encounters obstacles when it needs to be applied in practice. In Kennett and Payne (2014)'s terms, there is a disjuncture between the ideal world of the policy paradigm and the lived experience.

In sum, while we ought to recognize the global interconnectedness of different forms of inequalities, policy prescriptions should be able to adapt to the specifics of local, cultural, social, and economic contexts. In this chapter we have seen how 'gender troubles' in work–family tensions, in trafficking, in migration, or in poverty have come to the fore in national and international political arenas. Women are often the subjects of intervention and action as victims and also as the source of solutions since they seem to produce 'effective returns'. Meanwhile discussion of men within these systems, the relational aspects of gender inequality and the need to change these relational dynamics as a way to solve at least some of the issues are relatively lacking. Finally, as has been addressed in other chapters in this volume, dealing with social 'disadvantage' more generally means focusing on the ways in which 'advantage' is created and reproduced, on how and how much the gains of some elucidate the loss of so many others.

References

Adkins, L. and Skeggs, B. (2004). *Feminism after Bourdieu*. Oxford: Blackwell.

Albrecht, J., Björklund, A., and Vroman, S. (2001). 'Is There a Glass Ceiling in Sweden?' Discussion Paper N. 282, April 2001, <http://ftp.zew.de/pub/zew-docs/div/gender/vroman.pdf> last accessed 2 February 2015.

Anderson, B. (2000). *Doing the Dirty Work? The Global Politics of Domestic Labour.* London: Zed Books.

Anderson, B. and Shutes, I. (2013). *Migration, Diasporas and Citizenship*. Basingstoke: Palgrave Macmillan.

Béland, D. and Cox, R. H. (2010). *Ideas and Politics in Social Science Research*. New York: Oxford University Press.

Benería, L. (2008). 'The Crisis of Care, International Migration, and Public Policy'. *Feminist Economics,* 14(3): 1–21.

Bernstein, E. (2014). 'Introduction: Sexual Economies and New Regimes of Governance'. *Social Politics,* 21(3): 345–54.

Boje, T. and Ejnraes, A. (2011). 'Family Policy and Welfare Regime'. In H. Dahl, M. Keranen, and A. Kovalainen (eds), *Europeanisation, Care and Gender* (pp. 77–93). Basingstoke: Palgrave Macmillan.

Blossfeld, H. P. and Hakim, C. (1997). *Between Equalization and Marginalization: Women Working Part-time in Europe*. Oxford: Oxford University Press.

Blossfeld, H. P. and Drobnic, S. (2001). *A Cross-National Comparative Approach to Couples' Careers*. Oxford: Oxford University Press.

Breen, R. and Cooke L. P. (2005). 'The Persistence of Gendered Division of Domestic Labour'. *European Sociological Review*, 21(1): 43–57.

Brewster, K. L. and Rindfuss, R. R. (2000). 'Fertility and Women's Employment in Industrialized Nations'. *Annual Review of Sociology*, 26: 271–96.

Buchmann, C. and DiPrete, T. (2006). 'The Growing Female Advantage in College Completion: The Role of Family Background and Academic Achievement'. *American Sociological Review*, 7(4): 515–41.

Chang, M. L. (2000). 'The Evolution of Sex Segregation Regimes'. *American Journal of Sociology*, 105(6): 1658–701.

Chant, S. (2008). 'The "Feminisation of Poverty" and the "Feminisation" of Anti-poverty Programmes: Room for Revision?' *Journal of Development Studies*, 44(2): 165–97.

Crompton, R., Lewis, S., and Lyonette, C. (2007). *Women, Men, Work and Family in Europe*. Basingstoke: Palgrave Macmillan.

Dahlerup, D. (ed.) (2006). *Women, Quotas and Politics*. New York and London: Routledge.

Daly, M. (2011). 'What Adult Worker Model? A Critical Look at Recent Social Policy Reform in Europe from a Gender and Family Perspective'. *Social Politics: International Studies in Gender, State & Society*, 18(1): 1–23.

Davis, K. (2008). 'Intersectionality as Buzzword: A Sociology of Science Perspective on What Makes a Feminist Theory Successful'. *Feminist Theory*, 9(1): 67–85.

Drobnic, S. and León, M. (2013). 'Agency Freedom for Work-life Balance in Germany and Spain'. In H. Hobson (ed.), *Work–Life Balance: The Agency and Capabilities Gap across European and Asian Societies* (pp. 126–52). Oxford: Oxford University Press.

Esping-Andersen, G. (1990). *The Three Worlds of Welfare Capitalism*. Princeton, NJ: Princeton University Press.

Esping-Andersen, G. (2009). *The Incomplete Revolution. Adapting to Women's New Roles.* Cambridge and Malden: Polity Press.

Eurostat (2015). *Database of European Statistics*, Eurostat, EU.

Fausto-Sterling, A. (1992). *Myths of Gender: Biological Theories about Women and Men*, 2nd edn. New York: Basic Books.

Fraser, N. (2005). 'Reframing Justice in a Globalizing World'. *New Left Review*, 36(Nov/Dec): 56–80.

Fraser, N. (2009). 'Feminism, Capitalism and the Cunning of History'. *New Left Review*, 56(Mar/Apr): 97–117.

Gershuny, J. (1992). 'Changes in the Domestic Division of Labour in the UK 1975–87: Dependent Labour versus Adaptive Partnership'. In N. Abercrombie and A. Warde (eds), *Social Change in Contemporary Britain* (pp. 70–94). Cambridge: Polity Press.

Gauthier, A. (2007). 'The Impact of Family Policies on Fertility in Industrialized Countries: A Review of the Literature'. *Population Research and Policy Review*, 26(3): 323–46.

Giddens, A. (1984). *The Constitution of Society: Outline of the Theory of Structuration*. Oakland, CA: University of California Press.

Glucksmann, M. A. (1995). 'Why "Work"? Gender and the "Total Social Organization of Labour"'. *Gender, Work & Organization*, 2(2): 63–75.

Haas, L., Allard, K., and Hwang, P. (2002). 'The Impact of Organizational Culture on Men's Use of Parental Leave in Sweden'. *Community, Work and Family*, (5)3: 319–42.

Hernes, H. (1987). *Welfare State and Woman Power: Essays in State Feminism*. Oslo: Norwegian University Press.

Hobson, B. (2014). *Worklife Balance. The Agency and Capabilities Gap*. Oxford: Oxford University Press.

Hobson, B. and Ólah, L. (2006). 'Birthstrikes? Agency and Capabilities in the Reconciliation of Employment and Family'. *Marriage and Family Review*, 39(3–3): 197–227.

Hochschild, A. R. (2000). 'Global Care Chains and Emotional Surplus Value'. In W. Hutton and A. Giddens (eds), *On The Edge: Living with Global Capitalism* (pp. 130–46). London: Jonathan Cape.

Huber, J. and Stephens, E. (2000). 'Partisan Governance, Women's Employment, and the Social Democratic Service State'. *American Sociological Review*, 65(3): 323–42.

Jenson, J. (2009). 'Lost in Translation: The Social Investment Perspective and Gender Equality'. *Social Politics*, 16: 446–83.

Jenson, J. (2010). 'Diffusing Ideas for after Neoliberalism: The Social Investment Perspective in Europe and Latin America'. *Global Social Policy*, 10(1): 59–84.

Jackson, C. (1996). 'Rescuing Gender from the Poverty Trap'. *World Development*, 24(3): 489–504.

Kamerman, S. B. and Moss, P. (2009). *The Politics of Parental Leave Policies: Children, Parenting, Gender, and the Labour Market*. Bristol: Policy Press.

Kennett, P. and Lendvai, N. (2014). 'Policy Paradigms, Gender Equality and Translation: Scales and Disjuncture'. *Journal of International and Comparative Social Policy* 30(1): 17–27.

Kennet, P. and Payne, S. (2014). 'Gender Justice and Global Policy Paradigms'. *Journal of International and Comparative Social Policy*, 30(1): 1–15.

Kremer, M. (2007). *How Welfare States Care: Culture, Gender and Parenting in Europe.* Amsterdam: Amsterdam University Press.

Krizsan, S. H. and Squires, J. (2014). 'The Changing Nature of European Equality Regimes: Explaining Convergence and Variation'. *Journal of International and Comparative Social Policy*, 30(1): 53–68.

Krugman, P. (2008). 'For Richer'. In H. S. Sharpiro and D. E. Purpel (eds), *Critical Issues in American Education: Democracy and Meaning in a Globalizing World* (pp. 7–22). London: Taylor and Francis.

León, M. (2011). 'The Quest for Gender Equality'. In A. M. Guillén and M. León (eds), *The Spanish Welfare State in European Context* (pp. 59–76). Aldershot: Ashgate.

León, M. (ed.) (2014). *The Transformation of Care in European Societies.* Basingstoke: Palgrave Macmillan.

León, M., Pavolini, E., and Rostgaard, T. (2014). 'Cross-national Variations in Care'. In León (ed.), *The Transformation of Care in European Societies* (pp. 34–62). Basingstoke: Palgrave Macmillan.

Lewis, J. (2001). 'The Decline of the Male Breadwinner Model: Implications for Work and Care'. *Social Politics*, 8(2): 152–69.

Liff, S. and Ward, K. (2001). 'Distorted Views through the Glass Ceiling: The Construction of Women's Understanding of Promotion and Senior Management Positions'. *Gender, Work and Organizations*, 8(1): 19–36.

Lister, R. (1995). 'Dilemmas in Engendering Citizenship'. *Economy and Society*, 24(1): 35–40.

Lister, R., Williams, R., Anttonen, A., Bussemaker, J., Gerhard, U., Heinen, J., Johansson, S., Leira, A., Siim, B., Tobio, C., and Gavanas, A. (2007). *Gendering Citizenship in Western Europe: New Challenges for Citizenship Research in a Cross-National Context.* Bristol: The Policy Press.

Lombardo, E., Meyer, P., and Verloo, M. (2009). *The Discursive Politics of Gender Equality: Stretching, Bending and Policymaking.* London: Routledge.

Maestripieri, L. (2015). 'Gendering Social Vulnerability: The Role of Labour Market De- standardisation and Local Welfare'. In D. Kutsar and M. Kuronen (eds), *Local Welfare Policy Making in European Cities* (pp. 51–67). Berlin: Springer.

Mandel, H. and Semyonov, M. (2006). 'A Welfare State Paradox: State Interventions and Women's Employment Opportunities in 22 Countries'. *American Journal of Sociology*, 111(6): 1910–49.

Mandel, H. (2012). 'Winners and Losers: The Consequences of Welfare State Policies for Gender Wage Inequality'. *European Sociological Review*, 28(2): 241–62.

McCall, L. (2005). 'The Complexity of Intersectionality'. *Signs*, 30(3): 1771–800.

Morel, N., Palier, B., and Palme, J. (2012). *Towards a Social Investment Welfare State? Ideas, Policies and Challenges.* Bristol: The Policy Press.

OECD (2015). *Statistics Database*, <http://stats.oecd.org/Index.aspx?DataSetCode=LFS_SEXAGE_I_R>, accessed 3 September 2015.

Orloff, S. (2005). 'Social Provision and Regulation: Theories of States, Social Policies and Modernity'. In J. Adams, E. S. Clemens, and A. S. Orloff (eds), *Remaking Modernity: Politics, History, and Sociology* (pp. 190–224). Durham, NC: Duke University Press.

Orloff, A. S. and Palier, B. (2009). 'The Power of Gender Perspectives: Feminist Influence on Policy Paradigms, Social Science, and Social Politics'. *Social Politics*, 16(4): 405–12.

Parrenas, R. (2001). *Servants of Globalization: Women, Migration and Domestic Work*. Stanford, CA: Stanford University Press.

Pfau-Effinger, B. (2005). 'Culture and Welfare State Policies: Reflections on a Complex Interrelation'. *Journal of Social Policy*, 34(1): 3–20.

Piketty, T. (2014). *Capital in the Twenty-First Century*. Harvard: Harvard University Press.

Siim, B. (2014). 'Conflicts and Negotiations about Framings of Gender Equality and Diversity by Political Actors within the European Public Sphere'. *Journal of International and Comparative Social Policy*, 30(1): 17–27.

Stetson, D. and Mazur, A. (1995). *Comparative State Feminism*. London: Sage.

Van Hooren, F. (2014). 'Migrant Care Work in Europe'. In M. León (ed.), *The Transformation of Care in European Societies* (pp. 62–82). Basingstoke: Palgrave Macmillan.

Walby, S. (2011). 'Is the Knowledge Society Gendered?' *Gender, Work & Organization*, 18(1): 1–29.

Waring, M. (1988). *If Women Counted: A New Feminist Economics*. New York: Harper and Row.

West, C. and Zimmerman, C. W. (1987). 'Doing Gender'. *Gender and Society*, 1(2): 125–51.

Williams, F. (2012). 'Converging Variations in Migrant Care Work in Europe'. *Journal of European Social Policy*, 22(4): 363–76.

12

'Race' and Ethnicity

Coretta Phillips and Lucinda Platt

In much of the literature on poverty, exclusion, and power, 'race' has come to seem synonymous with the experience of advantage and disadvantage, with a wealth of research charting the disadvantage minority groups face across the Western world relative to the affluence, status, and power of majority populations. Across the world, race and ethnicity remain persistent stratifying features of societies, typically accompanied by differential access to resources, power, and status, and sometimes leading to conflict (Smith, 1991; Stewart, 2008). Yet the processes by which racial and ethnic inequalities are produced and sustained are complex. The contestation of the very terms 'race' and 'ethnicity' are one part of that complexity, requiring us to understand the boundaries by which different groups are defined in official categorizations and those formulated in research studies—and how those come to be meaningful and linked to relative positions of economic status in particular locations and historical contexts. At the outset, it is important to underline the multifarous manifestations of advantage and disadvantage that exists across the globe, with huge variation in positions and status, linked to race, ethnicity, indigeneity, skin colour, faith, and culture. For the sake of brevity, our focus in this chapter will remain on diverse experiences of ethnic groups in the US, the UK, and in other parts of Europe.

Processes of ethnic and racial disadvantage are also fundamentally relational, in that majority, often white advantage is the mirror of, and made possible by, minority ethnic disadvantage. Similarly the advantage of particular ethnic groups can only be evaluated relative to the disadvantage of others. Yet, as we argue in this chapter, it is potentially misleading to locate the sources of disadvantage exclusively *within* racial or ethnic groups. There remains a persistent tendency among not only those wishing to maintain their superior status but also some researchers and policymakers to draw on cultural and/or hereditary accounts of ethnic differences. Whilst attractive because of their simplicity, the empirical reality is typically rather different. Group distinctions inhere in processes of inclusion and exclusion rather than in intrinsic cultural differences (Barth, 1969); and what is recognized as 'ethnicity' displays different degrees of social closure, political salience, cultural distinctiveness, and historical stability' (Wimmer, 2008: 970) and is dependent on how shared understandings of boundaries arise.

Moreover, boundaries themselves are not fixed but are linked to forms of recognition, which are fluid and open to negotiation and redefinition. Thus, the expansion of the privileged 'white' category came to incorporate, over time, previously racialized groups such as the Irish and Italians (Ignatiev, 1995), while also contracting to exlude non-European white identities (Bonnett, 1998). This highlights the complexity of identifying those interlocking factors that lead to contemporary configurations of ethnic and racialized disadvantage and advantage.

As contemporary patterns of advantage and disadvantage cannot be understood solely in relation to characteristics of the ethnic and racial groups themselves, we must therefore look to the historial emergence of racial hierarchies and patterns of exclusion which marked some minority ethnic groups—both disasporic and indigenous—as culturally inferior. Examples of historical processes of colonialism and imperialism include the enslavement of African populations transported to the US, Caribbean, and Latin America, the cultural extermination or forced assimilation of indigenous populations, and the indenture of workers from India in East Africa and the Caribbean. In the present, we also need to attend to relational processes reinforcing perceived cultural superiority and inferiority through discrimination and racism, as directed against immigrants to European nations (see also Chapter 13), those of non-majority faiths (see also Chapter 14), as well as those often referred to as settled minorities whose primary immigration occurred several decades ago. Historical processes of colonialism and forced migration may also be implicated in differentials in social, economic, or human capital associated with particular groups (cf. Chapter 4). For example, migrants from prosperous nations typically move with high levels of capital, while those moving from low-income and developing countries typically start with a relative deficit. And, of course, history, discrimination, and resources interact in complex ways at different historical times and with wider economic, social, and demographic processes, such that 'successful' groups may lose their advantage through systematic discrimination or conflict, and disadvantaged minority groups may succeed or face reduced opportunities depending on the accidents or structures that located them in particular industries or particular regions at times of economic expansion or contraction.

This is not to say that there are not differences of behaviour, attitude, belief, or 'culture' across (some) ethnic groups that may be identified and subject to exploration. Indeed, at the heart of the multiculturalism debate is the extent to which the state should recognize such differences and develop social policies accordingly, for example, through providing cultural exemptions, where to not do so might indirectly discriminate against some cultural minorities (Parekh, 2006; Taylor, 2003). For traditional liberalists, such as Barry (2001), such practices defy the neutrality of the state and thus risk undermining equality for all and creating division and conflict in society between competing cultural groups. The former position carries the risk of essentializing and reifying ethnic and cultural identities while the latter approach can have material consequences when the state itself is implicated in perpetuating ethnic inequalities in access to goods and services (see also Fraser, 2000 on questions of redistribution). Neither perspective is particularly well suited to recognizing hybrid and sycretic identities in Britain, particularly of young people, borne out of complex patterns of migration, diasporic connections, and globalizing influences (Back, 2002; Brah, 1996; Sharma, Hutnyk, and Sharma, 1996). At the same time, we would not wish to argue, *pace* Cox (1959), that racial distinctions can be simply 'reduced' to class. Rather, as our illustrations and particularly our discussion of the 'underlass debate' makes clear, we demonstrate how reducing ethnic difference to 'culture' or 'ethnicity' is likely to provide a very limited account of how and why racial and ethnic advantage and disadvantage emerges and persists.

In what follows we expand upon these points. First we discuss the highly contingent nature of racial and ethnic classification and the allocation of people to 'groups', focusing primarily on practice within the US and UK. This is important as it reveals both how perceptions of the drivers of inequality are themselves implicated in how race and ethnicity are conceptualized and measured, but also how state recognition of identities and processes of ascription may relate only partially to individuals' self-evaluations. We then review some of the arguments relating to relative economic disadvantage of minorities and its persistence over time. We draw particularly on those that have been used to explore the experience of relatively recent migrants and their descendants in Europe. We provide examples of the position of the UK's ethnic groups to illustrate some of these arguments. Specifically, we focus on how historical, generational, and structural processes, including relational processes of discrimation, rather than cultural practices and behaviours, can lead to both economic disadvantage and to spatial segregation. In the final section of the chapter we explore how cultural and structural accounts have competed in attempting to explain the extreme economic disadvantage and racial segregation that characterise areas identified with the 'underclass'. As the discussion illustrates, and as comparative analysis reveals, while racialized processes may lead to an 'underclass', neighbourhood disadvantage (which is discussed in Chapter 15) is neither 'caused' by ethnicity nor is it limited to particular ethnic or racial groups. However, by recognizing those factors which have contributed to particular constellations of disadvantage it becomes possible to develop ways in which they might be addressed or compensated for in policy formulations.

12.1 What are 'Race' and Ethnicity?

It is now accepted that racial groups do not exist. Banton (1998) traces the contemporary use of race to the discredited theories of 'racial types' which assumed immutable heritable phenotypical characteristics, such as skin colour, had corresponding fixed cognitive and behavioural characteristics such as low intelligence and immorality (Eze, 1997). Racism, a relational process by which inferiority inheres to some groups is most commonly directed to those distinguished as originating from Africa, Asia, and Latin America. Yet the complexity of global migration patterns in recent times (see Chapter 13) suggests this term can also now be attached to those of white Eastern European origin, and others considered non-white or non-European in many Western nations, such as Hispanics in the US, or Turks in Germany, England, and the Netherlands.

The rejection of 'race' as an objective analytical category has led some to argue that its continued use is damaging and continues to perpetuate attitudes of racial superiority and hierachy (Gilroy, 2000; Song, 2004). However, the fact that people continue to act as if 'race' is meaningful renders the terminology of race and racism salient in social scientific analysis as well as popular discourse. Racism does not evaporate into thin air just because of the rejection of race by social scientists. Hence the categorization of 'races' and the analysis of difference across them is both an anachronism and a necessary, if blunt, instrument for those studying social inequalities in life chances.

In the UK, the language of 'ethnicity' has tended to supercede that of race, though some have argued that it has in the process lost much of its analytical purchase and become merely a synonym for what elsewhere might be described as 'race' (see Fenton, 2003). Weber (1968: 389) described ethnic groups as 'those human groups that entertain a subjective belief in their common descent because of similarities of physical type or of customs or both, or because of memories of colonization and migration'. Ethnic group is a flexible concept and, unlike race, is not tied to specific physical or cultural attributes. Yet in the same way as 'race', such uses of ethnicity and ethnic groups enable inequalities between those of different (racialized) ethnicities to be recognized and enumerated, albeit also risking essentializing such differences. Here and throughout this chapter we use the term 'racialization' and its derivatives descriptively, to identify how issues—such as immigration, unemployment, and 'underclass'—become imbued with meaning based on ideologies of racial inferiority and superiority. These are not fixed in time or space, but are contingent and specific to particular configurations (for more on the concept of racialization see Murji and Solomos, 2005; Rattansi, 2005).

The bluntness of our tools of categorization is also underlined by the lack of fit between racial and ethnic monitoring by the state, in attempting potentially to open up inequalities to scrutiny, and the degree to which official categorizations are meaningful to those they represent (Office for National Statistics, 2009). While as Prewitt (2005) acknowledges, individuals are increasingly asserting as a positive selfhood, a right to choose how they identify, rather than allowing this to be imposed by the state (Hall, 1991/2000), social scientists seeking to understand inequalities require stable categories to assess them. There remains an ongoing tension between social scientific understandings of ethnicity and its fluid, contingent and self-ascribed nature, and the more fixed and atheoretical categories used by the state to monitor experiences across different population groups (Coleman and Salt, 1996; Perlmann and Waters, 2002). For example, Figure 12.1 shows how race and ethnicity questions are differentiated in the US Census, where Hispanic Latino identification is explicitly distinguished from the race question and is identified as ethnicity. The US distinction between race and ethnicity means that many Hispanics identify and are identified as racially 'white'; many others perceive both their race and ethnicity to be Hispanic (Logan, 2004). Yet there is substantial diversity within the Hispanic population in terms of life chances, with those of Cuban origin experiencing relative advantage

Is this person of Hispanic, Latino, or Spanish origin?		
No, not of Hispanic, Latino, or Spanish origin		
Yes, Mexican, Mexican American, Chicano		
Yes, Puerto Rican		
Yes, Cuban		
Yes, another Hispanic, Latino, or Spanish origin–*Print origin, for example, Argentinean, Colombian, Dominican, Nicaraguan, Salvadoran, Spaniard, and so on*		
What is this person's race? *Mark one or more boxes*		
White		
Black, African American or Negro		
American Indian or Alaska Native–*Print name of enrolled or principal tribe*		
Asian Indian	Japanese	Native Hawaiian
Chinese	Korean	Guamanian or Chamorro
Filipino	Vietnamese	Samoan
Other Asian–*Print race*		Other Pacific Islander–*Print race*
Some other race–*Print race*		

Figure 12.1. US Census Hispanic identity and race questions
Source: US Census Bureau

What is your ethnic group?		
*Choose **one** section from A to E, then tick **one** box to describe your ethnic group*		
A	**White**	
	English/Welsh/ Scottish/ Northern Irish/ British	
	Irish	
	Gypsy or Irish Traveller	
	Any other White background,*write in*	
B	**Mixed/ multiple ethnic groups**	
	White and Black Caribbean	
	White and Black African	
	White and Asian	
	Any other mixed / multiple ethnic group background,*write in*	
C	**Asian/ Asian British**	
	Indian	
	Pakistani	
	Bangladeshi	
	Chinese	
	Any other Asian background,*write in*	
D	**Black/ African/ Caribbean / Black British**	
	African	
	Caribbean	
	Any other Black/African/Caribbean background,*write in*	
E	**Other ethnic group**	
	Arab	
	Any other ethnic group,*write in*	

Figure 12.2. England and Wales 2011 Census ethnic group questions
Source: Office for National Statistics

(Ennis, Ríos-Vargas, and Albert, 2011), which is not shared by the largest group of Hispanics, those of Mexican heritage (Telles and Ortiz, 2009). Such differences in life chances correspondingly provide different claims on or access to the status of majority white ethnicity (Duncan and Trejo, 2008).

In the UK census categories (Figure 12.2), national origins (e.g. Indian, Pakistani, Chinese) alongside aggregates such as as 'Black African' are described as 'ethnic groups', rather than 'races'. And instead of allowing multiple responses as in the US Census, there are separate 'mixed' ethnicity categories. One problem is that broad categorizations such as Black African may mask significant internal variation between groups with different national origins, relationships to the former colonial powers, primary reasons for migration, dominant religions, as well as diversity in official national languages. For example, UK Somalis and Ghanaians differ in all these aspects (Aspinall and Chinoyab, 2008). On the other hand, facilitating greater 'granularity' as Aspinall (2009: 1421) refers to it, or ever finer distinctions of identity, such as national origins, can present methodological problems of small sub-sample sizes which may obscure the systematic inequalities the categorization is intended to reveal.

Despite the differences between the categories, in both monitoring systems, there is a tendency to see whiteness as an undifferentiated racial norm against which all other ethnic groups are compared, thus upholding the normative sense of whiteness and the othered nature of minority ethnic identities (Bulmer, 1996; Coleman and Salt, 1996). This can also operate to exclude white minorities who may have experiences and opportunities distinct from the white majority ethnic group and who may be distinguished by language and accent. Such immigrants can easily become racialized and, despite their apparent privileged 'whiteness', can face discrimination and hostility. For example, the large-scale immigration from Eastern Europe to the UK, substantially changed the profile of the White Other aggregate category from a successful and privileged immigrant group to a much less well-paid and more marginal group facing substantial challenges in the labour market (Drinkwater, Eade, and Garapich, 2009), as well as hostile responses from the settled population (Duffy and Frere-Smith, 2014). Similarly, as non-Europeans, Turks have historically been excluded from 'white status' in the UK (Bonnett, 1998), and other parts of Europe, such as Germany where Turkish immigration has been extensive.

The incorporation of groups into, or exclusion of groups from, the dominant and privileged category of 'white' has had a long and complex history (see for example, Bonnett (2000); Bonnett and Carrington (2000); Ignatiev (1995); Sacks (1994)), but in the European context, groups such as the Turks, are regarded as a distinctive 'immigrant' group where the language of *immigration* largely substitutes for the US and UK paradigms of race and ethnicity. Immigration status is steadfastly durable such that the children of immigrants retain classification as (2nd generation) immigrants, and in the case of Germany, up until changes in nationality law in 2000, they were largely without access to German citizenship even if born there. Here it is assumed or observed *cultural* rather than *physical* difference that still renders such populations 'non-white' whether through dress, language, religious practice, ethnic consumption and resources, community organization, neighbourhood concentration, or some combination thereof. The shift from biological to cultural racism, that is, from a conception of difference and superiority located in a belief in racial types and hierarchies to one associated with perceptions of cultural incompatibility and inferiority, has been regarded as a key feature of race discourses in late modernity. This flexibility permits exclusion and discrimination beyond the realm of race and ethnicity, particularly extending to religion (Barker, 1981; Bonilla-Silva, 2006; Lentin, 2012) (and see Chapter 14 in this volume). Either way, group differences are once again explained as sets of cultural practices and behaviours, rendering marginalized groups the apparent authors of their own disadvantage—and majority groups as entitled to their advantage.

We turn now to reviewing some of the key forms of racialized advantage and disadvantage in employment in the UK, considering how inequalities persist, increase, or reduce over time and between family generations. Next we move to examine patterns of residential settlement and material disadvantage in the US. Clearly, these two arenas of labour market and area are interlinked; employment opportunities may be structured by where people live (see Chapters 6, 9, and 15). Two caveats must also be acknowledged:

- First, much analysis of ethnic inequalities still uses the white majority as the key comparator for the experience of ethnic groups which problematically reinforces whiteness as the normative benchmark. This approach also undermines claims of acculturation (Sam and Berry, 2010) and the new assimilation theories (Alba and Nee, 1997) which see such processes as two-way and evolving over time. Nevertheless, to the extent that the majority population captures the experience of the population as a whole such comparisons do illustrate the extent to which there is commonality or how unequally inequalities are distributed across societies.

- Second, it is important to note that *within-group* diversity in disadvantage typically exceeds that found between groups (Hills et al., 2010). To give a simple example, as Figure 12.3 shows, while the mean incomes of Bangladeshi and Pakistani women in the UK are far lower than all other ethnic groups, there remains a proportion that still have an income that is above that of some of those from majority and minority ethnic groups we might consider to be relatively advantaged (Nandi and Platt, 2010).

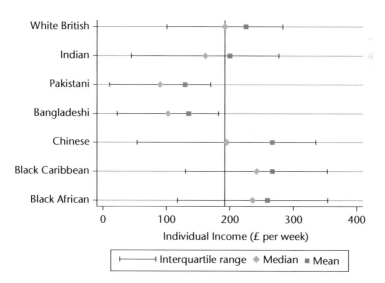

Figure 12.3. The dispersion of women's incomes, by ethnic group

Note: Incomes represent all income sources attributable to individual women, not household incomes. The largest component will typically be earnings from employment.
Source: Family Resources Survey 2004–9, from Nandi and Platt, 2010

12.2 Economic Outcomes and Penalties among Minorities

In understanding the economic positions occupied by different ethnic groups, reformulations of assimilation theory by Alba and Nee (1997) place weight on economic integration from a disadvantaged initial immigrant generation to a more equal position through subsequent generations. In contrast, the theory of segmented assimilation (Portes and Zhou, 1993) understands differential trajectories as simultaneously distinct and following an assimilative path (Portes and Rumbaut, 2001). Rather than taking a national majority reference point, it is argued that different groups relate their outcomes by reference to those who form their immediate context or reference population, although the context of reception into the 'host society' also plays a part, with some ethnic groups more positively received than others. The degree to which immigrants can access opportunities from successful co-ethnics will also play a significant role in progression for the immigrant and subsequent generations.This model has been used to account for the particular success of Chinese minorities—even from very disadvantaged origins—in the US, and the relatively poor employment outcomes of Caribbean men in the UK, despite their much greater levels of integration on other measures, such as marriage to partners from the white majority (Peach, 2005).

In the UK, the concept of the ethnic penalty was introduced by Heath and McMahon (1997) in their analysis of the 1991 Census, and has since been extended to work on exploring employment discrimination (Heath and Cheung, 2006) and research on the position of the second generation (Heath and Cheung, 2007) in both the UK and Europe more widely. Such analyses acknowledge improvements in educational qualifications for most, but not all, ethnic groups, but they also find that these qualifications do not always lead to the occupational rewards one might expect, even if penalties are somewhat smaller for the second than immigrant generation (cf. Cheung, 2013). Both direct discrimination by employers and occupational segregation are likely to be implicated in this disadvantage. In a recent study, using job applications matched on education, skills, and work history, but varying by applicants' names used to convey particular minority ethnic identities, Wood et al. (2009) found 39 per cent of minority ethnic applicants received a call-back for an interview compared with 68 per cent of white applicants. Similarly, studies by Longhi and Platt (2008) and Longhi et al. (2009, 2013) on wages, suggested that the most successful ethno-religious groups, such as Indian Hindus, nevertheless faced lower pay than would be expected based on their qualifications and experience. Notwithstanding, the less successful minority ethnic groups, such as Pakistani Muslims, were somewhat protected by minimum pay floors in the face of quite severe absolute disadvantage. Such studies also point to the significance of trying to understand ethno-religious experiences, rather than examining ethnicity and religion separately.

Additionally it is important to take account of social class background (see Chapter 4). The longer-term economic trajectories of minority ethnic groups in the UK show a positive upward trend in general, once we take account of the typically poorer starting points of the immigrant generation. Thus while they are not, in many cases, getting the returns to education in the form of equal employment chances (Heath and Cheung, 2007), compared with those of similarly advantaged or disadvantaged origins, they are by and large in an equivalent position to other ethnic groups (Zuccotti, 2015). Zuccotti's analysis, building on earlier work by Platt (2007) shows that taking account of the typically more disadvantaged class origins of minorities alongside their achieved education substantially explains the ethnic penalty in labour market outcomes, and this helps us to understand how minority ethnic disadvantage can be structurally perpetuated across generations.

Within this overall story, there are persistently higher risks of unemployment or non-employment among black men, and to a degree among Pakistani, Bangaldeshi, and Black African women (See Table 12.1). Employer discrimination is undoubtedly part of the explanation; self-reported racial

Table 12.1. Employment status across selected ethnic groups, by sex, England and Wales 2011, row %

	Employed	Unemployed	Retired	Student	Looking after home/family	Long-term sick or disabled	Other inactive
Women							
White UK	53.8	3.2	27.4	3.9	5.9	3.8	1.9
Other White	66.5	4.6	8.8	6.6	8.7	1.7	3.2
Mixed groups	55.8	8.4	5.7	13.7	8.3	4.2	3.9
Indian	57.4	5.3	12.0	7.9	10.1	3.5	3.8
Pakistani	30.3	7.1	6.4	11.0	29.6	5.8	9.7
Bangladeshi	28.7	8.6	6.0	10.8	30.9	5.1	9.8
Chinese	47.6	4.5	8.2	27.3	8.1	1.0	3.4
Black African	53.7	11.9	3.5	14.2	8.5	2.7	5.5
Black Caribbean	58.2	7.9	16.2	6.1	4.4	4.1	3.1
Men							
White UK	63.3	5.1	20.7	4.3	0.7	4.3	1.6
Other White	78.3	4.5	5.7	6.8	0.7	1.8	2.3
Mixed groups	59.0	11.6	4.6	14.5	1.0	5.1	4.2
Indian	70.6	5.9	9.0	9.0	0.7	2.6	2.3
Pakistani	62.3	9.7	6.3	11.9	1.5	4.1	4.2
Bangladeshi	62.0	11.1	5.3	11.6	2.0	4.0	4.1
Chinese	53.1	4.5	6.6	31.1	0.9	0.9	2.8
Black African	60.7	13.7	2.6	14.3	1.1	2.5	5.0
Black Caribbean	56.0	12.4	14.9	6.0	1.1	5.3	4.3

Source: ONS 2011 Census, Table DC6201EW

Table 12.2. Child poverty rates by ethnic group, 2010/11–2012/13

	Poverty rate (BHC below 60% of median) %
White British	15
Indian	22
Pakistani	45
Bangladeshi	44
Chinese	34
Black Caribbean/African/British	24

Note: For an explanation of the calculation of the poverty rate, see Chapter 7.
Source: Department for Work and Pensions (2014)

prejudice by managers and employers is higher in those industrial sectors where ethnic penalities are most common (Heath and Cheung, 2006). But it is also the case that demand for labour in areas with minority ethnic concentrations is likely to be lower and opportunities fewer. On the supply side, transport and childcare needs may present obstacles to accessing the labour market (HM Government, 2001). That said, on average, pay is high among Indian men, though there is substantial diversity across the group in overall incomes (Nandi and Platt, 2010). Moreover, child and family poverty rates may be particularly affected by households containing only a single earner, and this may even be the case for those seen as successful minorities (see Table 12.2).

In the analysis of ethnic penalties, it is important to consider not only the inequalities implied by unequal returns to education and qualifications—and social class background, but also the underlying differences in educational attainment that may themselves be shaped by discrimination within the school system. See also Chapter 6. These operate alongside the long-term consequences of earlier generations of discrimination that locate parents of the second generation in a poorer economic position. For example, research points to how the important role of negative stereotyping by white teachers (Burgess and Greaves, 2009; Youdell, 2003) is likely to impact on school attainment in a form of 'self-fulfilling prophecy'. So while students from some groups are expected to perform well, those from others tend to have their abilities underrated.

The nature and degree of the occupational clustering of ethnic groups within particular labour market sectors is striking (Blackwell and Guinea-Martin, 2005) and can also help explain patterns of disadvantage. To a degree these patterns reflect the structural effects of deindustrialization of certain specific sectors (textiles in Yorkshire and the motor industry in the Midlands), which have particularly affected certain minority groups, such as those of Pakistani origin. Hence the meaning of the concentration of ethnicity and disadvantage arises and takes shape through broader macroeconomic processes. Figure 12.4, for example, illustrates the over-representation of Bangladeshis and Chinese in England and Wales in catering and of Pakistanis in

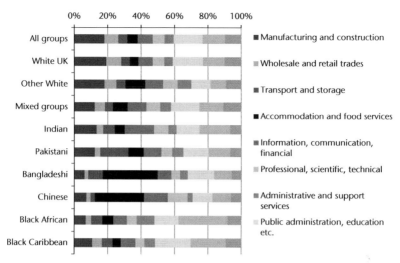

Figure 12.4. Sector of employment by ethnic group, England and Wales, 2011
Note: Some standard sectors of industry have been combined for simplicity.
Source: ONS 2011 Census, Table DC6211EW

transport, while Black Africans are strongly represented in the care sector (health and social work), all of which are associated with low pay and have undoubtedly been part of the shift from manufacturing to service-based employment (Longhi et al., 2013). Moreover, occupational and geographical clustering can be implicated in one another (Catney and Sabater, 2015); and the extent of geographical clustering and neighbourhood concentration is one route by which persistent ethnic inequalities are maintained.

12.3 Neighbourhoods and Minorities

Spatial concentration of minorities and its tendency to coincide with neigh-bourhood deprivation has often been a source of political concern, while as Bolt and others (2009) point out, the relationship between concentration, segregation, and economic outcomes is complex. The overrepresentation of minorities in poorer areas is regarded as both one aspect of their disadvantage (Phillips, 1998), but also potentially separating them from not only future opportunities but also more mainstream engagement and contexts (Bolt and van Kempen, 2009; Rex and Moore, 1967). Interestingly, geographical con-centration of wealth is subject to less political and academic scrutiny than geographical concentration of poverty, though they are the same processes which feed into the perpetuation of social divisions. While Massey and Denton (1993) illustrated the ways in which cumulative small-scale exclusionary decision processes could result in extreme residential segregation (aligning with disadvantaged areas), the negative connotations of 'ghettoes' out of step with normative culture and practices in the US have also been emphasized. In the UK, a debate has raged on the extent and measurement of ethnic segregation, and whether it is increasing or declining (Simpson, 2005), but there have also been claims about the existence of self-segregation with consequent selection into disadvantage and exclusionary cultural environments (Battu and Zenou, 2010), although this tends to be considered as more problematic than arguably similar processes of 'white flight' which increases this segregation through exclusion or exit (Amin, 2002).

There are, broadly speaking, three models of minority neighbourhood concentration and its evolution over time: spatial assimilation, place stratification, and enclave effects. Spatial assimilation involves people moving out of more concentrated to less concentrated areas over time, and is broadly the pattern that is found in the UK for most groups, albeit that the pace of this movement outwards is rather slow and somewhat variable across minority ethnic groups. Place stratification refers to the constraints on movement presented by historical discrimination in housing markets which has had long-term negative consequences in the UK (Karn, Kemeny, and Williams, 1985). Enclave effects represent the positive features of concentrations of co-ethnics for employment and networks (Borjas, 1995), but also the negative feature of minorities' self-employment because of labour market exclusion (Clark and Drinkwater, 2000) or because concentration reduces the threat of racist hostility which might be experienced in predominantly white neighbourhoods. Where the latter effects predominate, neighbourhood-level disadvantage becomes entrenched alongside ethnic clustering.

The UK is, however, far from the extremes of place stratification witnessed in particular for African Americans in the US who were seemingly rarely able to be spatially dispersed into the suburbs from cities' urban cores (Peach, 1996). In the US, debates have centred on the extent to which the resultant residential segregation and economic disadvantage results from structural changes in society, particularly relating to deindustrialization, or whether there are specific behavioural traits which exist among those cultural groups located in such areas. It is to this debate that we turn next.

12.4 Race, Ethnicity, and the 'Underclass'

Although not the first to use the term 'underclass', Charles Murray has been most closely associated with its cultural and racialized formulation in recent times (see Chapter 1 for the wider background). Murray (1994) documented both absolute and relative (to whites) declines since the 1960s and 1970s in young black employment and college enrolment, alongside increases in homicide arrests and illegitimate births in the US. Murray took these as indicators of distinct and problematic cultural behaviours among the poor black population, resulting from social disorganization, individualism, poor socialization, and the excessive generosity and disincentivizing effects of welfare benefits. The absence of role models demonstrating legitimate and constructive work was a particular feature of such underclass communities, according to Murray. In his limited foray into the politics of poverty in the UK, the markers of underclass—voluntary unemployment, illegitimacy, and violence—were in evidence in white not black communities (Murray, 1990). Murray's (2012) subsequent focus in the US envisaged an increasingly whitened underclass there too, influenced by vulgar and hopelessly violent black cultural practices that he perceived to be becoming part of the normative character of American society. Murray also described a narrow elite of professionals, advantaged by wealth, high incomes, and highly developed cognitive abilities, who were also spatially clustered, but these were typically white and Asian and rarely black or Latino.

Murray's work has been subject to an abundance of critical commentary on conceptual, theoretical, and empirical grounds (Dixon, Carrier, and Dogan, 2005; Ellwood and Summers, 1986; Lister, 1996; Marks, 1991; Peterson, 1991). It can be contrasted with the work of William Julius Wilson (1987) who instead attached greater emphasis to structural and demographic features of US society as producing entrenched urban poverty and the associated pathologies of black underclass life. For Wilson, chronic joblessness resulted from: the loss of low-education jobs in US cities, which in turn affected marriage and family stability; historically racist housing and zoning policies contributing to segregation and concentrated disadvantage in public housing; a youthful age structure stemming from South–North migration (particularly relevant in relation to crime and unemployment), and the flight of the middle-class professional buffer that had previously maintained informal social control, provided job networking opportunities, and acted as role models.

A slew of ethnographic studies have provided important insight by capturing the complex ways in which the urban poor live their lives, finding support for the arguments of both cultural determinists such as Murray and structural proponents like Wilson (Marks, 1991). MacLeod's (2009) *Ain't No Makin' It*, for example, found depressed aspirations for social mobility in a low-income housing project among mainly *white* young men whereas the mainly *black* young men were conspicuous by their conventionality and investment in the dominant legitimate culture. MacLeod's follow-up research found that ultimately even the latter group had in fact failed to achieve social mobility through hard work and educational commitment, not because of their cultural failings but because of structural circumstances beyond their control. Venkatesh's

255

(2008) work in Chicago, similarly warned against simplistic binary accounts of illegal cultures, recognizing that legitimate businesses and residents in poor minority neighbourhoods often have equivocal relationships with hustlers and gang members who they may profit from as they bring customers and trade into the neighbourhood. Finally, Goffman's (2009) ethnography of a Philadelphia neighbourhood underlined the amplificatory effects of aggressive police surveillance on young men who were, or had been, subject to criminal justice supervision, which also contributed, albeit not entirely, to young men struggling to meet their familial responsibilities.

This connection to the actions of agents of the criminal justice system is a central theme in the work of Loïc Wacquant (2008: 93) who preferred to use the neo-Marxist term 'subproletariat' to challenge the 'vague and morally pernicious neologism' of cultural understandings of the underclass. Wacquant regarded the degraded wastelands of black 'hyperghettoes' as containing those experiencing economic exclusion and marginality, victims of neoliberal policies of welfare retrenchment of both public and third sector provisions and services (but see also Wilson, 2009). Concentrated and extreme poverty, bare subsistence and hustling, drug dealing, and fatal violence—all contributed to a pervasive sense of insecurity and fear on the streets of urban black neighbourhoods. According to Wacquant (2009), urban marginality has become subject to disciplinary modes of governance and punishment. This is achieved through 'workfare'—the use of more stringent eligibility criteria for welfare benefits and the imposition of sanctions—and through 'prisonfare' and the massive increase in the use of incarceration. Wacquant claims we are witnessing a meshing of the 'assistantial' (welfare) and 'carceral' (prison, probation, and parole) functions of the neoliberal state, with the hyperghetto and the prison cyclically producing compliant workers for the deregulated labour market, which maintains high profits through low wages, poor benefits, and job insecurity in largely service-sector employment. Wacquant's work has courted criticism on a variety of conceptual, theoretical, and methodological grounds (Daems, 2008; Dawson, 2014; Jones, 2010; Lacey, 2010; Newburn, 2010; Sampson, 2012; Small, 2007; Wilson, 2014), but like that of others, such as Garland (1985, 2001), it deserves careful consideration for its description of the elision between welfare and penal state functions.

12.5 Concluding Comments

Cumulative disadvantage in education, employment, and residential settlement is faced by many minority ethnic groups, even though it is less marked after the immigrant generation. Nevertheless, diversity within minority experiences is a key part of the picture in the UK and Europe, with some, in absolute terms, excelling compared to the white majority (though not necessarily to the degree their qualifications would suggest). It is also clear that discrimination plays a role in disadvantage, and more so for some groups such as the African American population in the US.

The longer-term prospects for those who experience chronic joblessness in localities without access to legitimate alternatives face a bleak outlook. There are striking rates of low pay faced by some White groups, such as Polish immigrants to the UK (Campbell, 2013), and concentrated pockets of extreme disadvantage faced by predominantly White communities, for example in the North East of England. Nevertheless, these counterweights to an oversimplified story of the patterning of advantage and disadvantage by ethnicity and race do not overturn the overall persistence of white advantage. The need for greater levels of educational attainment to reach an equivalent level of success, the much greater risks of unemployment for similarly qualified minorities compared to their majority group peers, and the challenges facing the further upward mobility of the 'successful' groups, all act as a reminder of the relative advantage implicit in being 'white'. This, of course, does not mean that there is no white poverty or deprivation, but whiteness as an evolving marker of privileged, majority status remains a significant structural feature of life chances in many countries. While the nature and extent of this advantage and its exact configuration, including the enduring issue of who is included within the privileged category itself is variable and somewhat fluid, the underlying persistence of this specific advantage continues to be felt. Future explorations beyond Western states will also bring to the fore contexts in which majority privilege is not unequivocally linked to whiteness, and where power dynamics are structured through other allegiances and boundaries such as tribe, clan, caste, and sect.

References

Alba, R. and Nee, V. (1997). 'Rethinking Assimilation Theory for a New Era of Immigration'. *International Migration Review*, 31(4): 826–74.

Amin, A. (2002). 'Ethnicity and the Multicultural City: Living with Diversity'. *Environment and Planning A*, 34(6): 959–80.

Aspinall, Peter J. (2009). 'The Future of Ethnicity Classification'. *Journal of Ethnic and Migration Studies*, 35(9): 1417–35.

Aspinall, P. and Chinoyab, M. (2008). 'Is the Standardised Term "Black African" Useful in Demographic and Health Research in the United Kingdom?' *Ethnicity & Health*, 13(3): 183–202.

Back, L. (2002). 'The Fact of Hybridity: Youth, Ethnicity and Racism'. In D. T. Goldberg and J. Solomos (eds), *A Companion to Racial and Ethnic Studies* (pp. 439–54). Oxford: Blackwell.

Banton, M. (1998). *Racial Theories*. Cambridge: Cambridge University Press.

Barker, M. (1981). *The New Racism: Conservatives and the Ideology of the Tribe*. London: Junction Books.

Barry, B. (2001). *Culture & Equality*. Oxford: Polity Press.

Barth, F. (1969). *Ethnic Groups and Boundaries: The Social Organisation of Culture Difference*. London: Allen & Unwin.

Battu, H. and Zenou, Y. (2010). 'Oppositional Identities and Employment for Ethnic Minorities: Evidence from England'. *The Economic Journal*, 120(542): F52–F71.

Blackwell, L. and Guinea-Martin, D. (2005). 'Occupational Segregation by Sex and Ethnicity in England and Wales, 1991 to 2001'. *Labour Market Trends*, 13(12): 501–11.

Bolt, G., Özüekren, A. S., and Phillips, D. (2009). 'Linking Integration and Residential Segregation'. *Journal of Ethnic and Migration Studies*, 36(2): 169–86.

Bolt, G. and van Kempen, R. (2009). 'Ethnic Segregation and Residential Mobility: Relocations of Minority Ethnic Groups in the Netherlands'. *Journal of Ethnic and Migration Studies*, 36(2): 333–54.

Bonilla-Silva, E. (2006). *Racism without Racists: Color-blind Racism and the Persistence of Racial Inequality in the United States*. 2nd edn. Lanham, MD: Rowman & Littlefield.

Bonnett, A. (1998). 'Who Was White? The Disappearance of Non-European White Identities and the Formation of European Racial Whiteness'. *Ethnic and Racial Studies*, 21(6): 1029–55.

Bonnett, A. (2000). *White Identities: Historical and International Perspectives*. Harlow: Pearson Education.

Bonnett, A. and Carrington, B. (2000). 'Fitting into Categories or Falling between Them? Rethinking Ethnic Classification'. *British Journal of Sociology of Education*, 21(4): 487–500.

Borjas, G. J. (1995). 'Ethnicity, Neighborhoods and Human-capital Externalities'. *American Economic Review*, 85: 365–90.

Brah, A. (1996). *Cartographies of Diaspora*. London: Routledge.

Bulmer, M. (1996). 'The Ethnic Group Question in the 1991 Census of Population'. In D. Coleman and J. Salt (eds), *Ethnicity in the 1991 Census: Volume One: Demographic Characteristics of the Ethnic Minority Populations* (pp. 33–62). London: HMSO.

Burgess, S. and Greaves, E. (2009). 'Test Scores, Subjective Assessment and Stereotyping of Ethnic Minorities'. CMPO Working Paper Series 09/221.

Campbell, S. (2013). 'Over-education among A8 Migrants in the UK'. DoQSS Working Paper No. 13–09. London: Institute of Education.

Catney, G. and Sabater, A. (2015). *Ethnic Minority Disadvantage in the Labour Market: Participation, Skills and Geographical Inequalities*. York: Joseph Rowntree Foundation.

Cheung, S. Y. (2013). 'Ethno-religious Minorities and Labour Market Integration: Generational Advancement or Decline?' *Ethnic and Racial Studies*, 37(1): 140–60.

Clark, K. and Drinkwater, S. (2000). 'Pushed out or Pulled in? Self-employment among Ethnic Minorities in England and Wales'. *Labour Economics*, 7: 603–28.

Coleman, D. and Salt, J. (1996). 'The Ethnic Group Question in the 1991 Census: A New Landmark in British Social Statistics'. In D. Coleman and J. Salt (eds), *Ethnicity in the 1991 Census: Volume One: Demographic Characteristics of the Ethnic Minority Populations* (pp. 1–32). London: HMSO.

Cox, O. C. (1959). *Caste, Class, and Race: A Study in Social Dynamics*. New York: Monthly Review Press.

Daems, T. (2008). *Making Sense of Penal Change*. Oxford: Oxford University Press.

Dawson, M. D. (2014). 'The Hollow Shell: Loïc Wacquant's Vision of State, Race and Economics'. *Ethnic and Racial Studies*, 37(10): 1767–75.

Department for Work and Pensions (2014). 'Households below Average Income 1994/5–2012/13'. London: Department for Work and Pensions.

Dixon, J., Carrier, K., and Dogan, R. (2005). 'On Investigating the "Underclass": Contending Philosophical Perspectives'. *Social Policy and Society*, 4(1): 21–30.

Drinkwater, S., Eade, J., and Garapich, M. (2009). 'Poles apart? EU Enlargement and the Labour Market Outcomes of Immigrants in the United Kingdom'. *International Migration*, 47(1): 161–90.

Duffy, B. and Frere-Smith, T. (2014). *Perceptions and Reality: Public Attitudes to Immigration*. London: Ipsos MORI.

Duncan, B. and Trejo, S. J. (2008). 'Ancestry versus Ethnicity: The Complexity and Selectivity of Mexican Identification in the United States'. IZA Discussion Paper No. 352. Bonn: IZA.

Ellwood, D. T. and Summers, L. H. (1986). 'Is Welfare really the Problem?' *Public Interest*, (83): 57–78.

Ennis, S. R., Ríos-Vargas, M., and Albert, N. G. (2011). 'The Hispanic Population: 2010'. Report Number: C2010BR-04. Washington, DC: United States Census Bureau.

Eze, E. (1997). *Race and The Enlightenment: A Reader*. Oxford: Blackwell.

Fenton, S. (2003). *Ethnicity*. Cambridge: Polity.

Fraser, N. (2000). 'Rethinking Recognition'. *New Left Review*, 3(May–June): 107–20.

Garland, D. (1985). *Punishment and Welfare: A History of Penal Strategies*. Aldershot: Gower.

Garland, D. (2001). *The Culture of Control*. Oxford: Oxford University Press.

Gilroy, P. (2000). *Between Camps: Nations, Cultures and the Allure of Race*. Harmondsworth: Allen Lane/The Penguin Press.

Goffman, A. (2009). 'On the Run: Wanted Men in a Philadelphia Ghetto'. *American Sociological Review*, 74(3): 339–57.

Hall, S. (1991/2000). 'Old and New Identities, Old and New Ethnicities'. In L. Back and J. Solomos (eds), *Theories of Race and Racism* (pp. 144–53). London: Routledge.

Heath, A. and Cheung, S. Y. (2006). *Ethnic Penalties in the Labour Market: Employers and Discrimination*. Department for Work and Pensions Research Report 341. Leeds: Corporate Document Services.

Heath, A. and McMahon, D. (1997). 'Education and Occupational Attainments: The Impact of Ethnic Origins' In V. Karn (ed.), *Ethnicity in the 1991 Census: Volume Four: Employment, Education and Housing among the Ethnic Minority Populations of Britain* (pp. 91–113). London: HMSO.

Heath, A. F. and Cheung, S. Y. (eds) (2007). *Unequal Chances: Ethnic Minorities in Western Labour Markets*. Oxford: Oxford University Press.

Hills, J., Brewer, M., Jenkins, S. (2010). *An Anatomy of Economic Inequality in the UK: Report of the National Equality Panel*. London: Government Equalities Office/Centre for Analysis of Social Exclusion.

HM Government (2001). *Ethnic Minorities and the Labour Market: Interim Analytical Report*. London: Cabinet Office.

Ignatiev, N. (1995). *How the Irish became White*. Abingdon: Routledge.

Jones, M. (2010). '"Impedimenta State": Anatomies of Neoliberal Penality'. *Criminology and Criminal Justice*, 10(4): 393–404.

Karn, V., Kemeny, J., and Williams, P. (1985). *Home Ownership in the Inner City: Salvation or Despair?* Aldershot: Gower.

Lacey, N. (2010). 'Differentiating among Penal States'. *British Journal of Sociology*, 61(4): 778–94.

Lentin, A. (2012). 'Post-race, Post Politics: The Paradoxical Rise of Culture after Multiculturalism'. *Ethnic and Racial Studies*, 37(8): 1268–85.

Lister, R. (1996). *Charles Murray and the Underclass: The Developing Debate*. London: IEA Health and Welfare Unit in association with *The Sunday Times*.

Logan, J. R. (2004). 'How Race Counts for Hispanic Americans'. *Sage Race Relations Abstracts*, 29(1): 7–19.

Longhi, S., Nicoletti, C., and Platt, L. (2009). 'Decomposing Wage Gaps across the Pay Distribution: Investigating Inequalities of Ethno-religious Groups and Disabled People. Report commissioned by the National Equality Pane. ISER Working Paper 2009–32. Colchester: Institute for Social and Economic Research, University of Essex.

Longhi, S., Nicoletti, C., and Platt, L. (2013). 'Explained and Unexplained Wage Gaps across the Main Ethno-religious Groups in Great Britain'. *Oxford Economic Papers*, 65(2): 471–93.

Longhi, S. and Platt, L. (2008). *Pay Gaps Across Equalities Areas*. EHRC Research Report 9. Manchester: Equalities and Human Rights Commission.

MacLeod, J. (2009). *Ain't No Makin' It: Aspirations and Attainment in a Low-income Neighbourhood*. 3rd edn. Boulder, CO: Westview Press.

Marks, C. (1991). 'The Urban Underclass'. *Annual Review of Sociology*, 17(August): 445–66.

Massey, D. S. and Denton, N. A. (1993). *American Apartheid: Segregation and the Making of the Underclass*. Cambridge, MA: Harvard University Press.

Murji, K. and Solomos, J. (eds) (2005). *Racialization: Studies in Theory and Practice*. Oxford: Oxford University Press.

Murray, C. A. (1990). *The Emerging British Underclass*. London: Institute for Economic Affairs.

Murray, C. A. (1994). *Losing Ground: American Social Policy, 1950–1980*. 2nd. edn. New York, NY: Basic Books.

Murray, C. A. (2012). *Coming apart: The State of White America, 1960–2010*. New York, NY: Crown Forum.

Nandi, A. and Platt, L. (2010). *Ethnic Minority Women's Poverty and Economic Well Being*. London: Government Equalities Office.

Newburn, T. (2010). 'Diffusion, Differentiation and Resistance in Comparative Penality'. *Criminology and Criminal Justice*, 10(4): 341–52.

Office for National Statistics (2009). 'Final Recommended Questions for the 2011 Census in England and Wales: Ethnic Group'. London: ONS.

Parekh, B. (2006). *Rethinking Multiculturalism: Cultural Diversity and Political Theory*. Basingstoke: Palgrave Macmillan.

Peach, C. (1996). 'Does Britain Have Ghettos? *Transactions of the Institute of British Geographers*, 21: 216–35.

Peach, C. (2005). 'Social Integration and Social Mobility: Segregation and Intermarriage of the Caribbean Population in Britain'. In G. C. Loury, T. Modood, and S. M. Teles (eds), *Ethnicity, Social Mobility and Public Policy: Comparing the US and UK* (pp. 178–203). Cambridge: Cambridge University Press.

Perlmann, J. and Waters, M. (2002). *The New Race Question: How the Census Counts Multi-racial Individuals*. New York: Russell Sage.

Peterson, P. E. (1991). 'The Urban Underclass and the Poverty Paradox'. *Political Science Quarterly*, 106(4): 617–37.

Phillips, D. (1998). 'Black Minority Ethnic Concentration, Segregation and Dispersal in Britain'. *Urban Studies*, 35(10): 1681–702.

Platt, L. (2007). 'Making Education Count: The Effects of Ethnicity and Qualifications on Intergenerational Social Class Mobility'. *The Sociological Review*, 55(3): 485–508.

Portes, A. and Rumbaut, R. (2001). *Legacies: The Story of the Immigrant Second Generation*. Berkeley, New York: University of California Press and Russell Sage Foundation.

Portes, A. and Zhou, M. (1993). 'The New Second Generation: Segmented Assimilation and its Variants'. *Annals of the American Academy*, 530(November): 74–96.

Prewitt, K. (2005). 'Racial Classification in America: Where Do We Go from Here?' *Daedalus* 134(1): 5–17.

Rattansi, A. (2005). 'The Uses of Racialization: The Time-spaces and Subject-objects of the Raced body'. In K. Murji and J. Solomos (eds), *Racialization: Studies in Theory and Practice* (pp. 271–301). Oxford: Oxford University Press.

Rex, J. and Moore, R. (1967). *Race, Community, and Conflict: A Study of Sparkbrook*. Oxford: Oxford University Press.

Sacks, K. B. (1994). 'How Did Jews Become White Folks?' In S. Gregory and R. Sanjek (eds), *Race* (pp. 78–102). New Brunswick, NJ: Rutgers University Press.

Sam, D. L. and Berry, J. W. (2010). 'Acculturation: When Individuals and Groups of Different Cultural Backgrounds Meet'. *Perspectives on Psychological Science*, 5(4): 472–81.

Sampson, R. J. (2012). *Great American City: Chicago and the Enduring Neighbourhood Effect*. Chicago, IL: University of Chicago Press.

Sharma, S., Hutnyk, J., and Sharma, A. (eds) (1996). *Dis-Orienting Rhythms: The Politics of the New Asian Dance Music*. London: Zed Books.

Simpson, L. (2005). 'On the Measurement and Meaning of Residential Segregation: A Reply to Johnston, Poulsen and Forrest'. *Urban Studies*, 42(7): 1229–30.

Small, M. L. (2007). 'Is There Such a Thing as "the Ghetto"? The Perils of Assuming that the South Side of Chicago Represents Poor Black Neighbourhoods'. *City*, 11(3): 413–21.

Smith, A. D. (1991). *National Identity*. Harmondsworth: Penguin.

Song, M. (2004). 'Who's at the Bottom? Examining Claims about Racial Hierarchy'. *Ethnic and Racial Studies*, 27(6): 859–77.

Stewart, F. (2008). *Horizontal Inequalities and Conflict: Understanding Group Violence in Multiethnic Societies*. Basingstoke: Palgrave Macmillan.

Taylor, C. (2003). 'The Politics of Recognition'. In J. Stone and R. Dennis (eds), *Race and Ethnicity: Comparative and Theoretical Approaches*. Oxford: Blackwell.

Telles, E. E. and Ortiz, V. (2009). *Generations of Exclusion: Mexican Americans, Assimilation, and Race*. New York: Russell Sage Foundation.

Venkatesh, S. A. (2008). *Off the Books: The Underground Economy of the Urban Poor*. Cambridge, MA: Harvard University Press.

Wacquant, L. (2008). *Urban Outcasts: A Comparative Sociology of Advanced Marginality*. Cambridge: Polity.

Wacquant, L. (2009). *Punishing the Poor: The Neoliberal Government of Social Insecurity*. Durham, NC: Duke University Press.

Weber, M. (1968). *Economy and Society*. Translated by Guenther Roth and Claus Wittich. Berkeley, CA: University of California Press.

Wilson, W. J. (1987). *The Truly Disadvantaged: The Inner City, the Underclass, and Public Policy*. Chicago, IL: University of Chicago Press.

Wilson, W. J. (2009). *More than Just Race: Being Black and Poor in the Inner City*. New York: W. W. Norton.

Wilson, W. J. (2014). 'Marginality, Ethnicity and Penality: A Response to Loïc Wacquant'. *Ethnic and Racial Studies*, 37(10): 1712–18.

Wimmer, A. (2008). 'The Making and Unmaking of Ethnic Boundaries: A Multilevel Process Theory'. *American Journal of Sociology*, 113(4): 970–1022.

Wood, M., Hales, J., Purdon, S., Sejersen, T., and Hayllar, O. (2009). 'A Test for Racial Discrimination in Recruitment Practice in British Cities'. Department for Work and Pensions Research Report 607. London: Her Majesty's Stationery Office.

Youdell, D. (2003). 'Identity Traps or How Black Students Fail: The Interactions between Biographical, Sub-cultural, and Learner Identities'. *British Journal of Sociology of Education*, 24(1): 3–20.

Zuccotti, C. (2015). 'Do Parents Matter? Occupational Outcomes among Ethnic Minorities and British Natives in England and Wales (2009–2010)'. *Sociology*, 49(2): 229–51.

13

Citizenship and Migration

Isabel Shutes

International migration is a manifestation of global structures of social advantage and disadvantage. Who migrates, from where, to where, why, how, and to what effect are linked to the inequalities of class, gender, race, and ethnicity that have traditionally underpinned the analysis of advantage and disadvantage in society. However, international migration also highlights the significance of inequalities between the so-called global north and south, within regions, such as Europe, and the salience of citizenship in structuring advantage/disadvantage. While the movement of people has long shaped societies, international migration has become a defining feature of contemporary processes of globalization: more and more countries and regions have been affected by large population movements, and by different types of movements (Castles and Miller, 2009).The total number of people who are counted as migrants across the world ('living outside their country of usual residence' according to the United Nations definition) has continued to increase since the post-Second-World-War period and into the twenty-first century, although there have been both increases and decreases in certain types of migration at different points in time, for example, with respect to refugee movements (Castles and Miller, 2009). Migrants are from among the most advantaged and disadvantaged in terms of economic, social, political, and environmental change, among the wealthiest and poorest groups across the world, living in the wealthiest and poorest of countries. 58 per cent of migrants in the world are living in the most developed regions; 42 per cent in less developed regions (United Nations, 2013). In addition, despite the traditional image of migrants as male migrant workers, migrants are increasingly women (Piper, 2007). At latest estimates, 48 per cent of the total stock of migrants in the world were women (United Nations, 2013). These women migrate not only as the family members of male migrants who have settled in different countries, but also as workers.

The increasing mobility of people across the world has been accompanied by increasing attempts to control the borders of nation states (Massey and Pren, 2012). There has been a major expansion of national and supranational systems in the governance of migration since the post-war period (Betts, 2011; Cornelius et al., 2004). Those systems, notwithstanding their limits, have facilitated migration for some, while severely restricting migration for others (Cornelius et al., 2004). Immigration policies of high-income countries, shaped by varying interests and pressures, are often framed in policy debate in terms of need for specific types of migrant labour—to select migrants who are seen as contributing to national economies (Ruhs and Anderson, 2010b). But they are also framed in terms of resources—to protect welfare states from being 'burdened' by migrants (Bommes and Geddes, 2000). Citizenship as a marker of entitlement/belonging within an area of residence has, within this context, become a major axis of advantage and disadvantage within and across the borders of nation states. Nationality and immigration laws confer different rights on citizens of a country and non-citizens (foreign nationals). Those rights include rights of entry to a country, entitlements to employment and state welfare provisions, and rights of residence. At the same time, there has been increasing diversification of the legal status and rights and entitlements of different categories of non-citizens since the post-Second-World-War period, including workers, family members, students, asylum seekers, EU citizens, and Third Country Nationals (Spencer, 2011). State and inter-state policies on immigration have thus given rise to new forms of stratification at both the national and global levels. This raises significant questions for social policy. The social rights of citizenship, with the development of welfare states, were conceived as a means of ameliorating forms of disadvantage in capitalist economies: endowing citizens with rights and entitlements to social provisions. Migration-related forms of stratification have implications for differential access to labour markets and to social provisions, and thus for inequalities in relation to work, poverty, and welfare. International migration, therefore, brings into question the boundaries of social citizenship, and the potential transformation of those boundaries.

This chapter examines how immigration systems (policies on immigration and naturalization) structure social advantage and disadvantage. The first section considers definitions of migrants and non-migrants, citizens and non-citizens, in both legislation and data sources, and the implications of different definitions for the analysis of social advantage and disadvantage. Section 13.2 then outlines the ways in which immigration and naturalization policies structure advantage and disadvantage between citizens and non-citizens, and among non-citizens, with respect to the differentiation of their rights and entitlements. Section 13.3 interrogates inequalities between citizens and non-citizens in relation to work, poverty, and welfare. The chapter concludes by reflecting on the implications of international migration and migration-related inequalities for social citizenship.

13.1 Who is a Migrant?

Definitions of a 'migrant' vary according to national and international legislation and data sources (see Anderson and Blinder, 2014). There is no legal definition of a 'migrant'. Rather, a distinction is made in nationality legislation between those who are citizens of a territory and those who are not. The acquisition of citizenship, however, varies across countries, shaped by the different historical trajectories of the development of nation states. Citizenship may be acquired by birth in the territory of the country (*ius solis*) or by descent from a citizen of the country (*ius sanguinis*) (Castles and Miller, 2009). Citizenship can also be acquired through naturalization: non-citizens can apply to become citizens of a country, depending on the criteria for granting citizenship (e.g. length of residence in a country, employment, language proficiency), which also vary across countries. In addition to nationality, the development of the European Union (EU) has created a cross-national form of European citizenship with regard to the status of the EU citizen (nationals of the EU member states), as distinct from the non-EU citizen or 'Third Country National' (nationals of countries outside the EU).

The ways in which citizens and non-citizens are legally differentiated has implications for their rights. Fundamental to the rights of citizens of a particular country is the right of residence in that country. Those who are not citizens do not automatically have a right of residence in that country. However, not all non-citizens are equally restricted. Non-citizens are differentiated by their nationality and immigration status on or following entry to a country. They may enter, for example, on a student visa, a work visa, as an asylum seeker, as the family members of a citizen/permanent resident, or as a national of an EU member state, or they may enter as an 'undocumented' migrant (without being legally admitted to a country). However, immigration status is not static. People can move from legal status to becoming 'undocumented' after admission to a country (e.g. by over-staying their entry visa), and vice versa (e.g. undocumented migrants may subsequently be granted legal residence). Likewise, people may be 'semi-compliant': they may be legally resident in a country but working in violation of the employment restrictions attached to their immigration status (Ruhs and Anderson, 2010a). They may also apply to become a permanent resident or a citizen after a period of time in a country.

The rights and entitlements of different categories of non-citizens are subject to the terms and conditions of their immigration status. Those who are permanent residents, who have been granted permanent residency, generally have rights that are similar to those of citizens in the country in which they reside (Baubock, 1994). EU citizens and their family members have rights to freedom of movement and residence in the EU member states (Directive 2004/38/EC), although those rights are not equivalent to those of national citizens of the respective countries (Kleinman, 2002). Non-citizens are therefore stratified according to their nationality and immigration status, with some more advantaged or disadvantaged than others. Non-citizens with permanent residence have far greater rights than those who are 'undocumented', who are among the most disadvantaged with respect to their rights, including entitlement/lack of entitlement to state welfare provisions. At the same time, those who are 'stateless', who are not recognized as citizens by a nation state (neither by their country of origin nor the country in which they reside), are entirely excluded from the legal status and rights of citizenship (Blitz and Lynch, 2011).

Turning to definitions within data sources, a migrant may be defined in varying ways, including by nationality (foreign national), but also by country of birth (foreign-born) and length of stay. Different definitions are not inter-changeable and result in very different groups of people being referred to as 'migrants' in research (see Anderson and Blinder, 2014, for further discussion). This has implications for the analysis of social advantage and disadvantage. For example, data on the foreign-born population of a country include foreign-born people who are citizens of that country. As citizens, they are not subject to the restrictions of immigration controls. Similarly, data on foreign nationals in a particular country do not distinguish people who are permanent residents from those who have been granted temporary residence and may face far greater restrictions on their rights. In some contexts, data on 'migrants' may also include people who have not migrated at all, as is the case where people born in a country, who are citizens of that country, whose parents were born abroad, are referred to as 'second generation migrants'. The latter is sometimes the case where ethnicity is defined in immigration terms (see Chapter 12, this volume). At the same time, nationality may differ from country of birth, for example, someone living in the UK who was born in Brazil but has Portuguese nationality. Figure 13.1 shows the percentage of the population in each of the EU-15 countries who are foreign nationals: those who are citizens of an EU member state or citizens of a country outside the EU. The EU-15 includes countries that were members of the EU prior to 2004 (data for the EU-27 countries is available from Eurostat migration and migrant population statistics—see link to data source below Figure 13.1). However, within countries, there is significant regional variation in the share of foreign nationals in the population: in London 22 per cent of the population are non-UK citizens (Rienzo and Vargas-Silva, 2014).

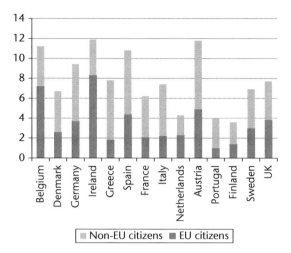

Figure 13.1. Foreign national population in the EU-15 countries, by citizenship, 2013 (% of total population)

Note: Luxembourg is excluded as it is a particular case in terms of the share of foreign nationals in the population (foreign nationals make up 45% of the total population).
Source: Eurostat, 2014a, Table 4: Non-national population by group of citizenship and foreign-born population by country of birth, 1 January 2013
<http://ec.europa.eu/eurostat/statistics-explained/index.php/Migration_and_migrant_population_statistics>

Across the EU-15, there is variation in the share of EU and non-EU nationals among the foreign-born population. While in Belgium and Ireland EU nationals make up around two-thirds of the foreign national population, in other countries (e.g. Greece, Italy, Austria, and Portugal), non-EU nationals form a greater share of the foreign national population. While EU and non-EU nationals have different rights and entitlements in those countries, there is variation in rights and entitlements among EU nationals as well as among non-EU nationals, shaped by EU and national policies towards EU and non-EU citizens.

Different data sources may be used to examine forms of advantage and disadvantage as they impact on migrants and non-migrants, citizens and non-citizens. Quantitative data from general population surveys (e.g. Census data) may provide data on citizens and non-citizens on the basis of nationality but, for non-citizens, are rarely able to provide adequate data on people's immigration status (whether they hold a work visa or are an asylum seeker, for example), including the terms and conditions of their status. However, surveys of migrants have enabled the identification of migrants by legal status (e.g. Fasani, 2014). In addition, given the rapid changes in immigration legislation in many countries over recent years, changes in the terms and conditions of a particular status result in groups of people with the same status but with different terms and conditions attached to their status, according to when it was issued by national immigration authorities. General population surveys also tend to under-represent 'undocumented' migrants—those who have no legal rights to be in a country, including, for example, those who have over-stayed their entry visa or asylum seekers whose application has been refused (see e.g. Font and Méndez, 2013). Qualitative data has, in this respect, been better able to capture the complexities with respect to immigration status, although qualitative studies also have their limitations (e.g. comparisons across multiple groups according to status). Notwithstanding these data limitations, examining the effects of restrictions applied through immigration controls to different groups of non-citizens is critical to understanding how immigration systems structure forms of (dis)advantage and explaining the consequences.

Definitions are not simply methodological issues. And citizenship is not simply a legal status. The use of the terms 'migrant' and 'citizen' in political debate and the media is highly normative, underpinned by divisions of class, gender, race, ethnicity, and religion, which interconnect in distinguishing who is the wanted and unwanted migrant, the included and excluded citizen. For example, wealthy non-EU investors are rarely depicted as migrants, in contrast to EU migrants from Eastern Europe, whose migration may be problematized in debates about so-called 'poverty migration'. Social groups who are citizens by law may still be constructed as the 'failed citizen' in public debate (Anderson, 2013), for example, benefits claimants. Likewise, some social groups who are citizens by law may experience being treated as 'third-class citizens' with respect to experiences of social divisions, such as race/ethnicity (Gilroy, 2002: 326).

13.2 Citizenship and Social Rights

According to Marshall's conception of citizenship, with the expansion of welfare states during the twentieth century, citizens acquired social in addition to political and civil rights (Marshall, 1950; and see Chapter 3, this volume). Social rights, involving the role of the state in the provision of social security, health care, education, housing, among other social provisions, were considered to form the basis for ameliorating the class-based inequalities that underpinned the development of capitalist economies. To this extent, they were a means of redressing forms of social disadvantage shaped by the market, providing, for example, income maintenance to those out of work due to unemployment, sickness, or old age. However, variation across welfare states in citizens' entitlements to state welfare provisions has had varying effects on levels of decommodification (the ability of individuals to meet their welfare needs independent of the market) and levels of stratification (class-based inequalities) within countries (Esping-Andersen, 1990). Liberal welfare regimes, typified by more minimal social rights, have been represented as being aimed at providing a minimum of means-tested assistance to those in need. By contrast, corporatist regimes are typified by differentiated social rights, aimed at maintaining existing differences in income status, while social-democratic regimes are exemplified by more universal social rights, aimed at promoting greater equality through more generous provisions to all citizens (Esping-Andersen, 1990).

Underlying analyses of social rights and welfare regimes were the assumptions, first, that social rights should be granted on the basis of citizenship, and, second, that citizenship denotes equality of status and equality of rights among individuals. Feminist scholarship has emphasized the ways in which full rights of citizenship were premised on the citizen being a male, full-time worker (Lister, 2003). Social rights were fundamentally shaped by gender-based inequalities in relation to paid and unpaid work (Lewis, 1992; Lister, 2003; see also Chapter 11, this volume). While men were granted social rights on the basis of their contributions through paid work, women's social rights often derived from their status as mothers and wives as much as workers, the assumption being that they were provided for through the wages/social benefits accrued to the male breadwinner (Lewis, 1992).

In addition to gender, inequalities of race/ethnicity and nationality among citizens as well as between citizens and non-citizens, were identified as also central to understanding the ways in which social rights, in principle and in practice, were exclusionary 'from within' the nation as well as 'from without' (Lister, 2003; Williams, 1989; see also Chapter 12, this volume). With the development of the welfare state in the UK in the post-war period, changes in citizenship legislation formed the basis for the exclusion of certain groups from the nation. Citizenship was defined under the 1948 British Nationality Act as including citizens of the UK, colonies, and newly independent colonies (Commonwealth countries). Those who had previously been subjects of the British Empire were thus still granted broadly the same rights (see Anderson, 2013). Migration to the UK from the former colonies in the post-war period gave rise to changes in British nationality legislation in the 1960s and 1970s that aimed to exclude Black and Asian Commonwealth citizens from rights of entry and residence in the UK (Joppke, 1999; Solomos, 2003). But changes in citizenship, immigration, and asylum legislation since the 1990s also formed the basis for the exclusion of migrant groups 'from within' the nation—for example, access to state welfare provisions for asylum seekers in the UK was made increasingly restrictive (Sales, 2002). These issues are treated next.

13.2.1 *Immigration and Social Rights*

The inclusion and exclusion of non-citizens from the rights of citizenship have been fundamentally shaped by the immigration systems of nation states (Faist, 1995; Morris, 2001; Sainsbury, 2012). Immigration and naturalization policies, which vary considerably across countries (Baubock, 1994), structure forms of advantage and disadvantage in relation to who is granted entry to a country; the conditions of admission to a country; and the conditions for acquiring permanent residence or citizenship within that country.

Historically, there were relatively few restrictions on the movement of people across different territories (Anderson, 2013). The expansion of immigration controls, set in the context of the development of nation states, led to increasing restrictions on the mobility of people across countries over the course of the twentieth century, processes that were profoundly shaped by, and shaped, divisions of race (Anderson, 2013; Ngai, 2004; see also Chapter 12, this volume). Border control systems have created increasing inequalities with respect to mobility: facilitating greater freedom of mobility for some groups, while heavily restricting mobility for others (Mau et al., 2012). As regards entry to a country, non-citizens may be included or excluded on the basis of their labour or economic status. There has been a shift in the immigration policies of high-income countries towards selecting workers whose labour is high-skilled and high-waged, and restricting the entry of low-skilled and low-waged workers (Ruhs and Anderson, 2010b). Some countries, such as Australia, Canada, and the UK, operate a points-based system on this basis, whereby migrants applying to enter the country accrue points according to their level of qualifications, employment experience, and other criteria. Similarly, the EU has introduced a 'Blue Card' system for facilitating the entry of high-skilled non-EU migrants to European labour markets (Directive 2009/50/EC). At the same time, immigration policies in several countries, such as Canada, the Netherlands, Spain, and the UK have aimed to facilitate the entry of the most affluent in society, establishing entry routes specifically for investors (e.g. Mitchell, 2001).

The expansion of immigration controls has entailed not only restrictions on who is admitted across the borders of a nation state, but restrictions on the rights of migrants after they are admitted. The immigration policies of high-income countries may, for example, be open to certain types of migrant labour, but at the same time be highly restrictive with regard to the rights of migrant workers granted temporary residence (Ruhs, 2013). Those restrictions include the terms and conditions of access to the labour market as well as restrictions on access to state welfare provisions. Economic independence may form a condition of admission to a country, excluding migrants from entitlements to social benefits. Taking the UK as an example, non-EU citizens who are subject to immigration controls in the UK are not entitled to claim non-contributory social benefits (Section 115, Immigration and Asylum Act, 1999). The legislation does not exclude those subject to immigration controls from claiming contribution-based benefits. However, contribution-based benefits are contingent on length of time in employment, which may be limited for those subject to immigration controls. At the same time, citizens/permanent residents in the UK are required to demonstrate that they have a certain level of resources to maintain non-EU family members, as a condition of the admission of family members to the UK (Immigration Rules, 2014). Following changes to the Immigration Rules in 2012, applicants must demonstrate a minimum gross annual income of £18,600 when applying for a spouse/partner to join them, and an additional amount for children (Immigration Rules, 2014, Appendix Family Members). Based on the earnings of a sample of applicants prior to the introduction of the new income threshold, it was estimated that just under half would have failed to meet the income criteria (Migration Advisory Committee, 2011). This has the effect of requiring non-citizens without permanent residence to be dependent on the market to meet their welfare needs or on the family/male breadwinner, with gendered implications. The majority of non-EU family members joining UK citizens/permanent residents are female spouses (Blinder, 2013) who, as a result of the terms and conditions of their entry visa, are made dependent on their husbands/partners for financial support.

Different immigration regimes (policies on the entry and settlement of migrants in a nation state) and their intersection with different welfare regimes have resulted in varying forms of inclusion and exclusion with respect to the social rights of non-citizens in different national contexts (Sainsbury, 2012). In some European countries, such as Germany, non-EU citizens may, in principle, be entitled to social benefits. However, in practice, claiming social benefits can be used as grounds for refusing applications for permanent residence, in effect restricting access to social rights (Morris, 2001). In other countries, such as Spain, there is variation at the sub-national level in the entitlement of non-EU citizens to social benefits: some regions provide some form of assistance, and others do not (Price and Spencer, 2014). The social rights of non-citizens have been seen to fare better in welfare states that are more universal, where entitlements to social benefits are based more on citizenship (social democratic regimes) than on contributions through work (corporatist regimes), and where immigration policy has conferred rights on non-citizens on the basis of residence (Sainsbury, 2012). However, since the 1990s there have been increasing divisions between wanted and unwanted forms of migration, which have placed pressure on residence as a basis for social rights (Geddes, 2003).

The conditions for acquiring permanent residence or citizenship have become increasingly selective in some countries. Permanent residence may be restricted according to the number of years of residence required to qualify, for example. In the UK, in addition to length of residence criteria, permanent residence has become tied to the economic status of the individual (cf. Chapter 11, this volume). With respect to those entering under the points-based system, only 'high-value' migrants (Tier 1 applicants, such as investors and entrepreneurs) and skilled workers (Tier 2 applicants) are potentially able to apply for permanent residence in the UK, subject to the criteria. All other categories of workers are only granted temporary residence (SN/HA/06037, 15 March 2012). This includes domestic workers, the majority of whom are women (Anderson, 2007), who are only permitted temporary stay for six months, without the option of renewal of their visa or permanent settlement (SN/HA/4786, 20 March 2012). Additionally, a minimum income threshold will be introduced in 2016, requiring non-EU Tier 2 applicants for permanent residence to have a minimum salary of £35,000 (SN/HA/06037), a higher level of pay than the median gross annual earnings of all (full-time) workers in the UK (£27,200 in 2014) (Office for National Statistics, 2014). For naturalization, length of residence criteria may vary for different groups, resulting in some groups being more advantaged/disadvantaged than others in accessing the status and rights of the citizen. The use of citizenship tests, which include language tests, in countries such as the Netherlands and the UK, forms another mechanism by which nation states selectively grant citizenship to applicants.

The creation of EU citizenship, within the context of the development of the EU as a market and the mobility of EU citizens as workers, has created a new divide between the EU and the non-EU citizen. The Single European Act of 1993 required immigration controls to be removed for European Community citizens, who have rights of movement and residence within the EU (Directive 2004/38/EC). EU citizenship, while creating an ideal of equal status among EU citizens, has entailed differentiation in the status and the rights and entitlements of EU citizens with respect to residence, work, and access to social benefits in EU member states—between nationals of the member state, economically active EU citizens, and non-economically active EU citizens (Kleinman, 2002). EU citizenship is premised on the EU citizen being a worker, with gendered implications since carers are excluded from claiming social rights (Ackers, 2004).

Increasing international migration since the post-war period has thus been marked by the stratification of citizens and non-citizens through national and supranational systems for governing the boundaries of national and regional territories, their labour markets, and welfare states. Immigration policies in the context of many high-income countries have become increasingly selective regarding the entry of certain categories of non-citizens and the rights of non-citizens admitted entry. This has resulted in increasing differentiation in the legal status and rights and entitlements of different groups of migrants, creating divisions not simply between migrants and non-migrants, citizens and non-citizens, but between national citizens, EU and non-EU citizens; and between different groups of non-EU citizens, for example, workers, family members, asylum seekers. At the same time, there is differentiation among EU and non-EU citizens according to their economic status. For example, EU citizens in secure types of employment, are more able to exercise rights of residence on the basis of their status as workers, compared to EU citizens whose relationship to the labour market is more precarious. At the same time, divisions exist among non-EU citizens, between, for example, high-skilled corporate workers, wealthy investors, and so-called low-skilled workers, such as domestic workers, whose labour may be central to national economies but does not afford them the privileged status of other types of workers.

13.3 Inequalities of Work, Poverty, and Welfare

The dimensions of advantage and disadvantage that citizenship and migration entail are wide-ranging and interconnect with forms of advantage and disadvantage discussed elsewhere in this volume. This section focuses on inequalities between citizens and non-citizens in relation to work, poverty, and the provision of income maintenance by the state (social benefits). As noted previously, citizens and non-citizens have different rights of residence, and different rights to work and to state welfare provisions. It should be emphasized, however, that inequalities between citizens and non-citizens in relation to work, poverty, and welfare may be affected by multiple factors in addition to differences in their legal rights. Indeed, inequalities among citizens are clearly evident in spite of the assumed equality of status conferred by citizenship, including inequalities of class, gender, race, and ethnicity (see Platt, 2011 and Chapters 4, 5, 11, and 12, this volume).

13.3.1 *Work*

Labour market inequalities between citizens and non-citizens are evident with respect to levels of employment and unemployment. Table 13.1 shows the employment rates for national citizens, EU citizens, and non-EU citizens in the EU-15 countries, distinguishing the rates for men and women of working age (Eurostat, 2014b). Across those countries, non-EU citizens have lower employment rates compared to EU citizens and national citizens (citizens of the respective country). There are also important gender differences in the

Table 13.1. Employment rates in the EU-15 countries of national citizens, EU citizens, and non-EU citizens (aged 20–64), by sex, 2013 (%)

	National citizens		EU citizens		Non-EU citizens	
	Males	Females	Males	Females	Males	Females
Belgium	73.6	63.9	68.9	57.9	50.1	29.6
Denmark	79.4	73.9	79.6	69	63.6	53.9
Germany	82.7	74.7	83.6	65.8	70.3	47.2
Ireland	70.8	60.9	75.1	62	63.5	46.4
Greece	63.2	43.5	59.4	47.2	59.6	38.8
Spain	64.4	53.8	61.6	54.5	53.2	46.7
France	74.2	67.1	75.8	64.3	63	36.2
Italy	69.5	49.6	75.3	59.4	72	48.4
Luxembourg	74.9	62.5	82.1	67.1	72.9	52.5
Netherlands	82	72.6	81.7	68.6	60.2	41.7
Austria	81	72.6	82	70.2	70.6	50.7
Portugal	69	62.6	71.9	50.9	60.4	56.9
Finland	74.9	72.6	73.6	69.1	64	42
Sweden	83.4	79.1	80.1	70.9	59	41.3
UK	80.6	70.2	87.1	71.9	72.2	52

Source: Eurostat (2014b)

employment rates of national citizens and non-EU citizens, with larger gaps in the employment rates of citizen women and non-EU citizen women, compared with the employment rates of citizen men and non-EU citizen men. By contrast, the employment rates of EU citizens (men and women) are broadly the same or slightly higher than those of national citizens in several countries, consistent with their construction as workers. While EU citizens have the right to work in another EU member state—indeed, their right of residence (after an initial three-month period) in another member state is conditional on being economically active or economically independent (Directive 2004/38/EC)—non-EU citizens may not have a right to work or they may experience significant employment restrictions, as explored below.

Non-EU citizens are more at risk of unemployment than citizens: the unemployment rate for non-EU citizens in Europe (at 21.5 per cent in 2013), is 11.5 per cent higher than the rate for national citizens (10 per cent in 2013) (Eurostat, 2014b). The unemployment rate for EU citizens (12.4 per cent) is 2.4 per cent higher than the rate for national citizens (Eurostat, 2014b). Non-EU citizens have also experienced larger increases in unemployment over the course of the economic recession (Eurostat, 2014b) (see Papademitriou et al., 2011, for discussion of migration and the effects of the economic crisis).

Inequalities are also evident with respect to the inclusion of non-citizens within the labour market. Across Europe, non-EU citizens are more likely than national citizens to be in temporary work: 20.4 per cent of non-EU citizens who are employees are in temporary work compared with 16.6 per cent of EU citizens and 12.4 per cent of national citizens (Eurostat, 2014b). Temporary work is one indicator of insecurity in the labour market (OECD, 2014). Analysis of national and regional data sets in the UK (Jayaweera and Anderson, 2008) shows evidence of other indicators of insecurity among, in particular, recent migrants to the UK, including being paid below the minimum wage, the absence of a written contract of employment, and non-standard hours of work. Non-standard hours include both excessive hours of work and non-voluntary under-employment at lower occupational levels, as well as shift and unsocial patterns of work. In addition to inequalities in wages between EU citizens from the new member states and national citizens, research has also found inequalities among EU citizens in the labour market (Campbell, 2013). EU citizens from the new EU member states working in the UK are more likely to be over-educated (to have a level of education that is higher than the standard level of education within the occupation in which they are employed) compared to other EU citizens. Access to employment for some groups of migrants, EU and non-EU citizens, may thus entail other forms of disadvantage within the labour market in terms of experiences of low-waged and less secure types of work (cf. Chapter 9, this volume).

Multiple factors contribute to these labour market inequalities. The structure of the labour market contributes to differences in the labour market outcomes of migrants in different countries (Kogan, 2006). Language barriers are identified as contributing to the labour market disadvantage of some migrants, as well as difficulties in transferring qualifications and employment experience obtained in other countries (Bloch, 2002). Various studies have found that education, language proficiency, and time spent in a country have a positive effect on the wages of foreign-born workers in a country (Dustmann et al., 2003). A reliance on co-ethnic social networks in limiting range of employment opportunities can also shape the experiences of migrants (Anderson et al., 2006). Discrimination on grounds of race, ethnicity, and nationality also contributes to experiences of labour market disadvantage (Shutes and Walsh, 2012). Indeed inter-generational inequalities for some ethnic minority groups indicate that labour market disadvantage can persist for so-called 'second generation' groups (individuals whose parents are foreign-born) (Heath et al., 2008; Platt, 2005).

These factors interconnect with the effects of immigration controls on labour market disadvantage. As noted in the previous section, immigration controls restrict the mobility of migrants not only across national borders but within labour markets. The terms and conditions attached to the immigration status of different categories of migrants construct groups of people with different rights in relation to paid work. As regards access to employment, non-citizens who are not legally entitled to work (as is the case for undocumented migrants, but also asylum seekers in some countries) may have few options but to enter irregular types work that offer low wages and poor working conditions. For those who are entitled to work, the terms and conditions of access to the labour market may be highly restrictive. Work permits may tie migrant workers to particular sectors of the labour market, to particular occupations, and to particular employers, restricting the mobility of non-citizens compared with citizens. Fear and insecurity concerning temporary immigration status can also further limit the ability of migrant workers to leave an employer. This has been the case for migrant workers whose ability to apply for permanent residence in the future was dependent on the renewal of a temporary work permit by an employer (Shutes, 2012). For undocumented migrants, fear of being reported to immigration authorities and of deportation has been found to contribute to experiences of forced labour, whereby employers are able to use the threat of denouncing a worker's irregular status to not only retain the worker but to force compliance with poor working conditions, including excessive hours of work, payment of low wages (below the national minimum wage) and delayed or non-payment of wages (Anderson, 2010; Bloch, 2013). As such, immigration controls have been found to limit the ability of migrant workers to voice individual or collective complaint over working conditions (Bloch, 2013; Shutes, 2012). The 'institutionalized uncertainty' (Anderson, 2010) of temporary immigration status thus creates a particular form of disadvantage for non-citizens in the labour market. However, differences among non-citizens are evident with respect to insecurity of status, and the consequences of that insecurity: between high-skilled and high-income groups (e.g. investors and transnational corporate employees) who may be granted privileged access to permanent residence, in contrast to low-income groups.

13.3.2 *Poverty and Income Maintenance*

Unemployment, employment in low-waged and less secure types of work, alongside restrictions on employment rights and on entitlements to social benefits have implications for the risk of poverty (see Pemberton, Phillimore, and Robinson, 2014, for further discussion). Analyses of EU SILC data show that migrants (identified on the basis of country of birth or nationality) are more likely to be at risk of poverty than citizens or those born in the respective country (Eurostat, 2011; Lelkes, 2007). For example, 31 per cent of people aged 25–54 born outside their country of residence in the EU in 2008 were at risk of poverty compared with 20 per cent of people born within their country of residence (Eurostat, 2011: 61). Among the foreign-born, the risk of poverty is greater for those born outside the EU (of whom 35 per cent were at risk of poverty) compared with those born within the EU (Eurostat, 2011: 61). Analysis of the data according to citizenship indicate that among the non-EU born population, the risk of poverty is greater for those who are non-citizens compared with those who are citizens of the country in which they reside (Lelkes, 2007).

Other cross-national studies show that non-citizens are more likely to be at risk of poverty than citizens, irrespective of the variance in welfare systems across countries (Morrissens and Sainsbury, 2005). Using the Luxembourg Income Study, Morrissens and Sainsbury compare levels of poverty among migrant households and citizen households across different European countries (Denmark, Sweden, France, Germany, UK) and the USA, countries which have been defined according to different welfare regimes (social democratic, conservative/corporatist, liberal). Migrant households are identified as households headed by a person who is foreign-born and a non-citizen; citizen households are identified as households headed by a person who is a citizen of the country (see Morrissens and Sainsbury, 2005: 642 for discussion regarding the problems of these indicators, including problems of comparability across countries; see also Lambert and Penn, 2001, on issues of definition). They find that migrant households are more likely to be below the poverty line (defined as below 50 per cent of the median income adjusted to family size) compared with citizen households across the countries. At the same time, migrant households have lower utilization rates than citizen households for pensions and unemployment benefits, and higher utilization rates for social assistance. As noted previously, non-citizens may be at a disadvantage with respect to contribution-based benefits, given greater risks of unemployment and shorter employment histories compared with citizens. In terms of the effect of social benefits on levels of poverty, the analysis suggests that citizen households are more likely to be lifted above the poverty line by social benefits than migrant households when comparing levels of poverty among pre-transfer and post-transfer households. This is partly explained by migrants' more limited access to unemployment benefits and pensions, and a greater reliance on social assistance, compared to citizens.

Permanent residence is a means of gaining access to social rights for non-citizens (Faist, 1995). However, as noted earlier, conditions for attaining permanent residence vary across countries, and may be more or less restrictive with respect to length of residence, employment, language proficiency, and other requirements. There has been limited research that has explored the effects of restrictions on the attainment of residence on differential poverty rates between citizens and non-citizens. The MIPEX (Migrant Integration Policy Index) dataset comprises indicators of the immigration policies of European countries, with a growing body of work using it to examine the relationship between immigration policies and migrant outcomes. The dataset has been used to construct an index of the level of conditionality EU member

277

states impose on non-EU migrants to attain permanent residency (Corrigan, 2014). Analysis of the MIPEX dataset along with EU SILC data suggests that deprivation experienced by non-EU citizens in European countries is greatest where conditions for attaining permanent residence are more restrictive and where social benefits are less generous (for citizens and non-citizens alike) (Corrigan, 2014).

Access to welfare provisions for non-citizens is not only affected by their legal status. Where particular groups are entitled to social benefits and other state welfare provisions, their access may be restricted by discrimination, language barriers, and lack of understanding of welfare entitlements and systems of provision (Sales, 2002). A range of informal sources of support through social networks, as well as support through voluntary and community organizations, have developed in response to the absence or inadequacies of state provision to address the welfare needs of migrant groups (Zetter et al., 2006).

13.4 Conclusion

Nationality and immigration legislation confer different rights on citizens and non-citizens. Immigration controls have contributed not simply to the exclusion of particular groups of non-citizens from nation states, but to forms of exclusion from within. Immigration controls have stratifying effects between citizens and non-citizens, and between different groups of non-citizens, with respect to their rights and entitlements. Inequalities are evident across countries with regard to the experiences of citizens and non-citizens in relation to work, poverty, and welfare. However, it is important to recognize that significant differences exist among those identified as 'non-citizens'—those who are not citizens of the country in which they reside—in terms not only of their legal status, rights, and entitlements, but also their economic and social characteristics, which have implications for the overall patterning of advantage and disadvantage among non-citizens. Moreover, there are significant differences cross-nationally with regard to the legal status and rights and entitlements of non-citizens, differences which reflect important national variation in histories of migration and immigration systems. In order to understand how immigration systems shape social advantage and disadvantage, therefore, it is important to develop analyses that further examine those differences.

International migration raises further issues, beyond the scope of this chapter, regarding the extent to which systems for meeting welfare needs have also become more transnational, including informal mechanisms of social protection, and the effects on global inequalities (Faist, 2014). The remittances of migrants in the global north form a major source of finance in meeting welfare needs in less developed countries, with potentially highly inequitable effects (Datta et al., 2007). There has also been an 'international transfer of caretaking' (Parrenas, 2001), whereby the labour market participation of women in the high-income countries of the global north has depended on the low-paid care labour of non-citizen women, employed as domestic workers and care workers by families and by home care and residential care providers, who in turn rely on the lower-paid and unpaid work of women in lower-income countries in caring for their own children, older relatives, and other family members (Anderson and Shutes, 2014; see also Chapter 11, this volume). These processes point to the interactions of immigration systems and the restructuring of welfare systems in shaping experiences of advantage and disadvantage within and across national borders.

Social citizenship—the granting of rights to state welfare provisions on the basis of citizen status—has for long been at the heart of social policy debate concerning the extent to which welfare states might ameliorate the class-based inequalities of the capitalist economies of the global north. Increasing international migration since the post-war period of the modern welfare state has called into question the boundaries of social citizenship. Immigration has been cast as a threat to social citizenship—non-citizens being perceived as a potential 'burden' on the resources of welfare states, undermining the solidarity required for generous welfare provisions (Alesina and Glaeser, 2004). At the same time, immigration has prompted calls for de-limiting the boundaries of social citizenship, to extend social rights to non-citizens 'from within' the nation state (Bolderson, 2011), and to extend social rights 'from without', at the global level, on the basis of our shared social needs as opposed to nationality (Dean, 2011; 2014). Indeed, it has been argued that a 'postnational' citizenship is evident insofar as certain rights have been extended beyond national citizenship through international law, giving people entitlements to certain basic rights independent of their nationality (Soysal, 1994). Supranational forms of governance have brought about some level of international recognition of the rights of certain groups of migrants, such as the UN and the ILO conventions on migrant workers, but often to limited effect (Ruhs, 2013). The international arena is also considered to have provided limited space for migrant rights activism, given the dominance of national legislation (Grugel and Piper, 2011). Nevertheless, political mobilizations at the local, national, and international levels around migrants' rights have constituted important forms of contestation of the exclusions of national citizenship. At the same time, they connect with broader concerns in global social policy debate for reframing social rights as issues of global social justice (Williams, 2014).

Data sources on migration

United Nations migration statistics
<http://esa.un.org/migration/>

Eurostat migrant integration statistics
<http://ec.europa.eu/eurostat/statistics-explained/index.php/Migrant_
integration_statistics_-_overview>
OECD migration data
<http://www.oecd.org/migration/mig/oecdmigrationdatabases.htm>

Migration Observatory
<http://migrationobservatory.ox.ac.uk/>

MIPEX
<http://www.mipex.eu/>

References

Ackers, L. (2004). 'Citizenship, Migration and the Valuation of Care in the European Union'. *Journal of Ethnic and Migration Studies*, 30(2): 373–96.

Alesina, A. and Glaeser, E. (2004). *Fighting Poverty in the US and Europe: A World of Difference*. New York: Oxford University Press.

Anderson, B. (2007). 'A Very Private Business: Exploring the Demand for Migrant Domestic Workers'. *European Journal of Women's Studies*, 14(3): 247–64.

Anderson, B. (2010). 'Migration, Immigration Controls and the Fashioning of Precarious Workers'. *Work, Employment & Society*, 24(2): 300–17.

Anderson, B. (2013). *Us and Them? The Dangerous Politics of Immigration Control*. Oxford: Oxford University Press.

Anderson, B. and Blinder, S. (2014). 'Who Counts as a Migrant? Definitions and their Consequences'. Oxford: Migration Observatory, University of Oxford.

Anderson, B., Ruhs, M., Rogaly, B., and Spencer, S. (2006). 'Fair enough? Central and East European Migrants in Low-wage Employment in the UK'. Oxford: Centre on Migration, Policy and Society, University of Oxford.

Anderson, B. and Shutes, I. (eds) (2014). *Migration and Care Labour: Theory, Policy and Politics*. Basingstoke: Palgrave Macmillan.

Baubock, R. (ed.) (1994). *From Aliens to Citizens: Redefining the Status of Immigrants in Europe*. Aldershot: Avebury.

Betts, A. (2011). *Global Migration Governance*. Oxford: Oxford University Press.

Blinder, S. (2013). 'Non-European Migration to the UK: Family Unification and Dependants'. Oxford: Migration Observatory, University of Oxford.

Blitz, B. K. and Lynch, M. (2011). *Statelessness and Citizenship: A Comparative Study on the Benefits of Nationality*. Cheltenham: Edward Elgar.

Bloch, A. (2002). *Refugee Migration and Settlement in Britain*. Basingstoke: Palgrave Macmillan.

Bloch, A. (2013). 'The Labour Market Experiences and Strategies of Young Undocumented Migrants'. *Work, Employment & Society*, 27(2): 272–87.

Bolderson, H. (2011). 'The Ethics of Welfare Provision for Migrants: A Case for Equal Treatment and the Repositioning of Welfare'. *Journal of Social Policy*, 40(2): 219–35.

Bommes, M. and Geddes, A. (eds) (2000). *Immigration and Welfare: Challenging the Borders of the Welfare State*. London: Routledge.

Campbell, S. (2013). 'Over-education amongst A8 Migrants in the UK'. Working Paper No. 13–09. London: Department of Quantitative Social Science, Institute of Education, University of London.

Castles, S. and Miller, M. J. (2009). *The Age of Migration: International Population Movements in the Modern World*. Basingstoke: Palgrave Macmillan.

Cornelius, W. A., Martin, P. L., and Hollifield, J. F. (eds) (2004). *Controlling Immigration: A Global Perspective*. Stanford, CA: Stanford University Press.

Corrigan, O. (2014). 'Migrant Deprivation, Conditionality of Legal Status and the Welfare State'. *Journal of European Social Policy*, 24(3): 223–39.

Datta, K., McIlwaine, C., Wills, J., Evans, Y., Herbert, J., and May, J. (2007). 'The New Development Finance or Exploiting Migrant Labour? Remittance Sending among Low-paid Migrant Workers in London'. *International Development Planning Review*, 29(1); 43–67.

Dean, H. (2011). 'The Ethics of Migrant Welfare'. *Ethics and Social Welfare*, 5(1): 18–35.

Dean, H. (2014). 'A Post-Marshallian Conception of Global Social Citizenship'. In E. F. Isin and P. Nyers (eds), *Routledge Handbook of Global Citizenship Studies* (pp. 128–38). Abingdon: Routledge.

Dustmann, C., Fabbri, F., Preston, I., and Wadsworth, J. (2003). *Labour Market Performance of Immigrants in the UK Labour Market*. Home Office Online Report, Volume 05/03. London: Home Office.

Esping-Andersen, G. (1990). *The Three Worlds of Welfare Capitalism*. Cambridge: Polity.

Eurostat. (2011). *Migrants in Europe: A Statistical Portrait of the First and Second Generation*. Luxembourg: Publications Office of the European Union.

Eurostat. (2014a). *Migration and Migrant Population Statistics*, <http://ec.europa.eu/eurostat/statistics-explained/index.php/Migration_and_migrant_population_statistics>, accessed 20 August 2015.

Eurostat. (2014b). *Migration Integration Statistics*, <http://ec.europa.eu/eurostat/statistics-explained/index.php/Migrant_integration_statistics_-_employment>, accessed 20 August 2015.

Faist, T. (1995). 'Boundaries of Welfare States: Immigrants and Social Rights'. In R. Miles and D. Traenhardt (eds), *Migration and European Integration* (pp. 177–95). London: Pinter.

Faist, T. (2014). 'On the Transnational Social Question: How Social Inequalities are Reproduced in Europe'. *Journal of European Social Policy*, 24(3): 207–22.

Fasani, F. (2014). 'Understanding the Role of Immigrants' Legal Status: Evidence from Policy Experiments'. London: Centre for Research and Analysis of Migration, University College London.

Font, J. and Méndez, M. (2013). *Surveying Ethnic Minorities and Immigrant Populations: Methodological Challenges and Research Strategies*. Amsterdam: IMISCOE-Amsterdam University Press.

Geddes, A. (2003). 'Migration and the Welfare State in Europe'. *The Political Quarterly*, 74(1): 150–62.

Gilroy, P. (2002). *There Ain't no Black in the Union Jack: The Cultural Politics of Race and Nation*. London: Routledge.

Grugel, J. and Piper, N. (2011). 'Global Governance, Economic Migration and the Difficulties of Social Activism'. *International Sociology*, 26(4): 435–54.

Heath, A., Rothon, C., and Kilpi, E. (2008). 'The Second Generation in Western Europe: Education, Unemployment and Occupational Attainment'. *Annual Review of Sociology*, 34: 211–35.

Jayaweera, H. and Anderson, B. (2008). *Migrant Workers and Vulnerable Employment: a Review of Existing Data*. London: TUC Commission on Vulnerable Employment.

Joppke, C. (1999). *Immigration and the Nation-State: The United States, Germany, and Great Britain*. Oxford: Oxford University Press.

Kleinman, M. (2002). *A European Welfare State? European Union Social Policy in Context*. Basingstoke: Palgrave.

Kogan, I. (2006). 'Labour Markets and Economic Incorporation among Recent Immigrants in Europe'. *Social Forces*, 85(2): 697–721.

Lambert, P. and Penn, R. (2001). 'SOR Models and Ethnicity Data in LIS and LES: Country by Country Report'. Luxembourg Income Study Working Paper.

Lelkes, O. (2007). *Poverty among Migrants in Europe*. Vienna: European Centre for Social Welfare Policy and Research.

Lewis, J. (1992). 'Gender and the Development of Welfare Regimes'. *Journal of European Social Policy*, 2(3): 158–73.

Lister, R. (2003). *Citizenship: Feminist Perspectives*. Basingstoke: Palgrave Macmillan.

Marshall, T. H. (1950). *Citizenship and Social Class and Other Essays*. Cambridge: Cambridge University Press.

Massey, D. and Pren, K. (2012). 'Unintended Consequences of U.S. Immigration Policy: Explaining the Post-1965 Surge from Latin America'. *Population Development Review*, 38(1): 1–29.

Mau, S., Brabandt, H., Laube, L., and Roos, C. (2012). *Liberal States and the Freedom of Movement: Selective Borders, Unequal Mobility*. Basingstoke: Palgrave Macmillan.

Migration Advisory Committee. (2011). 'Review of the Minimum Income Requirement for Sponsorship under the Family Migration Route'. London: Migration Advisory Committee.

Mitchell, K. (2001). 'Transnationalism, Neo-Liberalism, and the Rise of the Shadow State'. *Economy and Society*, 30: 165–89.

Morris, L. (2001). 'Stratified Rights and the Management of Migration: National Distinctiveness in Europe'. *European Societies*, 3: 387–411.

Morrissens, A. and Sainsbury, D. (2005). 'Migrants Social Rights, Ethnicity and Welfare Regimes'. *Journal of Social Policy*, 34(4): 637–60.

Ngai, M. (2004). *Impossible Subjects: Illegal Aliens and the Making of Modern America*. Princeton, NJ: Princeton University Press.

OECD. (2014). *OECD Employment Outlook 2014*. Paris: OECD Publishing.

Office for National Statistics. (2014). *Annual Survey of Hours and Earnings, 2014: Provisional Results*. London: ONS.

Papademitriou, D., Sumption, M., and Terrazas, A. (2011). *Migration and the Great Recession: The Transatlantic Experience*. Washington, DC: Migration Policy Institute.

Parrenas, R. (2001). *Servants of Globalization*. Stanford, CA: Stanford University Press.

Pemberton, S., Phillimore, J., and Robinson, D. (2014). 'Causes and Experiences of Poverty among Economic Migrants in the UK'. Working Paper Series No. 4/2014. Birmingham: Institute for Research into Superdiversity, University of Birmingham.

Piper, N. (ed.) (2007). *New Perspectives on Gender and Migration: Livelihoods, Rights and Entitlements*. Abingdon: Routledge.

Platt, L. (2005). 'New Destinations? Assessing the Post-migration Social Mobility of Minority Ethnic Groups in England and Wales'. *Social Policy and Administration*, 39(6): 697–721.

Platt, L. (2011). *Understanding Inequalities: Stratification and Difference*. Cambridge: Polity Press.

Price, J. and Spencer, S. (2014). *City-level Responses to Migrant Families without Recourse to Public Funds: A European Pilot Study*. Oxford: Centre on Migration, Policy and Society, University of Oxford.

Rienzo, C. and Vargas-Silva, C. (2014). 'Migrants in the UK: An Overview'. Oxford: Migration Observatory, University of Oxford.

Ruhs, M. (2013). *The Price of Rights: Regulating International Labor Migration*. Princeton: Princeton University Press.

Ruhs, M. and Anderson, B. (2010a). 'Semi-Compliance and Illegality in Migrant Labour Markets: An Analysis of Migrants, Employers and the State in the UK'. *Population, Space and Place*, 16(3): 195–221.

Ruhs, M. and Anderson, B. (eds) (2010b). *Who Needs Migrant Workers? Labour Shortages, Immigration and Public Policy*. Oxford: Oxford University Press.

Sainsbury, D. (2012). *Welfare States and Immigrant Rights: The Politics of Inclusion and Exclusion*. Oxford: Oxford University Press.

Sales, R. (2002). 'The Deserving and Undeserving? Refugees, Asylum Seekers and Welfare in Britain'. *Critical Social Policy*, 22(3): 456–78.

Shutes, I. (2012). 'The Employment of Migrant Workers in Long-Term Care: Dynamics of Choice and Control'. *Journal of Social Policy*, 41(1): 43–59.

Shutes, I. and Walsh, K. (2012). 'Negotiating User Preferences, Discrimination and Demand for Migrant Labour in Long-Term Care'. *Social Politics*, 19(1): 78–104.

SN/HA/4786. (2012). 'Immigration: Migrant Domestic Workers'. Standard Note: SN/HA/4786, 20 March. London: Home Affairs Section.

SN/HA/06037. (2012). 'Immigration: Permanent Settlement Reforms (Workers)'. Standard Note: SN/HA/06037, 15 March. London: Home Affairs Section.

Solomos, J. (2003). *Race and Racism in Britain*. Basingstoke: Palgrave Macmillan.

Soysal, Y. (1994). *Limits of Citizenship: Migrants and Postnational Membership in Europe*. Chicago: University of Chicago Press.

Spencer, S. (2011). *The Migration Debate*. Bristol: Policy Press.

United Nations. (2013). *International Migration Report 2013*. Geneva: United Nations Department of Economic and Social Affairs, Population Division.

Williams, F. (1989). *Social Policy: A Critical Introduction*. Cambridge: Polity Press.

Williams, F. (2014). 'Global Social Justice, Ethics and the Crisis of Care'. In A. Kaasch and P. Stubbs (eds), *Transformations in Global and Regional Social Policies* (pp. 85–107). Basingstoke: Palgrave Macmillan.

Zetter, R., Griffiths, D., and Sigona, N. (2006). 'Integrative Paradigms, Marginal Reality: Refugee Community Organisations and Disperal in Britain'. *Journal of Ethnic and Migration Studies*, 32(5): 881–98.

14

Religious Advantage and Disadvantage

Malcolm Torry

Emil Durkheim defines a religion as a:

> Unified set of beliefs and practices relative to sacred things, that is to say, things set apart and forbidden—beliefs and practices which unite into one single moral community called a Church all those who adhere to them.   (Durkheim, 1915: 47)

Religion is 'a collective thing' that can 'classify and systematize' practices and ideas (Durkheim, 1915: 47, 429), which suggests that for someone to identify themselves as religious requires that they participate in the activities of a 'church': or rather, in this multi-faith world, in the activities of a congregation.

But this is only one of the ways in which someone might identify themselves with a religion. The 2011 Census results show that over 33 million people living in England and Wales identify themselves as Christians (that is, well over half of the population), nearly 3 million as Muslims, nearly 1 million as Hindus, and nearly half a million as Sikhs. A UK time-use survey suggests that less than 7 per cent of the population attend a church service on any given Sunday (Bruce and Glendinning, 2013: 4); and my experience of the Royal Borough of Greenwich (which has a population of nearly a quarter of a million) suggests that the number of people who participate in some way in the activities of a congregation (of whatever religion) must be less than 10 per cent of that population. Whether all of those attendees believe a required set of beliefs and undertake prescribed practices is doubtful.

Participation in a religion must therefore be treated as a spectrum. At one end will be the self-identification invited by a census question that requires a choice to be made between boxes labelled 'Christian', 'Jewish', and so on, and at the other end will be active participation in a faith community (for instance, by attending a weekly act of worship).

For the purposes of this chapter I shall employ a two-part working definition:

1. People 'actively participate' in a religion if they identify with that religion, if they attend a congregation of that religion (even if only very occasionally), and if they exhibit behaviours related to that religion. Such active participation will be a social reality and not merely a private one.

2. People 'identify' with a religion if they tick the relevant box on a census form. This identification can be entirely private and will not necessarily impinge on the way in which the individual functions in society.

Two further points need to be made before we leave this section on the nature of religion.

There are religions, but there is no such thing as non-specific religion. Religions might share a variety of characteristics—for instance, gathering for worship—but the ways in which Jews, Christians, Muslims, Sikhs, and Hindus worship when they gather are in many ways radically different. This means that generalization will often be impossible. If we find a pattern of disadvantage and advantage in relation to one religion then we shall not be able to assume that the same pattern applies to another religion unless we can provide evidence that it does.

Different people's experience of their religion can be very different. Someone born into a Muslim family in a largely Muslim country is likely to regard themselves as a Muslim and to be regarded by others as a Muslim, regardless of the extent to which they are active participants in religious activity. Someone living in a largely secular country who converts to Islam, prays five times a day, attends the Mosque on Fridays, and keeps the Ramadan fast, will have a very different experience of his or her religion. Two people who identify with the same religion might therefore have experiences of religion that are more different than the experiences of another two people who identify with different religions.

14.1 Ethnicity and Religion

Every individual who identifies with a religion also belongs to an ethnic group, so we might need to decide whether any disadvantage or advantage that they experience relates to their ethnicity, their religion, or both:

> An ethnic group is, theoretically, one where the association with both a particular origin and specific customs is adopted by people themselves to establish a shared identity. (Platt, 2007: 17)

A religious group might be similarly described as 'one where the association with both a particular religion and specific customs is adopted by people themselves to establish a shared identity'.

As we have seen in Chapter 12, ethnicity is a complex reality. The ways in which people describe their ethnicities will have a variety of roots: their countries of residence, their places of origin, other countries in which they have lived, and their parents' places of origin and understandings of their ethnicities. If these factors point in a variety of different directions, then a person's ethnicity might be self-chosen within a set of constraints. People's religious affiliations might have similar sources and might be similarly complex.

Any society is a layered set of communities, with each person constructing their sense of identity within the diverse and 'discursively constructed citizenship of postmodernity' (Dean, 2002: 37; cf. Taylor, 1998; Foresight, 2013: 3); so each of us belongs at a particular position in a multi-dimensional matrix of communities, and, to make the situation even more complex, each ethnic and each religious community will construct a different matrix, and the layers of those matrices might be interrelated. Platt finds that a shared religion is often a 'core element in ethnic identification' (Platt, 2007: 17), and for some communities (for instance, Jews) religion largely determines ethnicity; for others, religion might be one of several foundations of ethnicity (as for Greek Orthodox Christians); and for yet others there might be many ethnic groups linked to a religion (for instance, the Latin American, Philippino, Irish, Italian, and Polish Roman Catholics) (Hammond, 2000: 118–19).

Just as nationality and ethnicity might be elements of a single complex identity (Foresight, 2013: 1), as in 'black British', so religion and ethnicity might be inextricable elements of an identity, as for those who define themselves as 'Pakistani Muslims' (Platt, 2011: 73; Georgiadis and Manning, 2011)—which leads Bradford and Forsyth to use the term 'ethno-religious group' (Bradford and Forsyth, 2006: 120) in their study of labour market participation.

A further complexity is that relationships between ethnic and religious identities will change if religion and ethnicity are experienced as in conflict with each other (Modood et al., 1994: 62), as migrants spend longer in a secularizing country such as the UK (Modood and Berthoud, 1997: 306), as one generation succeeds another (Modood et al., 1994: 57), and as more members of a community are UK-born rather than born elsewhere (Georgiadis and Manning, 2011): so whether ethnicity or religion is the more significant aspect of an individual's identity might change over time (Cornell and Hartmann, 1998: 50). Not only is each person differently located on an identity matrix, but each person's matrix is also differently constructed, and each person will face different matrices at different times (Alam and Husband, 2006: 50).

Two surveys in the US that measured the intensity of people's ethnic identity and the intensity of their religious affiliation have found that 'religion and ethnicity maintain a significant relationship in late twentieth-century America' (Hammond, 2000: 126) to differing extents for different ethno-religious groups; that both length of residence in a secularizing country, and increasing individualism, lead to declines in both ethnic and religious identification (Hammond, 2000: 127); and that decline in ethnic identity tends to precede decline in religious loyalty (Hammond, 2000: 126). However, for some, religious identity might be more significant than ethnic identity (for instance, when choosing someone to marry: Platt, 2009: 8), and in general secularization has affected the Muslim community less than it has affected other faith communities:

> There may be several reasons for this trend, including a component of religious revival, a reaction against perceived hostility towards Muslims, and the impact of international events.   (Foresight, 2013: 20; cf. Voas and Fleischman, 2012)

In Britain, for Pakistani young men in particular religion can be a more significant category than ethnicity:

> The greater significance of religion can be understood if we bear in mind, first, that these young people distinguish between the universalism of Islam and the particularism of their Pakistani or Asian ethnicity; and, secondly, that the social boundaries defining the young people's religious identities have a clarity and pervasiveness that protects and enhances the minority religion, whereas the boundaries delineating their ethnic identities are far less clear-cut, reflecting and contributing to a decline in the distinctiveness of the minority community. (Jacobson, 1997: 253)

'Debates about minority ethnic groups in Britain have a shifting nomenclature from "colour" in the 1950s and 1960s, to "race" in the 1960s–80s, to "religion" since the 1990s' (Jawad, 2012: 99): which suggests that in the long run ethnic identity might become less significant and less stable than religious affiliation (Platt, 2005: 31; Modood, 2014a: 122). But, however the different relationships evolve, they will always remain complex, and religion and ethnicity will continue to relate to each other in complex ways: which means (dis)advantage is more likely to relate to complex ethno-religious identities than to purely religious ones.

14.2 Religious (Dis)advantage?

If we employ our second working definition of religion, then 2011 Census data for England and Wales certainly appear to show some clear correlations between economic activity and identification with a religion. Christians and Muslims exhibit the lowest levels of economic activity (with 'economic activity' defined as the percentage of people aged 16 or over who are employed or unemployed, and 'unemployed' defined as 'actively seeking and available for work') (Office for National Statistics, 2013). Sikhs, Hindus, and those with no religion exhibit the highest levels of economic activity. Being Hindu or Jewish offers a better chance of being in a professional social class than being a Christian, and being a Sikh or a Muslim offers a worse chance (Platt, 2005: 31). Unemployment is highest among Muslims and lowest among Jews, and Muslims are generally paid less than any other religious group (Longhi et al., 2009).

Similarly, if poverty is defined as household disposable income below 60 per cent of median equivalized household disposable income, then we find a correlation between identification with a religion and poverty. In the UK, 49 per cent of Muslims, 27 per cent of Sikhs, and 22 per cent of Hindus, are in poverty, whereas all other religious groups are within 3 per cent of the overall poverty rate of 18 per cent (Heath and Li, 2014: 34). In order to suggest that there might be causal connections underlying these correlations, we need to hypothesize possible mechanisms.

Might religious discrimination in the labour market be a factor? The problem here is that we cannot separate racial and religious discrimination (Tackey et al., 2006: 2). Islamophobia might be an increasing problem (Modood, 2013: 41; Singh and Cowden, 2011: 359), and such discrimination might now be as much religious as ethnic, but still it is not clear whether this shift has increased the level of discrimination already suffered by, for instance, Pakistanis and Bangladeshis (Tackey et al., 2006: 95), most of whom are Muslims. For any individual, community and individual cultural, religious and ethnic factors will together influence economic opportunities and activity (Platt, 2002: 124), so proving the existence of a religious penalty that is not also an ethnic or cultural penalty would be quite difficult.

Might employer attitudes to religious practice be a causal mechanism? Many Muslims are perfectly happy to fit the midday prayers into their lunch break, even if that is not at exactly at the right time, and are happy to wait until they get home before they perform the afternoon prayers; and a younger generation of Muslim women are well able to combine childcare and other domestic responsibilities with employment (Dale, 2002): but employers might still assume that employing a Muslim will mean that absence for culturally prescribed childcare or at the religiously prescribed times for prayer may cause disruption (Tackey et al., 2006: 93).

Heath and Li suggest that 'historically contingent factors such as low qualifications or lack of fluency in the English language ... factors which may be more intrinsic to particular religious traditions, such as traditional family values which may encourage women to stay at home ... factors such as prejudice and discrimination ... lack of "bridging social capital" ... the number of dependent children' (Heath and Li, 2014: 35–6) might be causes of high poverty rates among some religious groups; and by comparing poverty rates of Muslims with the poverty rates of people with other religious affiliations within the same ethnic groups, Heath and Li attempt to disaggregate poverty rates into ethnic and religious components, and then conclude that religious affiliation contributes 18 per cent of the Muslim poverty rate, 8 per cent of the Sikh poverty rate, and 5 per cent of the Hindu poverty rate (Heath and Li, 2014: 35). In relation to a similar research project using 2001 Census data on qualifications and occupation, Khattab argues that 'ethnicity per se is not an important factor but operates as a proxy...skin colour and culture (religion) are to a greater extent probably the main mechanisms that operate to reinforce disadvantage among some groups or to facilitate social mobility amongst others' (Khattab, 2009: 319; cf. National Equality Panel, 2010: 227). Religious affiliation appears, superficially, to be an independent variable with both clear effects and hypothesized mechanisms. However, each of those religious groups is made up of a variety of ethno-religious groups, and each of those will have its own relationship with economic activity and poverty rates. The rates for individual faith communities are amalgams of rates for a collection of ethno-religious groups. We are still as likely to be seeing the outcomes of ethno-religious groups' histories and cultures rather than a purely religious effect (Longhi et al., 2013).

Yet one more complexity is the fact that we can hypothesize a causal link from economic disadvantage to religious practice. In countries in which people experience more economic security we find less religious belief and practice than we find in countries in which people experience less economic security (Inglehart, 2005: 27). Many of the functions previously supplied by religion are no longer required in more economically secure societies. For instance, the family is no longer the only source of economic assistance in difficult times, so religion's family-affirming elements are no longer required to the extent that they were (Inglehart et al., 1998: 11). In the UK context, recent migrants are economically insecure and might therefore regard religion as a resource, and they might value the sense of security that they already know can be supplied by the religious belief and practice that they have brought with them. More settled communities no longer have the same need for religion to supply a basis for economic security. The fact that economic insecurity correlates positively with levels of religious belief and practice might be just as likely to represent economic insecurity's effect on religious practice as to represent religious practice's effect on economic disadvantage.

14.3 Ethno-religious Disadvantage

Just as there appears to be evidence for religious disadvantage, there would also appear to be evidence for ethnic disadvantage, as we have discovered in

Chapter 12. Relevant to this chapter is the fact that when we specifically control for religious affiliation the 'ethnic penalty' remains substantial. Pakistani and Bangladeshi Muslim women have higher poverty rates than Indian Muslim women (Nandi and Platt, 2010: 4; Bradford and Forsyth, 2006: 113; Platt, 2007: 74), and Pakistani and Bangladeshi Muslim men are twice as likely to be unemployed as Indian Muslim men (Brown, 2000; Platt, 2007: 74). Here a complex bundle of factors might be in play. Since independence and the partition of the Indian subcontinent into Pakistan and India in 1946, Muslims have been a minority in the more secular and largely Hindu India and have suffered significant disadvantage there (Stewart, 2009: 319, 328). For the relatively better-off and better-educated Indian Muslim, emigration has been an important route out of disadvantage. Pakistan and Bangladesh have regarded themselves as Muslim societies, and education has often been more about learning the Qur'an than about the liberal arts and the natural sciences, both of which have sometimes experienced suspicion from religious authorities. Lack of education will have labour market consequences. Women from a more traditional Muslim culture might find that domestic responsibilities, limited education, poor spoken and written English, and cultural pressure to remain within the home and its environs unless accompanied by a male family member, make it difficult to be employed in anything other than low-paid home-working (Platt, 2007: 74). In all of these cases it might be historic religious and cultural factors, perpetuated within a family, that are causing disadvantage in the labour market for first-generation immigrant communities (Platt, 2002: 91; Clark and Drinkwater, 2007: 48; Longhi et al., 2013): disadvantage not experienced by succeeding generations as they benefit from educational opportunities and social capital generated by the extended family (Longhi et al., 2013; Thapar-Bjorkertand Sanghera, 2010: 261). It is surely of interest that Bangladeshi girls are doing better in school than Bangladeshi boys (Cassen and Kingdon, 2007: 14).

Similar historic religious and cultural factors are probably the reason for Indian Sikhs experiencing greater disadvantage in the labour market than Indian Hindus (Brown, 2000; Lindley, 2002). Sikhism was partly a reaction to the Indian caste system, and still today Sikhs in India tend to be from the lower castes: so they tend to have fewer educational opportunities and achievements, to have fewer skills, and to be in low-paying occupations. Sikhs who emigrate to the UK, and their descendants, might therefore possess less social and personal capital than the higher-caste Hindus who emigrate. Religious affiliation in India is intimately connected with a social class system: so again we are left asking to what extent current religious affiliation is a determining factor in relation to economic activity.

A complex picture emerges. Indian Hindus do better than Indian Sikhs, Indian Sikhs and Hindus do better than Indian Muslims (Platt, 2005: 32), and they in turn do better than Pakistani and Bangladeshi Muslims (Brown, 2000; Longhi et al., 2009; Platt, 2007: 74). Reasons for each of these relationships can be found in the histories and cultures of the countries from which these ethno-religious groups have emigrated.

Just as the causal direction between religious affiliation and poverty is not always clear, so the causal direction in some of the suggested mechanisms for differential labour market outcomes might not be clear. Take, for instance, the links between religion, education, and labour market outcomes (Clark and Drinkwater, 2007: 15). As we have already seen, women from more traditional communities might lack educational opportunities and therefore be disadvantaged in the labour market. In the other direction, belonging to a religious organization might improve someone's personal and social capital, enhance their intellectual skills, and provide them with educational opportunities and with network connections with economic opportunities, thus contributing to educational and economic advantage. In a different direction: participation in a higher education institution will open an individual's mind to the variety of the world's religions, might relativize their own religion, and might therefore lead to practical secularization, cultural secularization, and the secularization of ideas: and these shifts in mindset and behaviour might have economic consequences (Torry, 2010: 1). Alternatively, the experience of higher education might lead to a reaction against a more liberal previous generation and a secular world, and therefore to a more committed religious practice with somewhat different economic effects. It is therefore as likely that educational experience will affect both religious affiliation and economic activity as it is that religious affiliation will affect both educational experience and economic activity. So even when we study active participation in a religion, rather than mere identification with one, considerable care must be taken when drawing conclusions about the causal links between religious affiliation, educational activity, and economic (dis)advantage.

In order to suggest that some relatively independent religious factor is significant in relation to economic advantage or disadvantage, a hypothesis will need to be offered as to what the causal mechanism might be (Lindley, 2002). We might be able to do this in individual cases. For instance: a Muslim family might regard it as essential to send their children to private Arabic lessons (Platt, 2007: 54), religious buildings might need to be paid for (Alam and Husband, 2006: 12), more conservative Muslims might have their labour market options constrained by their wish to pray at the prescribed times five times a day, or religiously motivated avoidance of family planning methods might lead to larger families, thus reducing disposable income.

However, as we have seen, and as Heath and Li conclude, in relation to a faith community 'it is impossible to be sure whether we are observing a religious or an ethnic difference [in poverty rates]' (Heath and Li, 2014: 34), and even if religious and ethnic affiliation do generate separate effects, those separate effects will be difficult to separate from such factors as cultural histories, so we are still more likely to be able to draw conclusions about ethno-religious groups' relationship with economic disadvantage than about purely religious groups' relationship with it (cf. National Equality Panel, 2010: 227).

Given such uncertainty, we might wonder whether this book *should* contain a chapter on religion and (dis)advantage. However, if it did not contain one, then it would need to contain a chapter on ethno-religious disadvantage: and such disadvantage matters for society as a whole (Stewart, 2014). If we cannot isolate a religious penalty then we need to take seriously the ethno-religious penalty that we have discovered (Longhi et al., 2013).

But having said that, there *are* reasons for including a chapter on purely religious (dis)advantage in this book: and we discover them if we broaden our understanding of (dis)advantage.

14.4 A Broader Concept of (Dis)advantage

At a meeting in December 2013 members of the Greenwich Faith Community Leaders spoke from the experience of their own faith communities and identified a number of disadvantages of belonging to a faith community: prejudice, discrimination, anti-Semitism, being misunderstood, having their faith buildings attacked, and being physically attacked themselves: an experience that made some of them hesitate to wear such religiously identifiable clothing as skull caps. In other parts of the world—as in Iraq at the time of writing—violence between people of different religions has complex ethnic, tribal, and religious roots, and can be deadly; and in some parts extreme persecution—for instance, of Baha'is in Iran—is the severest possible social disadvantage and is clearly *religious* disadvantage. The kinds of disadvantage experienced in most countries bear no resemblance to that, although, as we know from Northern Ireland, lower-level religious disadvantage can become a motive for violence later on.

Less severe, but still significant, is the disadvantage suffered by faith communities in some European countries. For France's secular élite, secularism is more important than freedom of religious practice, so the élite find it both legitimate and necessary to ban the wearing of full-face veils in public places such as schools (Seckinelgin, 2012: 273). In a Swiss referendum, a majority of 57 per cent voted for a ban on the construction of minarets on mosques (Seckinelgin, 2012: 274). Such changes have social consequences (Seckinelgin, 2012: 268). Separating out the religious and ethnic factors in the accompanying public debates would be difficult, but because religion is perceived by all of the debate's participants to be an important factor, it is one.

As well as listing examples of disadvantage, members of the Greenwich Faith Community Leaders listed some of the advantages of belonging to faith communities: opportunities to be useful to the faith community and to the wider community, support from other community members (particularly during bereavement), opportunities to offer support, a source of identity, the opportunity to nurture one's religious faith (itself a source of hope and of a sense of purpose), an opportunity to learn new social skills, a sense of belonging, and a defence against isolation.

The members of this representative borough group were employing a sense of disadvantage and advantage broader than the economic, and a definition of belonging to a faith community at the 'active participation' end of the spectrum rather than at the 'identification' end. This suggests that by using a definition of religious belonging that involves attending a congregation (even if only very occasionally) and exhibiting behaviours related to that religion, and by employing broad definitions of social advantage and social disadvantage, we can begin to speak about genuinely religious advantage and disadvantage, and then search for further examples.

Among less overt non-economic disadvantages might be cultural pressures on women to remain in the home and only to go beyond it in the company of a male member of the family (Dean and Kahn, 1997: 201–2). Such practices will inevitably restrict access to education, culture, friendships, and political engagement. Whether such practices should be regarded as generating *religious* disadvantage is an important question, given that such practices vary widely within faith communities. Perhaps we should speak of cultural-religious groups? Faith communities are inevitably highly diverse, so *any* particular practice or belief will to some extent be cultural and a result of group or individual history: but if the practice or belief is believed by a significant subgroup to be intimately connected with a religion then it would probably be best to count it as religious.

We have identified some disadvantages and some advantages of active participation in a religion, and some particular practices that generate disadvantage or advantage: but there might be some religious practices that can be interpreted as generating both advantage and disadvantage. Take the Muslim prohibitions of gambling and drinking alcohol. Some might see such prohibitions as disadvantages, because they restrict freedom, and because they might deter Muslims from seeking employment in bars and restaurants (Tackey et al., 2006: 94, 268): but others might see the prohibitions as advantageous because they prevent any possible slide into addiction and they make time and financial resources available for other pursuits. An interesting question is the extent to which the Muslim prohibition against lending or borrowing money at interest disadvantages Muslims. Islamic banks take deposits which they then lend out for the purposes of trade, and depositors then share in the proceeds of the trade undertaken. The religious preference for employing money in trade, and the avoidance of other religiously less legitimate ways of making money, is a positive ('pull') reason for so many Muslim families engaging in small family trading businesses. (A 'push' reason for the high proportion of self-employment amongst Muslims is the difficulty experienced when they seek employment) (Clark and Drinkwater, 2000). The small profits usually generated by small trading businesses are one of the reasons for Muslims' low average earned income (Longhi et al., 2009).

This question, and the questions that we have already raised, make clear how complex the concept of disadvantage really is. Is it preferable to be a member of a tight-knit extended family running a chain of barely profitable shops, to be a Muslim accountant working for an import and export business that borrows from mainstream banks to fund investment, to be a schoolteacher, or to be a taxi driver and therefore able to pray every day at the prescribed times? I know all of these Muslims. They might disagree about which of them is the most disadvantaged and which the most advantaged. In relation to the different but related question of the choice of a life partner, is a woman disadvantaged if there is an expectation that she will marry a man introduced to her by her parents? The answer must surely be: not necessarily, provided the British cultural norm of the woman's right to decide who to marry is also a factor. In the UK, Muslim women have the lowest rate of partnership with someone of a different religion: 3 per cent—and this is as true in younger cohorts as in older ones; whereas for other religious groups more inter-religious partnership is in evidence (Platt, 2009: 9). Again, ethnic and cultural norms will be complicating factors. Muslims, Sikhs, and Hindus from families originally from the Indian subcontinent are more likely to have experienced family pressure in relation to the choice of a marriage partner. If a woman educated in the UK finds herself married to a less well educated man who has moved from the Indian subcontinent rather than someone with whom she was at university then she might find herself multiply disadvantaged: economically, educationally, culturally, and in terms of personal relationships and engagement with society—the kind of multiple exclusions and disadvantages experienced by women in such religiously conservative countries as Saudi Arabia, where attempting to make choices outside those prescribed by social norms can risk increased exclusion from society and thus even more disadvantage.

Membership of any corporate body can of course offer the security of belonging, a sense of purpose, social capital, and the potential for assistance in times of difficulty; and, as we have heard from members of the Greenwich Faith Community Leaders, membership of a religious organization will offer all of these advantages and also a moral structure for one's life, a sense of identity (Modood et al., 1994: 46, 51), and a sense of belonging—a kind of belonging that is in fact unique because it grants authority within the organization as well as the experience of belonging to a corporate body subject to a variety of other sources of authority (Torry, 2005: 124–8; Torry, 2014: vol. 1, 82–6). Religious affiliation can grant both higher social self-esteem and better psychological adjustment: correlations interestingly stronger in more religious countries than in less religious ones (Gebauer et al., 2012). Religious belonging offers all of the advantages of belonging to a 'club': a concept that Jordan employs to describe the ways in which dominant social groups exclude minority ethnic groups from social benefits (Jordan, 1996: 9–13; and see discussion in Chapter 1 of this volume) but which can equally well be employed to describe the way in which the Muslim global community, the *Ummah*, functions for its members, or the ways in which ethno-religious groups construct positive identities for themselves (Taylor, 1998), particularly when other identities might imply disadvantage. As we have seen, in the UK, Pakistanis might prefer to call themselves Muslims in the cause of seeking:

> Psychological security in affirming an alternative identity to the one they are being excluded from, and a solidarity with a culture or community that they know something of and that is part of their biography, even if it is not an accurate description of their current way of living.   (Modood et al., 1994: 107)

Apart from Hinduism in India, most religions recognize a fundamental human equality (Inglehart, 2005: 290). To identify with a community in which the wealthy and secure are subject to the same religious obligations as the poor and insecure, and in which the wealthy have to account for inequality, whether in this life or in the next, can offer an understandable escape from the highly unequal economic and labour market world.

Religious affiliation, and particularly active membership of a religious organization, can be a significant resource during periods of poverty, illness, or disability. There might be religious charities designed to serve the economic, care, and cultural needs of a faith community (Jawad, 2012: 108); and sometimes a broad-based bundle of values and activities might provide for a wide variety of psychological, social, and economic needs. The large black majority New Wine Church in Woolwich makes substantial demands on its members, both in terms of their time and of their financial resources, but it also provides them with a firm structure for their lives (by offering a variety of regular activities on Sundays and weekdays for family members of all ages), a hierarchical structure within which every individual can find a place, opportunities for developing such skills as public speaking and group leadership (cf. Torry, 2005: 151–61), and assistance with employment opportunities (the church runs 'careerbuilders' for its members), as well as providing a firm structure of belief and practice within which life can be lived (cf. Iannaccone, 1994; Torry, 2005: 124). Similarly, the Islamic Zakat—the requirement that annually a proportion of every Muslim's wealth should be given to those in greater need (either through an institution or to individuals) (Dean and Kahn, 1997)—improves the economic position of poorer Muslims and reduces inequality in the Muslim community, thus providing both economic and social benefits. The outcome, in both of these examples, is a combination of 'capitals', all of which overlap to some extent: human capital, social capital, cultural capital, spiritual capital (a faith basis, a value system, and a moral vision), and religious capital (practical action motivated by spiritual capital)— for the individual, for the faith community, and for society as a whole (Baker, 2009: 111; and see the discussion of human and cultural capitals in Chapter 4). While some might experience a relatively rigid social structure as restrictive, for New Wine Church members the ubiquitous structure can be experienced as freedom from the constant need to choose activities and priorities that many members of our modern secular society find to be such a source of stress. Members of the Greenwich Islamic Centre experience the same sense of freedom in relation to the beliefs, practices, and organizational structures of their own religion.

To experience a broadly defined well-being is to be advantaged, and within a religious organization and tradition:

> The emphasis on morality and duty as the basis for protecting social justice and our social obligations towards others advances a notion of wellbeing which is much more deeply related to the human character, human nature and human identity.   (Jawad, 2012: 83)

An organization with members of a particular ethnic group might provide some of the benefits of a religious organization in terms of a sense of belonging, a sense of security provided by a shared culture, and assistance in times of difficulty; and a variety of voluntary organizations will provide a sense of purpose. Religious organizations will provide these benefits and also a moral and religious structure, opportunities for the exercise of religious obligations of service to others, a structure within which life's crises can be managed (Jawad, 2012: 142, 154, 179–82), and an opportunity to exercise a degree of religious authority. All of this raises interesting questions in relation to those organizations in which ethnic and religious criteria for membership coincide. Being a Jew is both an ethnic and a religious category, and for each individual Jew the balance between the two will be different, and will shift over time: so explicitly Jewish faith-based organizations will need to encompass trustees, staff, volunteers, and users differently located both on the religious–secular spectrum and within a religiously fragmented Jewish community (Harris, 1997: 9–10; Harris and Rochester, 2001), creating tensions which might push organizations in a more secular direction.

While it remains true that every faith community is made up of a variety of ethno-religious groups, and that broader disadvantage and advantage might have cultural and ethnic characteristics and roots as well as religious ones, we have seen that by employing broader definitions of advantage and disadvantage, and a definition of religious affiliation that includes active participation, we have discovered a variety of disadvantages and advantages that we might be able to term religious.

14.5 Implications for Social Policy

Does social policy have any business getting mixed up with religion? And is this debate part of the 'multiculturalism' debate?—that is, debate about whether the government of a state and other institutions of civil society should protect and promote each of a number of different cultures, should ignore them as none of their business, or should attempt to eradicate visible cultural differences?

The concept of multiculturalism encompasses the diversity of religious, ethnic, and cultural identities in our society, and somewhat confusingly is both a recognition of 'group difference within the public sphere' and a political term seeking 'active support for cultural difference' (Modood, 2013: 2, 59). In relation to the latter meaning of the term, Singh and Cowden blame such multiculturalism for 'social fragmentation on one level and the rise of fundamentalist Islamic groups on the other' (Singh and Cowden, 2011: 344); the Dutch government has backed away from active support for different cultures because it has come to believe that the policy increased minorities' social exclusion (Entzinger, 2006); and Modood suggests that someone chooses their religion, whereas they do not choose their ethnicity, sexuality, gender, disability, or age, so religious identity should not be a public policy issue in the same way as someone's other identities might be (Modood, 2013: 65). However, as we have seen, religion will often not be chosen by the individual, and will be as much an element of their heritage as any other aspect. This means that 'multiculturalism' might be as relevant to religious identity as to any other kind, and that we might see a commitment to multiculturalism as an affirmation that religion is as much a public policy issue as is any other human characteristic. The relationship between the state and faith communities is clearly a policy issue (Modood, 1998: 397; 2010; 2013: 73; 2014b: 136); and in any local context the relationship between the local authority and faith communities will also be a legitimate matter for policy debate. The more that faith communities work together in a locality, and the closer their relationships with local authorities and with other civil society institutions, the less isolated, and the more secure, each faith community will be (Torry and

Thorley, 2008). If no regular gathering of representatives of faith communities in a borough exists, then the local authority might usefully facilitate such a gathering. In the national context, the Interfaith Network UK has an active presence, and there are university departments that study religious activity and the relationship between religion and society, but the religious sector does not enjoy the kind of organizational and academic infrastructure that the private, public, and voluntary sectors experience. A religious equivalent of the voluntary sector's National Council for Voluntary Organizations, and university centres to provide organizational expertise and management training appropriate to religious and faith-based organizations, would again reduce the isolation of religious organizations, strengthen relationships between civil society institutions and faith communities, and reduce the social disadvantage experienced by faith communities and their members.

In relation to social disadvantage, social policy has a clear role to perform. It might be no business of social policy to interfere in the beliefs, practices, and organizations of a faith community (unless they are causing problems in other aspects of society): but if social disadvantage is being suffered by members of faith communities then social policy needs to address that fact. So after growing concern about the discrimination and abuse experienced by Muslims largely because they were Muslims (Ansari, 2002), in 2010 the UK's equalities legislation recognized religion as a protected status alongside gender, ethnicity, disability, age, and sexual orientation. We have already discussed the question as to whether ethnicity and religion are overlapping categories (Platt, 2011: 72), but it is surely as right to provide protection for people who define themselves religiously as it is to provide protection for people who define themselves ethnically.

It might be no business of social policy to decide what a particular individual or family might perceive as advantages or disadvantages: but if some individual or family decides to leave behind disadvantages currently experienced, and to pursue new social, economic, or psychological advantages, and to do that through education or training, by moving geographically, occupationally or culturally, by making new relationships, or by crossing any other boundaries: then social policy needs to understand as problems to be solved any difficulties that they might experience in crossing those boundaries.

To take a few particular examples: universities and other higher education establishments might make themselves more attractive to the conservatively religious by ensuring that they can continue to practise their faith once they arrive; and state community schools might facilitate the practice of religion *in school*, rather than leave that to schools attached to individual faith communities (Flint, 2009), because only schools that mirror the society that we seek to create can be the right approach if we are to build a tolerant and multi-faith society. The task is to create porous boundaries across which deeper understanding can travel, and that would create the conditions for families and individuals to make their own transitions—culturally, occupationally, educationally, and religiously—if they wish to do so. Heath and Li suggest that English language lessons, appropriately provided childcare, and opportunities for civil engagement, would similarly reduce the isolation of faith communities and their members (Heath and Li, 2014: 35). It is a proper role for social policy to open the boundaries of society's different 'clubs' (Jordan, 1996: 8–11) so that understanding and resources can travel between them, and so that individuals, families and communities can, if they wish, seek new situations within which disadvantages can be abandoned and new advantages can be sought.

14.6 Conclusion

We can conclude that economic disadvantage appears to attach to certain ethno-religious groups in our society (where religious belonging is defined as someone's self-identification with a religion), and that advantages and disadvantages more broadly defined attach more closely to religion if religious belonging is defined as active participation in a religious congregation and in religious practices. We have discussed the ways in which social policy might address religious disadvantage broadly defined. At various points we have touched on how society and its institutions might best relate to religious identity and practice in order to reduce religious disadvantage, and I have suggested that a more robust institutional infrastructure might be helpful. Modood's prescription for a more plural relationship between religion and the state than that currently found in the UK would be a better context within which to construct such an infrastructure than Singh and Cowden's suggestion of a more secularist framework (2014: 130). State recognition of religious identity and of active religious practice will remain an important context within which to tackle the disadvantage suffered by members of faith communities (Modood, 2010: 8) and within which to construct a society comfortable with its diversity (Modood, 2010: 12, 13).

References

Alam, M. Y. and Husband, C. (2006). *British-Pakistani Men from Bradford: Linking Narratives to Policy*. York: Joseph Rowntree Foundation.
Ansari, H. (2002). *Muslims in Britain*. London: Minority Rights Group International.

Baker, C. (2009). 'Blurred encounters? Religious Literacy, Spiritual Capital and Language'. In A. Dinham, R. Furbey, and V. Lowndes (eds) *Faith in the Public Realm: Controversies, Policies and Practices* (pp. 105–22). Bristol: Policy Press.

Bradford, B. and Forsyth, F. (2006). 'Employment and Labour Market Participation'. In J. Dobbs, H. Green, and L. Zealey (eds) *Focus on Ethnicity and Religion* (pp. 111–58). Basingstoke: Palgrave Macmillan.

Brown, M. S. (2000). 'Religion and Economic Activity in the South Asian Population'. *Ethnic and Racial Studies*, 23(6): 1035–61.

Bruce, S. and Glendinning, T. (2013). 'The Extent of Religious Activity in England'. *FutureFirst*, 29: 1, 4, <http://brierleyconsultancy.com/images/ff29.pdf>, accessed 18 August 2015.

Cassen, R. and Kingdon, G. (2007). *Tackling Low Educational Achievement*. York: Joseph Rowntree Foundation.

Clark, K. and Drinkwater, S. (2000). 'Pushed Out or Pulled In? Self-employment among Ethnic Minorities in England and Wales'. *Labour Economics*, 7(5): 603–28.

Clark, K. and Drinkwater, S. (2007). *Ethnic Minorities in the Labour Market*. Bristol: Policy Press, for the Joseph Rowntree Foundation.

Cornell, S. and Hartman, D. (1998). *Ethnicity and Race: Making Identities in a Changing World*. Thousand Oaks, CA: Pine Forge Press.

Dale, A. (2002). 'Social Exclusion of Pakistani and Bangladeshi Women'. *Sociological Research Online,* 7(3), www.socresonline.org.uk/7/3/dale.html, accessed 18 August 2015.

Dean, H. (2002). *Welfare Rights and Social Policy*. Harlow: Pearson.

Dean, H. and Khan, Z. (1997). 'Muslim Perspectives on Welfare'. *Journal of Social Policy*, 26(2): 193–209.

Durkheim, E. (1915). *The Elementary Forms of the Religious Life*. London: George Allen and Unwin.

Entzinger, H. (2006). 'The Parallel Decline of Multiculturalism and the Welfare State in the Netherlands'. In K. Banting and W. Kymlicka (eds) *Multiculturalism and the Welfare State: Recognition and Redistribution in Contemporary Democracies* (pp. 177–201). Oxford: Oxford University Press.

Flint, J. (2009). 'Faith-based Schools: Institutionalising Parallel Lives?' In A. Dinham, R. Furbey, and V. Lowndes (eds) *Faith in the Public Realm: Controversies, Policies and Practices* (pp. 163–82). Bristol: Policy Press.

Foresight (2013). *Future Identities*. London: Government Office for Science.

Gebauer, J. E., Sedikides, C., and Neberich, W. (2012). 'Religiosity, Social Self-esteem, and Psychological Adjustment: On the Cross-cultural Specificity of the Psychological Benefits of Religiosity'. *Psychological Science*, 23(2): 158–60.

Georgiadis, A. and Manning, A. (2011). 'Change and Continuity among Minority Communities in Britain'. *Journal of Population Economics*, 24(2): 541–68.

Hammond, P. E. (2000). *The Dynamics of Religious Organizations: The Extravasation of the Sacred and Other Essays*. Oxford: Oxford University Press.

Harris, M. (1997). *The Jewish Voluntary Sector in the United Kingdom: Its Role and its Future*. London: Institute for Jewish Policy Research.

Harris, M. and Rochester, C. (2001). *Governance in the Jewish Voluntary Sector*. London: Institute for Jewish Policy Research. <http://www.bjpa.org/Publications/details.cfm?PublicationID=4329>, accessed 18 August 2015.

Heath, A. and Li, Y. (2014). 'Religion and Poverty'. In *Reducing Poverty: A Collection of Evidence Reviews* (pp. 33–6). York: Joseph Rowntree Foundation.

Iannaccone, L. R. (1994). 'Why Strict Churches Are Strong'. *American Journal of Sociology*, 99(5): 1180–211.

Inglehart, R., Basañez, M., and Moreno, A. (1998). *Human Values and Beliefs: A Cross-cultural Sourcebook*. Ann Arbor, MI: University of Michigan Press.

Inglehart, R. (2005). *Modernization, Cultural Change, and Democracy: The Human Development Sequence*. New York: Cambridge University Press.

Jacobson, J. (1997). 'Religion and Ethnicity: Dual and Alternative Sources of Identity among Young British Pakistanis'. *Ethnic and Racial Studies*, 20(2): 238–56.

Jawad, R. (2012). *Religion and Faith-based Welfare: From Wellbeing to Ways of Being*. Bristol: Policy Press.

Jordan, B. (1996). *A Theory of Poverty and Social Exclusion*. Cambridge: Polity Press.

Khattab, N. (2009). 'Ethno-religious Background as a Determinant of Educational and Occupational Attainment in Britain'. *Sociology*, 43(2): 304–22.

Lindley, J. (2002). 'Race or Religion? The Impact of Religion on the Employment and Earnings of Britain's Ethnic Communities'. *Journal of Ethnic and Migration Studies*, 28(3): 427–42.

Longhi, S., Nicoletti, C., and Platt, L. (2009). 'Decomposing Pay Gaps across the Wage Distribution: Investigating Inequalities of Ethno-religious Groups and Disabled People'. Working Paper Series 2009–31. Colchester: Institute for Social and Economic Research, University of Essex.

Longhi, S., Nicoletti, C., and Platt, L. (2013). 'Explained and Unexplained Wage Gaps across the Main Ethno-religious Groups in Great Britain'. *Oxford Economic Papers*, 65(2): 471–93.

Modood, T. (1998). 'Anti-essentialism, Multiculturalism, and the "Recognition" of Religious Groups'. *Journal of Political Philosophy*, 6(4): 378–99.

Modood, T. (2013). *Multiculturalism: A Civic Idea*. 2nd edn. Cambridge: Cambridge University Press.

Modood, T. (2010). 'Moderate Secularism, Religion as Identity and Respect for Religion'. *Political Quarterly*, 81(1): 4–14.

Modood, T. (2014a). 'Multiculturalism and Religion: A Three Part Debate. Part One: Accommodating Religions: Multiculturalism's New Fault Line'. *Critical Social Policy*, 34(1): 121–7.

Modood, T. (2014b). 'Multiculturalism and Religion: A three part debate. Part three: The Fault Lines of Multiculturalism: A Rejoinder'. *Critical Social Policy*, 34(1), 136–9.

Modood, T., Beishon, S., and Virdee, S. (1994). *Changing Ethnic Identities*. London: Policy Studies Institute.

Modood, T. and Berthoud, R. (1997). *Ethnic Minorities in Britain: Diversity and Disadvantage*. London: Policy Studies Institute.

Nandi, A. and Platt, L. (2010). 'Ethnic Minority Women's Poverty and Economic Well Being'. Colchester: Institute for Social and Economic Research, University of Essex.

National Equality Panel. (2010). *An Anatomy of Economic Inequality in the UK: Report of the National Equality Panel.* London: Government Equalities Office.

Office for National Statistics. (2013). 'What Does the Census Tell Us about Religion in 2011?' <http://www.ons.gov.uk/ons/infographics/what-does-the-census-tell-us-about-religion-in-2011-/index.html>, accessed 18 August 2015.

Platt, L. (2002). *Parallel Lives?* London: Child Poverty Action Group.

Platt, L. (2005). *Migration and Social Mobility: The Life Chances of Britain's Minority Ethnic Communities.* Bristol: Policy Press, for the Joseph Rowntree Foundation.

Platt, L. (2007). *Poverty and Ethnicity in the UK.* Bristol: Policy Press, for the Joseph Rowntree Foundation.

Platt, L. (2009). *Ethnicity and Family: Relationships within and between Ethnic Groups: An Analysis using the Labour Force Survey.* Colchester: Institute for Social and Economic Research, University of Essex, for the Equality and Human Rights Commission.

Platt, L. (2011). *Understanding Inequalities: Stratification and Differences.* Cambridge: Polity Press.

Seckinelgin, H. (2012). 'Peoples' Europe and the Limits of the European Public Sphere and Civil Society'. *Journal of Civil Society*, 8(3): 267–83.

Singh, G. and Cowden, S. (2011). 'Multiculturalism's New Fault Lines: Religious Fundamentalisms and Public Policy'. *Critical Social Policy*, 31(1): 343–64.

Singh, G. and Cowden, S. (2014). 'Multiculturalism and Religion: A Three Part Debate. Part Two: Response to Tariq Modood—Accommodating Religions: Who's Accommodating Whom?' *Critical Social Policy*, 34(1): 128–34.

Stewart, F. (2009). 'Horizontal Inequality: Two Types of Trap'. *Journal of Human Development and Capabilities*, 10(3): 315–40.

Stewart, F. (2014). 'Why Horizontal Inequalities are Important for a Shared Society'. *Development*, 57(1): 46–54.

Tackey, N. D., Casebourne, J., Aston, J., Ritchie, H., Sinclair, A., Tyers, C., Hurstfield, J., Willison, R., and Page, R. (2006). *Barriers to Employment for Pakistanis and Bangladeshis in Britain.* London: Department for Work and Pensions.

Taylor, D. (1998). 'Social Identity and Social Policy: Engagements with Postmodern Theory'. *Journal of Social Policy*, 27(3): 329–50.

Thapar-Bjorkert, S. and Sanghera, G. (2010). 'Social Capital, Educational Aspirations and Young Pakistani Muslim Men and Women in Bradford, West Yorkshire'. *Sociological Review*, 58(2): 244–64.

Torry, M. (2005). *Managing God's Business: Religious and Faith-based Organizations and their Management.* Aldershot: Ashgate.

Torry, M. (2010). *Bridgebuilders: Workplace Chaplaincy: A History.* Norwich: Canterbury Press.

Torry, M. (2014). *Managing Religion: The Management of Christian Religious and Faith-based Organizations.* Basingstoke: Palgrave Macmillan.

Torry, M. and Thorley, S. (eds) (2008). *Together and Different: Christians Working with People of Other Faiths.* Norwich: Canterbury Press.

Voas, D. and Fleischmann, F. (2012). 'Islam Moves West: Religious Change in the First and Second Generations'. *Annual Review of Sociology*, 38: 525–45.

15

Social Disadvantage and Place

Neil Lee

Social disadvantage is highly uneven across space. Disparities are evident at all scales and for most indicators of disadvantage. For example, a male in the Scottish city of Glasgow can expect to live to the age of 73, while one in the affluent London suburb of Harrow to live to 82 (ONS, 2014). In the US, a young person born to parents with incomes in the bottom quintile in San Jose has a 13 per cent chance of reaching the top quintile of incomes; a young person born in Charlotte has only a 4 per cent chance (Chetty et al., 2014). In Spain in 2013, the unemployment rate in Andalusia was over 36 per cent, but only 16 per cent in the Basque country (OECD, 2014). These disparities are not only wide but they are also, generally, increasing. Between 1995 and 2010, regional disparities in economic output (GDP per capita) increased in twenty out of thirty-three OECD economies (OECD, 2013). In the UK, geographical inequalities in mortality have been increasing since the early 1970s (Thomas et al., 2010).

Geographical disparities in social disadvantage matter for a number of reasons. First, the geography of social disadvantage influences the policy response to it. When patterns of social disadvantage change so should the support offered to the disadvantaged. Moreover, many policies are explicitly 'area based'—such as the neighbourhood focus of much of the UK's urban renewal polices of the late 1990s and 2000s (Lupton et al., 2013). A second, related reason is that local policymakers are often being given increased funding, powers, and flexibilities to address social disadvantage locally. The past twenty years has seen a growing, albeit far from universal, trend to devolve power to the local level (Rodríguez-Pose and Gill, 2003). One aim of devolution is to help policy reflect local specificities and so address the problems of the most disadvantaged places.

A third reason why place may matter is the concern that it can be a causal factor in disadvantage. If this is so, then concentrations of disadvantage can actually perpetuate that disadvantage. For example, if disadvantaged groups live in areas with unfavourable neighbourhood characteristics such as poor quality schools or transport links, they may find it harder to gain employment and progress in employment (Glennerster et al., 1999). The relationship between disadvantage and place may be dynamic. For example, access to the best state schools is often allocated on the basis of proximity. Yet proximity is determined by the housing market which is itself influenced by incomes, meaning that spatial factors can reinforce inequality (Hamnett and Butler, 2011). Some have also argued, controversially, that the simple concentration of disadvantaged residents may result in further disadvantage—'neighbour-hood effects'. These effects may arise if a lack of role models or restricted social networks worsen outcomes for people living in disadvantaged areas, irrespective of the other characteristics of those areas.

Yet, despite very visible spatial disparities, others argue the link between place and social disadvantage has been overstated (Gibbons et al., 2010). According to this view, who you are is more important than where you live and an individual's chances of social disadvantage or advantage are determined more by characteristics such as their education or personal background than their location. If this is correct, spatial disparities are simply reflections of the geography of socially disadvantaged people. Policy may then be better addressed at helping people with characteristics likely to lead to social disadvantage, regardless of the location of the disadvantaged.

This chapter considers the relationship between social disadvantage and advantage and place. It considers two principal spatial scales: cities and neighbourhoods. This is not to deny the importance of rural poverty, which remains a significant problem, but simply to reflect recent policy agendas in much of the world. The chapter is structured as follows. First, it considers the geography of social disadvantage and how this has changed using examples from both the global north and south. It focuses on urban areas and considers how economic change and changing housing markets have led to changes in the geography of poverty. Next, it outlines the key debates about the linkages between 'place' and social disadvantage and, in particular, the key causal question—is spatial variation in social disadvantage a cause or a consequence of inequality and poverty? Finally, it develops some of the key implications of the changing geography of poverty for policy and practice.

15.1 The Geography of Social Disadvantage

There is a long tradition of researching social disadvantage using geographical methods. Charles Booth, in his study of poverty in London, mapped poverty at a street level and categorized blocks of houses according to the social status of their inhabitants: red for the 'well-to-do'; black for 'semi-criminal'. Other seminal works have focused on 'place', such as Frederick Engels considering the slums of Manchester or George Orwell on the problems faced in Northern England in the depression. Much recent research in geography, social policy, and economics has focused on two spatial scales: the city, which is seen as economically important and the context for much disadvantage, and the neighbourhood, with researchers following Booth in the tradition of small area analysis of the nature of poverty. This section will consider both.

15.1.1 *Urban Poverty in Developed and Developing Countries*

Cities are increasingly seen as important units of economic analysis (World Bank, 2009). Policymakers in both the developed world and global south have highlighted the economic benefits of urban agglomeration, which allows the sharing of costly infrastructure, helps match workers into the appropriate employment and allows specialized economic actors to benefit from exchanges of knowledge and information (Duranton and Puga, 2004). Many countries have seen a resurgence of the city (at least rhetorically) and some central cities have experienced an influx of population and growing economic importance (Champion and Townsend, 2010; Turok and Mykhnenko, 2007). In the global south, this economic role was highlighted in the seminal 2009 World Development Report: *Reshaping Economic Geography*. The report was one of the most important attempts to highlight the links between 'place' and economic growth. It argued that cities were one of the three 'main catalysts of progress in the developed world over the past two centuries' (World Bank, 2009: xx) and highlighted the important role strong urban economies could play in reducing poverty.

This new narrative for cities focuses on their economic importance and potential for growth. Yet, while cities are important for economic growth, they also remain significant locations of social disadvantage (Lee et al., 2014). In many countries of the global north, long-term economic restructuring from the 1970s and 1980s worsened city economies and resulted in significant concentrations of urban poverty. Declining manufacturing employment and, in some smaller cities, extractive industries, left some cities in a state of economic deterioration (Lupton et al., 2013; Power et al., 2010; Turok and Edge, 1999). Local economies built on manufacturing often lacked the capacity to adapt to economic change: workforce skills were not suited to new industries, central cities contained dated industrial buildings and infrastructure, and a legacy of large employers meant there were too few growth-focused small- and medium-sized enterprises (SMEs). Cities such as Bradford in the UK or Wuppertal in Germany became exemplars of these trends as a declining textile industry led to long-term economic problems, reduced employment and eventually population loss (Turok and Mykhnenko, 2007). The most famous case of urban decline is Detroit, where declining employment in automobile manufacturing resulted in a vicious cycle of population decline, reduced local demand, falling tax revenues and the physical deterioration of the city. But cases of such stark decline are rare.

There is no single measure of the geography of disadvantage, but poverty is one potential indicator. Indicators of poverty at a city level are notoriously poor in the UK, but Fenton (2013) proposes an indicator based on benefits claiming. This is a good proxy for income poverty and one which is reliable at a local level and, unlike the more complex and recently introduced English Index of Multiple Deprivation (mentioned in Chapter 1, this volume), is comparable across time (Lee et al., 2014). Figure 15.1 maps this measure of poverty in the largest British cities—those defined in the government's State of the English Cities Database plus the major cities of Scotland and Wales (data is not available for Northern Ireland). The results show something of a core-periphery pattern, with cities nearer London and in the South of the UK tending to have the lowest rates of poverty. Reflecting the long-term legacy of industrial decline, poverty rates tend to be higher in cities in the north east of the country and in the cluster of cities in the North West and Yorkshire. Yet the results are far more complicated than a simple North-South divide. London itself has relatively high rates of poverty amongst the population as does Hastings on the south coast, while cities like York and even Leeds in the north perform better on this measure.

Some argue that disparities between cities with strong economies and the ex-industrial cities will continue to grow: a process of divergence of incomes between regions within countries which has occurred even as incomes have converged between countries (Storper, 2013). The main reasons for this are the increased premium placed on skills and the tendency of skilled workers to cluster in cities with already highly qualified populations (Duranton and Monastiriotis, 2002). Interlinked processes of globalization, technological change, and industrial change have raised the wage premium on skills as skilled workers have been particularly important for the economy. For low-skilled workers, faced with low-wage competition from abroad, it has proven difficult to secure employment. Employment opportunities for low-skilled workers have been increasingly in service work such as working as security guards, cleaning, or personal services—all jobs reliant on proximity to high-skilled workers) (Autor and Dorn, 2013; and see Chapter 9, this volume). Yet at the same time, skilled workers have been moving to cities and regions which have already high skill levels—with these cities and regions have been those which have experienced economic growth. The result has been a Catch-22 for cities with high concentrations of social disadvantage: cities need skilled workers for employment and economic growth, yet skilled workers are

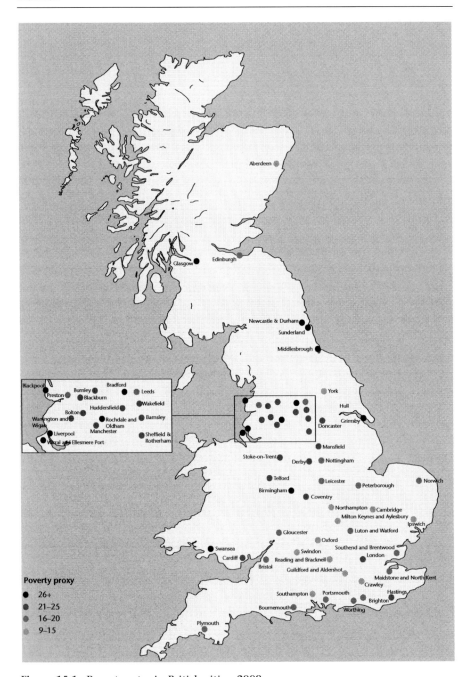

Figure 15.1. Poverty rates in British cities, 2008

Note: Measure of poverty is the unadjusted means-tested benefits rate (UMBR) developed by Fenton (2013)—the share of households in a city claiming the most important means tested benefits, a close proxy with other measures of income poverty. 'Cities' are travel-to-work areas.
Source: Lee et al., 2014

increasingly moving to cities with other skilled workers. One outcome has been rising economic disparities between places.

These patterns of urban change have led to a disconnect between the cities experiencing growth and those with the highest rates of poverty, in the UK at least (Lee et al., 2014). Over the 2000s, the cities with the greatest population in poverty experienced the lowest growth levels over the subsequent period. Output growth (measured in terms of Gross Value Added per capita) was concentrated in the relatively affluent cities near to London or cities with financial services (Edinburgh) or extractive economies (Aberdeen). There was a reduction in poverty in the most deprived cities over this period, but this was unrelated to the strength of the local economy—local economic conditions are less important than national changes to the benefits system.

Patterns in the global south have differed. While there has been significant variation between countries, the growth of cities in countries such as China and India has resulted in higher average incomes in core agglomerations than in rural areas (World Bank, 2009). This income differential has encouraged the socially disadvantaged to move to cities (UN Habitat, 2008). The result has often been slums, unpleasant places to be, and visible sites of disadvantage. Yet the association between urbanization and economic growth has not been uniform, and while it has been apparent in Asia many African countries have experienced urbanization without the same progress in development (Turok, 2013). Concern about the growth of disadvantaged slums were obvious in the UN Habitat (2003) report *The Challenge of Slums*, which highlighted the issues faced by 924 million urban slum dwellers worldwide—a figure the report predicted will increase significantly. Social policy has often reflected this changing geography of poverty. In some cases, social policy has had to be reconfigured to meet the needs of the urban poor. Appleton et al. (2010) document how anti-poverty programmes were traditionally focused on rural areas, before the rise of a 'new urban poverty' in the late 1990s led to growing concerns among policymakers about the urban poor, although they argue that increases in absolute numbers of the urban poor were overstated, in China at least.

Yet the counter argument is that for many people living conditions in the slums are better than they would otherwise expect living in rural poverty. So while there are now more poor people living in cities than before, this is because of the potential of urban areas to reduce social disadvantage rather than because they increase disadvantage (UN Habitat, 2008). Urban areas increasingly present a contrast between highly visible poverty and affluence at close quarters, with nearby gated communities often a visible sign of the lack of integration between different parts of the urban economy (Turok, 2013). Cities—and even the slums they often contain—are not simply sites of social disadvantage but also can play a role in improving the living standards of their residents.

15.1.2 *The Suburbanization of Poverty*

There have also been important changes in the geography of social disadvantage within cities. One phenomenon in many OECD countries has been the suburbanization of poverty. Poverty has traditionally been viewed as an inner-city problem (Madden, 1996). The inner cities often had the cheapest housing and had born the cost of industrial decline. In his seminal research on poverty, Wilson (1996) famously documented the problems faced by the inner city poor of the US: technological and industrial change was reducing the wages of manual workers, employment was suburbanizing and low-income inner city residents lacked the transport (and skills) needed to get to the new jobs being created in suburbs. At the same time, those residents with the means to do so were leaving—and the predominantly black inner city community was left socially disrupted and in a paradoxically isolated position.

Yet this view of cities as the sites of poverty has also been challenged: both the US and UK have seen increased suburbanization of poverty. This has been due in part to a limited 'resurgence' of many inner cities—improved transport, declining crime and reduced pollution have made it viable to live in or close to city centres. While city centres were once locations of production, they are increasingly seen as sites for consumption with changing preferences for urban living and increased disposable incomes amongst some residents. House prices in inner areas have often risen and the economies of inner areas were doing relatively better (Kneebone and Berube, 2013). Thus, as the central city became more desirable it became more expensive; less well-off residents have often been moved into suburban areas which were, at the same time, seeing their economies decline.

The US has been the exemplar of this trend. Between 2000 and 2010 the number of poor individuals in US suburbs grew by 5.3 million, a rate of increase of 53 per cent—double that of the rate of increase in cities, 23 per cent (Kneebone and Berube, 2013). In 2011, for the first time, there were more poor Americans living in suburbs than living in cities: 16.4 million relative to 13.4 million poor urban dwellers. While they still have many poor residents, the longstanding view of poverty as an inner city concern has been challenged.

These trends have not been apparent in all European cities, where poverty was often already a suburban issue as large housing estates built on the edge of the city containing relatively deprived residents (Power, 2012). In her seminal book on housing estates, Anne Power (1997) sets out how one of the consequences of rebuilding in the long period after the Second World War was the development of mass housing often in peripheral parts of cities. Surveying twenty estates across five countries, she shows how many estates had experienced long-term physical decline but that decline was neither uniform nor unchallenged by local residents who often acted to address these problems.

Many of the estates Power considered were historically located in the periphery of cities. Yet further suburbanization of disadvantage has been clear more recently in cities like London, patterns had been different and much of London's inner areas were inhabited by disadvantaged residents with relatively affluent suburbs around them, particularly to the West. A changing preference for urban living and changing housing policy led to significant increases in poverty rates in the outer boroughs. Lupton et al. (2013) consider the period 2001–11 and show small declines in one measure of poverty in Inner London but increases across all three areas of outer London.

Shifts in the geography of social disadvantage have some implications for policy. Kneebone and Berube (2013) set out three of these. First, they can lead to greater distance between the socially disadvantaged and potential employment. This 'jobs mismatch' may make it harder for people to access employment. Geographical shifts such as this matter as population dispersion leads to problems such as lack of access to transport and so employment opportunities (Power, 2012). Second, such patterns can distance the socially disadvantaged from potential support. Urban areas of the US are more likely to have charities which will support the socially disadvantaged and public services better targeted to provide help and advice to disadvantaged groups. This problem is underpinned by a third factor, with an out-dated perception of suburban areas as affluent meaning they receive too little support.

15.1.3 Neighbourhood Dynamics and Spatially Concentrated Disadvantage

Social disadvantage is most noticeable at the neighbourhood level and classic studies have considered poor neighbourhoods and contrasted them with more affluent areas. Charles Booth had considered the relationship between the poverty of the East End of London and the far more affluent West of the city (Briggs, 1968). Some of the research focus has been on the dynamics of neighbourhood change. In her seminal work, Jane Jacobs discussed the dynamics of neighbourhood decline and the potential for 'vicious circles' in the 'slums' of US cities in the 1960s (Jacobs, 1969). She describes how population change and physical decline work as reinforcing processes: less affluent populations move in, areas become neglected, and the remaining population leave.

The seminal approach to categorizing neighbourhoods in this fashion comes from Lupton and Power (2002). They suggest three ways of understanding the characteristics of neighbourhoods. First, there are intrinsic characteristics—such as location, the housing stock, and transport infrastructure. These characteristics can be hard (or, at least, expensive) for policy to change. Second, these processes will be exacerbated by spatial sorting of residents into particular neighbourhoods. As they have fewer choices about where to live, and sometimes due to allocation of social housing, the 'least advantaged areas become populated by the least advantaged people' (2001: 133). Finally, this concentration of deprivation can exacerbate the area's problems: for example, by developing a negative area reputation, crime, or worse local environment.

But there has been a stronger focus in the literature on processes of gentrification, in some ways the reverse process. Affluent incomers (the ironic term 'gentrification' is based on the notion of the Victorian 'gentry') would improve the housing stock of a particular neighbourhood (Hamnett, 2003). This would result in the opposite type of circle, with owners moving in and house prices rising—eventually pricing out the original occupants. Not the same 'vicious circle' which Jacobs had considered, but certainly one which could be vicious for the existing residents. While some have suggested that gentrification is an aggressive process driven by the middle classes, others have interpreted it as the inevitable result of changing population characteristics and a growing share of well-educated, professional workers (Hamnett, 2003).

If the residents of a place are disadvantaged, this does not mean that they will remain disadvantaged over the long term. Jacobs (1969) also highlighted the transitory nature of place, and the fact that low-income neighbourhoods often operate as transitory neighbourhoods from which people move upwards. Robson et al. (2008) divide deprived neighbourhoods into four categories, on the basis of where residents move to before or after. Places are either: (1) transit areas—where people come from less deprived areas and move to less deprived areas, residents live in these neighbourhoods for temporary periods; (2) escalators—which serve as a stepping stone for residents moving upwards (3) isolated areas—which take residents from other deprived areas, and lose residents to similarly deprived areas, with no upwards progression (4) improver areas—to which people move from less deprived neighbourhoods, in a similar process to gentrification.

Thinking about deprived areas as dynamic places has some implications. First, it is no longer enough to think of neighbourhoods as lying on a simple spectrum between 'deprived' and 'affluent'. Places are more complicated than that and many places may serve as transit points for social advantage over the long term (even Robson et al.'s typology misses significant variation between deprived places). Second and similarly, empirical work which focuses only on 'deprivation' as a measure may be missing significant variation. Finally, this raises significant issues for policy which should focus on the particular characteristics of local areas, rather than simply the level of deprivation of those residents who live there in one point in time. Clearly, the most important spatial focus is likely to be places were residents remain poor, not those which simply serve as stepping-stones in the lives of residents.

15.2 The Relationship between Place and Social Disadvantage

Changes in the geography of social disadvantage are interesting in a purely academic sense, but they also have implications for social policy. This section considers two of the most policy-relevant facets of the relationship between place and social disadvantage or advantage, focusing on local service provision and the potential existence of a causal relationship.

15.2.2 Local Public Services

'Place' influences the availability and quality of public services. Some services, such as schools, are often offered on geographically specific terms, such as catchment areas or selection by distance. Other services, such as transport, are inherently geographical and will shape the extent to which individuals can participate in society. Some important studies have considered this relationship and shown that the relationship between access to public services and social disadvantage is two-way: affluent people tend to move to areas with better public services, but also disadvantaged communities can also put a strain on public service provision resulting in worse outcomes. One example is schooling in East London, a case considered by Hamnett and Butler (2011). Distance is used to decide the allocation of school places. Because affluent residents have more choice in the housing market, they are better able to find homes near better schools and fulfil their choice. The structural features of income inequality are replicated, through the housing market, in disadvantage in the allocation of schooling, and so the eventual reinforcing of disadvantage. The result is a situation where 'geography is becoming the basis for rationing access to some forms of welfare' (2011: 479).

A second example of the relationship between place and public services is how transport links—often an 'intrinsic' place characteristic—influence access to work (Lupton and Power, 2002). Those in disadvantaged communities which are some distance from others can face a double disadvantage, as they are both unable to access opportunities through public transport but also less able to afford alternatives such as cars (Power, 2012). For example, access to employment is often dependent on the availability of suitable transport: the routes must be appropriate, timings must be compatible with shift-work, early or late starts, and the cost must not be prohibitive (Owen et al., 2012). Because of this problem, lack of transport is not just seen as a discrete problem, but as potentially a causal factor in a number of different areas of social policy, including poor health outcomes, low educational attainment, and labour market disadvantage (Lucas, 2012). Yet transport is intrinsically related to place, and changing geographical patterns of poverty will require new policies aiming at addressing this problem.

15.2.3 *Limitations of a 'Place-based' Perspective*

There are two important limitations to a place-based perspective. The first of these is the tendency to make generalizations about the characteristics of all residents based on the aggregate characteristics of the place: the ecological fallacy. Assuming all residents of a deprived neighbourhood are poor may ignore the affluence of some residents; similarly, there may be many living in poverty in rich neighbourhoods. For example, while London has a very high average income it would be wrong to label all residents as affluent—as Figure 15.1 shows, it has many residents in poverty.

The ecological fallacy has implications for both research on the link between social disadvantage and place and policy. It implies a need to consider not just average measures of local disadvantage in area studies, but also where the disadvantaged may be 'hidden' in averages. Otherwise, place-based policies risk ignoring many socially disadvantaged residents or providing benefits to many who do not need them. One example is the British Sure-Start programme which aimed to improve life chances for children growing up in some of the most deprived neighbourhoods of the UK. Area-based policy was explicitly included in the programme design and, to avoid stigma, all residents of the areas targeted were eligible for their services, regardless of whether they were disadvantaged themselves (Department for Education, 2011). Yet early evaluations suggested that residents with higher levels of human capital were often able to take advantage of this programme, meaning it was often a poorly targeted policy (Department for Education, 2005: 33).

Spatial scale is a second important issue when considering the relationship between place and social advantage or disadvantage. Aggregating at different scales will yield different results. Relationships are normally starkest at the smallest spatial scale, such as the neighbourhood, and will tend to show pronounced differences between places. Measures of social disadvantage will differ according to the boundaries used, making this a significant problem for research (this is sometimes referred to as the Modifiable Areal Unit Problem). In work on the impact of the neighbourhood on local school performance, for example, it has proven a difficult matter to define the 'neighbourhoods' which may be important for local residents, rather than the administrative boundaries on which research is based (Weinhardt, 2013).

A further complication is spatial sorting. Individuals move from place to place, and these moves are not random but determined by a range of factors including the nature of the place and the individual characteristics. As discussed above with relation to neighbourhoods, one important implication of this spatial sorting is that neighbourhood social disadvantage does not always mean most residents are disadvantaged in the long term. While the neighbourhood may remain poor, individuals may sort in and out of it according to their life stage and current incomes. A second implication of this spatial sorting is that it has led a number of authors to challenge the importance of area effects as determinants of social disadvantage. If individuals move to neighbourhoods because of particular characteristics—such as access to cheap housing—this complicates any relationships and leads to a challenge to the simple causality which suggests place has a causal role in disadvantage. Instead, the causal factors may be reversed as those at risk of disadvantage are sorted into the worst locations.

An example of this effect is the debate about the causes of the higher poverty rate outside of US metropolitan areas than within them. Two reasons have been suggested for this—a lack of jobs, which represents an area effect, or the tendency for residents with relatively lower incomes to sort into non-metropolitan areas. In research using US panel data, Fisher (2007) shows that both effects are important in explaining poverty rates. In a similar study which investigates wage disparities between UK cities, Gibbons et al. (2010) show that sorting of individuals into different areas explains the lion's share of disparities between places—although they consider wages rather than poverty and their estimation strategy makes a number of assumptions about the nature of individual's movements. In practice, few researchers would claim that area effects are the dominant cause of disparities between places.

15.2.4 *Place as a Causal Factor in Social Disadvantage*

Given the highly visible concentrations of disadvantage in many cities and neighbourhoods, and the fact that these disparities are widening in many countries, a dominant question has been the extent to which the geography of social disadvantage is a causal factor in perpetuating disadvantage, or more simply a reflection of existing patterns. This has not been a new argument (Glennerster et al., 1999), but it acquired particular salience in the UK when the New Labour government's policy focus on deprived neighbourhoods was based at least partly on the apparent assumption that concentrated disadvantage restricted social mobility. In a famous speech at the start of his period in Office in 1997, Prime Minister Tony Blair declared that: 'no one in future decades should be seriously disadvantaged by where they lived' (Lupton et al., 2013: 4).

The focus of research in this area has been on the neighbourhood and the idea of 'neighbourhood effects', where outcomes are worse for individuals living in deprived neighbourhoods beyond what would be expected given their other characteristics. In the UK, while the heyday of neighbourhood-focused policy was under the New Labour government (Lupton et al., 2013), the belief that neighbourhood matters for social advantage has remained entrenched. In the foreword to the UK Social Mobility Strategy of 2011, the Deputy Prime Minister argued that: 'In Britain today, life chances are narrowed for too many by the circumstances of their birth: the home they're born into, the neighbourhood they grow up in or the jobs their parents do.' (HM Government, 2011: 4).

Despite the focus of policymakers on reducing neighbourhood effects, studies considering whether they exist or not have yielded mixed results. Qualitative researchers and those using non-experimental quantitative methods have tended to find that neighbourhood effects exist (Weinhardt, 2013). Yet this interpretation has been challenged by evidence using an experimental research design, famously building on the 'Moving to Opportunity' (MTO) programme which began in the United States in 1994. The programme saw households in some deprived areas randomly allocated into either housing in better neighbourhoods, social housing in a deprived area, or nothing. The random allocation of households into the programme meant MTO is seen by many as the best possible way of demonstrating causal links between neighbourhood status and educational outcomes.

The findings from the MTO study have been the subject of considerable debate. In particular, in the absence of other experimental evidence and given the mixed and often positive evidence which exists for neighbourhood effects elsewhere, some have suggested that rejecting the existence of neighbourhood effects based on results from a single policy, with its own biases and problems, may not be a valid conclusion. Others have highlighted other problems with research using MTO: the relatively small sample size, the challenge of identifying effects which were not large in magnitude, and the often minor changes in neighbourhood which were experienced by participants (Quigley et al., 2008).

Yet the neighbourhood is not the only scale at which 'place' may matter for social disadvantage. More recent work has considered the impact of larger areas on life chances. In an important US study, Chetty et al. (2014) have considered the geography of intergenerational mobility in US cities using data on child and parental income. They show pronounced differences in mobility between cities. A child in Charlotte whose parents are in the bottom 20 per cent of incomes have only a 4.4 per cent chance of reaching the top 20 per cent. Yet the chances of such upward mobility are much higher for children born in Salt Lake City (10.8 per cent) or San Jose (12.9 per cent). More importantly, these differences seem to be partially explained by the characteristics of the city itself. Relatively unequal cities tend to have lower upward mobility with inequality limiting the extent to which individuals are able to progress up (or down) the income scale relative to their parents. Local community networks, involvement or other measures of 'social capital' (see Chapter 4 in this volume) also seem associated with greater inter-generational mobility, as are a smaller share of single parents. Geographical factors at the city level are also important and, in a result which partially supports the view that neighbourhood factors matter, they find segregation is negatively associated with upward mobility, although they argue that their analysis cannot be considered causal. Moreover, the local labour market does not seem to matter significantly in determining mobility.

A second point related to these causal analyses is that it is entirely possible that place matters more for some groups than others. Chetty et al. (2014) find that many of the effects they observe about inter-generational mobility are greatest for low-income children, that is, place matters more for those on lowest incomes. Other studies show that 'place' matters more for outcomes for some groups than others. Green and Owen (2006) show that the variations between employment rates across British regions are far higher for low-skilled workers than those educated to degree level or above. Low-skilled workers are less likely to move to economically successful places and their chances of employment are more reliant on local economic strength than skilled workers, who tend to be in employment wherever they live.

15.3 Conclusions: Implications for Policy and Practice

This chapter has considered the relationship between 'place' and social advantage or disadvantage. Both concepts are broad and open to interpretation, and no chapter could be comprehensive about the developments in all neighbourhoods or cities. Instead, it has highlighted some of the key trends in the geography of social disadvantage, the arguments around them and the implications for social policy.

The chapter first considered some of the key geographical scales at which social disadvantage may be evident. At a city level, there has been considerable discussion about the nature of industrial decline in many developed economies and the fact that, while some cities have been resurgent, others have found it harder to cope with economic change. The residents of these cities are more likely to experience social disadvantage than those elsewhere. Most forecasts suggest that the prospects of a significant economic resurgence in these cities are slim, in the short term at least. Analysis at a neighbourhood level also reveals changes in the geography of poverty and related patterns of gentrification of inner cities and suburbanization of social disadvantage. Disparities between rich and poor neighbourhoods are not new phenomena, but neighbourhood-based measures of social disadvantage are important because many policies to address disadvantage are delivered at a neighbourhood level (Lupton and Power, 2002). Some also argue that living in a deprived neighbourhood can play a causal role in disadvantage, although the existence of these 'neighbourhood effects' has been challenged by other researchers.

The chapter then considered the relationship between social disadvantage and place. It highlighted a number of analytical challenges faced by researchers working in this field—the dynamic nature of cities or neighbourhoods and the problems in adequately demarcating boundaries of areas for study. It suggested that while much recent work suggests neighbourhood effects are unimportant, other evidence suggests that place—in the form of city of birth—matters significantly for life chances over the long-term. Moreover, as policy is often best delivered at a local level, 'place' remains important.

Much of the literature on social disadvantage and place has considered the potential existence of 'neighbourhood effects'. Yet the geography of social disadvantage has important implications for policy, regardless of whether 'neighbourhood effects' exist. There is a distinction between policies focused on area outcomes, such as the UK's neighbourhood renewal policy, which relied to some extent on the existence of neighbourhood effects, and policy focused on particular areas which may be the best form of public services regardless. The changing geography of suburban poverty in the US, for example, highlights the importance of ensuring that provision matches need. Similarly, given concern about the potential for spatial markets, such as housing, to reinforce existing inequalities some form of place-based solution may be the only possible one. Moreover, many policies which address poverty will need to consider local context, regardless of whether 'place' has any causal role in disadvantage (Glasmeier et al., 2008). For example, local labour market context needs to be considered when planning employment interventions. While 'place' is only one factor explaining social advantage or disadvantage, understanding the geography of social disadvantage is an important part of any attempt to reduce it.

References

Appleton, S., Song, L., and Xia, Q. (2010). 'Growing out of Poverty: Trends and Patterns of Urban Poverty in China 1988–2002'. *World Development*, 38(5): 665–78.

Autor, D. H. and Dorn, D. (2013). 'The Growth of Low-Skill Service Jobs and the Polarization of the US Labor Market'. *American Economic Review*, 103(5): 1553–97.

Briggs, A. (1968). *Victorian Cities*. Harmondsworth: Penguin.

Champion, T. and Townsend, A. (2010). 'The Fluctuating Record of Economic Regeneration in England's Second-order City-regions, 1984–2007'. *Urban Studies*, 48(8): 1539–62.

Chetty, R., Hendren, N., Kline, P., and Saez, E. (2014). 'Where Is the Land of Opportunity? The Geography of Intergenerational Mobility in the United States'. *Quarterly Journal of Economics*, 129(4): 1553–623.

Department for Education and Skills (2005). *Early Impacts of Sure Start Local Programmes on Children and Families*. London: HMSO.

Department for Education (2011). *The Impact of Sure Start Local Programmes on Seven-year-olds and Their Families*. London: HMSO.

Duranton, G. and Monastiriotis, V. (2002). 'Mind the Gaps: The Evolution of Regional Earnings Inequalities in the UK, 1982–1997'. *Journal of Regional Science*, 42(2): 219–56.

Duranton, G. and Puga, D. (2004). 'Micro-foundations of Urban Agglomeration Economies'. In J. V. Henderson and J. F. Thisse (eds), *Handbook of Regional and Urban Economics* (pp. 2064–117). London: Elsevier B.V.

Fenton, A. (2013). *Small-area Measures of Income Poverty*. London: Centre for Analysis of Social Exclusion.

Fisher, M. (2007). 'Why Is U.S. Poverty Higher in Nonmetropolitan than in Metropolitan Areas?' *Growth and Change*, 38(1): 56–76.

Gibbons, S., Overman, H. G., and Pelkonen, P. (2010). 'Wage Disparities in Britain: People or Place?' Spatial Economics Research Centre Working Paper No. 60 (October).

Glasmeier, A., Martin, R., Tyler, P., and Dorling, D. (2008). 'Poverty and Place in the UK and the USA'. *Cambridge Journal of Regions, Economy and Society*, 1(1): 1–16.

Glennerster, H., Lupton, R., Noden, P., and Power, A. (1999). 'Poverty, Social Exclusion and Neighbourhood: Studying the Area Bases of Social Exclusion'. CASEpaper 22. London: Centre for the Analysis of Social Exclusion, LSE.

Green, A. E. and Owen, D. (2006). *The Geography of Poor Skills and Access to Work*. York: Joseph Rowntree Foundation.

Hamnett, C. (2003). 'Gentrification and the Middle-class Remaking of Inner London, 1961–2001'. *Urban Studies*, 40(12): 2401–26.

Hamnett, C. and Butler, T. (2011). '"Geography matters": The Role Distance Plays in Reproducing Educational Inequality in East London'. *Transactions of the Institute of British Geographers*, 36: 479–500.

HM Government. (2011). *Opening Doors, Breaking Barriers: A Strategy for Social Mobility*. London: HMSO.

Jacobs, J. (1969). *The Economy of Cities*. New York: Random House.

Kneebone, E. and Berube, A. (2013). *Confronting Suburban Poverty in America*. Washington, DC: Brookings Institution Press.

Lee, N., Sissons, P., Hughes, C., Green, A., Adam, D., Atfield, G., and Rodriguez-Pose, A. (2014). *Cities, Growth and Poverty: Evidence Review*. York: Joseph Rowntree Foundation.

Lucas, K. (2012). 'Transport and Social Exclusion: Where Are We Now?' *Transport Policy*, 20: 105–13.

Lupton, R., Fenton, A., and Fitzgerald, A. (2013). *Labour's Record on Neighbourhood Renewal in England: Policy, Spending and Outcomes 1997–2010*. London: Centre for Analysis of Social Exclusion, LSE.

Lupton, R. and Power, A. (2002). 'Social Exclusion and Neighbourhoods'. In J. Hills, J. Le Grand, and D. Piachaud (eds), *Understanding Social Exclusion* (pp. 118–40). Oxford: Oxford University Press.

Lupton, R., Vizard, P., Fitzgerald, A., and Fenton, A. (2013). 'Prosperity, Poverty and Inequality in London 2000/01–2010/11'. Social Policy in a Cold Climate Research Report. London: Centre for the Analysis of Social Exclusion, LSE.

Madden, J. (1996). 'Changes in the Distribution of Poverty across and within the US Metropolitan Areas, 1979–89'. *Urban Studies*, 33(9): 1581–600.

OECD (2013). *OECD Regions at a Glance 2013*. Paris: OECD.

OECD (2014). OECD.StatExtracts. Retrieved from <http://stats.oecd.org/>, accessed 8 April 2015.

Office of National Statistics (ONS) (2014). *Life Expectancy at Birth and at Age 65 by Local Areas in the United Kingdom, 2006–08 to 2010–12*. Newport: ONS.

Owen, D., Hogarth, T., and Green, A. E. (2012). 'Skills, Transport and Economic Development: Evidence from a Rural Area in England'. *Journal of Transport Geography*, 21: 80–92.

Power, A. (1997). *Estates on the Edge: The Social Consequences of Mass Housing in Northern Europe*. New York, NY: St Martin's Press.

Power, A. (2012). 'Social Inequality, Disadvantaged Neighbourhoods and Transport Deprivation: An Assessment of the Historical Influence of Housing Policies'. *Journal of Transport Geography*, 21: 39–48.

Power, A., Plöger, J., and Winkler, A. (2010). *Phoenix Cities: The Fall and Rise of Great Industrial Cities*. Bristol: Policy Press.

Quigley, J. M., Raphael, S., Sanbonmatsu, L., and Weinberg, B. A. (2008). 'Neighborhoods, Economic Self MTO Program Sufficiency, and the MTO Program'. *Brookings-Wharton Papers on Urban Affairs*, 3: 1–46.

Robson, B., Lymperopoulou, K., and Rae, A. (2008). 'People on the Move: Exploring the Functional Roles of Deprived Neighbourhoods'. *Environment and Planning A*, 40(11): 2693–714.

Rodríguez-Pose, A. and Gill, N. (2003). 'The Global Trend towards Devolution and its Implications'. *Environment and Planning C: Government and Policy*, 21(3): 333–51.

Storper, M. (2013). *Keys to the City: How Economics, Institutions, Social Interaction and Politics Shape Development*. Princeton, NJ: Princeton University Press.

Thomas, B., Dorling, D., and Smith, G. D. (2010). 'Inequalities in Premature Mortality in Britain: Observational Study from 1921 to 2007'. *British Medical Journal*, 341: 1–6.

Turok, I. (2013). 'Securing the Resurgence of African Cities'. *Local Economy*, 28(2): 142–57.

Turok, I. and Edge, N. (1999). *The Jobs Gap in Britain's Cities: Employment Loss and Labour Market Consequences*. York: Joseph Rowntree Foundation.

Turok, I. and Mykhnenko, V. (2007). 'The Trajectories of European Cities, 1960–2005'. *Cities*, 24(3): 165–82.

UN Habitat. (2003). *The Challenge of Slums: Global Report on Human Settlements 2003*. London: Earthscan.

UN Habitat. (2008). *State of the World's Cities 2008/9: Harmonious Cities*. Nairobi: UN Habitat.

Weinhardt, F. (2013). 'Neighbourhood Quality and Student Performance'. IZA Discussion Paper No. 7139.

Wilson, W. J. (1996). *When Work Disappears: The World of the New Urban Poor.* New York: Alfred A. Knopf.

World Bank. (2009). *World Development Report 2009: Reshaping Economic Geography.* Washington, DC: World Bank.

16

Social Disadvantage, Crime, and Punishment

Tim Newburn

Criminologists have long assumed that socio-economic conditions and social inequality play an important role both in why particular individuals become involved in criminal activity and in determining levels of crime within particular societies. The huge rises in crime that occurred from the 1950s to the early 1990s ended any easy assumptions about rising prosperity inevitably leading to falls in crime, and the crime decline in recent years has similarly put paid to the idea of any simple connection between economic crises and crime levels. Criminological theory, of various stripes, has focused on social disadvantage as central to explanation—not least as a consequence of the fact that criminal justice systems are focused primarily on the crimes of the disadvantaged rather than the 'crimes' of the socially privileged. Indeed, as Reiner (2007: 341) notes, the etymology of the terms 'villain' and 'rogue'—the former deriving from the medieval French for peasant and the latter from the Latin for beggar—is an indicator of the fact that this is an age-old association. In what follows I explore some of the complex associations between crime, punishment, and various manifestations of social (dis)advantage. The chapter has four broad questions at its heart. First, how, and in what ways, do economic conditions affect levels of crime? Are, for example, unemployment levels or economic upturns or downturns linked to changing levels and patterns of crime? Second, and relatedly, what is the relationship between social inequality and crime rates? Does rising social inequality inevitably lead to rising crime, and vice versa? Third, in what ways are material and social disadvantage related to patterns of offending and victimization? Finally, does the operation of the criminal justice and penal systems affect social inequality?[1]

---

[1] I am grateful to Coretta Phillips for comments on an earlier version of this chapter.

16.1 Economic Conditions and Crime

There is by now a quite considerable econometric literature on the relationship between prevailing economic conditions and crime. What one quickly discovers in this field, however, is that the relationships between income, wealth, crime, and victimization, though showing some fairly clear patterns, are far from straightforward. This can be illustrated, for example, by looking at property crime risks at the household level, and rates of property crime at the national level. First, as we will see below, the risk of burglary varies inversely with household income (Rosenfeld and Messner, 2013). That is to say, domestic burglary rates are substantially higher in poorer households. However, at the national level rates of burglary tend to increase according to the wealth, as measured by Gross Domestic Product (GDP). Why would this be the case? The simplest answer to this conundrum is most likely that at the national level a measure like GDP is broadly indicative of the level of criminal *opportunities* (how much there is of value to steal), whereas at the household level, patterns of burglary are determined by other factors including the proximity of people with the *motivation* to want to steal and the presence or absence of basic security measures.

In one of the earliest reviews, Box (1987) examined fifty major econometric studies of the relationship between economic conditions and crime. He found that slightly under two thirds appeared to show a positive relationship between rising unemployment and crime, the remainder showing the reverse. Even this far from overwhelming result was further diminished by doubts about the robustness of the data being used in many of the studies and by the fact that the positive relationships uncovered were generally weak. Cantor and Land (1985), while confirming a generally weak relationship between unemployment and crime argue that some of the confusion in this field derives from a failure to distinguish two separate causal links: a *positive* motivational relationship (unemployment increases the attractiveness of certain forms of crime) and a *negative* opportunity effect (unemployment keeps people at home and increases *guardianship* and also reduces the availability of goods through reduced consumption). As a consequence they argue that the relationship between unemployment rates and crime levels can be positive, negative, or null depending on the crime type under consideration. Hale and Sabbagh (1991), by contrast, found a significant positive relationship with burglary, theft, and robbery.

Dissatisfaction with unemployment as a measure—and increasing doubts about unemployment data—led scholars to begin to consider the relationship between macroeconomic changes and crime levels in a variety of different ways. In this regard, and building on Cantor and Land's work, Arvanites and Defina (2006), examined the impact of business cycles on levels of street crime. In particular, using inflation-adjusted, per capita gross state product as their measure, they argue that the strong economy in the United States in the 1990s reduced the number of property crimes in that period, all consistent with a motivation effect rather than an opportunity effect and a 'degree of social strain and control' (2006: 161). Similar results were found by Rosenfeld and Fornango (2007) who found that 'consumer sentiment' was significantly related to regional property crime trends and, in parallel, Rosenfeld's (2009) study of acquisitive crime and homicide rates between 1970 and 2006 found that collective perceptions of economic conditions affect acquisitive crime— such as motor theft, robbery, and burglary—and that this, indirectly, affects homicide rates.

That the very substantial declines in crime that appear to have been under-way for at least two decades appear not to have been reversed by the financial crisis of recent times, raises interesting questions about the relationship between crime and the economy. Intriguingly, while there is a growing body of work that sheds some light on the general economic underpinnings of crime trends, the continued crime drop remains something of a mystery. Research by Field (1990) argued that the relationship between property crime levels and consumption are much stronger than that between property crime and unemployment. He found that rates of property crime growth were closely linked to economic growth and, more particularly, when consumption grew quickly, property crime growth tended to slow down or reverse. The opposite, he argued, was true during economic recessions. Field's explanation for this general trend focused on motivation rather than opportunity, increases in consumption being argued to reflect the declining attractiveness of crime for gain. Field's conclusions were largely restricted to short-term changes in levels of property crime. Subsequently, Pyle and Deadman (1994) have pointed to the likelihood of longer-term relationships between property crime levels and economic factors such as consumption levels and GDP, but have been strongly criticized by Hale (1998) whose own analysis reasserted that significant relationships existed between unemployment and crime in the short run and that, in particular, changes in unemployment levels were significantly and positively related to changes in burglary, theft, and robbery rates. Hale (1998) concludes that consumption appears to have a dual role in explaining both trends and changes in property crime, with an explanation that focuses on both opportunity and motivation. If we accept the arguments of routine activities and opportunity theorists (for example, Felson, 2010) that for a crime to occur there must be three elements present—a motivated offender, a suitable target, and a lack of guardianship—then, as Hale puts it:

> The *level* of personal consumption measures the increasing availability of targets in the long term, the opportunity effect, whilst *changes* in the level of consumption

capture the impact of the business cycle upon the numbers of offenders, the motivation effect. (1998: 696)

In a somewhat similar vein, and revising his earlier conclusions, in a follow-up study Field argued that levels of theft and burglary were actually linked to the stock of crime opportunities 'represented by the sum of real consumers' expenditure in the each of the last four years' (Field, 1990). For every one per cent increase in the stock of opportunities, he calculated, burglary and theft were likely to increase by about two per cent.

There remains what Chiricos (1987) calls a 'consensus of doubt' about the relationship between unemployment and crime. Whilst there have been some interesting studies focusing on more particular economic measures such as consumption, this is a general field in which clear relationships remain hard to detect. Moreover, criminologists have been far less preoccupied with the economic aspects of crime than with biological, psychological, and socio-logical studies of, or reflections on, the causes of crime. The sociological criminology that became increasingly dominant in the second half of the twentieth century has taken a broadly social democratic perspective on crime, 'seeing it as shaped by social deprivation and inequality' (Reiner, 2006: 28). The next step is to consider some of the evidence for such a relationship.

16.2 Social Inequality and Crime Rates

A range of studies has pointed to a relationship between economic inequality and crime (both violent and property crime), within and across countries (Kelly, 2000; Demombynes and Ozler, 2005). Such studies have tended to use income inequality as their primary measure. Blau and Blau (1982), study-ing 125 US metropolitan areas found a strong relationship between economic inequality and violent crime, but once economic inequality was controlled for, poverty exerted no influence on rates of criminal violence. Nevertheless, writing in the early 1990s, Hsieh and Pugh said that at that point there was 'a growing consensus that resource deprivation in general is an underlying cause of violent crime' (1993: 182). More recently, work by Fajnzylber et al. (1998, 2002a, 2002b) found what appears to be a strong relationship between income inequality and rates of both homicide and robbery or violent theft (see also Messner and Rosenfeld, 1997). A study by Elgar and Aitken (2011) found a strong association between income inequality and international variations in homicide levels, and linked this to the lower levels of interpersonal trust they identified in societies characterized by relatively high income inequality. Such work perhaps speaks most directly to some of the Chicago School-influenced criminological theory which points to social organization, population turn-over, and the nature and condition of local neighbourhoods as key determin-ants of differential levels of violence (Shaw and McKay, 1942; Sampson and Wilson, 1995; Sampson et al., 2005). Their argument finds some support from Kennedy et al. (1998: 15) whose study shows that the strong relationship between income inequality and the incidence of homicide and other violent crimes may be attributable to the 'depletion of social capital' (see Chapter 4, this volume).

Much of the early work in this field was influenced by Gary Becker's (1968) economic theory, essentially a rational choice approach positing that growing inequality is likely to lead to more crime as a consequence of the changing balance between the costs and anticipated benefits of such activity. Such a theory has always appeared more obviously suited to explaining acquisitive crime and, indeed, work by a number of authors has cast doubt on its ability to explain patterns of violent crime (for example, Neumayer 2003, 2005). Kelly (2000) found violent crime to be little influenced by poverty, but strongly influenced by inequality, whereas inequality had little impact on property crime but that poverty did. As a consequence he suggests that Becker's eco-nomic theory is not especially helpful here and argues that strain theory (focusing on the gap between socially approved goals and the availability of legitimate opportunities for achieving them), and varieties of control theory (focusing on the relative strength or weakness of family and community ties) are likely to be more helpful.

In the UK, using data from police force areas, Machin and Meghir (2004) found that relative falls in the wages of low-wage workers between 1975 and 1996 led to increases in crime, particularly vehicle and property crime. On this basis they argue that it may be the nature of the low-wage labour market that exerts a greater effect on crime rates than levels of unemployment. Nilsson's (2004) work in Sweden, while finding a similar link between an increase in the proportion of the population on low incomes was associated with higher rates of property crime, also found that higher levels of unemployment tended to be linked with increases in overall crime, auto thefts, and robbery. Witt et al. (1999) found that high wage inequality associated with the distribution of weekly earnings of full-time manual men (arguably of decreasing significance in the late modern economy) was associated with high crime. Recently pub-lished research by Hicks and Hicks (2014) addresses this issue slightly differ-ently, abandoning income inequality in favour of measures of the distribution of visible consumption and criminal behaviour within US states over a twenty-year period. First and foremost, their results reinforce Kelly's (2000) finding that different patterns appear to apply to violent and property crime. The relationship they identity between property crime and consumption holds only for inequality in visible expenditure, not for inequality in total expenditure. On this basis they argue that 'visibility' is an important factor in decisions to offend and suggest that relative deprivation theories fit most closely with their data (see Runciman, 1966 and Chapter 1, this volume), whereas traditional economic theory, as Kelly had illustrated, has only a limited fit.

The relationship between inequality and crime has also been demonstrated at the sub-national level. An analysis using police-recorded crime data in England and Wales found inequality (measured using the Gini coefficient for Crime and Disorder Reduction Partnerships (CDRPs) weighted according to each Middle Layer Super Output Area's total population in 2005) to be positively and 'fairly strongly' correlated with burglary, robbery, violence, vehicle crime, and, though to a lesser extent, criminal damage (Whitworth, 2011). Whitworth's results were strongest for acquisitive crimes: 'other things equal, a one per cent increase in inequality within a CDRP is associated with a 0.20 per cent increase in the rate of burglary, a 0.28 per cent increase in the rate of robbery and a 0.27 per cent increase in the rate of vehicle crime' (2011: 32–3). On the basis of his analysis of a wide range of variables, Whitworth argues that his results fit more comfortably with elements of both social disorganization and strain theory than they do with Becker's economic theory.

In a systematic review Rufrancos et al. (2013) conclude that 'although there is some evidence to the contrary . . . a strong argument can be made for the existence of a longitudinal inequality-property crime relationship.' Though the explanation of violent crime is significantly more complex they neverthe-less conclude that 'homicide, murder and robbery are determined, to some extent, by changes in income inequality, whilst crimes such as assault and rape are determined to a considerably lesser extent and are likely obscured by reporting differences and/or different determinants'.

16.3 Social Disadvantage, Offending, and Victimization

We now turn our attention to questions of the relationship between material and social disadvantage and patterns of offending and victimization? Begin-ning with offending, it is as close to an established criminological 'fact' as exists that the vast majority of crimes dealt with by the criminal courts are committed by people of relatively impoverished means. Indeed, the predom-inance of people of lower social status in offending can be seen irrespective of how offending is measured. Braithwaite (1979: 62), for example, noted that 'lower-class adults commit those types of crime which are handled by the police at a higher rate than middle-class adults'. Before we turn to attempts to explain this relationship, what about the crimes of the socially advantaged?

A body of hugely important work within criminology in recent years has attempted to shift the focus of academic (and social) attention to 'social harms'—whether these be physical, psychological, emotional, or economic. Such an approach, it is argued, allows attention to be paid to otherwise ignored problems such as workplace injury and death, environmental offences, corporate 'offences' and other forms of white-collar crime, and the 'crimes' committed by states among much else (Davis et al., 2014). The gaze of the state, and that of academic criminologists, tends to focus on the crimes of the powerless, rather than the powerful, despite the very great harms caused by the latter. As Tombs and Whyte (2015: 3–4) observe, it is surely remarkable 'that, more than six years on from the great financial crash of 2007/08, we live in societies that have not fundamentally restructured the control of the corporate sector generally, nor the financial sector in particular. Indeed, given what has unfolded since then, we are yet to see a concerted effort or "war" against corporate crime. In fact, we have seen precisely the opposite'.

So, it is with a heavy heart that we must return to the more traditional focus of the relationship between material and social disadvantage and crime as ordinarily understood. Having focused earlier in this chapter on the broad structural relationships between socio-economic factors and offending, here the concern is more with the lives of individuals. In the past quarter century or so increasing attention has come to be paid to what tend to be referred to as 'risk', 'promotive', and 'protective' factors in offending. *Risk* factors are those that predict an increased probability of later offending. They tend to work cumulatively and in interaction with each other. *Promotive* factors are those that predict the absence of offending, and *protective* factors are those that predict desistance among groups of known offenders. Risk factors can be identified in a variety of domains: the individual level, but also the family level, school level, and neighbourhood level.

There is a sizeable body of research in this tradition that has examined the nature of the relationship between socio-economic status (SES) and offending. The Cambridge Study of Delinquent Development, for example, found low family SES when a boy was aged between 8–10 was predictive of later self-reported offending, but not officially recorded offending. Low family income and poor housing were predictive of both officially recorded and self-reported offending for juvenile and adults (Farrington, 1992). There are similar results in relation to serious persistent offending from the Pittsburgh Youth Study (Stouthamer-Loeber et al., 2002; see also Flood-Page et al., 2000 for the UK). Perhaps predictably there is much research that suggests that there are potentially a number of mediating factors, including parent management skills (Larzelere and Patterson (1990)), physical punishment styles, family size, and conduct problems including truancy and 'delinquent' peers (Fergusson et al., 2004) which may themselves be related both to SES and to the likelihood of offending. Living in a poor and/or high crime area is also a regularly identified risk factor for later offending. Fabio et al. (2011), for example, found that rates of violence among boys in disadvantaged neighborhoods rose to higher levels and were sustained significantly longer than those among their peers in more advantaged areas (see also, Wikstrom and Loeber, 2000). To this extent at least, there is evidence which appears to support both conventional wisdom and significant elements of criminological theory which posit that economic stress motivates people affected by it to offend (Cloward and Ohlin, 1960; Merton, 1968).

What of demographic differences? Sampson et al. (2005) in their study of Chicago neighbourhoods sought an explanation for the fact that the odds of perpetrating violence were 85 per cent higher for Blacks compared with Whites, whilst Latino-perpetrated violence was 10 per cent lower. They found the neighbourhood social context to be a highly significant factor in explaining such disparities and concluded that their findings were 'consistent with the hypothesis that Blacks are segregated by neighborhood and thus differentially exposed to key risk and protective factors' (2005: 230). In truth, the relationship between individual, group and structural factors in offending is a field of study in which there remains considerable room for development. Explaining the relationship between crime and social (dis)advantage—in essence the direction of causation—has and continues to be a source of controversy. In the 1980s in particular, debates raged between 'left realists' (for whom relative deprivation was seen as key to understanding crime and victimization; Lea and Young, 1984) and 'right realists' and underclass theorists (for whom offending was more a reflection of individual characteristics, propensities, and choices; Murray, 1990). Both perspectives have had considerable policy and political traction at different times—with those on the left tending to place greater emphasis on structural 'solutions' and those on the right focusing more obviously on individual responsibility (though the differences between governments have often been relatively slight).

Just as offending is unevenly socially distributed, so is criminal victimization. Early and influential research identified the importance of lifestyles and routine activities (how people organize and spend their lives) in helping to explain victimization risks (Hindelang et al., 1978; Cohen and Felson, 1979) in contrast to social disorganization theories which argued areas characterized by high population density, ethnic heterogeneity, and residential mobility tended to be characterized by higher rates of crime (Shaw and McKay, 1942). There are a number of reasons why, in principle, it is expected that there will be a relationship between social inequality and crime victimization. First, social disadvantage is associated with the likelihood of living in high crime areas. Second, the socially disadvantaged are likely to have fewer resources to protect themselves against the possibility of criminal victimization. Finally, it is also hypothesized that people who are disadvantaged socio-economically are also anticipated to be more vulnerable to the negative effects of criminal victimization.

The availability of victimization data since the 1970s in the US, and the early 1980s in England and Wales, allows the social distribution of crime to be examined in a more accurate manner than was hitherto possible. In short, much of this research has shown a variety of factors—including adverse socio-economic backgrounds such as living in social rented accommodation and multiple occupancy households, and lone parenthood—to be linked with an increased risk of criminal victimization (Grove et al., 2012). Research by Wohlfarth et al. (2001: 364), based on a representative sample of the Dutch population, found 'a clear relationship between social class and victimization, with the unemployed showing a higher rate (11%) compared to all other classes combined (6%).' There have been similar findings drawn from the Crime Survey for England and Wales (CSEW) showing, for example, the risks of being a victim of burglary, household theft, and personal theft, to be positively related to the level of unemployment in the victim's local community (Sampson and Wooldredge, 1987) and the risk of violent victimization to be inversely related to income (Brennan et al., 2010).

That some areas have chronically high levels of crime is, according to Trickett et al. (1992), 'one of the original and enduring issues in criminology'. Their analysis of crime survey data found prevalence of crimes against the person to be about eleven times as large in the poorest neighbourhoods as against the richest, with the comparison for property crimes being around a factor of four. They found that the vulnerability of victims (the number of crimes reported, on average, by each victim) in respect of both personal and property offences to be more than three times as high in the worst areas as in the best areas. Tseloni et al. (2002) found that household crime inequality is clearest in the inner city, whereas within more affluent areas, property crime is more evenly distributed. The greatest area inequality, they estimated, falls on households already most at risk—with higher incidence faced by residents of deprived areas generating increases in crime concentration more than increases in prevalence (i.e. through repeat and multiple victimization). Trickett et al. (1992), among others, show that the distribution of crime is different in 'low crime' and 'high crime' areas. In short, whereas crime is broadly randomly distributed across households in low crime areas it is disproportionately concentrated on a small number of households in areas with high levels of crime. In the top crime decile, by area, victims, on average, experience nearly three times as many personal crimes as would be the case were such crime randomly distributed. It is findings like that that have pushed criminologists to focus on the ideas of 'repeat' and 'multiple victimization'. Data from the 1998 British Crime Survey, for example, showed that whereas three-fifths of the population experienced no criminal victimization in the year under consideration, five per cent of the population experienced almost 44 per cent of all crime incidents (Farrell and Pease, 1993). Research by Hope (2001) estimated that around one-fifth of victims of household property crime live in the 10 per cent of residential areas with the highest crime rates, and suffer over one-third of the total household property crime. Over half of all property crime—and over one third of all property crime victims—are found in one fifth of communities in England and Wales and, conversely, the half of communities with the lowest crime rates suffer only 15 per cent of household property crime victimization (Hope, 1996, 1997).

What then of the impact of crime? Beyond the heightened risks of criminal victimization, there is also evidence that those living in areas with high levels of physical disorder, or those who perceive there to be high levels of anti-social behaviour in their local area, are much more likely to rate both crime generally, and fear of crime, as having a moderate or high impact on their quality of life (Nicholas et al., 2007). Recent work on the impact of anti-social behaviour (ASB) found that area deprivation was significantly and negatively associated with the likelihood of being a repeat and vulnerable ASB victim. They concluded that whilst 'the likelihood of being a repeat victim (RV) or a Repeat and Vulnerable Victim (RVV) is strongly associated with the situational vulnerability induced by local socio-demographic disadvantage, non-repeat and non-vulnerable victim status is associated with more advantageous socio-demographic characteristics including low area deprivation and home ownership' (Innes and Innes, 2013: 19).

Not only do those living in lower-crime neighbourhoods face lower risks as a consequence of where they live, they also often have the option, thanks to their material wealth, to increase their security. Indeed, a number of authors (Lab, 1990; Hope, 1995, 2000) have shown income and home-ownership to be among the most consistent predictors of the adoption of security measures, Hope (2000) showing this to include both physical security products (alarms, CCTV, locks) but also 'collective' services such as the arrangement of private contents insurance, membership of neighbourhood watch schemes, and free household security surveys offered by the police. In fact, Hope (1999, 2000) argues that, irrespective of the impact of access to security, it is access to the private housing market that offers the socially advantaged the greatest benefit, enabling them to mitigate risks 'through spatial and cultural distancing from "criminogenic" places and people' (2000: 102). As numerous commentators have identified, it is the urban enclavization—the rise of high crime, heavily policed ghettos alongside the gated, fortified communities of the wealthy—which potentially poses the greatest challenge. This future has been outlined in its most dystopian form in Mike Davis' (1990) description of postmodern Los Angeles, which he views as an increasingly militarized landscape, where much formerly public space is privatized and subjected to constant surveillance, and where the city, divided by wealth, becomes a 'halo of barrios and ghettos' surrounding an increasingly fortified core (Davis, 1995).

16.4 Punishment and Social Inequality

Scholars working in the field of the political economy of punishment have observed that contrasting penal practices are almost certainly a function of differences in the social, economic, and political organization of the countries concerned (Lacey, 2008). Whilst there is no suggestion in such accounts that penal differentiation can be reduced to matters of economic inequality, it is striking that there nevertheless appears to be quite a clear positive relationship between incarceration levels and income inequality in the developed world (Wilkinson and Pickett, 2010). Who, though, gets caught in the penal net? In 1979 Jeffrey Reiman wrote a book with the title, *The Rich Get Richer and the Poor Get Prison*. Though the title was intentionally provocative, it nevertheless spoke to a number of criminological truths. First, as the title implies, the 'crimes' of the wealthy are rarely punished in the same way, or to a comparable extent, to the crimes of the poor. Second, it is clear that the poor are significantly over-represented in police and prison cells. There is, in fact, relatively little by way of socio-demographic details on those that are arrested by the police. American surveys of arrestees (usually to monitor drug use) report both high levels of unemployment prior to arrest (from 43 per cent to 69 per cent) and similarly high proportions of respondents without health insurance (as high as 73 per cent in Chicago) (Office of National Drug Control Policy, 2013). In England and Wales an 'arrestee survey' conducted in 2003–6 found 41 per cent of respondents to have been excluded from school temporarily and 23 per cent excluded permanently, and in its final year found 16 per cent of all respondents had spent some time in a foster home, children's home, or a young person's unit, 4 per cent were homeless at the time of their arrest and 10 per cent had slept rough at some point in the week leading up to their arrest.

There is much more consistent and robust collection of data on the prison population, though this clearly only represents one subset—and not a typical subset—of all those offenders that come into contact with the criminal justice system. Reinforcing earlier research (Caddle and Crisp, 1997; Dodd and Hunter, 1992), the Surveying Prisoner Crime Reduction (SPCR) study, a longitudinal cohort study which tracks the progress of newly sentenced adult (18+ years) prisoners in England and Wales, found 24 per cent of prisoners to have lived with foster parents or in an institution, or had been taken into care at some point as a child (Williams et al., 2012). In terms of living circumstances, SPCR found 16 per cent of prisoners reported having been homeless (either sleeping rough or in temporary accommodation) immediately prior to their incarceration, compared with the 3.5 per cent of the general population who have ever done so. Such living circumstances have potentially profound implications for there is clear evidence that those who were homeless prior to their imprisonment are more likely to be reconvicted upon release compared with those that report living in other forms of accommodation (79 per cent compared with 47 per cent in the first year, and 84 per cent compared to 60 per cent in the second year) (Williams et al., 2013).

The potentially *reinforcing* nature of the experience of crime is illustrated in a number of studies of prisoners. Boswell and Wedge's (2002) study of imprisoned fathers, though small in scale, indicated substantial minorities had been physically abused by their own fathers and had witnessed their father abusing their mother. One third of imprisoned mothers in Poehlmann's (2005) research reported physical or sexual abuse, and more than two-thirds reported having witnessed domestic violence in childhood, and there is some evidence that such experiences have adverse consequences for future offending and anti-social conduct (Glasser et al., 2001). The SPCR study, for example, found that prisoners who had experienced abuse or observed violence as a child were more likely than those who had not to be reconvicted after release (Williams et al., 2012).

Arguably the most interesting study in this field in the UK, though it is now sadly rather out of date, is that published by the government's Social Exclusion Unit in 2002. In summary, it observed '[b]efore they ever come into contact with the prison system, most prisoners have a history of social exclusion, including high levels of family, educational and health disadvantage, and poor prospects in the labour market' (Social Exclusion Unit, 2002: 18). From a variety of sources, they offered the comparisons shown in Table 16.1.

American research reinforces many such findings, not least in connection with a heightened prevalence of mental health issues among the incarcerated population. A recent study by Schnittker et al. (2012) found substantially higher lifetime and twelve-month prevalence of a wide range of psychiatric disorders. The relationship here is, of course, difficult to disentangle. Schnittker et al. (2012: 459) suggest that there is 'considerable overlap between the life-course determinants of crime and the life-course determinants of psychiatric outcomes'. Nevertheless, there does appear to be a persistent relationship between imprisonment and mood disorders (being associated, for example, with a 45 per cent increase in the odds of lifetime major depression).

Imprisonment also contributes to social disadvantage and social inequality. Prison expansion in the US—from half a million in 1980 to 2.2 million in 2012—has vastly, and unevenly, increased the lifetime likelihood of serving a prison sentence. The cumulative risk of imprisonment by age 30–34 for Black males is over 25 per cent, compared with just over 5 per cent for White males.

Table 16.1. Characteristics of prisoners and the general population

Characteristic	Percentage of prisoners	Percentage of general population
Taken into care as a child	27	2
Young fathers	25 (of young offenders)	4
Regularly truanted from school	30	3
Excluded from school	49 (male) 33 (female)	2
Have no qualifications	52 (male) 71 (female)	15
Literacy at or below that of Level 1 (expected of an 11-year-old)	65	23
Reading at or below that of Level 1	48	21–23
Writing at or below that of Level 1	82	No direct comparison
Unemployed	67 (in the four weeks before imprisonment)	5
Suffer from two or more mental disorders	72 (male) 70 (female)	5 (male) 2 (female)
Suffer from three of more mental disorders	44 (male) 62 (female)	1 (male) 0 (female)
In receipt of benefits	72 (immediately before imprisonment)	14 (of working age population)
Homelessness	32 (not living in permanent accommodation prior to imprisonment)	1 (households assessed to be statutorily homeless each year)
Long-standing illness or disability	46 (sentenced male prisoners aged 18–49)	29 (men aged 18–49)

Source: Social Exclusion Unit (2002)

The respective figures for Black and White high school drop-outs is 68 per cent and 28 per cent (Western and Pettit, 2010). Prison is now an extraordinarily powerful institutional influence on life chances, with a growing body of research that shows that ex-prisoners face very poor employment prospects on release from prison (Apel and Sweeten, 2010; Pager et al., 2009), and that the very different risks of incarceration contribute to racial inequality (Western, 2006). Western and Pettit's longitudinal research reached the general conclusion that 'serving time in prison was associated with a 40 per cent reduction in earnings,... reduced job tenure, reduced hourly wages, and higher unemployment' (2010: 13), and there is increasing evidence that mass imprisonment is contributing substantially to intergenerational inequality (Comfort, 2003; Wildeman, 2010).

Not only does imprisonment contribute to social inequality, but it may also mask it. Again, because of the scale of its imprisonment boom this can be illustrated most clearly by looking at research from the US. Recent detailed quantitative (Pettit, 2012) and ethnographic research (Goffman, 2014) has illustrated how much of the impact of America's penal experiment, despite its extraordinary consequences, remains largely hidden. Pettit's (2012) meticulous research has shown how the exclusion of prison inmates from social survey research has dramatically affected the picture of inequality in the US, significantly underestimating the estimated high school drop-out rate, employment rates among young, black, low-skilled men. The research by Pettit, Goffman, and others shows how America's most disadvantaged communities have been affected by the imprisonment boom; particularly through its dramatically negative effect on the health and well-being of children and families in those communities (see also Geller et al., 2012; Freudenberg, 2001).

16.5 Conclusion

Up until at least the 1970s criminology was much influenced by a social democratic-oriented sociological approach whose primary concerns were issues of social deprivation and inequality. It has been at least partially displaced by a number of other criminologies whose concerns are either narrowly pragmatic (crime prevention and the efficiency of the criminal justice system) or, certainly, much less influenced by broad matters of political economy. Why so? Is it that the social democratic analysis was proven wrong? As should be clear by now, though the relationships between social disadvantage and crime are complex—and issues of causation particularly so—it is hard to conclude that social inequality is anything other than of central importance in understanding crime, anti-social behaviour, criminal victimization, and state punishment. As Rosenfeld and Messner (2013: 4) observe, 'Whether we look at official statistics on arrest and incarceration, self-report studies of criminal offending, or surveys of crime victims, the same pattern emerges: lower socioeconomic status is associated with greater involvement with the criminal justice system, higher rates of criminal offending, and higher rates of various forms of victimization. The relationship between socioeconomic deprivation and involvement in crime and the justice system holds not only for individuals ... but also for neighbourhoods.' Where the picture becomes less clear is in connection with understanding crime *levels*. Here, although there is a growing body of econometric work linking changes in consumption and other economic trends to short-term shifts in property crime in particular, criminology continues to struggle. In particular, the two big movements in crime since the Second World War—the massive increases from the late 1950s onward which occurred despite rising prosperity, and the sizeable drops in crime since the mid 1990s (which have continued despite a massive economic recession)—were both largely unanticipated, and remain less than fully explained, by criminology. Great strides have been made in untangling the complex relationships between social (dis)advantage and crime, but there remains much still to be done.

References

Apel, R. and Sweeten, G. (2010). 'The Impact of Incarceration on Employment during the Transition to Adulthood'. *Social Problems*, 57(3): 448–79.

Arvanites, T. M. and Defina, R. H. (2006). 'Business Cycles and Street Crime'. *Criminology*, 44(1): 139–64.

Becker, G. (1968). 'Crime and Punishment: An Economic Approach'. *The Journal of Political Economy*, 76(2): 169–217.

Blau, J. and Blau, P. (1982). 'The Cost of Inequality: Metropolitan Structure and Violent Crime'. *American Sociological Review*, 47: 114–29.

Boswell, G. and Wedge, P. (2002). *Imprisoned Fathers and their Children*. London: Jessica Kingsley.

Box, S. (1987). *Recession, Crime and Punishment*. London: Macmillan.

Braithwaite, J. (1979). *Inequality, Crime and Public Policy*. London: Routledge.

Brennan, I. R., Moore, S. C., and Shepherd, J. P. (2010). 'Risk Factors for Violent Victimisation and Injury from Six Years of the British Crime Survey'. *International Review of Victimology*, 17: 209–29.

Caddle, D. and Crisp, D. (1997). *Imprisoned Women and Mothers*. Home Office Research Study 162. London: Home Office.

Cantor, D. and Land, K. C. (1985). 'Unemployment and Crime Rates in the Post-World War II United States: A Theoretical and Empirical Analysis'. *American Sociological Review*, 50: 317–32.

Chiricos, T. G. (1987). 'Rates of Crime and Unemployment: An Analysis of Aggregate Research Evidence'. *Social Problems*, 34: 187–212.

Cloward, R. A. and Ohlin, L. E. (1960). *Delinquency and Opportunity: A Theory of Delinquent Gangs*. New York: The Free Press.

Cohen, L. E. and Felson, M. (1979). 'Social Change and Crime Rates Trends: A Routine Activity Approach'. *American Sociological Review*, 44: 588–608.

Comfort, M. (2003). 'In the Tube at San Quentin: The "Secondary Prisonization" of Women Visiting Inmates'. *Journal of Contemporary Ethnography*, 32(1): 82.

Davis, M. (1990). *City of Quartz: Excavating the Future in Los Angeles*. London: Verso.

Davis, M. (1995). *Ecology of Fear: Los Angeles and the Imagination of Disaster*. New York: Metropolitan Books.

Davis, P., Francis, P., and Wyatt, T. (2014). *Invisible Crimes and Social Harms*, Basingstoke: Palgrave.

Demombynes, G. and Ozler, B. (2005). 'Crime and Local Inequality in South Africa'. *Journal of Development Economics*, 76: 265–92.

Dodd, T. and Hunter, P. (1992). *The National Prison Survey*. London: OPCS.

Elgar, F. J. and Aitken, N. (2011). Income Inequality, Trust and Homicide in 33 Countries'. *European Journal of Public Health*, 21(2): 241–6.

Fabio, A., Li-Chuan, T., Loeber, R., and Cohen, J. (2011). 'Neighbourhood Socioeconomic Disadvantage and the Shape of the Age-crime Curve'. *American Journal of Public Health*, 101(1): 325–32.

Fajnzylber, P., Lederman, D., and Loayza, N. (1998). *Determinants of Crime Rates in Latin America and the World: An Empirical Assessment*. Washington, DC: World Bank.

Fajnzylber, P., Lederman, D., and Loayza, N. (2002a). 'What Causes Violent Crime?' *European Economic Review*, 46(7): 1323–56.

Fajnzylber, P., Lederman, D., and Loayza, N. (2002b). 'Inequality and Violent Crime'. *Journal of Law and Economics*, 45(1): 1–40.

Farrell, G. and Pease, K. (1993). *Once Bitten, Twice Bitten: Repeat Victimization and its Implications for Crime Prevention*. London: Home Office.

Farrington, D. P. (1992). 'Explaining the Beginning, Progress and Ending of Antisocial Behaviour from Birth to Adulthood'. In J. McCord, (ed.) *Facts, Frameworks and Forecasts: Advances in Criminological Theory*, vol. 3 (pp. 253–86). New Brunswick, NJ: Transaction.

Felson, M. (2010). *Crime and Everyday Life*. Thousand Oaks, CA: Sage.

Fergusson, D. M., Swain-Campbell, N. R., and Horwood, L. J. (2004). 'How Does Childhood Economic Disadvantage Lead to Crime?' *Journal of Child Psychology and Psychiatry*, 45(5): 956–66.

Field, S. (1990). *Trends in Crime and their Interpretation: A Study of Recorded Crime in Postwar England and Wales*. London: Home Office.

Field, S. (1999). *Trends in Crime Revisited*. London: Home Office.

Flood-Page, C., Campbell, S., Harrington, V., and Miller, J. (2000). *Youth Crime: Findings from the 1998/99 Youth Lifestyles Survey*. London: Home Office.

Freudenberg, N. (2001). 'Jails, Prisons and the Health of Urban populations', *Journal of Urban Health*, 78(2): 214–35.

Geller, A., Cooper, C. E., Garfinkel, I., Schwartz-Soicher, O., and Mincy, R. B. (2012). 'Beyond Absenteeism: Father Incarceration and Child Development'. *Demography*, 49(1): 49–76.

Glasser, M., Kolvin, I., Campbell, D., and Glasser, A. (2001). 'Cycle of Child Sexual Abuse: Links between Being a Victim and Becoming a Perpetrator'. *British Journal of Psychiatry*, 179: 482–94.

Goffman, A. (2014). *On the Run: Fugitive Life in an American City*. Chicago: University of Chicago Press.

Grove, L., Tseloni, A., and Tilley, N. (2012). 'Crime, Inequality and Change in England and Wales'. In J. Van Dijk, A. Tseloni, and G. Farrell (eds) *The International Crime Drop: New Directions in Research* (pp. 182–99). Palgrave: Macmillan.

Hale, C. (1998). 'Crime and the Business Cycle in Post-war Britain Revisited'. *British Journal of Criminology*, 38(4): 681–98.

Hale, C. and Sabbagh, D. (1991). 'Testing the Relationship between Unemployment and Crime: A Methodological Comment and Empirical Analysis Using Time Series Data from England and Wales'. *Journal of Research in Crime and Delinquency*, 28: 400–17.

Hicks, D. L. and Hicks, J. H. (2014). 'Jealous of the Joneses: Conspicuous Consumption, Inequality, and Crime'. *Oxford Economic Papers*, 66: 1090–120.

Hindelang, M. J., Gottfredson, M. R., and Garofalo, J. (1978). *Victims of Personal Crime: An Empirical Foundation for a Theory of Personal Victimization*. Cambridge, MA: Ballinger.

Hope, T. (1995). 'Community Crime Prevention'. In M. Tonry and D. Farrington (eds) *Building a Safer Society: Strategic Approaches to Crime Prevention* (pp. 21–89). Chicago: University of Chicago Press.

Hope, T. (1996). 'Communities, Crime and Inequality in England and Wales'. In T. Bennett (ed.) *Preventing Crime and Disorder: Targeting Strategies and Responsibilities* (pp. 215–35). Cambridge: Institute of Criminology.

Hope, T. (1997). 'Inequality and the Future of Community Crime Prevention'. In S. P. Lab (ed.) *Crime Prevention at the Crossroads*. Cincinnati, OH: Anderson Publishing.

Hope, T. (1999). 'Privatopia on Trial? Property Guardianship in the Suburbs'. In K. Painter and N. Tilley (eds) *Surveillance of Public Space* (pp. 15–46). Monsey, NY: Criminal Justice Press.

Hope, T. (2000). 'Inequality and the Clubbing of Private Security'. In T. Hope and R. Sparks (eds) *Crime, Risk and Insecurity* (pp. 83–106). London: Routledge.

Hope, T. (2001). Crime victimization and inequality in risk society, in R. Matthews and J. Pitts (eds) *Crime, Disorder and Community Safety* (pp. 193–218). London: Routledge.

Hsieh, C. C. and Pugh, M. D. (1993). 'Poverty, Income Inequality and Violent Crime: A Meta-analysis of Recent Aggregate Data Studies'. *Criminal Justice Review*, 18(2): 182–202.

Innes, H. and Innes, M. (2013). 'Personal, Situational and Incidental Vulnerabilities to ASB Harm: A Follow-up Study'. Report to Her Majesty's Inspectorate of Constabulary, Cardiff: Universities Police Science Institute.

Kelly, M. (2000). 'Inequality and Crime'. *The Review of Economics and Statistics*. 82(4): 530–9.

Kennedy, B. P., Kawachi, I., Prothrow-Stith, D., Lochner, K., and Gupta, V. (1998). 'Social Capital, Income Inequality, and Firearm Violent Crime'. *Social Science and Medicine*, 47(1): 7–17.

Lab, S. (1990). 'Citizen Crime Prevention: Domains and Participation'. *Justice Quarterly*, 7: 467–92.

Lacey, N. (2008). *The Prisoners' Dilemma: Political Economy and Punishment in Contemporary Democracies*. Cambridge: Cambridge University Press.

Larzelere, R. E. and Patterson, G. R. (1990). 'Parental Management: Mediator of the Effect of Socioeconomic Status on Early Delinquency'. *Criminology*, 28(2): 301–24.

Lea, J. and Young, J. (1984). *What Is to Be Done about Law and Order?* Harmondsworth: Penguin.

Machin, S. and Meghir, C. (2004). 'Crime and Economic Incentives'. *Journal of Human Resources*, 39: 958–79.

Merton, R. K. (1968). *Social Theory and Social Structure*. Glencoe, IL: Free Press.

Messner, S. and Rosenfeld, R. (1997). 'Political Restraint of the Market and Levels of Criminal Homicide: A Cross-national Application of Institutional–Anomie Theory'. *Social Forces*, 75: 1393–416 .

Murray, C. (1990). *The Emerging British Underclass*. London: Institute of Economic Affairs.

Neumayer, E. (2003). 'Good Policy Can Lower Violent Crime: Evidence from a Cross-national Panel of Homicide Rates 1980–97'. *Journal of Peace Research*, 40(6): 619–40.

Neumayer, E. (2005). 'Is Inequality really a Major Cause of Violent Crime? Evidence from a Cross-national Panel of Robbery and Violent Theft Rates'. London: LSE research online.

Nicholas, S., Kershaw, C., and Walker, A. (2007). *Crime in England and Wales 2006/07*. London: Home Office.

Nilsson, A. (2004). 'Income Inequality and Crime: The Case of Sweden'. IFAU Working Paper No. 2004–6, Uppsala.

Office of National Drug Control Policy (2013). *ADAM II: Arrestee Drug Abuse Monitoring Programme II: 2013 Annual Report*. Washington, DC: Executive Office of the President.

Pager, D., Western, B., and Sugie, N. (2009). 'Sequencing Disadvantage: Barriers to Employment Facing Young Black and White Men with Criminal Records'. *Annals of the American Academy of Political and Social Sciences*, 623(1): 195–213.

Pettit, B. (2012). *Invisible Men: Mass Incarceration and the Myth of Black Progress*. New York: Russell Sage Foundation.

Poehlmann, J. (2005). 'Incarcerated Mothers' Contact with Children, Perceived Family Relationships, and Depressive Symptoms'. *Journal of Family Psychology*, 19(3): 350–7.

Pyle, D. J. and Deadman, D. F. (1994). 'Crime and the Business Cycle in Post-War Britain'. *British Journal of Criminology*, 34: 339–57.

Reiner, R. (2006). 'Beyond Risk: A Lament for Social Democratic Criminology'. In T. Newburn and P. Rock (eds) *The Politics of Crime Control: Essays in Honour of David Downes*, Oxford: Clarendon Press.

Reiner, R. (2007). 'Political Economy, Crime, and Criminal Justice'. In M. Maguire, R. Morgan, and R. Reiner (eds) *Oxford Handbook of Criminology* (pp. 341–80), 4th edn. Oxford: Oxford University Press.

Rosenfeld, R. (2009). 'Crime Is the Problem: Homicide, Acquisitive Crime and Economic Conditions'. *Journal of Quantitative Criminology*, 25: 287–306.

Rosenfeld, R. and Fornnago, R. (2007). 'The Impact of Economic Conditions on Robbery and Property Crime: The Role of Consumer Sentiment'. *Criminology*, 45: 735–69.

Rosenfeld, R. and Messner, S. F. (2013). *Crime and the Economy*. Los Angeles: Sage.

Rufrancos, H. G., Power, M., Pickett, K., and Wilkinson, R. (2013). 'Income Inequality and Crime: A Review and Explanation of the Time-series Evidence'. *Sociology and Criminology*, 1(1): 1–9.

Runciman, W. G. (1966). *Relative Deprivation and Social Justice: A Study of Attitudes to Social Inequality in 20th Century England*. Berkeley, CA: University of California Press.

Sampson, R. J., Morenoff, J. D., and Raudenbush, S. W. (2005). 'Social Anatomy of Racial and Ethnic Disparities in Violence'. *American Journal of Public Health*, 95: 224–32.

Sampson, R. J. and Wilson, W. J. (1995). 'Toward a Theory of Race, Crime, and Urban Inequality'. In J. Hagan and R. Peterson (eds) *Crime and Inequality* (pp. 37–54). Stanford, CA: Stanford University Press.

Sampson, R. J. and Wooldredge, J. D. (1987). 'Linking the Micro- and Macro-level Dimensions of Lifestyle: Routine Activity and Opportunity Models of Predatory Victimisation'. *Journal of Quantitative Criminology*, 3: 371.

Schnittker, J., Massoglia, M., and Uggen, C. (2012). 'Out and Down: Incarceration and Psychiatric Disorders'. *Journal of Health and Social Behaviour*, 53(4): 448–64.

Shaw, C. and McKay, H. (1942). *Juvenile Delinquency and Urban Areas,* Chicago: University of Chicago Press.

Social Exclusion Unit (2002). *Reducing Reoffending by Ex-Prisoners*. London: Office of the Deputy Prime Minister.

Stouthamer-Loeber, M., Loeber, R., Wei, E., Farrington, D. P., and Wikstrom, P.-O. (2002). 'Risk and Promotive Effects in the Explanation of Persistent Serious Delinquency in Boys'. *Journal of Consulting and Clinical Psychology*, 70: 111–23.

Tombs, S. and Whyte, D. (2015). 'Introduction to the Special Issue on "Crimes of the Powerful"'. *Howard Journal*, 54(1): 1–7.

Trickett, A., Osborn, D. R., Seymour, J., and Pease, K. (1992). 'What Is Different about High Crime Areas?' *British Journal of Criminology*, 32: 81–9.

Tseloni, A., Osborn, D. R., Trickett, A., and Pease, K. (2002). 'Modelling Property Crime Using the British Crime Survey: What Have We Learnt?' *British Journal of Criminology*, 42: 109–28.

Western, B. (2006). *Punishment and Inequality in America*. New York: Russell Sage Foundation.

Western, B. and Pettit, B. (2010). 'Incarceration and Social Inequality'. *Daedalus*, Summer: 8–19.

Whitworth, A. (2011). 'Inequality and Crime across England: A Multilevel Modelling Approach'. *Social Policy and Society*, 11(1): 27–40.

Wikström, P.-O. and Loeber, R. (2000). 'Do Disadvantaged Neighborhoods Cause Well-adjusted Children to Become Adolescent Delinquents? A Study of Male Juvenile Serious Offending, Risk and Protective Factors, and Neighborhood Context'. *Criminology*, 38: 1109–42.

Wildeman, C. (2010). 'Paternal Incarceration and Children's Physically Aggressive Behaviors: Evidence from the Fragile Families and Child Wellbeing Study'. *Social Forces*, 89(1): 285–309.

Wilkinson, R. and Pickett, K. (2010). *The Spirit Level: Why Equality Is Better for Everyone*. London: Penguin.

Williams, K., Papadopoulou, V., and Booth, N. (2012). 'Prisoners' Childhood and Family Backgrounds: Results from the Surveying Prisoner Crime Reduction (SPCR) Longitudinal Cohort Study of Prisoners'. London: Ministry of Justice.

Williams, K., Poyser, J., and Hopkins, K. (2013). 'Accommodation, Homelessness and Reoffending of Prisoners: Results from the Surveying Prisoner Crime Reduction (SPCR) Survey'. London: Ministry of Justice.

Witt, R., Clarke, A., and Fielding, N. (1999). 'Crime and Economic Activity: A Panel Data Approach'. *British Journal of Criminology*, 39(3): 391–400.

Wohlfarth, T., Winkel, F.W., Ybema, J. F., and van den Brink, W. (2001). 'The Relationship between Socio-economic Inequality and Criminal Victimisation: A Prospective Study'. *Social Psychiatry and Psychiatric Epidemiology*, 36: 361–70.

Part IV
Conclusion

17

Conclusions

Lucinda Platt and Hartley Dean

We live in an unequal world. There are dramatic differences in access to resources, life chances, educational opportunities, and mortality rates across the globe and within countries. These are, moreover, stratified by social group, with particular sections of national, global, and local populations being more advantaged than others. In this book, we have set out to articulate some of these inequalities, particularly, though not only, as they structure societies in the global north, through framing them in terms of the poles or continuum of advantage and disadvantage.

While there is a wealth of literature and policy analysis that focuses on aspects of disadvantage and the causes and consequences of poverty and social exclusion, the premise of this book is that we cannot properly understand the means by which disadvantage is created and sustained without also engaging with how it articulates with the perpetuation and maintenance of advantage. In relation to both better understanding the mechanisms underpinning social inequalities and finding ways of addressing them, we need not only to investigate the nature, risks, and circumstances of disadvantage and what we might do about it, but also to understand the (cumulative) advantage of the advantaged.

The advantage and disadvantage that we address are axiomatically *social*. Advantage and disadvantage may have material substance (in terms of income, assets, and resources) or geographical or biological dimensions (in terms of spatial or physical circumstances, or bodily attributes or impairments). But it is within a social context that they arise and in which their consequences have meaning. In human society some people have always been more or less fortunate than others. Inquiring into inequalities, Amartya Sen's famous question was 'inequality of what?' (Sen, 1992). We have inquired into substantive inequalities of income, wealth, opportunities, and life-course outcomes, but for Sen it was inequality of 'capabilities' (discussed in Chapter 2 of this volume) that matter, by which he was referring to personal freedoms. Personal freedoms, however, are exercised subject to social constraints; and though liberal societies have sought to establish and protect the freedoms of the less powerful from the more powerful, the rights of the least advantaged may be systemically ineffectual in the face of the freedoms secured by the most advantaged (see Chapter 3, this volume).

It has been argued that while inequality scholars are very good at describing inequalities in outcomes (such as income, education, mortality), and there is a developing body of understanding on how such differentiated outcomes arise, there remains much less research that focuses on their wider implications and solutions. This could in part be an issue of scale and complexity. This volume provides a wide-ranging account of advantage and disadvantage across areas of life (such as income, wealth, education) and a review of some of the most recent and relevant research on how individual circumstances, such as age, gender, and migration status structure life chances. At the same time, reading the chapters together cumulatively reveals the challenges of developing appropriate responses to nationally framed inequalities. This is because a) forms of advantage can contribute to reinforcing each other, which can undermine attempts to treat any one dimension of inequality in isolation, and b) there is considerable heterogeneity in outcomes across social groups and over time. Background and social position may be predictive but it is far from being deterministic; and disadvantages may not only accumulate but they may interact in distinctive ways (Browne and Mishra, 2003). Hence, ascertaining and prescribing relevant points of intervention, which from a narrower perspective appears less problematic, becomes challenging, even if possibly more revealing, when looking across the spectrum.

For example, poverty research and research focused on social exclusion or on the exclusion of particular social groups will aim to address the circumstances of the most deprived or marginalized, whether through social investment and skills, or income maintenance approaches. But developing approaches and interventions that aim to limit the possibilities for more advantaged groups to maximize their opportunities or those of their children, is much more challenging, not to say controversial. This brings clearly to the fore the issue of agency and the possibilities for action, albeit agency is shaped by context (Stones, 2005), an element often lacking from accounts of disadvantage (see also Chapters 5, 6, 15, 16). Focusing on advantage makes it much clearer how what people do can influence not only their own lives, but impact those of others around them. However, changing such actions is rarely straightforward.

Similarly, an emphasis on international inequalities can reveal the ways in which distinctions between insiders and outsiders, inclusion and exclusion, as operated by nation states can operate in apparently counter-intuitive ways, that may reinforce structural inequalities while providing equalizing opportunities. For example, Kogan (2006) has highlighted the ways in which labour migrants may do rather better in liberal rather than corporate—or social democratic—welfare states; while Mandel and Semyonov (2006) have discussed the paradox of more equal societies in relation to gender having levels of occupational segregation. Across the developed world, as Chapter 13 highlights, advantaged women often build greater gender equality for themselves on the basis of access to unequal global employment relations. Thus, group level inequalities also need to be considered from a distributional perspective.

In the remainder of this chapter, we first discuss distributional issues, and how looking across the distribution of resources and rewards is an essential first step to identifying and analysing how social advantage articulates with social disadvantage. We then move on to consider how a focus on both social advantage and disadvantage enhances—even as it complicates—our understanding of diversity in outcomes within as well as between groups. The following section reviews the implications for how we frame disadvantage and advantage in terms of cumulative, intersectional, and relational processes. Finally, we consider potential developments and gaps before drawing together our closing reflections.

17.1 Inequalities across the Distribution and Inequalities between Groups

17.1.1 Distributions of Advantage and Disadvantage

A focus on the continuum of advantage and disadvantage brings consideration of how and why the most advantaged are breaking away from the rest of the (national/global) population, and what might effectively be done about it (Atkinson, 2015). As we saw in Chapters 7 and 8 in relation to income and wealth, even at times of improving living standards overall, the most advantaged have been increasingly distinguished from the rest of the population. While these two chapters focus primarily on a single country (the UK), the patterns are replicated cross-nationally (see also Piketty, 2014). We also saw that in times of recession, the distinction between those at the top of the economic distribution and those at the bottom can become sharper, even if welfare state safety nets can provide some more equalizing impetus (Jenkins et al., 2012). These unequal distributions of resources focus attention on the relative positions of people at different points across the distribution. They demonstrate that gaps are substantial not just between rich and poor but between rich and the middle, with corresponding implications for solidarity and social status among those who do not count as 'deprived' in typical analysis. As Runciman (1972) pointed out in 1966, deprivation is experienced relationally, and even if the distinction between 'them and us' is a myth (Hills, 2014), we are likely to have a much better understanding of how those in a secure position, including analysts and researchers, nevertheless distance themselves from those they see as deprived if we recognize the ways in which the rich are increasingly separating themselves off from the rest of 'us' (Bischoff and Reardon, 2013, see also Chapter 15). The extremes of accumulation among the wealthy, and the potential to transmit that wealth across generations, enhancing subsequent generations' options and opportunities (see also the discussion in Chapter 5) is a critical part of contemporary society, and how people understand their place within it.

Chapters 6 and 9 also drew attention to the distribution of skills and opportunities in education and employment. While educational levels are rising and employment conditions in developed countries have moved a long way from the insecure low-paid wage labour that characterized much of the labour markets of the late nineteenth century, there are clear distinctions between those who are increasing their skills and qualifications, employment rewards and security and those who remain in the lower ranks of the distribution. The increasing attention paid to education as a 'positional good' (Van de Werfhorst, 2011) highlights the ways in which it is relative position in the distribution that can potentially provide a better explanation of labour market outcomes compared to the fact or type of qualifications themselves. Moreover, the social investment model is often predicated on an acceptance that forms of less-skilled employment can be ceded to other nations, creating or exacerbating divides between countries, even if they aim to reduce them within countries.

As ongoing South to North migration shows, low-wage jobs in OECD countries still offer returns that attract those living in poorer countries (Drinkwater et al., 2009), even when costs and barriers are high (Massey and Pren, 2012). Employment is thus structured not only on international lines between more and less vulnerable forms, but global inequalities are incorporated into national labour markets through migration and subsequent processes of labour market stratification and exclusion. These processes of labour market inclusion and exclusion are arguably driven on the ground not (solely) by forms of capitalist exploitation, but by workers aiming to protect their relative position within a divided labour market (Bonacich, 1972). At the same time, migrants may judge their economic returns favourably by comparison with others who remain in their countries of origin (Guveli et al., 2015), complicating their relative position in the overall distribution when viewed from a wider context. (See also Amelina and Faist's (2012) discussion of methodological nationalism.) We turn to consider the issue of advantaged and disadvantaged groups more explicitly in the next section.

17.1.2 *Advantage and Disadvantage across Groups*

The emphasis on balancing discussion of disadvantage with advantage is arguably even more important when we turn to exploring inequalities between social groups. Not only does an exclusive focus on disadvantaged groups tend to ignore highly salient inequalities within these same 'groups' (as discussed for example in Chapters 10, 12, and 13), but it also tends to normalize the experience of the comparator, majority group, implying that the minority groups face—or are—a problem, and that solutions are to be found by addressing that problem. For example, much discussion of gendered inequalities focuses on changes that women need to make or that are needed to accommodate women more effectively so that they can fulfil their potential. However, while it may seem like a truism to assert that if we want to shift, for example, gendered occupational segregation, it is not simply that we need more women engineers and fewer women to take time off for children, it is also necessary (perhaps more necessary) to encourage boys to aspire to the caring professions (Polavieja and Platt, 2014) and for more fathers to take on (and be supported in taking on) early child-rearing responsibilities, as discussed in Chapter 11. Such prescriptions are all too rarely either offered or followed in practice.

At the same time, 'groups' are not homogenous entities. Bringing us back to the distributional issue already raised, income and economic differences between individuals from the same social 'group'—whether women, minorities, older people, or combinations of these—dwarf average economic differences between groups. (See for example, Nandi and Platt, 2010.) Similarly, many 'disadvantaged' groups will include highly advantaged segments, whose experience may have little in common with the more disadvantaged members of the group. For example, women are increasingly surpassing men in terms of educational attainment (Diprete and Buchmann, 2013), and there are increasing numbers of independently wealthy women, whom it is hard to analyse in the same terms as the experience of those more marginalized and lower paid women who work for them, facilitating their working and family lives (Le Feuvre, 1999; see also the discussion in Chapter 11). Moreover, in some cases, the emphasis on disadvantage will occlude consideration of those members of the group who do not share in this disadvantage. For example, a feature of immigration to and within Europe (as discussed in Chapter 13) is that it comprises some of the most advantaged, highly skilled, and highly paid employees or entrepreneurs, as well as some of the most impoverished and badly paid. Advantaged immigrants often have considerable flexibility in their settlement options, and are also, typically, able to pass their advantages on to their children, wherever they settle. However, research and policy emphasis has tended to be on those who are more marginalized (and 'visible'), with the more advantaged migrants sometimes being effectively invisible in data sources or discussion. For example, in the UK, Germans are the fifth largest foreign-born group in the UK (after Indians, Poles, Pakistanis, and Irish), but while the other four groups are, and have been, subject to a huge volume of research and analysis, there is a dearth of studies on the (economic or social) experience of the German community in the UK, outside macro-economic accounts that emphasize the fiscal contribution of migration.

Such silence about or normalization of 'non-problematic' groups, is an issue that was raised in Chapter 12, in relation to the persistent articulation of minority status relative to the neutralized category of 'white' or 'majority'. Such use of a majority 'reference category' implicitly validates the cultural values, employment patterns, and family behaviours of the majority. For example, in a context of increasing employment participation among women in many Western societies (England, 2005), the comparatively low participation rates of women from particular minority groups in these countries are often problematized. Such an approach assumes that high participation rates are both natural and a positive development, simultaneously dehistoricizing the contemporary phenomenon and failing to address the complex transformation of gender relations of which labour market participation is just one part (Illich, 1982). By contrast, when attention focuses on women's economic position relative to men's, it is the unequal terms on which such labour market participation takes place that is brought to the fore. We also need to recognize the normalized understandings that underpin the very recognition of 'groups' as worthy of interrogation. If 'successful' groups cease to be measured *as* minorities or groups, for example upwardly mobile of Hispanic origin in the US (Duncan and Trejo, 2005), then we are likely to perpetuate a partial—deficit—model of minority status, as well as losing explanatory opportunities for addressing the conditions under which those who are relatively marginalized or lacking in resources or power, nevertheless attain a position of greater advantage.

The ways in which inequality *within groups* plays out may also lead to challenging our conception of groups (Platt, 2011a). That is, we need to consider the meaning and interpretation of aggregate categories such as women, children, older people, minorities, and migrants in relation to their distributions of life chances. Groups may combine both advantage as well as disadvantage. We note specifically the following issues:

- Great diversity within groups, in terms of the income, wealth, educational attainment, social class, spatial distribution, and political power may challenge the idea that the group is meaningfully considered as a group, and we need to pay more attention to implicit or explicit sub-populations, especially if we are to find appropriate ways of explaining group disadvantage.

- At the same time, the very diversity may be salutary in reminding us that group membership does not determine outcomes (not all minorities are poor, not all women are in low-paid work, not all children from disadvantaged backgrounds have low educational attainment); and in facilitating non-deterministic explanatory frameworks that can take account of variation in experience.

- Thirdly, recognition of diversity in disadvantage can turn attention away from explanations that seek their source in the group (what is it about women or about minorities that is particular?) and instead seek approaches that address the conditions under which differentiated outcomes arise. These varied outcomes may arise through cumulative advantage or disadvantage, the moderation of disadvantaged status through intersection with other characteristics, or the different relational processes that arise and shape experiences under specific conditions. It is to the potential for these approaches as contributing to understanding some of the empirical regularities outlined in this volume that we turn next.

17.2 Developing a Three-part Approach to Processes of Advantage and Disadvantage

There are, clearly, different ways of conceiving of the relationship between advantage and disadvantage that depend in part on whether it is distributional inequalities or inequalities between social groups that are at issue (Platt, 2011b). But an approach that combines the recognition of cumulative processes, intersectional processes, and relational processes can help in bringing these two different 'forms' of inequality together. That is, by using these three approaches to look at the distribution of advantage and disadvantage within as well as across social groups we are likely to be able to develop both better understanding and, potentially, solutions. Moreover, such a three-part approach takes us beyond the somewhat sterile, as well as contested, dichotomy between (equality of) opportunities and outcomes, since it recognizes how mutually implicated the two are.

First, it is important to recognize the role that accumulation plays in the distribution of advantage on any given measure. Chapter 8 drew explicit attention to the consequences of the accumulation of wealth within families and over time, and Chapter 9 highlighted the ways in which employment disadvantage can cluster. However, advantage also accumulates across domains: those with advantaged backgrounds, good educational outcomes, and living in highly resourced neighbourhoods (or nations) are likely to experience feedback effects, such that increasing advantage in one domain leads to or enhances advantage in another domain (see also the discussion in Chapter 4). Hence recognizing the role of accumulation can contribute to understanding the dispersion of outcomes within as well as across social groups.

At the same time, the literature on intersectionality has highlighted the ways in which categories (such as 'woman', or 'black') do not simply subsume all others within the category, but may interact with other categorizations and social positions. While intersectional perspectives (Taylor, 1998; McCall, 2005; Brah and Pheonix, 2004; see also Chapter 11) derive from analysis of differences among women, they can be extended to other conjunctions of categories, or social locations at the intersection of multiple categories. For example, as well as ethnicity, gender, and class, these could be citizenship, class, and age. Intersectional accounts provide both visibility for the intersections and an articulation of the distinctive experiences at those specific social locations. Hence, for example, they both describe the economic position of African American women and how it differs from that of African American men and white American women (Browne and Mishra, 2003), and they provide a purchase on how those differences arise, in the process potentially challenging and refining overarching accounts of both gender inequality and of racial inequality.

Intersectional approaches can also highlight the particular social contexts in which intersectional experiences arise, such as within families, communities, or nations. For example, within families individuals may experience themselves as workers (breadwinners), parents, children, carers, and so on, both concurrently and successively, and these intersecting identities may inform the negotiation of relationships and their external positioning on the spectrum of economic or status advantage. It is also significant that the intersections between ethnic, religious, and cultural identities are fluid over time and across generations, continually generating new or syncretic identities (e.g. Hall, 1996; Phillips, 2007).

By contrast with the cumulative approach to (dis)advantage, intersectional approaches may highlight contrasts and apparently counterintuitive findings. For example, there is substantial evidence that minorities' educational performance and social mobility is relatively insensitive to neighbourhood context or class background (for England see Burgess, 2014; Platt, 2005; see also Chapters 4 and 6). A story purely of cumulative disadvantage would suggest the opposite should apply. Conceiving of these intersections as meaningful in their own right can, instead, lead to theoretical accounts that are better able to explain these discrepancies. In doing so they have to pay attention to why (relative) success is possible in some situations rather than others.

Third, advantage and disadvantage are experienced relationally. We learn our social position from the experience and responses of those around us. While local comparisons, with work colleagues, kin, neighbours (Sharkey and Faber, 2014; see also Chapter 15) will tend to be the most salient, individual expectations are also shaped by those we see as linked to us through group membership and social structures. This can help to explain why those in positions of power and advantage endorse high boardroom salaries to a degree that can seem bewildering on the grounds of performance (see also the discussion in Piketty, 2014: 330–5). But since others' expectations are also based on what are seen as salient aspects of group membership, it can also facilitate stereotyping and 'self-fulfilling prophecies'. Hence, relational understandings of disadvantage and advantage can help to understand how individuals use information on their relative position, within a society or group, to make particular decisions that may have consequences for their future wellbeing— and that of others. Just as the experiences of the relatively disadvantaged are impacted by the conduct and prejudices of the relatively advantaged, so the identities and strategies of the relatively advantaged may be bolstered through their perceptions and fears of the 'otherness' of the relatively disadvantaged (Dean, with Melrose, 1999; and see Chapter 1, this volume).

17.2.1 *Issues of Method and Measurement*

It is also worth considering the implications of this agenda for questions of analysis and measurement. It is well accepted that the most advantaged in terms of power and wealth are also the most difficult to access for the purposes of analysis, and it is often argued that the poor, disenfranchised, and marginal are most intensively studied because they are least able to protect themselves from intrusion. The fetishization of misery has been claimed to be one of the consequences of this differential access to rich and poor. However, with the emerging use of for example tax data to investigate income and wealth (see Chapters 7 and 8) and increasing numbers of studies that take elite organizations, professions, and classes as their object, the degree of research material about those more advantaged on various dimensions is increasing. The challenge, nevertheless, still remains to bring it together effectively with the much greater number of studies on the poor and excluded.

To take account of the way advantage articulates with disadvantage across social groups, we also need to move away from comparison of average experiences. The average is not only a very partial summary, it may in fact not represent the experience of many of the group thus summarized. For example, average earnings of a particular group may conflate the bimodal experience of those with zero earnings and those with somewhat higher earnings. Instead, taking advantage as well as disadvantage seriously as a subject for analysis of inequalities requires that we are able to operationalize cumulative, intersectional, and relational perspectives through investigation of correspondingly fine-grained distributions of dimensions of experience (class, income, education, etc.) that allow us to locate individuals at different places on these distributions.

17.3 Areas for Development

There are positions of relative advantage and disadvantage that are worthy of additional treatment, beyond what has been possible in this book. These can be characterized in terms of coverage, forms of inequality and disadvantaged groups, and additional perspectives. Despite some attention to global inequalities and global processes (see, especially Chapters 11 and 13), this was not a major focus for many of the chapters which concentrated, in order to make the topic coherent and containable, on OECD countries, and often with a specific focus on the UK. Extending the reach of the book further to consider how far the patterns, premises, and explanations are applicable to other parts of the world would be an important and relevant development.

In relation to forms of inequality, other than in the context of the discussion in Chapter 3 of the role of rights as domains of advantage and disadvantage, the issues of politics and power have been left largely to one side in our analysis of socio-economic positions. Politics and power are, clearly, central to the perpetuation and accumulation of advantage. They are also implicated in the relative lack of attention paid to the role of the privileged in contributing to disadvantage faced by others. For example, while it may be possible to garner a reasonable level of democratic support for ensuring the amelioration of (extreme) poverty, it is politically more challenging to implement more comprehensive redistribution. While issues of power and command complement and intersect with economic divides (Weber, 1978; see also Chapter 4), they are not so often found at the heart of discussions of social disadvantage and exclusion. Issues of access to power, political control, lobbying and the relationship between class and economic advantage and political influence merit further incorporation into core discussions of inequality, if we are to gain a more comprehensive understanding of how it operates and is sustained.

In relation to group differences, a major lacuna in volume is the role of disability in both structuring life chances and being linked to disadvantaged origins (Parsons and Platt, 2013). Disability lies outside much of the class-based stratification literature but, arguably, it operates in a similar way in influencing life-course transitions and life chances. There is, moreover, beginning to be greater attention to life course perspectives on disability that link the fields of both child and adult disability (Janus, 2009; Priestley, 2003). Like other groups discussed in this volume there is substantial variation in both what is recognized as disabling (Shakespeare and Watson, 2002; Burchardt, 2003) and in the experience of disabled people across different dimensions of advantage and disadvantage. Investigation of how disability intersects with other forms of disadvantage and at different points in the life course in addition to later years (see Chapter 10) would pay dividends.

Finally, there are a number of additional perspectives that, in taking the topics discussed here further, would be worth paying more consideration. In particular, historical processes deserve greater attention than it has been possible to give them in the short chapters of this volume (cf. Atkinson, 2015). Many current systematic experiences of disadvantage have their roots in historically contingent circumstances that go back a long way. Seeking for explanations in the present is therefore liable to understate the long-term influences of these forces, or even prove misleading. For example, racial inequalities typically have their roots in processes of colonialization, slavery, and indentured labour, even when more recent migrations have not been forced movements. Gender socialization, moreover, does not 'simply' begin in the family, but is embedded in social organization that is of long standing (Illich, 1982). In addition to more attention to historical processes, examining the potential role of multicultural and group rights approaches (Phillips, 2011; Parekh, 2000; Kymlicka, 1996) could enhance our ways of thinking about how to address disadvantage and make claims of recognition from those in positions of advantage.

17.4 Final Reflections

Social advantage and disadvantage are apparently inescapable dimensions of the contemporary social world. Yet a recognition of historical processes and transformations reveals that the extent of the gap between those more and less advantaged is not fixed or necessary (Atkinson, 2015). There have, for example, been periods of lower income and wealth inequality than the present; and times when there was the will and the tools to reduce it. Similarly, boundaries between groups are neither immutable nor carry the same meanings over time. Ethnic and racial boundaries shift; and girls' educational disadvantage has shown a dramatic transformation into educational advantage over a number of countries and over a relatively short period. While socially advantaged groups maintain substantial ability to favour outcomes for their offspring, this has not resulted in the fossilizing of social change. The motor of cumulative advantage is a powerful one, but is not irreversible. However, as we have aimed to show, it is only by recognizing the divergence of fortunes between the better and worse off and developing an understanding of the ways in which social positions are attained and held on to that we are likely to find relevant policies to address these divides. Such policies might address Nancy Fraser's three Rs of redistribution, recognition, and representation (e.g. 2010): the redistribution of advantage; the recognition of social diversity; and the political representation of the interests of the least advantaged. Our priority in this book has been to contribute to an understanding of the processes by which social advantage is differentially distributed and by which disadvantage is misrecognized. This prepares the ground, at least, more actively to pursue the issue of representation and move beyond the realm of empirical inquiry, into the equally essential but contested realm of theory and normative debates concerning social justice.

References

Amelina, A. and Faist, T. (2012). 'De-naturalizing the National in Research Methodologies: Key Concepts of Transnational Studies in Migration'. *Ethnic and Racial Studies*, 35(10): 1707–24.

Atkinson, A. B. (2015). *Inequality: What Can Be Done?* Cambridge, MA: Harvard University Press.

Bischoff, K. and Reardon, S. F. (2013). 'Residential Segregation by Income, 1970–2009'. US2010 Project, Russell Sage Foundation and Brown University, <http://www.s4.brown.edu/us2010/data/report/report10162013.pdf>, accessed 10 August 2015.

Bonacich, E. (1972). 'A Theory of Ethnic Antagonism: The Split Labour Market'. *American Sociological Review*, 37: 537–59.

Brah, A. and Phoenix, A. (2004). '"Ain't I a Woman?" Revisiting Intersectionality. *Journal of International Women's Studies*, 5(3): 75–86.

Browne, I. and Mishra, J. (2003). 'The Intersection of Gender and Race in the Labour Market'. *Annual Review of Sociology*, 29: 487–513.

Burchardt, T. (2003). 'Disability, Capability and Social Exclusion'. In J. Millar (ed.) *Understanding Social Security: Issues for Policy and Practice* (pp. 145–66). Bristol: The Policy Press.

Burgess, S. (2014). 'Understanding the Success of London's Schools'. Centre for Market and Public Organisation (CMPO) Working Paper 14/333. Bristol: University of Bristol, CMPO.

Dean, H. with M. Melrose (1999). *Poverty, Riches and Social Citizenship*. Basingstoke: Macmillan.

DiPrete, T. A. and Buchmann, C. (2013). *The Rise of Women: The Growing Gender Gap in Education and What It Means for American Schools*. New York: Russell Sage.

Drinkwater, S., Eade, J., and Garapich, M. (2009). 'Poles apart? EU Enlargement and the Labour Market Outcomes of Immigrants in the United Kingdom'. *International Migration*, 47(1): 161–90.

Duncan, B. and Trejo, S. (2005). 'Ethnic Identification, Intermarriage, and Unmeasured Progress by Mexican Americans'. IZA Discussion Paper No. 1629. Bonn: IZA.

England, P. (2005). 'Gender Inequality in Labor Markets: The Role of Motherhood and Segregation'. *Social Politics: International Studies in Gender, State & Society*, 12(2): 264–88.

Fraser, N. (2010). *Scales of Justice: Reimagining Political Space in a Globalizing World*. New York: Columbia University Press.

Guveli, A., Ganzeboom, H. B. G., Platt, L., Nauck, B., Baykara-Krumme, H., Eroglu,Ş., Bayrakdar, S., Sözeri, E. K., and Spierings, N. (2015). *Intergenerational Consequences of Migration: Socio-Economic, Family and Cultural Patterns of Stability and Change in Turkey and Europe*. Basingstoke: Palgrave Macmillan.

Hall, S. (1996). *Critical Studies in Cultural Studies*. London: Routledge.

Hills, J. (2014). *Good Times, Bad Times: The Welfare Myth of Them and Us*. Bristol: The Policy Press.

Illich, I. (1982). *Gender*. New York: Pantheon.

Janus, A. L. (2009). 'Disability and Transition to Adulthood'. *Social Forces*, 88(1): 99–120.

Jenkins, S. P., Brandolini, A., Micklewright, J., and Nolan, B. (2012). *The Great Recession and the Distribution of Household Income*. Oxford: Oxford University Press.

Kogan, I. (2006). 'Labor Markets and Economic Incorporation among Recent Immigrants in Europe'. *Social Forces*, 85(2): 697–721.

Kymlicka, W. (1996). *Multicultural Citizenship: A Liberal Theory of Minority Rights*. Oxford: Clarendon.

Le Feuvre, N. (1999). 'Gender, Occupational Feminization, and Reflectivity: A Cross-National Perspective'. In R. Crompton (ed.) *Restructuring Gender Relations and Employment: The Decline of the Male Breadwinner* (pp. 150–78). Oxford: Oxford University Press.

Mandel, H. and Semyonov, M. (2006). 'A Welfare State Paradox: State Interventions and Women's Employment Opportunities in 22 Countries'. *American Journal of Sociology*, 111: 1910–49.

Massey, D. S. and Pren, K. A. (2012). 'Unintended Consequences of US immigration Policy: Explaining the post-1965 Surge from Latin America'. *Population and Development Review*, 38: 1–29.

McCall, L. (2005). 'The Complexity of Intersectionality'. *Signs: Journal of Women in Culture and Society*, 30(3): 1771–800.

Nandi, A. and Platt, L. (2010). *Ethnic Minority Women's Poverty and Economic Well-Being*. London: Government Equalities Office.

Parekh, B. (2000). *Rethinking Multiculturalism: Cultural Diversity and Political Theory*. Cambridge, MA: Harvard University Press.

Parsons, S. and Platt, L. (2013). 'Disability among Young Children: Prevalence, Heterogeneity and Socio-economic Disadvantage'. CLS Working Paper 2013/11, November 2013. London: Institute of Education.

Phillips, A. (2007). *Multiculturalism without Culture*. Princeton, NJ: Princeton University Press.

Phillips, C. (2011). 'Institutional Racism and Ethnic Inequalities: An Expanded Multilevel Framework'. *Journal of Social Policy*, 40(1): 173–92.

Piketty, T. (2014). *Capital in the Twenty-First Century*. Cambridge, MA: Belknap Press.

Platt, L. (2005). 'The Intergenerational Social Mobility of Minority Ethnic Groups'. *Sociology*, 39(3): 445–61.

Platt, L. (2011a). 'Inequality within Ethnic Groups'. JRF programme paper: Poverty and Ethnicity. York: Joseph Rowntree Foundation.

Platt, L. (2011b). *Understanding Inequalities: Stratification and Difference*. Cambridge: Polity.

Polavieja, J. and Platt, L. (2014). 'Nurse or Mechanic? Explaining Sex-typed Occupational Aspirations amongst Children'. *Social Forces*, 93(1): 31–61.

Priestley, M. (2003). *Disability: A Life Course Approach*. Cambridge: Polity Press.

Runciman, W. G. (1972 [1966]). *Relative Deprivation and Social Justice: A Study of Attitudes to Social Inequality in Twentieth-century England*. Harmondsworth: Pelican.

Sen, A. (1992). *Inequality Re-examined*. Oxford: Oxford University Press.

Shakespeare, T. and Watson, N. (2002). 'The Social Model of Disability: An Outdated Ideology?' *Research in Social Science and Disability*, 2: 9–28.

Sharkey, P. and Faber, J. W. (2014). 'Where, When, Why, and for Whom Do Residential Contexts Matter? Moving away from the Dichotomous Understanding of Neighborhood Effects'. *Annual Review of Sociology*, 40(1): 559–79.

Stones, R. (2005). *Structuration Theory*. Basingstoke: Palgrave Macmillan.

Taylor, D. (1998). 'Social Identity and Social Policy: Engagements with Post-modern Theory'. *Journal of Social Policy*, 27(3): 329–50.

Van de Werfhorst, H. G. (2011). 'Skills, Positional Good or Social Closure? The Role of Education across Structural–Institutional Labour Market Settings'. *Journal of Education and Work*, 24(5): 521–48.

Weber, M. (1978). *Economy and Society*. Edited by G. Roth and C. Wittich. Berkeley, CA: University of California Press.

Name Index

Abel-Smith, B. 12
Acheson, S. D. C. 68
Ackers, L. 272
Adkins, L. 235
Ainley, P. 190
Aitken, N. 325
Akee, R. K. 95
Alam, M. Y. 287, 292
Alba, R. 249–50
Albert, N. G. 247
Albrecht, J. 229
Aldridge, S. 67, 73
Alesina, A. 279
Alkire, S. 8, 28, 36
Allen, G. 102, 124
Allen, R. 116, 122, 124
Alston, P. 43
Althusser, L. 120, 125
Amelina, A. 346
Amin, A. 254
Anderson, B. 264–6, 268, 270, 275–6, 279
Anderson, B. 230
Anderson, P. 96
Ansari, H. 299
Apel, R. 334
Apple, M. 120
Appleton, S. 309
Arber, S. 213
Arendt, H. 180–1
Aristotle 180–1
Arulampalam, W. 193
Arvanites, T. M. 323
Aspinall, P. J. 247
Atkinson, A. B. 25, 148, 158, 167, 175, 193, 345, 353
Attias-Donfut, C. 213
Auletta, K. 18
Autor, D. H. 307
Averett, S. 95

Back, L. 244
Baker, C. 297
Baker, M. 97, 101
Ball, S. J. 117, 124, 127

Banton, M. 245
Barker, D. J. P. 91–3
Barker, M. 248
Barnes, C. 192
Barnes, M. 214
Baron, S. 66
Barrientos, A. 195
Barry, B. 244
Bartels, L. M. 158
Barth, F. 243
Battu, H. 254
Baubock, R. 266
Beck, U. 12, 194
Becker, G. 326
Beitz, C. 48
Belfield, C. 148–9
Bell, B. 154
Ben-Shlomo, Y. 86
Benería, D. 235
Bennett, F. 186
Berger, L. 101
Bergman, J. 15
Bernstein, B. 12
Bernstein, E. 237
Berry, J. W. 249
Berthoud, R. 194, 287
Berube 310–11
Besley 55
Betts, A. 264
Bian, Y. 78
Bischoff, K. 346
Bismarck 206
Björkland, A. 68
Black, S. E. 92
Blackwell, L. 252
Blair, T. 87, 124, 315–16
Blanchflower, D. 186, 215
Blanden, J. 75, 89, 91, 104
Blane, D. 212
Blau, P. 76
Blau, J. 325
Blau, P. 325
Blinder, S. 265–6, 271
Blitz, B. K. 266

Subject Index